THE MONSTROSITY OF CHRIST

THE MONSTROSITY OF CHRIST

PARADOX OR DIALECTIC?

Slavoj Žižek
John Milbank
edited by Creston Davis

THE MIT PRESS   CAMBRIDGE, MASSACHUSETTS   LONDON, ENGLAND

MIT Press books may be purchased at special quantity discounts for business or sales promotional use. For information, please email special_sales@mitpress.mit.edu or write to Special Sales Department, The MIT Press, 55 Hayward Street, Cambridge, MA 02142.

This book was set in Copperplate 33BC and Joanna by Graphic Composition, Inc. Printed and bound in the United States of America.

Library of Congress Cataloging-in-Publication Data
Žižek, Slavoj.
  The monstrosity of Christ : paradox or dialectic? / Slavoj Žižek and John Milbank ; edited by Creston Davis.
      p.   cm.—(Short circuits)
  Includes bibliographical references and index.
  ISBN 978-0-262-01271-3 (hardcover : alk. paper)
  1. Philosophical theology. 2. Christianity—Philosophy. 3. Hegel, Georg Wilhelm Friedrich, 1770–1831. 4. Milbank, John. 5. Žižek, Slavoj. I. Milbank, John. II. Davis, Creston.   III. Title.
  BT40.Z59 2009
  230—dc22
                                                                        2008035984

10 9 8 7 6 5 4 3 2 1

Contents

A short circuit occurs when there is a faulty connection in the network—faulty, of course, from the standpoint of the network's smooth functioning. Is not the shock of short-circuiting, therefore, one of the best metaphors for a critical reading? Is not one of the most effective critical procedures to cross wires that do not usually touch: to take a major classic (text, author, notion) and read it in a short-circuiting way, through the lens of a "minor" author, text, or conceptual apparatus ("minor" should be understood here in Deleuze's sense: not "of lesser quality," but marginalized, disavowed by the hegemonic ideology, or dealing with a "lower," less dignified topic)? If the minor reference is well chosen, such a procedure can lead to insights which completely shatter and undermine our common perceptions. This is what Marx, among others, did with philosophy and religion (short-circuiting philosophical speculation through the lens of political economy, that is to say, economic speculation); this is what Freud and Nietzsche did with morality (short-circuiting the highest ethical notions through the lens of the unconscious libidinal economy). What such a reading achieves is not a simple "desublimation," a reduction of the higher intellectual content to its lower economic or libidinal cause; the aim of such an approach is, rather, the inherent decentering of the interpreted text, which brings to light its "unthought," its disavowed presuppositions and consequences.

And this is what "Short Circuits" wants to do, again and again. The underlying premise of the series is that Lacanian psychoanalysis is a privileged instrument of such an approach, whose purpose is to illuminate a standard text or ideological formation, making it readable in a totally new way—the long history of Lacanian interventions in philosophy, religion, the arts (from the visual arts to the cinema, music, and literature), ideology, and politics justifies this premise. This, then, is not a new series of books on psychoanalysis, but a series of "connections in the Freudian field"—of short Lacanian interventions in art, philosophy, theology, and ideology.

"Short Circuits" wants to revive a practice of reading which confronts a classic text, author, or notion with its own hidden presuppositions, and thus reveals its disavowed truth. The basic criterion for the texts that will be published is that they effectuate such a theoretical short circuit. After reading a book in this series, the reader should not simply have learned something new: the point is, rather, to make him or her aware of another—disturbing—side of something he or she knew all the time.

Slavoj Žižek

THE MONSTROSITY OF CHRIST

INTRODUCTION: HOLY SATURDAY OR RESURRECTION SUNDAY? STAGING AN UNLIKELY DEBATE

Creston Davis

If the theological was marginalized in the age of Western secular modernity, it has now returned with a vengeance. Theology is reconfiguring the very makeup of the humanities in general, with disciplines like philosophy, political science, literature, history, psychoanalysis, and critical theory, in particular, feeling the impact of this return. There are many ways of accounting for this surprising development but one stands out, namely, the collapse of communism in the late 1980s and early 1990s and the subsequent global expansion of capitalism under the flag of the American Global Empire. So extensive and profound have been the effects of this development that some have celebrated it as the victory not merely of an economic order or ideology, but of life itself. We are told that life, history, humanity has attained its end.[1]

But just as humanity was said to be reaching the summit of its development, a feeling emerged in the collective consciousnesses of philosophers, critics, poets, and theologians. Something was being lost, forgotten. The exceeding depth of humanity was being overrun by the fiend of mindless material consumption, and the mysterious truths and hopes of humanity and history were being sold out to the markets: the new logic of this new world order was a crass conspicuous logic of the *nouveau riche*.

In response to the advent of this capitalist nihilism, thought—the act of thinking—was forced to find a new way forward, a new source of hope. It had to appeal to a tradition that could resist the hegemony of capitalism and its presupposition—the individual will-to-power. Thinkers of resistance to capitalist depredation could no longer appeal to the humanist-Marxist tradition alone, especially as the history of actually existing Marxism finally folded before the juggernaut of capitalism. This was the opening for the theological. The portal to theology was opened precisely because capitalism is ultimately a self-enclosed structure, and so theology gives us a way to transcend capital premised on relationality and not on Ego (the Hegelian "In-Itself").

Yet, this new thought could not simply embrace the theological and repudiate the older tradition of resistance. Not only because the theological is equivocal, and so not universally opposed to the advent of capitalist nihilism (as Marx duly noted), but also because the Marxist tradition, even in historic defeat, was not defeated without remainder. This is to say: even in its death, it retains a truth that exceeds the bureaucratic, nihilistic materialism or immanentism without remainder that was defeated with the fall of the Wall in 1989. That truth is that humanity is material; thus the material world cannot be written off in favor of some kind of retreat into an ethereal transcendence.[2] Thus accounts of human flourishing and resistance to capitalist nihilism must be thoroughly material. So, in the end, this new thought must be critical of the Marxist-Communist tradition without being dismissive.

This is the problematic that gives rise to a new logic that nurtures a world beyond a secular-immanentist humanism and its unavoidable conclusion:

capitalist indifference. By secular humanism I mean that which obeys the Kantian injunction to conceive of the possibilities of human experience without reference to transcendence. The basic idea here is to recover or reconnect transcendence with a militant materialism. Daniel Bell nicely summarizes this movement away from a self-enclosed humanistic-immanent worldview toward a properly transcendent but nevertheless revolutionary, material politics, when he writes:

> For a time it was fashionable in some revolutionary circles to suggest that liberation was to be found only beyond the confines of [transcendence]. If humanity was to overcome the afflictions of this present age, then a genuinely revolutionary politics must eschew, indeed escape, the constrictions of [transcendence]. Now . . . the dismissal of [transcendence] is being reconsidered. While totalizing discourse may be anathema and practice celebrated, it is recognized that liberation hinges upon a prior ontology that maps the trajectories of the constitutive power of life. [And] for a time it was also popular to espouse a militant atheism, to insist that liberation, if it is to be truly liberative, reject appeals to transcendence (and its handmaid, theology) in accord with the received prejudice that transcendence was but a species of opiate.[3]

Thus is the stage set upon which two of the most significant thinkers of our time meet. In the pages that follow, the orthodox Christian theologian John Milbank and the militant Marxist Slavoj Žižek engage one another around this revolutionary political problematic: How can the theological and the material unite to fund resistance to capitalist nihilism?

As an aid to the reader, in what follows I introduce the political-philosophical-theological currents and conundrums that help to stage and flesh out the background for the debate. I do this in three steps. In the first section, I show how modernity is premised on a false dichotomy between reason and faith which continues to plague contemporary forms of theology, especially Protestant and Catholic liberalism, and which a materialist philosophy-cum-theology of resistance seeks to overcome. What is of particular interest for our purposes is the fact that both Milbank and Žižek see the philosopher G. W. F. Hegel as crucial to developing a theology of resistance, albeit in different ways. For Žižek, Hegel helps to resolve this deadlock, whereas Milbank is convinced that Hegel (or at least half of Hegel) continues to perpetuate it, while other aspects of Hegel signal a way beyond dialectics into theological paradox. This first section will then develop the basic building blocks of a materialist theology and philosophy.[4]

In the second section, we turn to postmodernism and its relationship to theology. This section traces out what happens to philosophy and theology (and even to the foundations of logic) once Hegel is prematurely dismissed as a totalizing thinker. In short, what we observe is language overtaking metaphysics and theology, and finally falling prey to the powers of capitalism and

Empire. And it is helpful to register Alain Badiou's view that philosophy after the linguistic turn forgets its original desire.[5] What is at stake, then, is how Milbank and Žižek understand Hegel as a way of recovering from the ashes of philosophy in the twentieth century.

The third and final section shows how the need for a theology of resistance is necessarily dependent on the Žižek / Milbank debate, because it helps to open a passage beyond the deadlock of the twin ideological structures of capitalist Empire, namely postmodernism (philosophy) and Protestant and Catholic liberalism (theology). The movement beyond these ideological lacunas radically changes the coordinates of the very nature of theology. But then the question becomes: What is theology? Is theology essentially orthodox à la Milbank, or could it be that theology itself is radically heterodox, as Žižek zealously argues? In what sense could Žižek be right when, in his response to Milbank, he argues that he is more of a Christian than Milbank? The possibility that Christianity—in a Philip K. Dick twist—may have returned to its displaced origins, in which different communities wrestled over the very truth and meaning of Christianity and its practice, has become a viable thesis again.[6]

I. TOWARD A MATERIALIST THEOLOGY

In order to understand the operating coordinates on which theology is being reconceptualized through this Žižek/Milbank dialogue, we must first understand the background of this debate. Indeed, this debate makes sense only against the backdrop of two basic but interdependent logical relations: the relation between reason and myth in the epoch called modernity, and the breakdown of modernity's coherent thought structure in the wake of postmodernism. In what follows, I will frame the debate in light of these two epochs and their constitutive conditions, beginning with modernity.

For whatever the epoch of "modernity" really is—and I am convinced that we will struggle for a coherent conception of it for a long time to come—reason's stance against myth, superstition, and the theological in order to access reason, pure and autonomous reason,[7] has proved at least wanting, if not downright irrational.[8] If the Middle Ages failed to employ enough reason (which is debatable, if not a flat-out stereotype, in itself), then secular modernity has employed too much of it (even to the point of contradiction!). Thus, to hazard an admittedly premature conjecture (and this is my conjecture): the return to the theological in our time may be a call, once again, to strike a balance between reason and myth, between belief and faith, between political struggle and the secular state, and between the divine and the human.

But the attempt to strike such a balance between reason and faith has proved a very difficult business. How does one proceed? The question of striking a balance is always a question of mediation—it is, as Hegel reminds us, always a question of relation. We must therefore seek a way of relating two terms that were for centuries posed in opposition to each other. There are many examples of this, but let me give two. There are, on the one hand, the pure rationalists who are the culmination of the Enlightenment ideals about the primacy of reason. Although there are many examples of rationalists, we can name just three: there is François-Marie Arouet (Voltaire), James Clifford, and Ludwig Feuerbach. Voltaire, influenced by the empiricist John Locke and Isaac Newton, raged against any kind of mystery in the cosmos, preferring instead to settle for a cold universe driven by the machine of pessimistic reason. For Clifford the duty to reason led directly to an irrational maxim, viz. "it is wrong always, everywhere, and for anyone, to believe anything upon insufficient evidence."[9] The third example is Feuerbach's transformation of philosophy into anthropology, which, as Georg Lukács rightly pointed out, "caused man [sic] to become frozen in a fixed objectivity and thus dismissed both dialectics [relation between things] and history [as process beyond 'man']."[10] What remained for Lukács in the wake of Feuerbach's anthropological turn was a state of total reification and commodification in which the dynamic process of change and flux was arrested by a capitalist logic of reproduction of the same.

On the other side, there is the pure religious thinker, or, in more pejorative terms, the fideist of the Barthian or neo-Wittgensteinian ilk. The central axiom of the fideist tradition is the conviction that religious discourse is self-referential, intertextual, and autonomous, and thus sectarian. Denys Turner rightly explains this theology as "an autonomous and exclusive set of rules governing talk of religious objects, such talk makes sense . . . only in and for that language game. It does not make sense in terms of any other form of discourse or language game." And because fideism acquires meaning only from within itself, it cannot be understood by reference to historical realities, and so, "evidence is neither here nor there from the religious point of view."[11] In short, fideism becomes the systematic evacuation of material history, and takes two forms: Barthian (postliberal theology, Yale and Duke schools) and a certain variant of Bultmannianism.[12] In both cases, the collapsing of the religious within a delimited and self-referential linguistic economy, seen supremely in Barth's abandonment of a natural knowledge of God, is an unconditional concession to the truth and politics of the Enlightenment.

Thus, we have two polemically opposed positions within modernity: there is the atheist, rationalist stance on the one side, and, on the other side, there is Barthian/Bultmannian fideism. But for all their differences, there emerges one common feature that connects these oppositions at a deeper level. In both attempts to shore up their own internally coherent positions, they have done so at a great cost, a cost that is presupposed by their respective conceptual and linguistic configurations. For the rationalist, the mechanical world is wholly devoid of surprise, mystery, and wonder; the world is, in all its banal predictability,

Whereas for the fideist the world is mediated only through a linguistically guaranteed structure in which all is accounted for prior to saying it (in other words, the economy of meaning is secured even before words are used). Only for the fideist, what is accounted for is a dematerialized ghetto that cannot account for the material conditions within which its very existence makes sense.

The problem stated bluntly, therefore, is that each side (rationalist/fideist) is not only unable to speak to the other, but does not need to in order to persist. In other words, each side fails to risk its own stance in order to be open to something new: some new logic of connection (à la Hegel's nonreductive relation, which we will examine below), after the fortified structures of modernity, stands in all its melodramatic glory. Consequently, the commonality between the rational atheist and the irrational fideist is that there is nothing that cannot be accounted for within their respective structure of linguistic and rational articulation. The atheist and the theist may be absolutely opposed, but in a more fundamental sense, they operate on a logic of the unsurprising, eternal return of the same linguistic and concomitant conceptual and practical structure. In other words, the linguistic horizon (in the Heideggerian sense) becomes the transcendental a priori that is always assumed but never questioned. This is an internally self-referential structure: another way of saying that it is a self-mediating process (Hegel's "In-Itself"). And, insofar as there is a self-mediation process in the heart of their discourses, then these structures of thought really are unrescuably idealistic.

Reason versus Fideism

At first blush, the debate that has emerged between John Milbank and Slavoj Žižek is the most improbable of developments, and seems to fall into this dualism of rationalism (Žižek) and fideism (Milbank) that I have outlined above. Again, on the surface, these thinkers represent two visions that could not be more diametrically opposed. Žižek is a full-blooded militant atheist who represents the critical-materialist stance against religion's illusions beginning with Hegel, Marx, and Feuerbach up to the French structuralist tradition that reaches its apex in the thought of Louis Althusser and Jacques Lacan. By contrast, Milbank is an equally potent and provocative thinker who argues for the opposite thesis, namely that only theology gives us a true foundation on which knowledge, politics, and ethics can finally stand. A new materialist theology (not modern philosophy) alone stands against the shifting sands of liberal and cultural nihilism. Milbank arrives at this thesis by ingeniously appropriating central theological doctrines from such thinkers as Augustine, Aquinas, Nicholas of Cusa, Giambattista Vico, and Henri de Lubac.

So just as Žižek stirs up the grounds for a revival of atheism, Milbank argues for the opposite: a return to a robust and unadulterated theology. And as if this atheistic/theological opposition were not enough, each has an equally opposing outlook: for Žižek the world is an essentially dark place that embodies an inherent negativity, whereas for Milbank the world alights in the very excesses of God's infinite love for the world. For Žižek, existence is a struggle about tarrying with the negative, whereas for Milbank, it is about the movement of being's reconciliation with itself.

From these prima facie observations one would expect something akin to the repulsion exhibited by magnets. The result of this repulsion outstrips "conversation," and only resembles or simply repeats the fruitlessness and incommensurability of contemporary clashes of the "new atheists" and their Christian (theistic) opponents. Here I am thinking of the popularized version of the theistic/atheistic debate represented by such thinkers as Christopher Hitchens, Richard Dawkins, and Samuel Harris on the atheist side and Os Guinness, Alister McGrath, Norman Geisler, and R. C. Sproul on the theist side.

But for all the pomp and circumstance of this "debate," in the end, it only manages to recapitulate the same premises with which each side begins. Consequently, the debate over the truth of either stance can never be resolved through the arbitration of speculative reason—and this because each side *appears* to be different, but, on a deeper level, they share the exact same version of that which underlies their very thinking, viz. secular reason. Reason functions in this atheistic/theistic debate in a very limited, even reductionist way as it becomes the final arbiter of all truth forced into propositional form and thus sundered from everyday life. The primacy of the split between thought and action is maintained throughout this so-called debate. And this is the basic point that Simon Critchley makes in his short book Continental Philosophy: that modern thought, from its original inception, founds an intractable nihilism owing to its dualism structured and established between thinking and acting. For the Kantian critique of metaphysics ends up appealing to a fundamental alienation grounded in an austere mechanical universe that cannot give rise to freedom. Critchley nicely highlights the Kantian problem in the following way: "Doesn't Kant leave human beings in what Hegel and Marx might have called the amphibious position of being both freely subject to the moral law and determined by an objective world of nature that has been stripped of any value and which stands over against human beings as a world of alienation? Isn't individual freedom reduced to an abstraction in the face of an indifferent world of objects that are available to one—at a price—as commodities?"[13]

According to this view, all truth is disclosed within the limits of reason alone such that it remains disembodied, inert, and above all mechanical. It is no surprise that a pure atheistic naturalism would take up this version of secular reason. But what is more surprising still is that a theistic stance espouses such a prosaic view. Yet this surprise dissipates when you examine the version of theism that embraces a view of God as being nothing more than the idol of classical foundationalism.[14] God, under this view, becomes a perfect and predictable *deus ex machina* who guarantees the outcome of events before they happen. This version of God is what Lacanian psychoanalytic theory calls the big Other, a kind of guarantee of global meaning, which should be a solace as it gets us off the hook. So the ideological import is: if you believe in the God derived from secular reason, then paradoxically you don't have to believe in anything (external to the Imaginary order) at all. Thus, the worship of the God of Reason is less about a liturgy of the world unfolding through a tradition and a historic community called Church, and more about how this "God" is predictable within the limits of reason alone, and can justify the continual existence of an unjust political order. In the final analysis, the fideist "God" necessarily dissolves faith and lets you off the hook.

Žižek witnessed this kind of contemporary theistic ideology as it was perfectly distilled in a Church frontal sign in Chicago in spring 2006. The sign read: "We Don't Believe [in God], We Know God." Here the very notion of faith is altogether removed from the practice of religion insofar as knowledge hijacks *doxa* (belief). Thus paradoxically, for those modern "believers" who accept the terms of the dichotomy between faith and reason, God is known and therefore should *not* be believed in. With this we can see firsthand how knowledge and belief are totally sundered from each other, which is the basic matrix of ideology for Žižek's twist on the core, Marxist concept of ideology. Here Žižek submits that the rudimentary definition of ideology is taken from Marx's work, *Capital*: "They do not know it, but they are doing it."[15] Under the standard Marxist view, reality and how it appears to us (or how we learn to believe in this "reality") are dissociated from each other—and this gap is the very thing that helps to reproduce the social status quo without questioning it. Here we can see that religious knowledge is believed in without being arrived at through any kind of discursive process. In other words, the way by which such knowledge as "God exists" is derived is itself hidden from the very process through which such a claim is achieved. The identification of this mysterious "hidden" process of reasoning is precisely the meaning of the concept of ideology.

Žižek's twist on Marx's notion of ideology is helpful here in that it adds the additional idea that we humans within capitalism know full well that this "reality" presented to us is a total fake, but nevertheless we continue following it because we no longer believe in anything at all beyond the immediate appearance of things. Tony Myers nicely summarizes Žižek's twist on ideology, which "is located in what we do and not in what we know [or even how we come to know]. Our belief in an ideology is thus staged in advance of our understanding of the fact."[16] So, according to Myers, Žižek thinks that when we "convert to the Church, when we actually *believe we believe*, all we are doing is recognizing the fact that our belief has already been decided and pre-exists our knowledge of it."[17] This ideology is a problem for both Žižek and Milbank, but for the latter, the Church is not simply reducible to ideology, but is exactly that community by which such illusion is shattered by entering into a divine community beyond this world.[18] Consequently, the theistic "God" of McGrath et al. is thus not so much a being as much as a dematerialized logic that never touches, much less changes, the world. And this entails that the Incarnation (and, by extension, orthodox Christianity) is rendered impossible under this condition of secular "neutral" (and so, ideological) reason.

In short, although this Dawkins/McGrath debate looks genuine, and is certainly successful in terms of selling a great many books, it nevertheless is only a limited and not very intellectually significant debate. It is more an exercise in ideological (mis)interpretation of the same premises than a real debate, because it fails to risk forgoing the very existence of what both sides presuppose. For is it not the case that modernity's mode of reason—for all its worth—cannot bring reason under its own critique? Is not the Achilles heel of reason precisely the fact that it cannot be deployed against itself? This is because if you fold reason back against itself, it panics.[19] In this respect, like a person without a face, reason cannot tolerate the representation of its own mirror image. So, in the end, the atheist's and the secular theist's views of reason and how it functions remain more or less identical, and far from organizing a theology of resistance that overthrows the established order, this false debate only ever manages to perpetuate and reproduce it.

By contrast to this ideological debate, the conversation between Milbank and Žižek takes place on an entirely different plane, as they are not only concerned with how reason (Logos-Word) connects up and distinguishes between different concepts, but also—and perhaps more importantly—they interrogate the very foundation of reason as such, and help stage a theology that resists global capitalism. Here Milbank and Žižek radicalize both Theodor Adorno and Max Horkheimer's study that linked Enlightenment reason to capitalism in their *Dialectic of Enlightenment*. This debate goes beyond a critique of the culture industry; indeed, it risks everything, as it goes to the heart of the problem by never hedging. It asks simple but devastating questions such as: What is reason? How does reason function? What does reason *do*, and what are its limits? These are the questions that we must risk even as we toil with dispensing our enslaved tutelage of the reified Kantian individualism that undercuts our social connections (or, better, creates false ones). We must do this because if we are really honest about the status of reason in the history of philosophy and theology, we ineluctably encounter its terrifying hidden supplement, that is, reason's otherness that does not show its truth so long as we naively accept its face value (what Hegel called the "Ruse of Reason"). The unabashed demand to penetrate beyond the generic view of Enlightenment "reason" radically separates this debate from the Dawkins/McGrath one and many others besides. This desire to go beyond the impoverished Enlightenment view of reason is a central theme that permeates the whole thought structure of both Milbank and Žižek. This above all enables us to turn the standard view of Enlightenment on its head and fuse action with thought once again. In very specific ways, I believe this overturning of Enlightenment reason can be seen in Žižek's view of the term Word (*Logos*) derived from Schelling, in which the "subject finally finds himself [completes his desire for himself because] . . . in the Word, he directly attains himself."[20] But, and here is the radical twist, the subject finally attains himself at the cost of forever losing himself in the very Word or symbolization that takes place outside the self. This positing of the self through the Word that entails its absolute loss is a certain twist on the early Christian thinker Augustine, whose idea of "self" remains internally divided until it reaches its consummate rest in God. Indeed for Žižek, as for Augustine, there is no unified self or *cogito*, which is the standard reading of the famous Descartes statement "I think, therefore I am." Milbank agrees here: the subject is never the cause of itself, but is rather only ever a response to its cause in God. This raises the issue about how to grasp Descartes's foundation of the subject within the vascular domain of the *cogito*.

There are at least two different readings of Descartes's *cogito*. Either it reifies the subject as wholly centered on itself (the basic premise of liberalism or Nietzsche's "will-to-power") or else it gets swallowed up by forces external to it, and disappears altogether (antimetaphysics Levinas, middle Derrida, etc.). The former reading is the liberal "Kantian" reading in which the self is fundamentally autonomous, self-caused, and in need of no one, whereas the latter reading is totally enraptured by the postmodern view that, in the end, all reality is a construction of language such that the subject altogether vanishes in the name of the objectivity of language.

Žižek attends to this problem by formulating *how* Descartes arrives at the *cogito*—namely, through the method of doubt that is essentially a process of transformation between the objectivity of nature and the process of subjectivity in concrete language. Žižek describes this process of coming to subjectivity through the experience of total loss: at the kernel of the *cogito* there is an empty abyss of negativity. The subject is a total void, and therefore does not exist.

If for Žižek the subject is constituted in the gap between nature and its representation in the symbolic order,[21] then for Milbank the "subject" is itself an invention of modernity. It is true that Milbank and Žižek both agree that the subject (i.e., finite being) is not by itself substantially (in and of itself) anything at all, but each has radically different ways of unpacking this rather esoteric and heterodox stance. Indeed, Milbank's theology preserves genuine finitude and contingency, and so goes against Žižek arguing that every moment is a false reification of an esoteric process. So theology's ontology of paradox secures finite belonging to the infinite order of things in a way that is fully real, if totally paradoxical, because eternity and time merge.[22] Thus for Milbank, talk of the subject is already framed in terms of the secular order sundered from the true ground of all things in God. So, for orthodox theology it is better to think of the locus called "self" as always mediated not by a primordial violence against which the "subject" must struggle in order to exist, but rather through a more fundamental peace within which the self develops as an excessive gift unfolding within the plentitude of being as such, that is, the Trinitarian God of Christianity. Thus this true "self" is not so much a social construction à la Foucault, for Milbank, but has its being only insofar as it is participating in the infinite love of the Trinity (Father, Son, and Holy Spirit). Drawing on Aquinas and Dionysian paradox, Milbank argues that God, in a manner, exists outside God, which in this very excess births all finitude within which the self is born. Of course one should not mistakenly think of the self as possessing itself only in relation to a static God, like Aristotle's unmoved mover. For Milbank, following Aquinas, God is not substance in the sense of an isolated self-founding thing, as a substrate for something else and as substance in contract with accident. So Milbank accepts substance for God in a very negative sense of self-sufficiency. The picture here is inherently dynamic: The self for Milbank is thus never stabilized but unfolds into the infinite God who also unfolds as the creation of love. Therefore, unlike Žižek, for whom the subject happens between nature and culture and is only ever negatively defined, for Milbank the self is the materialization of God's love as gratuitous gift.

But unlike the world as an irrepressible positive moment of love that Milbank's theology articulates, Žižek's world is less romantic. They are both equally pessimistic about the foundations of modern philosophy because the latter, as each understands it, rests on a negative posture of being. This is the belief that the natural world is devoid of surprise, and that, in the words of Michael Hardt, "the existence of something is the active negation of something else."[23] But whereas for Milbank this negative stance is a mandate against the entire edifice of modern philosophy (whose apex is Hegel's violent ontology), Žižek sees redemption at the heart of this darkness in the purely negative movement of dialectical undoing. Again they both agree that modernity is radically contingent and always destabilized—in other words, the social and cultural spheres are shot through with anxiety. But the strategy that Žižek deploys to address this reality is called "the vanishing mediator" which acts as a conductor through which different stages of history unfold and after which the "conductor-epoch-bridge" disappears.[24] This strategy is a product of Hegel's dialectical truth (which I will address below), but is used by Žižek to further the Marxist revolutionary position. This happens because if history unfolds through different stages, and there is no fundamental ahistorical ground, then what you have in the heart of being, for Žižek, is that which can always reverse the dominant power structure through itself. It is this destabilization that proffers inherent revolutionary possibilities.

This question of the subject and the self is among the basic questions that have generated the debate between Milbank and Žižek. Indeed, it is only by daring to look into the Fort Knox of secular reason that such a debate emerges, and thought is freed from its chains. And the figure for directing our attention to the reinforcing foundation of reason is none other than Hegel himself. For both Milbank and Žižek it is Hegel who both brings modernity to an apex and, in that very moment, opens up a way beyond.

Hegel: The Crack in Reason

The debate in this book is principally framed by how Žižek and Milbank interpret and idiosyncratically appropriate Hegel in their respective ways. In my view, Hegel is not only the most important figure here, but the most significant thinker in modern and twenty-first-century philosophy and theology.[25] This may sound like an outlandish claim, but keep in mind that Hegel's importance was marginalized throughout twentieth-century philosophy because—and here I follow Alain Badiou—philosophy has announced a certain end to the quest for truth. Instead philosophy compromises itself by settling for prioritizing language as absolute.[26] But this antimetaphysical bias in recent philosophy has given way to a return to a quest for the Truth of Being-in-the-World (and Žižek and Milbank are two key figures in this return to Truth). Hegel's robust philosophical and theological structure stands in stark relief from the bashful and timid styles of thinking that have dominated the recent terrain of thought. The reason for this is that Hegel is a thinker of the "Whole," for "The True is the whole . . . [and] is nothing other than the essence consummating itself through itself as organic process."[27] Hegel arrives at a structure that demands a deep organic unity by overcoming surface fragmentation—or what David Harvey calls the "time–space compression" and Fredric Jameson calls "the postmodern condition."[28] To perceive the "Whole," however, is never easy, and most certainly cannot materialize by simple empirical observation of the world's isolated objects and facts (which are necessarily disassociated from nature).

The empirical (the immediate experience of sense) for Hegel is thus limited to simply repeating the world's fragmentation, and here we can begin to see the ligaments of Marx and Žižek's notion of ideology. Hegel thinks that the empirical sensing of an object tricks us because we do not question how the object's appearance becomes an "immediate certainty." He shows how the empirical view of knowledge traps us because it perceives the object as if it were not mediated through something else. The empirical thus only repeats fragmentation.[29] So to overcome fragmentation one must bypass the tyranny of the empirical, and Hegel does this by embracing a way to think about the world beyond the immediate presentation of itself—as an object already sundered from the subject.

So, rather than thinking about the world as an object (or a fragmented chain of reified things), Hegel overcomes the world's fragmentation by developing an idealism founded in unity. The basic premise of Idealism is that individuated objects such as a book, a cow, a house, a person, and so forth may not exist without the accompaniment of the idea the mind (consciousness) has about them.[30] So the object is always-already bound up in the complex mediating process of the subject's thinking it, and conversely, the subject's thinking the object is itself bound up in the object's very existence. This is what Hegel means when he says that substance is subject: "the living Substance is being which is in truth *Subject* [and] is in truth actual . . . in the moment of positing itself . . . [as] the mediation of its self-othering with itself."[31] The point here is that Hegel introduces into philosophy a way of reuniting the world (substance and subject, form and content, truth and its practice, etc.) through a process of ontological mediation. The premise is: Before anything there is relation. But this mediation of the world's parts is itself internally divided. This paradox that lies at the heart of Hegel's ontology springs forth, and the world is at once united in the "Whole" (consciousness), but in the very positing of the "Whole" there is from within it a "self-othering" rupture or fissure (or, as Lacan would say, a "cut") in being's very disclosure of itself. In other words, the "Whole" with which the world presents itself in its naked reality cannot appear—in its empirical manifestation—without compromising this unity. The paradox is that the "Whole" appears, and when it does, its very appearance ruptures it from within the very disclosure of itself.[32]

We can observe the history of philosophy and theology that takes a radical turn after Hegel's ontology—a turn so radical that its effects remain incalculable to this very day. For here, the foundation of reason qua reason is turned against itself and can no longer contain its own truths. This consequent forces a mediating way called "dialectical sublation."[33] Reason's fractured self-enclosed foundation introduces into thought an insidious and intractable panic: The question that thought asks in the wake of Hegel is this: If there really is no universal foundation of reason (what Heidegger properly called "onto-theology"), then is there anything at all? Responding to this question brings us to our second signpost, viz. the timid process called postmodernism.

II. POSTMODERNISM AND THEOLOGY: THE TWISTING OF HEGEL

In contrast to a self-enclosed structure of the rational and the linguistic fideist, we could think of postmodernism as being highly critical of the unity of the stable Saussurian sign[34]—a shift from the signified to the signifier that opens up a perpetual detour down the pathway to a truth that has lost all status and finality, not to mention creditability.[35] And once truth and the signified have lost security, suddenly securing the ground of all truth within a singular metaphysical structure is rendered impossible. The death of metaphysics delivers a deathblow to theology (especially the fideist Barthian project), because if

God (in the Christian sense) is the final ground of truth, the true signified by which all signification is guaranteed, then God is effectively castrated from the symbolic order and from all language as such. In the wake of this, postliberal theology must surrender even further from a common notion of historical knowledge, and this signals an even more devastating sign, viz., the fear of looking into the abyss of reason.

The metaphysical God is nailed to the Cross by the logic of the sign crucified. Yet, on the other hand, far from being the final blow to the theological, I argue (in contrast with Žižek, but with Milbank) that postmodernism can be seen as the first step in the smashing of the idol of language as such—demonstrating that the economy of the sign becomes itself a truth effect of its own logic such that the unfolding of the lines of signification, as a whole, sneaks the absolute foundation of the signified in through the back door. Thus, by deconstructing metaphysics, a new metaphysics of language is erected in its place. A metaphysics of language is substituted for a metaphysics of truth. Consequently, truth and any appeal to transcendence (and its handmaid, theology) is rendered impossible.

But far from the liquidation of theology, Milbank (but not Žižek) sees that postmodernism is a step that *can* return us to a theology and a more fundamental truth, albeit a necessary but insufficient step. It is a return to a process that cannot be captured by the self-enclosed logic of the omnipresence of an endless series of differing meaning. For is not différance the ken of a Kantian a priori that simply repeats itself identically? By contrast to this, the Milbank/Žižek debate, on my view, is a response to the reality that something is exceeding the essentially conservative stance of the postmodern structure of language as such. It is at this precise juncture that postmodernism has certainly done its work, but this work's critical stance nevertheless fails to transcend its own symptom of critique (again falling prey to the Ruse of Reason, which ironically is why Hegel must be dispensed with). And this is where the resuscitation of thought must be our first priority—a view that thinking itself must pass beyond this passive stance by articulating a positive structure that risks touching the infinite. And here I follow Alain Badiou when he maintains that "Philosophy must examine the possibility of a point of interruption—not because all this must be interrupted—but because thought at least must be able to extract itself from this circulation and take possession of itself once again as something other than an object of circulation."[36] The irruption of the tyrannical circulation of the sign is the sine qua non of the very existence of philosophy, theology, and thinking as ontological participation. And this is where Hegel, as the central figure of the Žižek/Milbank debate, directs us back to (and beyond) the ground of reason and logic.

As we have seen, it was Hegel who confronted the nihilism of modernity manifested in the Kantian dualism (that began with Scotus and nominalist theology which subsequently went through Descartes, as Milbank understands it) between duty and freedom, between form and content, and between the Is and the Ought. But the only way around this deadlock for Hegel was to penetrate beyond the crust of reason and into its very abyss. Hegel's dialectical method is founded on the deepest level of relation (beyond fragmented reason) that finally outflanks Kant's dualism. Consequently, Hegel's strong method gives us the coordinates for unifying the fragmented parts into a "Whole." This process attracts both Milbank and Žižek—only each thinker radically twists Hegel in his own unique ways. But before we delineate both Milbank's and Žižek's unique adaptation of Hegel's dialectical thinking, I want to first identify the very notion of the dialectic itself, and from here we will better see how their respective idiosyncratic twists are formulated.

The Dialectical Method

On Milbank's view, Hegel's dialectical method must be seen, in the first place, as a *method*. It is properly a *way* by which the world is constituted. But Milbank and Žižek will immediately diverge on the basic claim of the very *meaning* of method. For example, Milbank understands the dialectic as something wholly external to that about which it is applied, viz., the world. In effect, then, Milbank sees the dialectic as simply and irredeemably dualistic. There is the method and, set over against this, there is the world. And because the method is dualistic it is, for Milbank, not radical enough; it is too conservative and removed from the world, and acts as a kind of bourgeois academic observer overlooking the world from the safe distance of an armchair, second-order thinker who can only ever think *about* the world. The point of materially thinking the world is always and already to change the world, for Milbank. Moreover, the dialectical thinker is thus afraid of the world and so constructs a method *about* it behind which one can too easily hide—like the Wizard of Oz hiding behind the curtain. In this way, the science of perception (or phenomenology), especially as seen in Hegel and later in Edmund Husserl and his followers like Heidegger and Derrida (as glossed by Milbank), commits the error of erecting a privileged a priori elitist "vantage point" about the world which is *not* the world but nevertheless determines what the world is before it becomes, as it were, itself.

Where Žižek agrees with Milbank is precisely the truth about the dialectic: it is a methodology that approaches the world, but he would make an exception to Milbank's belief that thinking *about* the world (as method) is a misconstrual of both logic and being of the world. For Žižek, thinking *about* the world is always-already the world, so method is fused with reality and constructs reality in revolutionary becoming. In the end, the difference turns on the question: "What is method?" Does it hide a dualism, or does it overcome it through a dialectical process?

At best, Milbank's relation to Hegel is equivocal. The title of his chapter on Hegel in the classic text *Theology and Social Theory* testifies to this: "For and Against Hegel." That is to say, Milbank both appropriates Hegel's genealogical method whereby the fragments of history are synthesized into the "whole," are finally Christian, but also rejects Hegel's pure dialectical *method* as too ahistorical. Thus, what you have with Hegel, according to Milbank, is a relation between history and nonhistory, between the "whole" of historical synthesis and the identical repetition of ahistorical method. Milbank thus rejects Hegel because the dialectical method is situated outside the unfolding infinite plentitude of being's flux as it overflows in God's very being as pure act.

The point, if true, is fair enough: if one attempts to explain being from a static and ahistorical perspective of method, then that which it is trying to explain (viz. being) will explain nothing but the truths found in method, and know nothing of being's ways as they flow forth from within and beyond. In sum, for Milbank, Hegel is not radical enough, for he fails to throw himself into the very middle of being's making, and *from within the middle* arrive at its truth. Milbank concludes that "'Dialectics', which depend upon the myth of negation, is therefore another mode of the Cartesian arsenal. By its means, Hegel once more subordinates the contingencies of human making / speaking to the supposedly 'logical' articulation of a subjectivity [hidden within dialectical methodology] which is secretly in command throughout."[37]

Similarly for Žižek, whose work is increasingly drawing on aspects of Christian theology—even to the point where he refers to himself as a "materialist theologian"[38]—the fundamental reality of which he redefines through the kenosis of God in Christ. Christ on his view is the *monstrum* (monster)—that is, the exceptional that cannot be accounted for in rational terms alone—and is, paradoxically, that on which the rational itself rests. This is seen in the event of the death of Christ that gives humanity the possibility of resistance in the birth of the Church as embodied in the Holy Spirit. And Žižek, following Badiou and their master, Lacan, subscribes to the theme of the irruptive event. For in order for reality to reproduce itself, its reproduction (à la Hegel) must always contain its properly dialectical Other: "it has to rely on an inherent excess which grounds it," for the Real cannot be encountered directly, and the trauma of experiencing it is displaced by the freeze-framing of the Imaginary founded in the symbolic order.

As for the emerging postsecular theological horizon, the irruption of the world does not stand over against language, but is both imbued with it as the divine Word and yet is always also something that exceeds language, appears as an indefinable aporia that consistently disrupts the rational. As Milbank maintains, being is basically most paradoxical; it is always exceeding itself by bringing together the infinite and the finite without collapsing them into a monolithic process (or, more strictly, method). Therefore theology always resists being defined in terms of idealism, rationalism, or fideism—in a manner, theology always defines the world through itself. To put it differently: theology, for Milbank, always arrives in the monstrosity named the Incarnational Event, which is nonreductively reconciled not through the conservative domestic foundation of reason but, rather, via the Holy Spirit back to the unity with the Father. The whole of the cosmos (all time and space) basically happens between the unfolding love of Trinitarian relations. By contrast to this ontology, Žižek's "God" reveals himself in a radically self-emptying process, to the point where God's love for the world results in sacrificing his own transcendence—that is, his own distance from the world, if you will— in order to be more fully God. "This is why," as Žižek says, following Hegel, "what we have after crucifixion, namely, the resurrected God, is neither God the Father nor God the Son—it is the Holy Ghost."[39] And, as the Scriptures say, the Holy Ghost is love *between* believers—it is the spirit of the community of believers. These famous words of Christ: "whenever two or three are gathered together [in love] I am in the midst of you."[40] Žižek thinks we should all take this passage literally.[41]

And this hones in on a basic difference between Žižek and Milbank. This difference is that Žižek takes God's act of revelation without reservation—revelation means absolute kenosis, after which transcendence has now arrived in the heart of the material world completely devoid of the protection that transcendence guarantees. Milbank, on the other hand, sides with transcendence, which is fully revealed in God's kenosis in Christ, but is not compromised in the act of Incarnation; indeed, God's Incarnation in Christ, for Milbank, frees the world from itself by opening up the very portals beyond our realm. So, to hazard a thesis: For Milbank, God's act of Incarnation saves the world from itself by opening up a way beyond the material realm into the beyond of the infinite life of God, whereas for Žižek the same event signals the reality of a radical, even Kierkegaardian, leap of faith without guarantees—the abyss opens up, allowing for the coordinates of a life of real yet terrifying freedom for both God and human beings. This debate then orbits around these two irreconcilable versions of Christianity—between Milbank's orthodox Trinitarianism and Žižek's heterodox negativity. And despite these two different voices, one thing remains common: the terms of the debate are established not by the strict circulation of language, or by some abstract rule of reason, but by a new universal logic that connects us to each other once again. The universal for Milbank is his ontology of peace that reconciles differences in an eschatological harmony, whereas for Žižek it is courage to face the truth that God's transcendence diffused through the world confronts us in the monstrous exception that founds the truth of all things. It is the dawning of this new universal that transcends postmodernism, calling us to risk founding the new universal beyond pure-hyper fragmentation or the distancing ourselves from the world behind the mask of the a priori of différance. If nothing else, this debate lays out the coordinates for this risk—for touching the infinite beyond the malaise of capitalistic pretense and sheer boredom. For, in the final analysis, it is the monster of Christ that calls us to risk everything for the sake of the world.

III. Theology: Orthodox or Heterodox?

With the contextualization of both the modern epoch and the logic of post-modernism, we start to see the finer points of this debate as it reshapes the very terms of theology as we know it. Moreover, this debate between orthodox and heterodox theology is symptomatic of an epoch reached at the end of modernity, the end of mediating metanarratives that try to synthesize the whole of reality within a singular story. Badiou says that modernity is "the idea of the historical subject, the idea of progress, the idea of revolution, the idea of humanity and the ideal of science."[42] There can be no more arbitration employing ahistorical "reason," because reason (as grounded in the nontranscendent) is no longer credible. Ours is an age of uncompromising winner-takes-all. This encounter between Milbank and Žižek is the intellectual equivalent of Ultimate Fighting, because both partners in this debate are defining the terms of the very meaning of Christianity, the death of Christ, the Trinity, and the Church. In other words, to restate this: the very heart of theology itself is at stake. In this sense, we can see how this debate is fundamentally different than the rather domestic and apolitical debates about the truth of theism versus atheism, or science versus religion. This book is about not a disembodied belief but the true radical nature of Christianity and its political import. In other words, this debate is not merely about the rejection of reason for the sake of it; rather, it is better to see that it rejects a certain type of reason, namely, self-repeating, ideological reason that only reproduces the political and economic status quo.[43]

Both Žižek's and Milbank's critical thinking about the logic of secular reason has freed them to think otherwise—to think about new strategies of thought and connection. Consequently, to think differently about connection and ontology allows one to rethink the recent trends of modern Christianity. In this way, the debate also circulates around the question of what will replace the rejection of Christianity as defined by modernity (and, conversely, modernity in Christianity)? And this is where the rub lies as Milbank and Žižek differ on their respective answers. For the former, reason is recovered in the betweenness of being. For the latter, what replaces the vacuum of modern Enlightenment reason is the movement of the negative as the "parallax view" that "constantly shift[s] perspective[s] between two points between which no synthesis or mediation is possible."[44] In this respect, this debate offers something refreshing, something new and full of hope that risks questioning the systemic implementation and return of secular reason as status quo, or what Badiou calls the "state of the situation."[45]

The fact that it is not completely trapped in the *standard* "capitalist" Enlightenment's version of reason opens up the possibility that this debate is a portal not only to a way of understanding the far side of the state of the situation, but to a new engagement with a Christianity after the death of its supplement— Christian capitalist and cultural hegemony. Indeed, much of the social cohesion that binds conservative and liberal Christianity together is directly related to the breakup of modern Christianity's grip on culture. A logic that Niebuhr's "American" theology could not identify, much less reject. The argument is simple—once modern Christianity (i.e., Protestant liberalism) has lost its grip on culture, it creates a powerful "other" or enemy that charges conservative Christianity with the task of regaining its cultural imperialist stance and forgotten power. On the other hand, the answer that liberal Christianity provides is premised on the "same/otherness" logic of conservative Christianity, only the "other" (or opposite) for the liberal is anyone who actually believes there is truth in the world.[46] The problem is that, again, each of these two different sides of the debate agrees with the other. They agree that the logic of a particular kind of modernity dictates the coordinates of the debate itself. Fundamentalism and liberalism are thus inherently bound up in a type of modernity. Again, the problem here is that the theological debates, even between Schleiermacher and Barth, literally cannot afford to question their own premises—but differ in how these premises are cashed out and interpreted. Thus, Christianity in modernity is little more than modernity in Christianity, which continues to reproduce itself through polemical argumentation.

In short, the theoretical coordinates of thought, philosophy, and both liberal and confessional theologies indebted to the logic of modernity have all proven to be woefully unsatisfactory not only epistemologically and ontologically, but also on another basic level of life—the level of action. These theologies have all proven unable to resist the capitalistic global Empire along with the new security-emergency state that has emerged in the wake of 9/11. We can see this by understanding the basic structure of twentieth-century theology, which took two fundamental routes: either it circled the wagons and formulated a "ghetto" of fundamentalist-literalist ideals, or else it sold out to a utilitarian "America-corporate" logic that eventually became Empire. Although each of these two different routes in twentieth-century theology differs in its own respects, they remain joined on a most disturbing level. The theological orientation that left the world in order to preserve the truth of "Christianity" (a truth, on my view, that was indebted in method to modernity) failed to remain faithful to the radical universality of Agape. Thus truth for the fundamentalist became exclusive and premised on propositional truth claims that sucked the life out of the tradition.

The liberal theological orientation failed too, but not by retreating into the ghetto; rather, by disavowing any linkage to history, wisdom, and truth from the tradition itself. Christianity either gave up and retreated into its modernist box of propositional truth, or else it dissolved its authority by appealing to a politically disinterested outlook (premised on an abstract and dehumanizing market utilitarianism) totally unable to hold in check the rapid technological advancements and the growing thirst of atheistic capitalism and nationalist power.

Conclusion: Holy Saturday (Žižek) or Resurrection Sunday (Milbank)?

The significance of the Milbank/Žižek debate ultimately arises from the fact that modern Christianity has finally met its doom. So I want to conclude this Introduction by raising a fundamental question: What becomes of theology after secular Enlightenment reason has run its course? Is secular reason replaced with paradox or dialectics? Or, as may be the case for Žižek, is secular reason sublated by the dialectic? For Milbank it is the former, paradox, whereas for Žižek the parallax dialectical view is that which finally gives us the coordinates for a revolutionary faith.

Christianity as approached by both Žižek and Milbank uniquely proffers an emancipatory exit beyond the deadlock of capitalism and its supplement, liberalism—which in truth is a false politics sequestered by the owners of production in the name of freedom. But here, in this debate, the very terms of Christianity are themselves up for debate. This leaves us at the end of the line—with another either/or: Either Christianity is the plenitudal wave of love that takes us all up within the light of divine glory (the paradox of Resurrection Sunday), or else it is about an infinite freedom without teleology which is the ground for the emergence of a true, disillusioned, and disenchanted love (the dialectic of Holy Saturday). The monstrosity of Christ is the love either in paradox or in dialectics—and, I believe, may be the pathway beyond the current popular-absolutist rule of finance, spectacle, and surveillance.[47]

Notes

1. See Francis Fukuyama, "Reflections on The End of History, Five Years Later," in After History? Francis Fukuyama and His Critics, ed. Timothy Burns (Lanham, MD: Rowman & Littlefield, 1994).

2. For an excellent argument on the relation between transcendence and immanence, see Joshua Delpech-Ramey, "The Idol as Icon: Andy Warhol's Material Faith," Angelaki 12, no. 1 (2007).

3. Daniel M. Bell, Jr., "Only Jesus Saves: Toward a Theopolitical Ontology of Judgment," in Theology and the Political: The New Debate, ed. Creston Davis, John Milbank, and Slavoj Žižek (Durham: Duke University Press, 2005), p. 201.

4. For an excellent text on this, see Phillip Blond, Post-Secular Philosophy: Between Philosophy and Theology (London: Routledge, 1998).

5. Alain Badiou, "Philosophy and Desire," in *Infinite Thought: Truth and the Return to Philosophy*, trans. and ed. Oliver Feltham and Justin Clemens (London: Continuum, 2003).

6. See Ward Blanton, *Displacing Christian Origins: Philosophy, Secularity, and the New Testament* (Chicago: University of Chicago Press, 2007).

7. This is the view that Immanuel Kant maintained regarding reason. See his *Critique of Pure Reason*, trans. N. K. Smith (New York: St. Martin's, 1965).

8. Georg Lukács, "Reification and the Consciousness of the Proletariat," in *History and Class Consciousness* (Cambridge, MA: MIT Press, 1971), p. 182.

9. W. K. Clifford, *Lectures and Essays* (London: Macmillan, 1886), p. 346.

10. Lukács, "Reification and the Consciousness of the Proletariat," pp. 186–187.

11. Denys Turner, *Marxism and Christianity* (Oxford: Blackwell, 1983), p. 171.

12. Ibid.

13. Simon Critchley, *Continental Philosophy: A Very Short Introduction* (Oxford: Oxford University Press, 2001), p. 76.

14. Nicholas Wolterstorff, *Reason within the Bounds of Religion* (Grand Rapids: Eerdmans, 1984). For a standard version of the position that posits God as a scientific hypothesis, see Richard Swinburne's P-inductive argument for the existence of God in his *The Existence of God*, 2nd ed. (Oxford: Oxford University Press, 2004).

15. Slavoj Žižek, *The Sublime Object of Ideology* (London: Verso, 1989), p. 28.

16. Tony Myers, *Slavoj Žižek* (London: Routledge, 2003), pp. 68–69.

17. Ibid., p. 69. See Žižek, *The Sublime Object of Ideology*, p. 40.

18. John Milbank, *Being Reconciled: Ontology and Pardon* (London: Routledge, 2003), p. 105.

19. Just to be precise, the point is that the coherence of secular reason presupposes the absence of God, while the coherence of religious faith presupposes God's presence. Neither side can address the other's presuppositions. As Žižek points out, the deadlock is that neither side wants to "believe," but only to know. Thanks to Joshua Delpech-Ramey for several discussions on this.

20. Slavoj Žižek, *The Indivisible Remainder: An Essay on Schelling and Related Matters* (London: Verso, 1996), pp. 46–47. In this way, I claim that Žižek's thought cannot simply be reduced to extending the Enlightenment, as the very fact that this debate is taking place witnesses to this possibility.

21. For Žižek there is always an unbridgeable gap between the nature of the subject and the nature of the subject's representation.

22. Thanks to Joshua Delpech-Ramey for fleshing this out.

23. See Michael Hardt, *Gilles Deleuze: An Apprenticeship in Philosophy* (Minneapolis: University of Minnesota Press, 1993), p. 3.

24. Slavoj Žižek, *For They Know Not What They Do: Enjoyment as a Political Factor* (London: Verso, 1991), p. 185.

25. See Slavoj Žižek, Clayton Crockett, and Creston Davis's forthcoming book on Hegel (Columbia University Press, 2009).

26. See Badiou, "Philosophy and Desire," pp. 39–57.

27. G. W. F. Hegel, Phenomenology of Spirit, trans. A. V. Miller (Oxford: Oxford University Press, 1977), p. 11, section 20. Translation slightly modified.

28. See David Harvey, The Condition of Postmodernity (Oxford: Blackwell, 1990); and Fredric Jameson, Postmodernism, or, The Cultural Logic of Late Capitalism (Durham: Duke University Press, 1991).

29. See Hegel's critique of empiricism in the section on "Consciousness" in the Phenomenology of Spirit, pp. 58–103.

30. See Tony Myers's discussion of idealism in Slavoj Žižek, p. 16.

31. Ibid., p. 10.

32. See Alain Badiou's chapter 17, "Hegel and the Whole," in Theoretical Writings, ed. Ray Brassier and Alberto Toscano (London: Continuum, 2004).

33. Hegel's idea of sublation (Aufhebung) is the process by which oppositions are synthesized beyond their own identity into a higher order of becoming. It is a dialectical overcoming of the world's fragmentation in the process that moves from the In-Itself to a self-consciousness In-and-For-Itself.

34. Ferdinand de Saussure, Course in General Linguistics, trans. Wade Baskin, rev. ed. (London: Fontana, 1974).

35. Jean-François Lyotard, The Postmodern Condition: A Report on Knowledge, trans. Geoff Bennington and Brian Massumi (Minneapolis: University of Minnesota Press, 1979).

36. Badiou, "Philosophy and Desire," p. 49.

37. John Milbank, Theology and Social Theory: Beyond Secular Reason, 2nd ed. (Oxford: Blackwell, 2006), p. 158.

38. Materialism Today Conference, Birkbeck College, University of London, June 23, 2007.

39. Specs, vol. 1 (Winter Park, FL: Rollins College Press, 2008), pp. 122–133.

40. Matthew 18:20.

41. Taken from a lecture by Slavoj Žižek at Rollins College, November 4, 2008.

42. Badiou, "Philosophy and Desire," p. 44.

43. Of course Milbank and Žižek have different takes on how they understand the precise logic of reason—something to which a simple introduction cannot attend.

44. Slavoj Žižek, The Parallax View (Cambridge, MA: MIT Press, 2006), p. 4.

45. Peter Hallward defines Badiou's idea of the "state" or "the state of the situation" in Alain Badiou, Ethics: An Essay on the Understanding of Evil (London: Verso, 2001), p. ix.

46. For a reading of the "same/otherness" dialectic through the history of the United States, see James A. Morone, Hellfire Nation: The Politics of Sin in American History (New Haven: Yale University Press, 2003).

47. I would like to thank Dan Bell, Sarah Kate Moore, Ward Blanton, Joshua Delpech-Ramey, Clayton Crockett, Anthony Paul Smith, Adrian Johnston, John Milbank, and Slavoj Žižek for their helpful comments on this introduction.

The Fear of Four Words: A Modest Plea for the Hegelian Reading of Christianity

Slavoj Žižek

G. K. Chesterton concluded "The Oracle of the Dog" with Father Brown's defense of commonsense reality: things are just what they are, not bearers of hidden mystical meanings, and the Christian miracle of Incarnation is the exception that guarantees and sustains this common reality:

> People readily swallow the untested claims of this, that, or the other. It's drowning all your old rationalism and scepticism, it's coming in like a sea; and the name of it is superstition. It's the first effect of not believing in God that you lose your common sense and can't see things as they are. Anything that anybody talks about, and says there's a good deal in it, extends itself indefinitely like a vista in a nightmare. And a dog is an omen, and a cat is a mystery, and a pig is a mascot, and a beetle is a scarab, calling up all the menagerie of polytheism from Egypt and old India; Dog Anubis and great green-eyed Pasht and all the holy howling Bulls of Bashan; reeling back to the bestial gods of the beginning, escaping into elephants and snakes and crocodiles; and all because you are frightened of four words: He was made Man.[1]

It was thus his very Christianity that made Chesterton prefer prosaic explanations to all-too-fast resorts to supernatural magic—and to engage in writing detective fiction: if a jewel is stolen from a locked container, the solution is not telekinesis but the use of a strong magnet or some other sleight of hand; if a person vanishes unexpectedly, there must be a secret tunnel; and so on. This is why naturalistic explanations are more magic than a resort to supernatural intervention: how much more "magic" is the detective's explanation of a tricky deceit by means of which the criminal accomplished the murder in a locked room than the claim that he possessed the supernatural ability to move through walls!

I am even tempted to go a step further here, and give Chesterton's last lines a different reading—no doubt not intended by Chesterton, but nonetheless closer to a weird truth: when people imagine all kinds of deeper meanings because they "are frightened of four words: He was made Man," what really frightens them is that they will lose the transcendent God guaranteeing the meaning of the universe, God as the hidden Master pulling the strings— instead of this, we get a God who abandons this transcendent position and throws himself into his own creation, fully engaging himself in it up to dying, so that we, humans, are left with no higher Power watching over us, just with the terrible burden of freedom and responsibility for the fate of divine creation, and thus of God himself. Are we not still too frightened today to assume all these consequences of the four words? Do those who call themselves "Christians" not prefer to stay with the comfortable image of God sitting up there, benevolently watching over our lives, sending us his son as a token of his love, or, even more comfortably, just with some depersonalized Higher Force?

The axiom of this essay is that there is only one philosophy which thought the implications of the four words through to the end: Hegel's idealism—which is why almost all philosophers are also no less frightened of Hegel's idealism. The ultimate anti-Hegelian argument is the very fact of the post-Hegelian break: what even the most fanatical partisan of Hegel cannot deny is that something changed after Hegel, that a new era of thought began which can no longer be accounted for in Hegelian terms of absolute conceptual mediation; this rupture occurs in different guises, from Schelling's assertion of the abyss of prelogical Will (vulgarized later by Schopenhauer) and Kierkegaard's insistence on the uniqueness of faith and subjectivity, through Marx's assertion of the actual socioeconomic life process, and the full autonomization of mathematicized natural sciences, up to Freud's theme of "death drive" as a repetition that insists beyond all dialectical mediation. Something happened here, there is a clear break between before and after, and while one can argue that Hegel already announces this break, that he is the last of the idealist metaphysicians and the first of the postmetaphysical historicists, one cannot really be a Hegelian after this break; Hegelianism has lost its innocence for ever. To act like a full Hegelian today is the same as to write tonal music after the Schoenberg revolution.

The predominant Hegelian strategy that is emerging as a reaction to this scarecrow image of Hegel the Absolute Idealist is the "deflated" image of Hegel freed of ontological-metaphysical commitments, reduced to a general theory of discourse, of possibilities of argumentation. This approach is best exemplified by the so-called Pittsburgh Hegelians (Brandom, McDowell): no wonder Habermas praises Brandom, since Habermas also avoids directly approaching the "big" ontological question ("are humans *really* a subspecies of animals, is Darwinism true?"), the question of God or nature, of idealism or materialism. It would be easy to prove that Habermas's neo-Kantian avoiding of ontological commitment is in itself necessarily ambiguous: while Habermas and the Pittsburgh Hegelians treat naturalism as the obscene secret not to be publicly admitted ("of course man developed from nature, of course Darwin was right . . ."), this obscure secret is a lie, it covers up the idealist form of thought (the a priori transcendentals of communication which cannot be deduced from natural being). The truth here is in the form: just as in Marx's old example of royalists in the republican form, while Habermasians secretly think they are really materialists, the truth is in the idealist form of their thinking.

Such a "deflated" image of Hegel is not enough; we should approach the post-Hegelian break in more direct terms. True, there is a break, but in this break Hegel is the "vanishing mediator" between its "before" and its "after," between traditional metaphysics and postmetaphysical nineteenth- and twentieth-century thought. That is to say: something happens in Hegel, a breakthrough into a unique dimension of thought, which is obliterated, rendered invisible in its true dimension, by postmetaphysical thought. This obliteration leaves an empty space which has to be filled in so that the continuity of the development of philosophy can be reestablished—filled in with what? The index of this obliteration is the ridiculous image of Hegel as the absurd "Absolute Idealist" who "pretended to know everything," to possess Absolute Knowledge, to read the mind of God, to deduce the whole of reality out of the self-movement of (his) mind—the image which is an exemplary case of what Freud called *Deck-Erinnerung* (screen-memory), a fantasy-formation intended to cover up a traumatic truth. In this sense, the post-Hegelian turn to "concrete reality, irreducible to notional mediation," should rather be read as a desperate posthumous revenge of metaphysics, as an attempt to reinstall metaphysics, albeit in the inverted form of the primacy of concrete reality.

The next standard argument against Hegel's philosophy of religion targets its teleological structure: it openly asserts the primacy of Christianity, Christianity as the "true" religion, the final point of the entire development of religions.[2] It is easy to demonstrate how the notion of "world religions," although it was invented in the era of Romanticism in the course of the opening toward other (non-European) religions, in order to serve as the neutral conceptual container allowing us to "democratically" confer equal spiritual dignity on all "great" religions (Christianity, Islam, Hinduism, Buddhism . . .), effectively privileges Christianity—already a quick look makes it clear how Hinduism, and especially Buddhism, simply do not fit the notion of "religion" implied in the idea of "world religions." However, what conclusion are we to draw from this? For a Hegelian, there is nothing scandalous in this fact: every particular religion in effect contains its own notion of what religion "in general" is, so that there is no neutral universal notion of religion—every such notion is already twisted in the direction of (colorized by, hegemonized by) a particular religion. This, however, in no way entails a nominalist/historicist devaluation of universality; rather, it forces us to pass from "abstract" to "concrete" universality, i.e., to articulate how the passage from one to another particular religion is not merely something that concerns the particular, but is simultaneously the "inner development" of the universal notion itself, its "self-determination."

Postcolonial critics like to dismiss Christianity as the "whiteness" of religions: the presupposed zero level of normality, of the "true" religion, with regard to which all other religions are distortions or variations. However, when today's New Age ideologists insist on the distinction between religion and spirituality (they perceive themselves as spiritual, not part of any organized religion), they (often not so) silently impose a "pure" procedure of Zen-like spiritual meditation as the "whiteness" of religion. The idea is that all religions presuppose, rely on, exploit, manipulate, etc., the same core of mystical experience, and that it is only "pure" forms of meditation like Zen

Buddhism that exemplify this core directly, bypassing institutional and dog-matic mediations. Spiritual meditation, in its abstraction from institutional-ized religion, appears today as the zero-level undistorted core of religion: the complex institutional and dogmatic edifice which sustains every particular religion is dismissed as a contingent secondary coating of this core. The reason for this shift of accent from religious institution to the intimacy of spiritual experience is that such a meditation is the ideological form that best fits today's global capitalism.

THE TROUBLE WITH CHRIST IN ORTHODOXY . . .

Do the three main versions of Christianity not form a kind of Hegelian triad? In the succession of Orthodoxy, Catholicism, and Protestantism, each new term is a subdivision, split off from a previous unity. This triad of Universal–Particular–Singular can be designated by three representative founding figures (John, Peter, Paul) as well as by three races (Slavic, Latin, German). In Eastern Orthodoxy, we have the substantial unity of the text and the body of believers, which is why the believers are allowed to interpret the sacred text; the text goes on and lives in them, it is not outside the living history as its exempted standard and model—the substance of religious life is the Christian commu-nity itself. Catholicism stands for radical alienation: the entity which mediates between the founding sacred text and the body of believers, the Church, the religious Institution, regains its full autonomy. The highest authority resides in the Church, which is why the Church has the right to interpret the text; the text is read during the Mass in Latin, a language which is not understood by ordinary believers, and it is even considered a sin for an ordinary believer to read the text directly, bypassing the priest's guidance. For Protestantism, finally, the only authority is the text itself, and the wager is on every believer's direct contact with Word of God as delivered in the text; the mediator (the Particular) thus disappears, withdraws into insignificance, enabling the believer to adopt the position of a "universal Singular," the individual in direct contact with the divine Universality, bypassing the mediating role of the particular Institu-tion. This reconciliation, however, becomes possible only after alienation is brought to the extreme: in contrast to the Catholic notion of a caring and loving God with whom one can communicate, negotiate even, Protestant-ism starts with the notion of God deprived of any "common measure" shared with man, of God as an impenetrable Beyond who distributes grace in a totally contingent way.

The key doctrinal division between Orthodoxy and Western Christianity (both Catholicism and Protestantism) concerns the procession of the Holy Spirit: for the Latin tradition, the Holy Spirit proceeds from both Father and

Son, while for the Orthodox it proceeds from the Father alone. From this perspective of the "monarchy of the Father" as the unique source of the three divine "hypostases" (Father, Son, Holy Spirit), the Latin notion of double procession introduces an all too rational logic of relations into God: Father and Son are conceived as relating to each other in the mode of opposition, and the Holy Spirit then appears as their reunion, not genuinely as a new, third, Person. We thus do not have a genuine Trinity, but a return of the Dyad to One, a reabsorption of the dyad into One. So, since the principle of the sole "monarchy of the Father" is abandoned, the only way to think the Oneness of the divine triad is to depersonalize it, so that, in the end, we get the impersonal One, the God of philosophers, of their "natural theology."[3]

Apropos of this disputed question of the origin of the Holy Spirit, Hegel committed a weird slip of the tongue: he mistakenly claimed that for Orthodoxy, the Holy Spirit originates from both Father and Son, and for Western Christianity from the Son alone (from Christ's Resurrection in the community of believers); as he wrote, the disagreement between East and West concerns knowing "if the Holy Spirit proceeds from the Son, or from the Father and the Son, the Son being only the one who actualizes, who reveals—thus from him alone the Spirit proceeds."[4] For Hegel, it is thus not even thinkable for the Holy Spirit to proceed from the Father alone—and my point is that there is a truth in this slip of the tongue. Hegel's underlying premise is that what dies on the Cross is not only God's earthly representative-incarnation, but the God of beyond itself: Christ is the "vanishing mediator" between the substantial transcendent God-in-itself and God qua virtual spiritual community. This "shift from subject to predicate" is avoided in Orthodoxy, where God–Father continues to pull the strings, is not really caught in the process.

Orthodoxy accounts for the Trinity of divine Persons by positing a "real difference" in God himself: the difference between essence (*ousia*) and its personal "hypostases." God is one with regard to essence, and triple with regard to personality; however, the three Persons are not just united in the substantial oneness of the divine essence, they are also united through the "monarchy of the Father" who, as a Person, is the origin of the other two hypostases. The Father as Person does not fully overlap with his "essence," since he can share it with (impart it to) the other two Persons, so that the three are consubstantial: each divine Person includes in himself the whole of divine nature/substance; this substance is not divided in three parts.

This distinction between essence and its hypostases is crucial for the Orthodox notion of the human person, because it takes place also in the created/fallen universe. Person is not the same as individual: as an "individual," I am defined by my particular nature, by my natural properties, my physical and psychic qualities. I am here as part of substantial reality, and what I am I am at the expense of others, demanding my share of reality. But this is not what makes me a unique person, the unfathomable abyss of "myself." No matter how much I look into my own properties, even the most spiritual ones, I will never find a feature that makes me a person:

> "person" signifies the irreducibility of man to his nature—"irreducibility" and not "something irreducible" or "something which makes man irreducible to his nature" precisely because it cannot be a question here of "something" distinct from "another nature" but of *someone* who is distinct from his own nature.[5]

It is only this unfathomable void which accounts for my freedom, as well as for my unique singularity which distinguishes me from all others: what distinguishes me are not my personal idiosyncrasies, the quirks of my particular nature, but the abyss of my personality—this is why it is only within the Holy Spirit, as a member of the body of the Church, that I can attain my singularity. This is how man is made "in the image and likeness of God": what makes a human being "like God" is not a superior or even divine quality of the human mind. One should thus leave behind the well-known motifs of a human being as a deficient copy of divinity, of man's finite substance as a copy of the divine infinite substance, of analogies of being, etc.: it is only at the level of person, qua person, qua this abyss beyond all properties, that man is "in the image of God"—which means that God himself must also be not only an essential substance, but also a person.

Lossky links this distinction between (human) nature and person to the duality of Son and Holy Spirit, of redemption and deification: "The redeeming work of the Son is related to our nature. The deifying work of the Holy Spirit concerns our persons."[6] The divine dispensation of humankind has two aspects, negative and positive. Christ's sacrifice is only the precondition for our deification: it changes our nature so that it becomes open to grace and can strive for deification. In Christ, "God made Himself man, that man might become God,"[7] so that "the redeeming work of Christ . . . is seen to be directly related to the ultimate goal of creatures: to know union with God."[8] As such, Christ's sacrifice provides only a precondition for the ultimate goal, which is the deification of humanity: "the idea of our ultimate deification cannot be expressed on a Christological basis alone, but demands a Pneumatological development as well."[9] Orthodoxy thus deprives Christ of his central role, since the final prospect is that of the deification (becoming-God) of man: man can become by grace what God is by nature. This is why "the adoration of Christ's humanity is almost alien to Orthodox piety."[10]

From the strict Christian standpoint, the Orthodox symmetrical reversal (God became man so that man can become God) misses the point of Incarnation: once God became man, there was no longer a God one could return to or become—so one would have to paraphrase Irenaeus's motto: "God made Himself man, that man might become God *who made Himself man*." The point of Incarnation is that one cannot become God—not because God dwells in a transcendent Beyond, but because God is dead, so the whole idea of approaching a transcendent God becomes irrelevant; the only identification is the identification with Christ. From the Orthodox standpoint, however, the "exclusively juridical theology" of Western Christianity thus misses the true sense of Christ's sacrifice itself, reducing it to the juridical dimension of "paying for our sins": "Entering the actuality of the fallen world, He broke the power of sin in our nature, and by His death, which reveals the supreme degree of His entrance into our fallen state, He triumphed over death and corruption."[11] The message of Christ's sacrifice is "victory over death, the first fruits of the general resurrection, the liberation of human nature from captivity under the devil, and not only the justification, but also the restoration of creation in Christ."[12] Christ breaks the hold of (fallen) nature over us, thereby creating the conditions for our deification; his gesture is negative (breaking with nature, overcoming death), while the positive side is provided by the Holy Spirit. In other words, the formula "Christ is our King" is to be taken in the Hegelian sense of the monarch as the exception: what we humans are from grace, he is by nature—a being of the perfect accord between Being and Ought.

The primordial fact is the Oneness of essence/substance and the Trinity of persons in God—this Trinity is not deduced and relational, but an original unfathomable mystery, in clear contrast to the God of Philosophers, who see in him the primordial simplicity of the Cause. Antinomies in our perception of God must be maintained, so that God remains an object of awed contemplation of his mysteries, not the object of rationalist analyses. The opposition between positive and negative theology is thus grounded in God himself, in the real distinction in God between essence and divine operations of energies (the divine economy): "If the energies descend to us, the essence remains absolutely inaccessible."[13] The main mode of this descent of the divine energy is grace:

> Precisely because God is unknowable in that which He is, Orthodox theology distinguishes between the essence of God and His energies, between the inaccessible nature of the Holy Trinity and its "natural processions." . . . The Bible, in its concrete language, speaks of nothing other than "energies" when it tells us of the "glory of God"—a glory with innumerable names which surrounds the inaccessible Being of God, making Him known outside Himself, while concealing what He is in Himself. . . . And when we speak of the divine energies in relation to the human beings to whom they are communicated and given and by whom they are appropriated, this divine and uncreated reality within us is called Grace.[14]

This distinction between the unknowable essence of the Trinity and its "energetic manifestations" outside the essence fits the Hegelian opposition between In-Itself and For-us:

> Independently of the existence of creatures, the Trinity is manifested in the radiance of its glory. From all eternity, the Father is "the Father of glory," the Word is "the brightness of His glory," and the Holy Spirit is "the Spirit of glory."[15]

However, from the strict Hegelian standpoint, this move is deeply problematic: is not the very essence of the Son to enable God to manifest himself and intervene in human history? And, even more, is not the Holy Spirit the "personality" of the community itself, its spiritual substance? Lossky is aware of the problem:

> If . . . the name "Holy Spirit" expresses more a divine economy than a personal quality, this is because the Third Hypostasis is *par excellence* the hypostasis of manifestation, the Person in whom we know God the Trinity. His Person is hidden from us by the very profusion of the Divinity which He manifests.[16]

What remains unthinkable within this perspective is the full engagement of God in human history which culminates in the figure of the "suffering God": from a proper Christian perspective, this is the true meaning of the divine Trinity—that God's manifestation in human history is part of his very essence. In this way, God is no longer a monarch who eternally dwells in his absolute transcendence—the very difference between eternal essence and its manifestation (the divine "economy") should be abandoned. What we get in Orthodoxy instead of this full divine engagement, instead of the God who goes to the end and sacrifices himself for the redemption of humans, instead of the notion of the history of human redemption as a history in which the fate of God himself is decided, is a God who dwells in his Trinity beyond all human history and comprehension, where the Incarnation in Christ as a fully human mortal and the establishment of the Holy Spirit as the community of believers are just an echo, a kind of Platonic copy, of the "eternal" Trinity-in-itself totally unrelated to human history.

The key question here is: how does the distinction between essence and its manifestation (energy, economy) relate to the distinction between essence (qua substantial nature) and person, between *ousia* and *hypostasis* (in Hegelese, to the distinction between substance and subject)? What Orthodoxy is unable to do is to *identify* these two distinctions: God is a Person precisely and only in his mode of manifestation. The lesson of Christian Incarnation (God becomes man) is that to speak of divine Persons outside Incarnation is meaningless, at best a remainder of pagan polytheism. Of course, the Bible says "God sent and sacrificed his only Son"—but the way to read this is: the Son was not present in God prior to Incarnation, sitting up there at his side. Incarnation is the birth of Christ, and after his death, there is neither Father nor Son but "only" the Holy Spirit, the spiritual substance of the religious community. Only in this sense is the Holy Spirit the "synthesis" of Father and Son, of Substance and Subject: Christ stands for the gap of negativity, for subjective singularity, and in the Holy Spirit the substance is "reborn" as the virtual community of singular subjects, persisting only in and through their activity.

Orthodoxy thus falls short of the central fact of Christianity, the shift in the entire balance of the universe implied by the Incarnation: the notion of the "deification" of man presupposes the Father as the substantial central point of reference to which/whom man should return—Hegel's idea that what dies on the Cross is the God of Beyond itself is unthinkable here. And the supreme irony is that Lossky wrote a detailed analysis of Meister Eckhart, although his Orthodoxy is completely opposed to Eckhart's central tenet: the ex-centricity of God himself, on account of which God himself needs man in order to come to himself, to reach himself, to actualize himself, so that God is born in man, and man is the cause of God.

What unites them is nonetheless the refusal (or inability) to endorse Christ's full humanity: they both reduce Christ to an ethereal being foreign to earthly reality. Furthermore, what both Lossky and Eckhart share is the accent on via negativa, approaching God through negating all predicates accessible to us, and thus asserting his absolute transcendence.

. . . AND IN MEISTER ECKHART

What makes Meister Eckhart so unbearable for all traditional theology is that, in his work, "the most fundamental dualism is shattered, that between God and his creature, the self, the 'I'."[17] This is to be taken literally, beyond the standard platitudes about God becoming man, etc.: it is not just that God gives birth to—creates—man, it is also not merely that only through and in man, God becomes fully God; much more radically, it is man himself who gives birth to God. God is nothing outside man—although this nothing is not a mere nothing, but the abyss of Godhead prior to God, and in this abyss, the very difference between God and man is annihilated-obliterated. We should be very precise here, with regard to this opposition between God and God-head: it is an opposition not between two kinds/species, but between God as Some(Thing) and Godhead as Nothing: "One usually speaks of God in opposi-tion to the 'world' or to 'man': 'God' is opposed to 'non-God.' In the Godhead all opposition is effaced."[18] In Kantian terms, the relationship between God and Godhead involves the indefinite (and not a negative) judgment: it isn't that

Godhead "isn't God," it's that Godhead *is a non-God*, an "Ungod" (in the same sense as we talk of the "undead" who are neither living or dead, but the living dead). This does not mean that the asymmetry between God and man is abolished, that they are posited at the same level with regard to the "impersonal" abyss of Godhead; however, their asymmetry turns around the standard one: it is God who needs man in order to reach himself, to be born as God:

> God has such a need to seek us out—exactly as if all his Godhead depended on it, as in fact it does. God can no more dispense with us than we can dispense with him. Even if it were possible that we might turn away from God, God could never turn away from us.[19]

What this means is that just as, for Heidegger, human being is *Dasein*, the "there" of Being itself, the (only) site of its clearing, for Eckhart, I am the only "there" (site) of God:

> In my [eternal] birth all things were born, and I was cause of myself as well as of all things. If I had willed it, neither I nor any things would be. And if I myself were not, God would not be either: that God is God, of this I am a cause. If I were not, God would not be God. There is, however, no need to understand this.[20]

(Note the final qualification!) Or, as Reiner Schürmann concisely recapitulates Eckhart's point: "I do not reflect God, I do not reproduce him, I declare him."[21] ("Declare," of course, retains here all its *performative* strength.) What this paradox implies is Eckhart's fundamental insight: "while one's [human] being has a center outside of it, in God, God's [being] too has a corresponding eccentricity."[22] What this means is that the eccentric character of man, the fact that he has his Center outside himself, in God, should not be understood as the relationship between a perfect/uncreated and imperfect/created substance, between the Sun and its planets that circulate around it; this eccentricity decenters God himself, and it is with regard to this Otherness (Godhead) in God himself that man and God are related: God himself can relate to himself only through man, which is why "the difference between God and not-God is a cleft that splits man thoroughly."[23] The two clefts thus overlap: man is eccentric with regard to God, but God himself is eccentric with regard to his own ground, the abyss of Godhead, and it is only through man's detachment from all creatures that God himself reaches himself: "not only does grace make the Son be born within us in his divinity, but the human being engenders the Son in God."[24] It is again crucial to note the asymmetry here: insofar as we consider God and man as two substances, the perfect-infinite-uncreated one and the imperfect-finite-created one, there can be no relation of *identity* between the two, only an external relation (of analogy, of cause and effect . . .); it is only with regard to Godhead, to "*ungod/Unding*" in God, that man can be identical to God.

There is, however, a crucial (and, perhaps, structurally necessary) ambiguity in Eckhart with regard to the birth of God in man—to put it in brutally simplified terms: who/what is given birth to here, God or Godhead? Does God, through man's "releasement" (*Gelassenheit*), reach back to the void of Godhead, of the abyss of his own nature, or is God-Word born out of the abyss of Godhead? Compare these two passages from the same page of Schürmann's book:

> The glory of God is that man "breaks through" beyond the Creator. Then the Son is born in the paternal heart, and man finds his God, the Godhead.[25]

> God is nothing as long as man lacks the breakthrough to the Godhead. If you do not consent to detachment, God will miss his Godhead, and man will miss himself.[26]

What is it, then? In order to clarify this point, on which *everything* hangs, we should inquire more closely into what Eckhart actually means by God and Godhead. Their relationship is not that of Substance and Subject, i.e., it is not that Godhead is the chaotic impersonal substance/nature and God a Person: God is the (only) Thing, *ein Dinc*, it is "everything that is." This is what explains Eckhart's strange reading of the sense in which God suffered for us:

> Only that is poverty of spirit when one keeps oneself so clear of God and of all one's works that if God wants to act in the mind, he is himself the place wherein he wants to act—and this he likes to do. For if God finds man so poor, he operates his own work and man suffers God in him, and God is himself the site of this operation, since God is an agent who acts within himself.[27]

> He who suffers without being attached to his suffering has God bear his burden, making it light and gentle for him. To detach oneself from one's pain means to consider it not as one's own but as assumed by God himself. . . . A human being who is a "wife" gives back to God the suffering that has befallen him.[28]

The radicality of this reinterpretation of God's suffering for us is unheard-of. God (not Godhead) should be grasped as the Spinozan *deus sive natura*: a Substance in which all activity and passivity, all creating and being-created, all joy and suffering, all love and anguish and fear, take place. As such, contrary to the deceptive appearance generated by the word "God," God is not a person, even if one can attribute feelings and desires to him. There is no freedom in it, no choice, just a necessity—God qua Creator does what he *has* to do. So it is *God*, not *Godhead, who/which is the impersonal substance*. And God reaches his Godhead, actualizes it, only in and through man.

But—here is Eckhart's real breakthrough, the move that, in effect, points beyond Spinoza to German Idealism—this is not "all that is": what lies outside the Substance is Nothing itself, Godhead as the abyss of *Unding*. There is, in

Eckhart, no word about the divine suffering as the price paid by God for our sins, about all this judicial-penal aspect of the Way of the Cross. It is simply that, since God is (not, as Thomas Aquinas and others thought, the Supreme Substance, but) the only Substance, everything, all creatures and their relations, take place in him. So when, through releasement, we detach ourselves from creatureliness, from the reality of decay, and identify with the abyss of Godhead, we no longer suffer; all the suffering remains where it always was, in the divine Substance, only we are no longer there.

From this notion of God as a substance caught in its own necessity, Eckhart draws the inevitable radical conclusion: there is nothing for which we should be grateful to God: "I will never thank God that he loves me, for he cannot do otherwise, whether he wishes it or not; his nature forces him to it."[29] Since God is merely a thing (dinc), not only do I not have to ask or solicit him for anything; insofar as I return to the original poverty of the abyss that I am, I can even command him: "The humble man does not solicit (bitten) anything [from God], but he can indeed command (gebieten) him."[30]

When Eckhart writes that anyone who wants to receive Jesus must become as free of all representations "as he was when he was not yet," before his birth on earth, he is, of course, referring to Plato, to the Platonic notion of the soul prior to its bodily dwelling; however, in contrast to Plato, this preexistence does not involve a soul which, uncontaminated by the images of sensory things, beholds eternal ideas, but one which purifies itself of all "things," ideas included (and including God himself as a Thing)—more a kind of tabula rasa, an empty receptacle. Only in such a state of pure receptivity which is nothing in itself, and thus potentially (a place for) everything, am I truly free, ledic, "virgin" of all images. This is how Eckhart interprets the virginity of Mary: only a virgin (a soul purified of all creaturely things) is open to receive/conceive (empfangen) and then give birth to Jesus-Word. To introduce a later distinction here, freedom for Eckhart is "freedom from" as well as "freedom for": freedom from all creaturely images and, as such, freedom for conceiving and giving birth to God: ". . . he was big with nothingness as a woman is with a child. In this nothingness God was born. He was the fruit of nothingness. God was born in nothingness."[31]

So there is a freedom which is not just Spinozan "conceived necessity": when I rejoin the abyss of Godhead, I became free. Here, however, we reach the crux of the matter: what is the relationship between the two Nothings, the abyss of Godhead, the Origin-Source of everything, and the abyss of the poverty of man? So when Schürmann writes that, in this detachment, "the nuda essentia animae joins the nuda essentia dei,"[32] how are we to understand this? Are the two voids simply to be identified? The asymmetry is clear here: if they are to be identified, then one of them—the abyss of Godhead, the Nothingness of the Ungod—has priority, and what happens in detachment is that, in achieving the supreme "poverty," man rejoins the divine abyss. How, then, are we to think the difference between the two abysses? Only by distinguishing between the Nothingness of the primordial abyss ("Godhead") and the Nothingness of the primordial gesture of contraction (what Schelling called *Zusammen-ziehung*), the gesture of supreme egotism, of withdrawing from reality and reducing oneself to the punctuality of Self. (In the mystical tradition, it was Jacob Boehme who took this crucial step forward.) This withdrawal-into-self is the primordial form of Evil, so one can also say that Eckhart is not yet able to think the Evil aspect of divinity. And there is a necessity in this shift from Nothingness as the abyss of Godhead to Nothingness as the void of my Self, the necessity of the passage from potentiality to actuality: *the divine void is pure potentiality, which can actualize itself only in the guise of the punctuality of Evil*—and giving birth to the Son-Word is the way to move beyond this Evil.

Linked to this is a further inability of Eckhart, the inability to think the encounter with a Thing which would not be simply an encounter with a created object/substance. In this specific sense, Eckhart in effect misses the central feature of the Judeo-Christian tradition, in which man's encounter with divinity is not the result of withdrawal into the depths of my inner Self and the ensuing realization of the identity of the core of my Self and the core of Divinity (*atman–Brahman* in Hinduism, etc.). That is the overwhelming argument for the intimate link between Judaism and psychoanalysis: in both cases, the focus is on the traumatic encounter with the abyss of the desiring Other—the Jewish people's encounter with their God whose impenetrable Call derails the routine of daily existence; the child's encounter with the enigma of the Other's *jouissance*. This feature seems to distinguish the Jewish-psychoanalytic "paradigm" not only from any version of paganism and Gnosticism (with their emphasis on inner spiritual self-purification, on virtue as the realization of one's innermost potential), but no less also from Christianity—does the latter not "overcome" the Otherness of the Jewish God through the principle of Love, the reconciliation/unification of God and Man in the becoming-man of God? As for the basic opposition between paganism and the Jewish break, it is definitely well founded: both paganism and Gnosticism (the reinscription of the Jewish-Christian stance back into paganism) emphasize the "inner journey" of spiritual self-purification, the return to one's true Inner Self, the self's "rediscovery," in clear contrast to the Jewish-Christian notion of an *external* traumatic encounter (the divine Call to the Jewish people, God's call to Abraham, inscrutable Grace—all totally incompatible with our "inherent" qualities, even with our "natural" innate ethics). Kierkegaard was right here: it is Socrates versus Christ, the inner journey of remembrance versus rebirth through the shock of the external encounter. That is also the ultimate gap that forever separates Freud from Jung: while Freud's original insight concerns the traumatic external encounter with the Thing that embodies *jouissance*, Jung reinscribes the topic of the unconscious into the standard Gnostic problematic of the inner spiritual journey of self-discovery.

With Christianity, however, things get complicated. In his "general theory of seduction," Jean Laplanche provides the definitive formulation of the encounter with unfathomable Otherness as the fundamental fact of the psychoanalytic experience.[33] However, it is Laplanche himself who insists here on the absolute necessity of the move from the enigma of to the enigma in—a clear variation of Hegel's famous dictum apropos of the Sphinx: "The enigmas of the Ancient Egyptians were also enigmas for the Egyptians themselves":

> When one speaks, to take up Freud's terms, of the enigma of femininity (what is woman?), I propose with Freud to move to the function of the enigma in femininity (what does a woman want?). In the same way (but Freud does not make this move), what he terms the enigma of the taboo takes us back to the function of the enigma in the taboo. And still more so, the enigma of mourning takes us to the function of the enigma in mourning: what does the dead person want? What does he want of me? What did he want to say to me?
>
> The enigma leads back, then, to the otherness of the other; and the otherness of the other is his response to his unconscious, that is to say, to his otherness to himself.[34]

Is it not crucial to accomplish this move also apropos of the notion of *Dieu obscur*, of the elusive, impenetrable God: this God has to be impenetrable also to himself, he has to have a dark side, an otherness in himself, something that is in himself more than himself? Perhaps this accounts for the shift from Judaism to Christianity: Judaism remains at the level of the enigma *of* God, while Christianity moves to the enigma *in* God himself. Far from being opposed to the notion of *Logos* as the Revelation in/through the Word, Revelation and the enigma in God are strictly correlative, two aspects of one and the same gesture. That is to say: it is precisely because God is an enigma also *in and for himself*, because he has an unfathomable Otherness in himself, that Christ had to emerge to reveal God not only to humanity, but *to God himself*—it is only through Christ that God fully actualizes himself as God.—Along the same lines, we should also oppose the fashionable thesis on how our intolerance toward the external (ethnic, sexual, religious) other is the expression of an allegedly "deeper" intolerance toward the repressed or disavowed Otherness in ourselves: we hate or attack strangers because we cannot come to terms with the stranger within ourselves. . . . Against this topos (which, in a Jungian way, "internalizes" the traumatic relationship to the Other into the subject's inability to accomplish his "inner journey" of fully coming to terms with what he is), we should emphasize that the truly radical otherness is not the otherness in ourselves, the "stranger in our heart," but the Otherness of the other itself to itself. It is only within this move that properly Christian Love can emerge:

as Lacan emphasized again and again, love is always love for the other insofar as he is lacking—we love the other *because* of his limitation. The radical conclusion from this is that if God is to be loved, he must be imperfect, inconsistent in himself; there has to be something "in him more than himself." This is what Eckhart is unable to think: God as a traumatic Thing which cannot be reduced to a creaturely Something—for him, "Something alien falls into my mind with everything it learns about the outside."[35]

Schürmann formulates this ambiguity very precisely: is it that the "breakthrough" Eckhart is struggling to formulate is "a breakthrough beyond everything that has a name," or is the highest moment of detachment to "let the Son of God be born in you"?[36] Schürmann's solution is evental processuality.[37] There is a double movement in Eckhart: first, from substantial entities to process, to event, to becoming (in the interaction between teacher and pupil, the only true reality is the event of the rise of Knowledge, i.e., the fusion of two entities, teacher and pupil—or God and man—is not substantial, but evental); then, the shift from movement, process of becoming, to repose, but to the repose of this process as such. This is what *Gelassenheit* is: not a kind of peace above the evental flux, but peace in and of this flux itself.[38] Identity thus becomes identification, nothingness becomes annihilation—this is where the "ethical" dimension comes in: I have to strive to become what I always am.[39]

This solution is nonetheless inadequate. When Schürmann writes: "Breakthrough on the one hand, birth on the other, are reconciled in the itineracy of the detached man,"[40] the alternative remains: under the dominance of which of the two are they reconciled? Schürmann gives a clear answer: "Union with the Son is subordinated to union with the Godhead. The first union is the preparation and the motivation for the second. The Christian vocabulary and apprenticeship appear as a training, as an *exercitatio animi*, towards the breakthrough."[41] Is it possible to imagine the predominance of the other pole, so that breakthrough (achieving "poverty") fulfills itself in giving birth to Christ? This is why G. K. Chesterton opposed all claims about the "alleged spiritual identity of Buddhism and Christianity":

> Love desires personality; therefore love desires division. It is the instinct of Christianity to be glad that God has broken the universe into little pieces. . . . This is the intellectual abyss between Buddhism and Christianity; that for the Buddhist or Theosophist personality is the fall of man, for the Christian it is the purpose of God, the whole point of his cosmic idea. The world-soul of the Theosophists asks man to love it only in order that man may throw himself into it. But the divine centre of Christianity actually threw man out of it in order that he might love it. . . . All modern philosophies are chains which connect and fetter; Christianity is a sword which separates and sets free. No other philosophy makes God actually rejoice in the separation of the universe into living souls.[42]

And Chesterton is fully aware that it is not enough for God to separate man from himself so that mankind will love him—this separation has to be reflected back into God himself, so that God is abandoned by himself. It is thus not enough to reach the eventual identity of God and man in the abyss of Godhead; from this zero point, one has to return to Christ, i.e., the abyss of Godhead had to give birth to Christ in his singular humanity. Eckhart avoids the monstrosity of Christ's Incarnation, he is unable to accept Christ's full humanity: "When Eckhart speaks of Christ, he almost always stresses his divinity at the expense of his humanity. Even in scriptural texts clearly describing the humanity of Jesus, he still finds ways of reading his divine nature."[43] For example, when interpreting John's "God sent his only son into the world" (1 John 4:9), he finds a way out in mobilizing the old play of words between "mundus" (world) and "mundum" (pure):

> "He sent him into the world": in one of its usages mundum means "pure." Notice that no place is more proper for God than a pure heart and a pure mind; there the Father begets his Son such as he begets him in eternity, neither more nor less. What then is a pure heart? That heart is pure which is separated and detached from all creatures, for all creatures soil, since they are one nothingness. Nothingness is decay, and it soils the mind.[44]

But is the Incarnation not precisely Christ's descent among creatures, his birth as part of the "nothingness" submitted to corruption? No wonder, then, that love itself disappears here:

> When the mind experiences love or anguish it knows where these come from. But when the mind ceases to regress towards these outward things, it has come home and lives in its simple and pure light. Then it has neither love nor anguish nor fear.[45]

In a way that points forward to Walter Benjamin, Eckhart distinguishes between continued time or duration and discontinued time or the instant: when the mind withdraws from created reality and reaches "poverty," it "enters into the fullness of the instant, which is eternity."[46] Eternity is thus not "all the time," but is experienced only through the utter reduction of the temporal duration to the instant (what Benjamin called Jetzt-Zeit). And, again, what Eckhart cannot think is eternity which really is a punctual moment, a Now fully in time.

The trap to avoid apropos of Eckhart is to introduce the difference between the ineffable core of the mystical experience and what D. T. Suzuki called "all sorts of mythological paraphernalia" in the Christian tradition: "As I conceive it, Zen is the ultimate fact of all philosophy and religion. . . . What makes all these religions and philosophies vital and inspiring is due to the presence in them all of what I may designate as the Zen element."[47] In a different way, Schürmann makes exactly the same move, when he distinguishes between the core of Eckhart's message and the way he formulated it in the inappropriate terms borrowed from the philosophical and theological traditions at his disposal (Plato, Aristotle, Plotinus, Aquinas . . .); even more, Schürmann designates the philosopher who, centuries later, was finally able to provide the adequate formulation of what Eckhart was striving at, Heidegger: "Eckhart came too early in his daring design. He is not a modern philosopher. But his understanding of being as releasement prepares the way for modern philosophy."[48]

However, does this not obliterate the true breakthrough of Eckhart, his attempt to think Christology (the birth of God within the order of finitude, Incarnation) from the mystical perspective? There is a solution to this impasse: what if what Schürmann claims is true, with the proviso that the "modern philosopher" is not Heidegger, but Hegel? Eckhart's goal is withdrawal from the created reality of particular entities into the "desert" of the divine nature, of Godhead, the negation of all substantial reality, withdrawal into the primordial Void-One beyond Word. Hegel's task is exactly the opposite one: not from God to Godhead, but from Godhead to God, i.e., how, out of this abyss of Godhead, God qua Person emerges, how a Word is born in it. Negation must turn around onto itself and bring us back to determinate (finite, temporal) reality. The same holds for Freud apropos of Oedipus: the true task is not to uncover the pre-Oedipal primordial texture of drives that precedes the Oedipal order of the Law, but, on the contrary, to explain how, out of this primordial chaos of preontological virtualities, the Word (the symbolic Law) emerges. We are thereby not back to where we already were, since, in this return, Oedipus itself is "de-Oedipianized": in Kierkegaardese, we pass from the being-of-Oedipus (Oedipus as given horizon) to Oedipus-in-becoming; we pass from the given horizon of Word the very birth of the Word—only at this point, when we return to the Word, but on the opposite side of the Moebius band, as it were, we effectively "sublate" it. The crucial step toward God as absolute person was accomplished only by Jacob Boehme—here is Henry Corbin's precise formulation of the difference between Eckhart and Boehme, who saw the necessity of the passage to the *absolute person* which is "absolved of the indetermination of the original Absolute, the *Absconditum*":[49]

In both of them, we certainly encounter the same profound sentiment of the mystical Divinity as undetermined Absolute, immobile and unchangeable in his eternity. From this point on, however, the two masters diverge. For Meister Eckhart, the *Deitas* (*Gottheit*) transcends the personal God, and the latter must be transcended because it is the correlative of the human soul, the world, and the creature. The personal God, therefore, is only one step on the way of the mystic because this personal God is affected by limitation and negativity, by non-being and becoming; "He becomes and un-becomes" (*Er wird und entwird*). The "Eckhartian soul" strives to free itself of it in order to escape from the limits of being, from the nihil of finitude and everything that could fixate it. Therefore, it must escape from itself in order to dive into the abyss of divinity, into an Abgrund whose bottom (Grund) it can never reach. Jacob Boehme's conception and attitude are completely different. He is searching for liberation in the affirmation of the self, in the realization of the true self, of its eternal "idea." . . . Therefore, everything is reversed: it is not the personal God which is the step toward the Deitas, the undetermined Absolute. To the contrary, this Absolute is a step toward the generation, the eternal birth of the personal God.[50]

Eckhart was still unable to see that "the Absolute being absolved of all determination still remains to be absolved of this determination."[51] In a way, everything turns around the inner tension of "nothingness." There is an old Jewish joke, loved by Derrida, about a group of Jews in a synagogue, publicly admitting their nullity in the eyes of God. First, a rabbi stands up and says: "O God, I know I am worthless, I am nothing!" After he has finished, a rich businessman stands up and says, beating himself on the chest: "O God, I am also worthless, obsessed with material wealth, I am nothing!" After this spectacle, a poor ordinary Jew also stands up and also proclaims: "O God, I am nothing. . . ." The rich businessman kicks the rabbi and whispers in his ear with scorn: "What insolence! Who is that guy who dares to claim that he is nothing too!" There is thus also a "positive" nothingness which clears the space for creativity, and dwelling in this nothingness—"being" it—is more than being something. In the Western tradition, this tension was first clearly formulated in Kabbala, apropos of two terms for "(nothing)ness," ayin or afisah. In a first approach, nothingness is "the barrier confronting the human intellectual faculty when it reaches the limits of its capacity . . . there is a realm which no created being can intellectually comprehend, and which, therefore, can only be defined as 'nothingness.'"[52] However, this simple notion of nothingness as a negative designation of God's absolute transcendence is then developed in a much more unsettling way; first, on the basis of this concept, the traditional doctrine of creatio ex nihilo is transformed into "a mystical theory stating the precise opposite of what appears to be the literal meaning of the phrase."[53] In its traditional meaning, creatio ex nihilo implies that God created reality in a radical way: he did not only transform or (re)organize some preexisting stuff, he effectively posited the created universe "out of nowhere," relying on no preexisting reality. In its new meaning, it implies the "precise opposite": "the emergence of all things from the absolute nothingness of God."[54] The "nothingness" is the nothingness of (that is) God himself, i.e., creatio ex nihilo implies that a thing appears "out of nowhere," and is not caused by an identifiable ground. (In this sense, the miracle of creatio ex nihilo happens also in our ordinary reality, when a well-known object all of a sudden acquires, "out of nowhere," a new dimension.)

But there is even more to it. The underlying premise of the notion of "nothingness" as the first act of the divine (self-)manifestation is that "since in reality there is no differentiation in God's first step toward manifestation, this step cannot be defined in any qualitative manner and can thus only be described as 'nothingness.'"[55] This insight is a very refined one: prior to differentiating himself from his creatures, prior to positing the created entities as distinct from himself, God has to open up a void in himself, i.e., to create a space for creation: in other words, before determinate differences, there should be (what Gilles Deleuze called) a pure difference, a difference in pure intensity which cannot be pinned down to any distinction in qualities or properties. To get an idea of this, recall the common experience of how—say, when we fall in love—the object can mysteriously undergo a radical transubstantiation, "nothing is any longer the same," although it remains empirically exactly the same. This *je ne sais quoi* which "changes everything" is the Lacanian *objet petit a*.

What this means is that there is a Hegelian dialectical reversal to be accomplished here: the initial opposition—"nothingness" as the mode of appearance (to us, finite minds) of the infinite actuality of the creative power of God, i.e., as the "for-us" of the unfathomable divine In-Itself—should be turned around, so that God as the supreme Creator, as the highest being, is, on the contrary, the way "nothingness" has to appear to us, finite minds. From this perspective it is, rather, nothingness which stands for the divine In-Itself, and the mirage of God as the Highest Being for God in the mode of his appearance, in his "for-us."

"A MATTER MORE DARK AND AWFUL . . ."

What, then, is this "matter more dark and awful," as Chesterton put it, that neither Orthodoxy nor Eckhart is able to confront? Let us turn to Chesterton himself, to his religious thriller *The Man Who Was Thursday*. It tells the story of Gabriel Syme, a young Englishman who makes the archetypal Chestertonian discovery of how order is the greatest miracle and orthodoxy the greatest of all rebellions. The focal figure of the novel is not Syme himself, but a mysterious chief of a super-secret Scotland Yard department who is convinced that "a purely intellectual conspiracy would soon threaten the very existence of civilization":

> He is certain that the scientific and artistic worlds are silently bound in a crusade against the Family and the State. He has, therefore, formed a special corps of policemen, policemen who are also philosophers. It is their business to watch the beginnings of this conspiracy, not merely in a criminal but in a controversial sense. . . . The work of the philosophical policeman . . . is at once bolder and more subtle than that of the ordinary detective. The ordinary detective goes to pot-houses to arrest thieves; we go to artistic tea-parties to detect pessimists. The ordinary detective discovers from a ledger or a diary that a crime has been committed. We discover from a book of sonnets that a crime will be committed.

We have to trace the origin of those dreadful thoughts that drive men on at last to intellectual fanaticism and intellectual crime.[56]

As cultural conservatives would put it today, deconstructionist philosophers are much more dangerous than actual terrorists: while the latter want to undermine our politico-ethical order to impose their own religious-ethical order, deconstructionists want to undermine order as such:

> We say that the most dangerous criminal now is the entirely lawless modern philosopher. Compared to him, burglars and bigamists are essentially moral men; my heart goes out to them. They accept the essential ideal of man; they merely seek it wrongly. Thieves respect property. They merely wish the property to become their property that they may more perfectly respect it. But philosophers dislike property as property; they wish to destroy the very idea of personal possession. Bigamists respect marriage, or they would not go through the highly ceremonial and even ritualistic formality of bigamy. But philosophers despise marriage as marriage. Murderers respect human life; they merely wish to attain a greater fullness of human life in themselves by the sacrifice of what seems to them to be lesser lives. But philosophers hate life itself, their own as much as other people's. . . . The common criminal is a bad man, but at least he is, as it were, a conditional good man. He says that if only a certain obstacle be removed—say a wealthy uncle—he is then prepared to accept the universe and to praise God. He is a reformer, but not an anarchist. He wishes to cleanse the edifice, but not to destroy it. But the evil philosopher is not trying to alter things, but to annihilate them.[57]

This provocative analysis demonstrates the limitation of Chesterton, his not being Hegelian enough: what he doesn't get is that *universal(ized) crime is no longer a crime—it sublates (negates/overcomes) itself as crime and turns from transgression into a new order.* He is right to claim that, compared to the "entirely lawless" philosopher, burglars, bigamists, murderers even, are essentially moral: a thief is a "conditionally good man," he doesn't deny property as such, he just wants more of it for himself, and is then quite ready to respect it. The conclusion to be drawn from this, however, is that crime as such is "essentially moral," that it simply wants a particular illegal reordering of a global moral order which should remain. And, in a truly Hegelian spirit, we should bring this proposition (of the "essential morality" of the crime) to its immanent reversal: not only is crime "essentially moral" (in Hegelese: an inherent moment of the deployment of the inner antagonisms and "contradictions" of the very notion of moral order, not something that disturbs moral order from outside, as an accidental intrusion) but *morality itself is essentially criminal*—again, not only in the sense that the universal moral order necessarily "negates itself" in particular crimes, but, more radically, in the sense that *the way morality (in the case of theft, property) asserts itself is already in itself a crime*—"property is theft," as they used to say in the nineteenth century. That is to say, one should pass from theft as a particular criminal violation of the universal form of property to this form itself as a criminal violation: what Chesterton fails to perceive is that the "universalized crime" that he projects into "lawless modern philosophy" and its political equivalent, the "anarchist" movement that aims at destroying the totality of civilized life, *is already realized in the guise of the existing rule of law*, so that the antagonism between Law and crime reveals itself to be inherent to crime, the antagonism between universal and particular crime.

When one continues to read the novel, however, it becomes clear that this position of Syme is only the starting point: at the end, the message is precisely the identity of crime and law, the fact that the highest crime is law itself—that is to say, the end of the novel does explicitly posit the identity between Law and universalized/absolute crime—that is the very final twist of *The Man Who Was Thursday*, in which "Sunday," the arch-criminal, the anarchists' all-powerful leader, is revealed to be the mysterious chief of the super-secret police unit who mobilizes Syme into the fight against the anarchists (i.e., against himself). So let us proceed with our brief description of the novel and look at how, in a scene worthy of *Mission Impossible*, Syme is recruited by this mysterious chief, reduced to a voice in darkness, to become one of these "philosophical policemen":

Almost before he knew what he was doing, he had been passed through the hands of about four intermediate officials, and was suddenly shown into a room, the abrupt blackness of which startled him like a blaze of light. It was not the ordinary darkness, in which forms can be faintly traced; it was like going suddenly stone-blind.

"Are you the new recruit?" asked a heavy voice.

And in some strange way, though there was not the shadow of a shape in the gloom, Syme knew two things: first, that it came from a man of massive stature; and second, that the man had his back to him.

"Are you the new recruit?" said the invisible chief, who seemed to have heard all about it. "All right. You are engaged."

Syme, quite swept off his feet, made a feeble fight against this irrevocable phrase.

"I really have no experience," he began.

"No one has any experience," said the other, "of the Battle of Armageddon."

"But I am really unfit—"

"You are willing, that is enough," said the unknown.

"Well, really," said Syme, "I don't know any profession of which mere willingness is the final test."

"I do," said the other—"martyrs. I am condemning you to death. Good day."[58]

Syme's first duty is to penetrate the seven-member "Central Anarchist Council," the ruling body of a secret superpowerful organization bent on destroying our civilization. In order to preserve their secrecy, members are known to each other only by a name of a day of the week; through some deft manipulation, Syme gets elected as "Thursday." At his first Council meeting he meets "Sunday," the larger-than-life president of the Central Anarchist Council, a big man of incredible authority, mocking irony, and jovial ruthlessness. In the ensuing series of adventures, Syme discovers that all the other five regular members of the Council are also secret agents, members of the same secret unit as himself, hired by the same unseen chief whose voice they have heard; so they join forces and finally, at a lavish masked ball, confront Sunday. Here, the novel passes from mystery to metaphysical comedy: we discover two surprising things. First, that Sunday, president of the Anarchist Council, is the same person as the mysterious never-seen chief who hired Syme (and the other elite detectives) to fight the anarchists; second, that he is none other than God himself. These discoveries, of course, trigger a series of perplexed reflections in Syme and the other agents. Syme's first reflection concerns the strange duality he noticed when he first met Sunday: seen from the back he appears brutish and evil, while seen from the front, face to face, he appears beautiful and good. So how are we to read this dual nature of God, this unfathomable unity of Good and Evil in him? Can we explain the bad side as just conditioned by our partial, limited, view, or—a horrible theological vision—is the back really his face, "an awful, eyeless face staring at me," whose deceptive mask is the good jovial face?

> When I first saw Sunday . . . I only saw his back; and when I saw his back, I knew he was the worst man in the world. His neck and shoulders were brutal, like those of some apish god. His head had a stoop that was hardly human, like the stoop of an ox. In fact, I had at once the revolting fancy that this was not a man at all, but a beast dressed up in men's clothes. . . . And then the queer thing happened. I had seen his back from the street, as he sat in the balcony. Then I entered the hotel, and coming round the other side of him, saw his face in the sunlight. His face frightened me, as it did everyone; but not because it was brutal, not because it was evil. On the contrary, it frightened me because it was so beautiful, because it was so good. . . . When I see the horrible back, I am sure the noble face is but a mask. When I see the face but for an instant, I know the back is only a jest. Bad is so bad, that we cannot but think good an accident; good is so good, that we feel certain that evil could be explained.
> I was suddenly possessed with the idea that the blind, blank back of his head really was his face—an awful, eyeless face staring at me! And I fancied that the figure running in front of me was really a figure running backwards, and dancing as he ran.[59]

If, however, the first, more comforting, version is true, then "we have only known the back of the world": "We see everything from behind, and it looks brutal. That is not a tree, but the back of a tree. That is not a cloud, but the back of a cloud. Cannot you see that everything is stooping and hiding a face? If we could only get round in front—"[60]

However, things get even more complicated: God's essential goodness itself is held against him. When Sunday, asked who he really is, answers that he is the God of Sabbath, of peace, one of the enraged detectives reproaches him: "it is exactly that that I cannot forgive you. I know you are contentment, optimism, what do they call the thing, an ultimate reconciliation. Well, I am not reconciled. If you were the man in the dark room, why were you also Sunday, an offense to the sunlight? If you were from the first our father and our friend, why were you also our greatest enemy? We wept, we fled in terror; the iron entered into our souls—and you are the peace of God! Oh, I can forgive God His anger, though it destroyed nations; but I cannot forgive Him His peace."[61]

As another detective observes in a terse, English-style remark: "It seems so silly that you should have been on both sides and fought yourself."[62] If there ever was British Hegelianism, this is it—a literal transposition of Hegel's key thesis that, in fighting the alienated substance, the subject fights his own essence. The novel's hero, Syme, finally springs to his feet and, with mad excitement, spells out the mystery:

I see everything, everything that there is. Why does each thing on the earth war against each other thing? Why does each small thing in the world have to fight against the world itself? Why does a fly have to fight the whole universe? Why does a dandelion have to fight the whole universe? For the same reason that I had to be alone in the dreadful Council of the Days. So that each thing that obeys law may have the glory and isolation of the anarchist. So that each man fighting for order may be as brave and good a man as the dynamiter. So that the real lie of Satan may be flung back in the face of this blasphemer, so that by tears and torture we may earn the right to say to this man, "You lie!" No agonies can be too great to buy the right to say to this accuser, "We also have suffered."[63]

This, then, is the formula provided: "So that each thing that obeys law may have the glory and isolation of the anarchist." So that Law is the greatest transgression, the defender of the Law the greatest rebel. However, where is the limit of this dialectic? Does it also hold for God himself? Is he, the embodiment of cosmic order and harmony, also the ultimate rebel, or is he a benign authority observing from a peaceful Above, with bemused wisdom, the follies of mortal men struggling against each other? Here is God's reply when Syme turns to him and asks him: "Have you ever suffered?"—

As [Syme] gazed, the great face grew to an awful size, grew larger than the colossal mask of Memnon, which had made him scream as a child. It grew larger and larger, filling the whole sky; then everything went black. Only in the blackness before it entirely destroyed his brain he seemed to hear a distant voice saying a commonplace text that he had heard somewhere, "Can ye drink of the cup that I drink of?"[64]

This final revelation—that God himself suffers even more than us mortals—brings us to the fundamental insight of Orthodoxy, Chesterton's theological masterpiece (which belongs to the same period: he published it a year later than Thursday)—not only the insight into how orthodoxy is the greatest transgression, the most rebellious and adventurous thing, but a much darker insight into the central mystery of Christianity:

> When the world shook and the sun was wiped out of heaven, it was not at the crucifixion, but at the cry from the cross: the cry which confessed that God was forsaken of God. And now let the revolutionists choose a creed from all the creeds and a god from all the gods of the world, carefully weighing all the gods of inevitable recurrence and of unalterable power. They will not find another god who has himself been in revolt. Nay (the matter grows too difficult for human speech), but let the atheists themselves choose a god. They will find only one divinity who ever uttered their isolation; only one religion in which God seemed for an instant to be an atheist.[65]

Because of this overlapping between man's isolation from God and God's isolation from himself, Christianity is "terribly revolutionary. That a good man may have his back to the wall is no more than we knew already; but that God could have His back to the wall is a boast for all insurgents for ever. Christianity is the only religion on earth that has felt that omnipotence made God incomplete. Christianity alone has felt that God, to be wholly God, must have been a rebel as well as a king."[66] Chesterton is fully aware that we are thereby approaching "a matter more dark and awful than it is easy to discuss . . . a matter which the greatest saints and thinkers have justly feared to approach. But in that terrific tale of the Passion there is a distinct emotional suggestion that the author of all things (in some unthinkable way) went not only through agony, but through doubt."[67] In the standard form of atheism, God dies for men who stop believing in him; in Christianity, God dies for himself.[68]

Peter Sloterdijk[69] was right to notice how every atheism bears the mark of the religion out of which it grew through its negation: there is a specifically Jewish Enlightenment atheism practiced by great Jewish figures from Spinoza to Freud; there is the Protestant atheism of authentic responsibility and assuming one's fate through anxious awareness that there is no external guarantee of success (from Frederick the Great to Heidegger in Sein und Zeit); there is a Catholic atheism à la Maurras, there is a Muslim atheism (Muslims have a wonderful word for atheists: it means "those who believe in nothing"), and so on. Insofar as religions remain religions, there is no ecumenical peace between them—such a peace can develop only through their atheist doubles. Christianity, however, is an exception here: it enacts the reflexive reversal of atheist doubt into God himself. In his "Father, why have you forsaken me?",

Christ himself commits what is for a Christian the ultimate sin: he wavers in his Faith. While, in all other religions, there are people who do not believe in God, only in Christianity does God not believe in himself. This "matter more dark and awful than it is easy to discuss" is narratively presented as the identity of the mysterious Scotland Yard chief and the president of the anarchists in *Thursday*. The ultimate Chestertonian opposition thus concerns the locus of antagonism: is God the "unity of the opposites" in the sense of the frame containing worldly antagonisms, guaranteeing their final reconciliation, so that, from the standpoint of divine eternity, all struggles are moments of a higher Whole, their apparent cacophony a subordinate aspect of the all-encompassing harmony—in short, is God elevated above the confusion and struggles of the world in the way Goethe put it:

And all our days of strife, all earthly toil
Is peace eternal in God the Lord.[70]

—or is antagonism inscribed into the very heart of God himself, i.e., is the "Absolute" the name for a contradiction tearing apart the very unity of the All? In other words, when God appears simultaneously as the top policeman fighting crime and the top criminal, does this division appear only to our finite perspective (and is God "in himself" the absolute One without divisions), or is it, on the contrary, that the detectives are surprised to see the division in God because, from their finite perspective, they expect to see a pure One elevated above conflicts, while God in himself is the absolute self-division? Following Chesterton, we should conceive such a notion of God, the God who says "Can ye drink of the cup that I drink of?", as the exemplary case of the properly *dialectical* relationship between the Universal and the Particular: the difference is not on the side of particular content (as the traditional *differentia specifica*), but on the side of the Universal. The Universal is not the encompassing container of the particular content, the peaceful medium-background of the conflict of particularities; the Universal "as such" is the site of an unbearable antagonism, self-contradiction, and (the multitude of) its particular species are ultimately nothing but so many attempts to obfuscate / reconcile / master this antagonism. In other words, the Universal names the site of a Problem-Deadlock, of a burning Question, and the Particulars are the attempted but failed Answers to this Problem. For example, the concept of State names a certain problem: how to contain the class antagonism of a society. All particular forms of State are so many (failed) attempts to propose a solution to this problem. So it is not that particular "really existing states" are so many failed attempts to realize the ideal of the State: they are so many attempts to actualize an ideal (model) that would resolve the antagonism inscribed into the very notion of the State.

To put it even more pointedly: God is not only not the "unity of opposites" in the (pagan) sense of maintaining a balance between opposed cosmic principles, shifting the weight to the opposite sense when one pole gets too strong; God is not only not the "unity of opposites" in the sense of one pole (the good One) encompassing its opposite, using evil, struggle, difference in general, as means to enhance the harmony and wealth of the All; it is also not enough to say that he is the "unity of opposites" in the sense of being himself "torn" between opposite forces. Hegel is talking about something much more radical: the "unity of opposites" means that, in a self-reflexive short circuit, God falls into his own creation; that, like the proverbial snake, he in a way swallows/eats himself by his own tail. In short, the "unity of opposites" does not mean that God plays with himself the game of (self-)alienation, allowing evil opposition in order to overcome it and thus assert his moral strength, etc.; it means that "God" is a mask (a travesty) of "Devil," that the difference between Good and Evil is internal to Evil.[71]

FROM JOB TO CHRIST

What this Chestertonian identity of the good Lord and the anarchist Rebel enacts is the logic of the social carnival brought to the extreme of self-reflection: anarchist outbursts are not a transgression of Law and Order; in our societies, anarchism is already in power, wearing the mask of Law and Order—our Justice is a travesty of Justice, the spectacle of Law and Order is an obscene carnival—a point made clearly by arguably the greatest political poem in English, The Masque of Anarchy by Percy Bysshe Shelley, which describes the obscene parade of figures of power:

> And many more Destructions played
> In this ghastly masquerade,
> All disguised, even to the eyes,
> Like Bishops, lawyers, peers, or spies.

> Last came Anarchy: he rode
> On a white horse, splashed with blood;
> He was pale even to the lips,
> Like Death in the Apocalypse.

> And he wore a kingly crown;
> And in his grasp a sceptre shone;
> On his brow this mark I saw—
> "I AM GOD, AND KING, AND LAW!"

Although it is part of today's feminist Politically Correct rules to praise Mary, Shelley's wife, as the one who gained a deeper insight than her husband into the destructive potential of modernity, in *Frankenstein*, she stopped short of this radical identity of opposites. There is a dilemma faced by many interpreters of *Frankenstein*, the dilemma that concerns the obvious parallel between Victor and God on the one side and the monster and Adam on the other: in both cases, we are dealing with a single parent creating a male progeny in a nonsexual way; in both cases, this is followed by the creation of a bride, a female partner. This parallel is clearly indicated in the novel's epigraph, Adam's complaint to God: "Did I request thee, Maker, from my clay / To mould Me man? Did I solicit thee / From darkness to promote me?" (*Paradise Lost*, X, 743–745). It is easy to state the problematic nature of this parallel: if Victor is associated with God, how can he also be the Promethean rebel against God (recall the novel's subtitle: *or The Modern Prometheus*)? From Chesterton's perspective, the answer is simple: there is no problem here, Victor is "like God" precisely when he commits the ultimate criminal transgression and confronts the horror of its consequences, since *God IS also the greatest Rebel*—against himself, ultimately. The King of the universe is the supreme criminal Anarchist. Like Victor, in creating man, God committed the supreme crime of aiming too high—of creating a creature "in his own image," new spiritual life, precisely like scientists today who dream of creating an artificially intelligent living being; no wonder his own creature ran out of his control and turned against him. So what if the death of Christ (of himself) is the price God has to pay for his crime?

Mary Shelley withdrew from this identity of opposites from a conservative position; more numerous are the cases of such a withdrawal from a "radical" leftist position. An excellent illustration is *V for Vendetta*, a film which takes place in the near future when Britain is ruled by a totalitarian party called Norsefire; the film's main opponents are a masked vigilante known as "V" and Adam Sutler, the country's leader. Although *V for Vendetta* was praised (by none other than Toni Negri, among others) and, even more, criticized for its "radical"—pro-terrorist, even—stance, it does not go to the end: it shrinks from drawing the consequences from the parallels between V and Sutler.[72] The Norsefire party is, we learn, the instigator of the terror it is fighting—but what about the further identity of Sutler and V? In both cases, we never see the live face (except the scared Sutler at the very end, when he is about to die): we see Sutler only on TV screens, and V is a specialist in manipulating the screen. Furthermore, V's dead body is placed on the train with the explosives, in a kind of Viking funeral strangely evoking the name of the ruling party: Norsefire. So when Evey—the young girl who joins V—is imprisoned and tortured by V in order to learn to overcome fear and be free, is this not parallel to what Sutler does to the entire English population, terrorizing them so that they get free and rebel? Since the model of V is Guy Fawkes (he wears Guy's mask), it is even stranger that the film refuses to draw the obvious Chestertonian lesson of its own plot: the ultimate identity between V and Sutler.[73] In other words, the missing scene in the film is the one in which, when Evey takes off the mask of the dying V, we see Sutler's face beneath.[74]

However, the attentive reader will already have guessed that we do not have merely a duality, but a trinity of the features/faces of God: the whole point of the novel's final pages is that, to the opposition between the benevolent God of peace and cosmic harmony and the evil God of murderous rage, one should add a third figure, that of the suffering God. This is why Chesterton was right in dismissing Thursday as a basically pre-Christian book: the insight into the speculative identity of Good and Evil, the notion of God's two sides, peaceful harmony and destructive rage—the claim that, in fighting Evil, the good God is fighting himself (an internal struggle)—is still the (highest) pagan insight. It is only the third feature, the suffering God whose sudden emergence resolves this tension of God's two faces, that brings us to Christianity proper: what paganism cannot imagine is such a suffering God. This suffering, of course, brings us to the book of Job, praised by Chesterton, in his wonderful short "Introduction to Book of Job," as "the most interesting of ancient books. We may almost say of the book of Job that it is the most interesting of modern books."[75] What accounts for its "modernity" is the way in which the book of Job strikes a dissonant chord in the Old Testament:

> Everywhere else, then, the Old Testament positively rejoices in the obliteration of man in comparison with the divine purpose. The book of Job stands definitely alone because the book of Job definitely asks, "But what is the purpose of God? Is it worth the sacrifice even of our miserable humanity? Of course, it is easy enough to wipe out our own paltry wills for the sake of a will that is grander and kinder. But is it grander and kinder? Let God use His tools; let God break His tools. But what is He doing, and what are they being broken for?" It is because of this question that we have to attack as a philosophical riddle the riddle of the book of Job.

The real surprise, however, is that in the end, the book of Job does not provide a satisfying answer to this riddle: "it does not end in a way that is conventionally satisfactory. Job is not told that his misfortunes were due to his sins or a part of any plan for his improvement. . . . God comes in at the end, not to answer riddles, but to propound them." And the "great surprise" is that the book of Job

> makes Job suddenly satisfied with the mere presentation of something impenetrable. Verbally speaking the enigmas of Jehovah seem darker and more desolate than the enigmas of Job; yet Job was comfortless before the speech of Jehovah and is comforted after it. He has been told nothing, but he feels the terrible and tingling atmosphere of something which is too good to be told. The refusal of

God to explain His design is itself a burning hint of His design. The riddles of God are more satisfying than the solutions of man.

In short, God performs here what Lacan calls a *point de capiton*: he solves the riddle by supplanting it with an even more radical riddle, by redoubling the riddle, by transposing the riddle from Job's mind into "the thing itself"— he himself comes to share Job's astonishment at the chaotic madness of the created universe: "Job puts forward a note of interrogation; God answers with a note of exclamation. Instead of proving to Job that it is an explainable world, He insists that it is a much stranger world than Job ever thought it was." To answer the subject's interrogation with a note of exclamation: is this not the most succinct definition of what the analyst should do in a treatment? So, instead of providing answers from his total knowledge, God does a proper analytic intervention, adding a mere formal accent, a mark of articulation.

The ontological implications of such a reply are truly shattering. After Job is hit by calamities, his theological friends come, offering interpretations which render these calamities meaningful, and the greatness of Job is not so much to protest his innocence as to insist on the meaninglessness of his calamities (when God appears afterward, he sides with Job against the theological defenders of the faith). The structure here is exactly the same as that of Freud's dream of Irma's injection, which begins with a conversation between Freud and his patient Irma about the failure of her treatment due to an infected injection; in the course of the conversation, Freud gets closer to her, approaches her face and looks deep into her mouth, confronting the horrible sight of the livid red flesh. At this point of unbearable horror, the atmosphere of the dream changes, the horror all of a sudden lapses into comedy: three doctors, Freud's friends, appear and, in ridiculous pseudo-professional jargon, enumerate multiple (and mutually exclusive) reasons why Irma's poisoning by the infected injection was nobody's fault (there was no injection, the injection was clean . . .). So there is first a traumatic encounter (the sight of the raw flesh of Irma's throat), which is followed by the sudden change into comedy, into the exchange between three ridiculous doctors which enables the dreamer to avoid the encounter with the real trauma. The function of the three doctors is the same as that of the three theological friends in the story of Job: to obfuscate the impact of the trauma with a symbolic semblance.

Such resistance to meaning is crucial when we are confronting potential or actual catastrophes, from AIDS and ecological disasters to the Holocaust: they have no "deeper meaning." This explains the failure of the two Hollywood productions released to mark the fifth anniversary of the 9 / 11 attacks: Paul Greengrass's *United 93* and Oliver Stone's *World Trade Center*. The first thing that strikes us is that both try to be as anti-Hollywood as possible: both focus on the courage of ordinary people, with no glamorous stars, no special effects, no grandiloquent heroic gestures, just a terse, realistic depiction of ordinary people in extraordinary circumstances. However, both films contain notable formal exceptions: moments which violate this basic terse, realistic style. *United 93* starts with kidnappers in a motel room, praying, getting ready; they look austere, like some kind of angels of death—and the first shot after the title credits confirms this impression: it is a panoramic shot from high above Manhattan in the night, accompanied by the sound of the kidnappers' prayers, as if the kidnappers are roaming above the city, getting ready to descend on earth to glean their harvest. . . . Similarly, there are no direct shots of the planes hitting the towers in *WTC*; all that we see, seconds before the catastrophe, when one of the policemen is on a busy street in a crowd of people, is an ominous shadow quickly passing over them—the shadow of the first plane. (Plus, significantly, after the policemen-heroes are caught in the rubble, the camera, in a Hitchcockian move, withdraws back into the air to a "God's-eye view" of the whole of New York City.) This direct passage from down-to-earth daily life to the view from above confers on both films a strange theological reverberation—as if the attacks were a kind of divine intervention. What is its meaning? Recall the first reaction of Jerry Falwell and Pat Robertson to the 9 / 11 bombings, perceiving them as a sign that God withdrew his protection of the USA because of the sinful lives of the Americans, putting the blame on hedonist materialism, liberalism, and rampant sexuality, and claiming that America got what it deserved. The fact that the very same condemnation of "liberal" America as the one from the Muslim Other came from the very heart of l'*Amérique profonde* should give us food for thought.

In a concealed way, *United 93* and *WTC* tend to do the opposite: to read the 9 / 11 catastrophe as a blessing in disguise, as a divine intervention from above to awaken us from moral slumber and to bring out the best in us. *WTC* ends with the offscreen words which spell out this message: terrible events like the Twin Towers destruction bring out the worst and the best in people—courage, solidarity, sacrifice for community. People are shown to be able to do things they would never imagine being able to do. And, in effect, this utopian perspective is one of the undercurrents that sustain our fascination with catastrophe films: it is as if our societies need a major catastrophe in order to resuscitate the spirit of communal solidarity. The two films are not really about the War on Terror, but about the lack of solidarity and courage in our permissive late-capitalist societies.

The legacy of Job precludes such a gesture of taking a refuge in the standard transcendent figure of God as a secret Master who knows the meaning of what appears to us to be a meaningless catastrophe, the God who sees the entire picture in which what we perceive as a stain contributes to global harmony. When we are confronted with an event like the Holocaust, or the death of millions in Congo in recent years, is it not obscene to claim that these stains have a deeper meaning in that they contribute to the harmony of the Whole? Is there a Whole which can teleologically justify, and thus redeem/sublate, an event like the Holocaust? Christ's death on the Cross thus means that we should immediately ditch the notion of God as a transcendent caretaker who guarantees the happy outcome of our acts, the guarantee of historical teleology—Christ's death on the Cross is the death of this God, it repeats Job's stance, it refuses any "deeper meaning" that obfuscates the brutal reality of historical catastrophes.[76] This also allows us to provide the only consistent Christian answer to the eternal critical question: was God present in Auschwitz? How could he allow such immense suffering? Why didn't he intervene and prevent it? The answer is neither that we should learn to withdraw from our earthly vicissitudes and identify with the blessed peace of God, who dwells above our misfortunes, so that we become aware of the ultimate nullity of our human concerns (the standard pagan answer), nor that God knows what he is doing and will somehow recompense us for our suffering, heal our wounds, and punish the guilty (the standard teleological answer). The answer is found, for example, in the final scene of *Shooting Dogs*, a film about the Rwanda genocide, in which a group of Tutsi refugees in a Christian school know that they will soon be slaughtered by a Hutu mob; a young British teacher in the school breaks down in despair and asks his father figure, the elder priest (played by John Hurt), where Christ is now to prevent the slaughter; the priest's answer is: Christ is now present here more than ever, He is suffering here with us. . . . The very term "presence" should be read against this background: presence is, at its most radical, the presence of a spectral *objet a* which adds itself to objects which are here in reality: when a Christian is caught in a situation like the one in the film, objects in reality around him are *present*, but the *presence* is that of Christ. This is why, in spite of a fundamental difference that separates me from Caputo and Vattimo, I fully share the idea, common to both of them, of Christ as a weak God, a God reduced to a compassionate observer of human misery, unable to intervene and help (we should just be careful to strictly distinguish this idea from the notion of "weak thought"). I cannot fail to agree with Caputo's description of what is happening on the Cross:

> It is a mystification to think that there is some celestial transaction going on here, some settling of accounts between the divinity and humanity, as if this death is the amortization of a debt of long standing and staggering dimensions. If anything, no debt is lifted from us in this scene but a responsibility imposed on us.[77]

What, then, if this was what Job perceived and what kept him silent: he remained silent neither because he was crushed by God's overwhelming presence, nor because he wanted thereby to indicate his continuous resistance—the fact that God avoided answering his question—but because, in a gesture of silent solidarity, he perceived the divine impotence. God is neither just nor unjust, but simply impotent. What Job suddenly understood was that it *was not him, but God himself who was in effect on trial in Job's calamities*, and he failed the test miserably. Even more pointedly, I am tempted to risk a radical anachronistic reading: Job foresaw God's own future suffering—"Today it's me, tomorrow it will be your own son, and there will be no one to intervene for him. What you see in me now is the prefiguration of your own Passion!"[78]

I should add a further complication here. Let us return to Freud's basic question: why do we dream at all? Freud's answer is deceptively simple: the ultimate function of the dream is to enable the dreamer to prolong his sleep. This is usually interpreted as bearing upon the dreams we have just before awakening, when some external disturbance (noise) threatens to awaken us. In such a situation, the sleeper quickly imagines (in the guise of a dream) a situation which incorporates this external stimulus and thus succeeds in prolonging his sleep for a while; when the external signal becomes too strong, he finally wakes up. . . . However, are things really so straightforward? In another dream from *The Interpretation of Dreams* about waking up, a tired father, who is spending the night watching at the coffin of his young son, falls asleep and dreams that his son is approaching him all in flames, addressing to him the horrifying reproach: "Father, can't you see I am burning?" Soon afterward, the father wakes up and discovers that, due to an overturned candle, his dead son's shroud has in fact caught fire—the smoke that he smelled while asleep was incorporated into the dream of the burning son to prolong his sleep. So did the father wake up when the external stimulus (smoke) became too strong to be contained within the dream scenario? Was it not, rather, the other way around: the father first constructed the dream in order to prolong his sleep, i.e., to avoid the unpleasant awakening; however, what he encountered in the dream—literally the burning question, the creepy specter of his son making the reproach—was much more unbearable than external reality, so he woke up, escaped into external reality—why? To continue to dream, to avoid the unbearable trauma of his own guilt for his son's painful death.

In order to get the full weight of this paradox, we should compare this dream with the one about Irma's injection. In both dreams, there is a traumatic encounter (the sight of the raw flesh of Irma's throat; the vision of the burning son); in the second dream, however, the dreamer wakes up at this point, while in the first dream the horror is replaced by the inane spectacle of professional excuses. This parallel gives us the ultimate key to Freud's theory of dreams: the awakening in the second dream (the father awakens into reality in order to escape the horror of the dream) has the same function as the sudden change into comedy, into the exchange between three ridiculous doctors, in the first dream—that is to say, our ordinary reality has precisely the structure of such an inane exchange which enables us to avoid the encounter with the real trauma.

From here, we should return to Christ: is Christ's "Father, why have you forsaken me?" not the Christian version of Freud's "Father, can't you see I am burning?"? And is this not addressed precisely to God-Father who pulls the strings behind the stage and teleologically justifies (guarantees the meaning of) all our earthly vicissitudes? Taking upon himself (not the sins, but) the suffering of humanity, he confronts the Father with the meaninglessness of it all.

THE DOUBLE KENOSIS

The theological term for this identity of Job and Christ is double kenosis: God's self-alienation overlaps with the alienation from God of the human individual who experiences himself as alone in a godless world, abandoned by God, who dwells in some inaccessible transcendent Beyond. For Hegel, the co-dependence of the two aspects of kenosis reaches its highest tension in Protestantism. Protestantism and the Enlightenment critique of religious superstitions are the front and the obverse of the same coin. The starting point of this entire movement is the medieval Catholic thought of someone like Thomas Aquinas, for whom philosophy should be a handmaiden of faith: faith and knowledge, theology and philosophy, supplement each other as a harmonious, nonconflictual, distinction within (under the predominance of) theology. Although God in himself remains an unfathomable mystery for our limited cognitive capacities, reason can also guide us toward him by enabling us to recognize the traces of God in created reality—this is the premise of Aquinas's five versions of the proof of God (the rational observation of material reality as a texture of causes and effects leads us to the necessary insight into how there must be a primal Cause to it all; etc.). With Protestantism, this unity breaks apart: we have on the one side the godless universe, the proper object of our reason, and the unfathomable divine Beyond separated by a hiatus from it. Confronted with this break, we can do two things: either we deny any meaning to an otherworldly Beyond, dismissing it as a superstitious illusion, or we remain religious and exempt our faith from the domain of reason, conceiving it as an act of, precisely, pure faith (authentic inner feeling, etc.). What interests Hegel here is how this tension between philosophy (enlightened rational thought) and religion ends up in their "mutual debasement and bastardization."[79] In a first move, Reason seems to be on the offensive and religion on the defensive, desperately trying to carve out a place for itself outside the domain under the control of Reason: under the pressure of the Enlightenment critique and the advances of science, religion humbly retreats into the inner space of authentic feelings. However, the ultimate price is paid by enlightened Reason itself: its defeat of religion ends up in its self-defeat, in its self-limitation, so that, at the conclusion of this entire movement, the gap between faith and knowledge reappears, but transposed into the field of knowledge (Reason) itself:

> After its battle with religion the best reason could manage was to take a look at itself and come to self-awareness. Reason, having in this way become mere intellect, acknowledges its own nothingness by placing that which is better than it in a faith outside and above itself, as a Beyond to be believed in. This is what has happened in the philosophies of Kant, Jacobi and Fichte. Philosophy has made itself the handmaiden of a faith once more.[80]

Both poles are thus debased: Reason becomes mere "intellect," a tool for manipulating empirical objects, a mere pragmatic instrument of the human animal, and religion becomes an impotent inner feeling which can never be fully actualized, since the moment one tries to transpose it into external reality, one regresses to Catholic idolatry which fetishizes contingent natural objects. The epitome of this development is Kant's philosophy: Kant started as the great destroyer, with his ruthless critique of theology, and ended up with—as he himself put it—constraining the scope of Reason to create a space for faith. What he displays in a model way is how the Enlightenment's ruthless denigration and limitation of its external enemy (faith, which is denied any cognitive status—religion is a feeling with no cognitive truth value) inverts into Reason's self-denigration and self-limitation (Reason can legitimately deal only with the objects of phenomenal experience; true Reality is inaccessible to it). The Protestant insistence on faith alone, on how the true temples and altars to God should be built in the heart of the individual, not in external reality, is an indication of how the anti-religious Enlightenment attitude cannot resolve "its own problem, the problem of subjectivity gripped by absolute solitude."[81] The ultimate result of the Enlightenment is thus the absolute singularity of the subject dispossessed of all substantial content, reduced to the empty point of self-relating negativity, a subject totally alienated from the substantial content, including its own content. And, for Hegel, the passage through this zero point is necessary, since the solution is not provided by any kind of renewed synthesis or reconciliation between Faith and Reason: with the advent of modernity, the magic of the enchanted universe is forever lost, reality will forever remain gray. The only solution is, as we have already seen, the very redoubling of alienation, the insight into how my alienation from the Absolute overlaps with the Absolute's self-alienation: I am "in" God in my very distance from him.

The crucial problem is: how are we to think the link between these two "alienations," the one of the modern man from God (who is reduced to an unknowable In-Itself, absent from the world subjected to mechanical laws), the other of God from himself (in Christ, incarnation)? They are the same, although not symmetrically, but as subject and object. In order for (human) subjectivity to emerge out of the substantial personality of the human animal, cutting links with it and positing itself as the I=I dispossessed of all substantial content, as the self-relating negativity of an empty singularity, *God himself*, the universal Substance, has to "humiliate" himself, to fall into his own creation, to "objectivize" himself, to appear as a singular miserable human individual in all its abjection, i.e., *abandoned by God*. The distance of man from God is thus the distance of God from himself:

> The suffering of God and the suffering of human subjectivity deprived of God must be analysed as the recto and verso of the same event. There is a fundamental relationship between divine kenosis and the tendency of modern reason to posit a beyond which remains inaccessible. The *Encyclopaedia* makes this relation visible by presenting the Death of God at once as the Passion of the Son who "dies in the pain of negativity" and the human feeling that we can know nothing of God.[82]

This double kenosis is what the standard Marxist critique of religion as the self-alienation of humanity misses: "modern philosophy would not have its own *subject* if God's sacrifice had not occurred."[83] For subjectivity to emerge— not as a mere epiphenomenon of the global substantial ontological order, but as essential to Substance itself—the split, negativity, particularization, self-alienation, must be posited as something that takes place in the very heart of the divine Substance, i.e., the move from Substance to Subject must occur within God himself. In short, man's alienation from God (the fact that God appears to him as an inaccessible In-Itself, as a pure transcendent Beyond) must coincide with the alienation of God from himself (whose most poignant expression is, of course, Christ's "Father, why have you forsaken me?" on the Cross): finite human "consciousness only represents God because God represents itself; consciousness is only at a distance from God because God distances himself from himself."[84]

The topic of the divine kenosis, of God's emptying into the world, is crucial to a proper understanding of the Christian notion of divine love. Some theologians, reflecting on the mystery of the divine dispensation of mercy, have been brought to Lacan's formula of love: the ultimate proof that God loves us is that he "gives what he does not have."[85] If we are to grasp this properly, we should oppose to have and to be: God doesn't give what he has, he gives what he is, his very being. That is to say: it is wrong to imagine the divine dispensation as the activity of a wealthy subject, so abundantly rich that he can afford to cede to others a part of his possessions. From a proper theological perspective, God is the poorest of them all: he "has" only his being to give away. His whole wealth is already out there, in creation.

This is why standard Marxist philosophy oscillates between the ontology of "dialectical materialism" which reduces human subjectivity to a particular ontological sphere (no wonder Georgi Plekhanov, the creator of the term "dialectical materialism," also designated Marxism as "dynamized Spinozism") and the philosophy of *praxis* which, from the young Georg Lukács onward, takes as its starting point and horizon collective subjectivity which posits/mediates every objectivity, and is thus unable to think its genesis from the substantial order, the ontological explosion, "Big Bang," which gives rise to it.—So if Christ's death is "at once the death of the God-man and the Death of the initial and immediate abstraction of the divine being which is not yet posited as a Self,"[86] this means that, as Hegel pointed out, *what dies on the Cross is not only the earthly-finite representative of God, but God himself, the very transcendent God of beyond.* Both terms of the opposition, Father and Son, the substantial God as the Absolute In-Itself and the God-for-us, revealed to us, die, are sublated in the Holy Spirit.

The standard reading of this sublation—Christ "dies" (is sublated) as the immediate representation of God, as God in the guise of a finite human person, in order to be reborn as the universal/atemporal Spirit—remains far too inadequate. The point this reading misses is the ultimate lesson to be learned from the divine Incarnation: the finite existence of mortal humans is the only site of the Spirit, the site where Spirit achieves its actuality. What this means is that, in spite of all its grounding power, Spirit is a *virtual* entity in the sense that its status is that of a subjective presupposition: it exists only insofar as subjects *act as if it exists.* Its status is similar to that of an ideological cause like Communism or Nation: it is the substance of the individuals who recognize themselves in it, the ground of their entire existence, the point of reference which provides the ultimate horizon of meaning to their lives, something for which these individuals are ready to give their lives; yet the only thing that really exists are these individuals and their activity, so this substance is actual only insofar as individuals believe in it and act accordingly. The crucial mistake to be avoided is therefore to grasp the Hegelian Spirit as a kind of meta-Subject, a Mind, much larger than an individual human mind, aware of itself: once we do this, Hegel has to look like a ridiculous spiritualist obscurantist, claiming that there is a kind of mega-Spirit controlling our history. Against this cliché about the "Hegelian Spirit," I should emphasize how Hegel is fully aware that "it is in the finite consciousness that the process of knowing spirit's essence takes place and that the divine self-consciousness thus arises. Out of the foaming ferment of finitude, spirit rises up fragrantly."[87] This holds especially for the Holy Spirit: our awareness, the (self-) consciousness of finite humans, is its only actual site, i.e., the Holy Spirit also rises up "out of the foaming ferment of finitude." Badillon says in Paul Claudel's *L'otage*: "Dieu ne peut rien sans nous [God can do nothing without us]." This is what Hegel has in mind here: although God is the substance of our entire (human) being, he is impotent without us, he acts only in and through us, he is posited through our activity as its presupposition. This is why Christ is impassive, ethereal, fragile: a purely sympathetic observer, impotent in himself.

We can see apropos of this case how sublation (*Aufhebung*) is not directly the sublation of otherness, its return into the same, its recuperation by the One (so that, in this case, finite/mortal individuals are reunited with God, return to his embrace). With Christ's Incarnation, the externalization/self-alienation of divinity, the passage from the transcendent God to finite/mortal individuals, is a *fait accompli*, there is no way back, all there is, all that "really exists," from now on are individuals; there are no Platonic Ideas or Substances whose existence is somehow "more real." What is sublated in the move from the Son to Holy Spirit is thus God himself: after the Crucifixion, the death of God incarnate, the universal God returns as a Spirit of the community of believers, i.e., he is the one who passes from being a transcendent substantial Reality to a virtual/ideal entity which exists only as the "presupposition" of acting individuals. The standard perception of Hegel as an organicist holist who thinks that really existing individuals are just "predicates" of some "higher" substantial Whole, epiphenomena of the Spirit as a mega-Subject who effectively runs the show, totally misses this crucial point.

What, then, is "sublated" in the case of Christianity? It is not the finite reality which is sublated (negated—maintained—elevated) into a moment of ideal totality; it is, on the contrary, the divine Substance itself (God as a Thing-in-Itself) which is sublated: negated (what dies on the Cross is the substantial figure of the transcendent God), but simultaneously maintained in the transubstantiated form of the Holy Spirit, the community of believers which exists only as the virtual presupposition of the activity of finite individuals.

CHRIST WITH WAGNER

Such a virtual order of collective spirituality (what Hegel called the "objective spirit" and Lacan the "big Other") is, however, clearly already present in Judaism—where is its specifically Christian twist? Let us look for a reply to this key question in the two masterpieces of Alfred Hitchcock, a British Catholic like Chesterton.

In predigital times, when I was in my teens, I remember seeing a bad copy of *Vertigo*—its last seconds were simply missing, so that the movie appeared to have a happy ending: Scottie reconciled with Judy, forgiving her and accepting her as a partner, the two of them passionately embracing. . . . My point is that such an ending is not as artificial as it may seem: it is rather in the actual ending that the sudden appearance of the Mother Superior from the staircase below functions as a kind of negative *deus ex machina*, a sudden intrusion in no way properly grounded in the narrative logic, which prevents the happy ending. Where does the nun appear from? From the same pre-ontological realm of shadows from which Scottie himself secretly observes Madeleine at the florist's. And it is here that we should locate the hidden continuity between *Vertigo* and *Psycho*: the Mother Superior appears from the same void from which, "out of nowhere," Norman appears in the shower-murder sequence of *Psycho*, brutally attacking Marion, interrupting the reconciliatory ritual of cleansing.[88]

And we should follow this direction to the end: in a strange structural analogy with the between-two-frames dimension of a painting, many Hitchcock films seem to rely on a between-two-stories dimension. Here is a simple mental experiment with two of Hitchcock's late masterpieces: what if *Vertigo* were to end after Madeleine's suicide, with the devastated Scottie listening to Mozart in the sanitarium? What if *Psycho* were to end seconds prior to the shower murder, with Marion staring into the falling water, purifying herself? In both cases, we would get a consistent short film. In the case of *Vertigo*, it would be a drama of the destruction caused by violently obsessive male desire: it is the very excessive-possessive nature of male desire which makes it destructive of its object—(male) love is murder, as Otto Weininger knew long ago. In the case of *Psycho*, it would be a moral tale about a catastrophe prevented at the last minute: Marion commits a minor crime, escaping with the stolen money to rejoin her lover; on the way, she meets Norman, who is like a figure of moral warning, showing Marion what awaits her at the end of the line if she follows the path she has taken; this terrifying vision sobers her up, so she withdraws to her room, plans her return, and then takes a shower, as if to cleanse herself of her moral dirt. . . . In both cases, it is thus as if what we are first lured into taking as the full story is all of a sudden displaced, reframed, relocated into, or supplemented by, another story, something along the lines of the idea envisaged by Borges in the opening story of his *Fictions*, which culminates in the claim: "Un libro que no encierra su contralibro es considerado incompleto" (A book which does not contain its counter-book is considered incomplete). In his 2005–2006 seminar, Jacques-Alain Miller elaborated on this idea, referring to Ricardo Piglia.[89] Piglia quoted as an example of Borges's claim one of Anton Chekhov's tales whose nucleus is: "A man goes to the casino at Monte Carlo, wins a million, returns to his place and commits suicide":

> If this is the nucleus of a story, one must, in order to tell it, divide the twisted story in two: on the one hand, the story of the game; on the other, that of the suicide. Thus Piglia's first thesis: that a story always has a double characteristic and always tells two stories at the same time, which provides the opportunity to distinguish the story which is on the first plane from the number 2 story which is encoded in the interstices of story number 1. We should note that story number 2 only appears when the story is concluded, and it has the effect of surprise. What joins these two stories is that the elements, the events, are inscribed in two narrative registers which are at the same time distinct, simultaneous, and antagonistic, and the construction itself of the story is supported

by the junction between the two stories. The inversions which seem superfluous in the development of story number 1 become, on the contrary, essential in the plot of story number 2. . . .

There is a modern form of the story which transforms this structure by omitting the surprise finale without closing the structure of the story, which leaves a trace of a narrative, and the tension of the two stories is never resolved. This is what one considers as being properly modern: the subtraction of the final anchoring point which allows the two stories to continue in an unresolved tension.

This is the case, says Piglia, with Hemingway, who pushed the ellipse to its highest point in such a way that the secret story remains hermetic. One perceives simply that there is another story which needs to be told, but which remains absent. There is a hole. If one modified Chekhov's note in Hemingway's style, it would not narrate the suicide, but rather the text would be assembled in such a way that one might think that the reader already knew it.

Kafka constitutes another of these variants. He narrates very simply, in his novels, the most secret story, a secret story which appears on the first plane, told as if coming from itself, and he encodes the story which should be visible but which becomes, on the contrary, enigmatic and hidden.[90]

Back to Hitchcock's *Vertigo* and *Psycho*: is this not precisely the structure of the narrative twist/cut in both films? In both cases, story number 2 (the shift to Judy and to Norman) appears only when the story seems to have concluded, and it certainly has the effect of surprise; in both cases, the two narrative registers are at the same time distinct, simultaneous, and antagonistic, and the construction of the narrative itself is supported by the junction between the two stories. The inversions which seem superfluous in the development of story number 1 (like the totally contingent intrusion of the murdering monster in *Psycho*) become essential in the plot of story number 2.

One can thus well imagine, along these lines, *Psycho* remade by Hemingway or Kafka. An excellent example of Hemingway's procedure is "Killers," his best-known short story which, in a mere ten pages, reports in a terse style the arrival of two killers in a small provincial town; they go to a diner, awaiting a mysterious "Swede" whom they have to kill. Swede's young friend escapes from the diner and informs him that two killers are on the way to murder him, yet Swede is so desperate and resigned that he sends the boy off and calmly awaits them. The "second story," the explanation of this enigma (what happened to Swede that he is ready to calmly await his death), is never told. (The classic film *noir* based on this story tries to fill this void: in a series of flashbacks, the "second story," the betrayal of a *femme fatale*, is told in detail.) In Hemingway's version, Norman's story would remain hermetic: the spectator would simply perceive that there is another (Norman's) story which needs to be told, but remains absent—there is a hole. In Kafka's version, Norman's story would appear in the foreground, told as if coming from itself: Norman's weird universe would be narrated directly, in the first person, as something completely normal, while Marion's story would be encoded/framed by Norman's horizon, told as enigmatic and hidden. Just imagine the conversation between Marion and Norman in his private room, prior to the shower murder: the way we have it now, our point of identification is Marion, and Norman appears as a weird and threatening presence. What if this scene were to be reshot with Norman as our point of identification, so that Marion's "ordinary" questions would appear as what they often in fact are, a cruel and insensitive intrusion into Norman's world?

No wonder Borges loved the detective whodunit, a genre which exemplifies a double story: the whole point of the detective's investigation is that, at the end, he is able to narrate a counter-story ("what really happened") to the confused story of how the murder appears. Of special interest here are those detective stories which raise this procedure to a second-degree self-reflective level, like Erle Stanley Gardner's *The Case of the Perjured Parrot*, in which the denouement itself is redoubled: Perry Mason first offers one explanation (the narrative of what "really happened") and then, not satisfied with it, takes it back and offers a second, correct, solution. Agatha Christie plays a variation on the same game when the two versions, the novel and the play, of *Appointment with Death* provide different denouements to the same story. Christie is in general at her best when she explores all the formal possibilities of the denouement of a whodunit: that the murderer is the entire group of suspects (in *Murder on the Orient Express*—the necessary ideological consequence of this solution is that, since society as such cannot be guilty, the victim must coincide with the murderer, the true criminal, so that his violent death is not a crime but a justified punishment); that the murderer is the very person who discovers the murder (*Peril at End House*); that the murderer is Poirot himself (in *The Curtain*, quite appropriately the last Poirot novel, and, again, with a variation on the *Orient Express* theme of the victim as the true criminal); that Poirot investigates the indications that a murder will be committed and prevents it at the last moment, thus saving the soul of a nice guy who, in a desperate situation, plans a murder ("Wasp's Nest"); and, finally, that the murderer is the very naive narrator of the story, the figure of commonsense decency (in *The Murder of Roger Ackroyd*). Here I should mention *Who Killed Roger Ackroyd?*, Pierre Bayard's excellent literary study in which, armed with logic and psychoanalysis, he conclusively demonstrates that the solution provided by Poirot is false, that Poirot becomes a victim of his own paranoia and imposes a construction which leaves too many clues unaccounted for.[91] Bayard's solution is that the real murderer is the narrator's sister, a spinster who knows all the secrets of the small town—the explanation that the narrator confesses to the murder in order to protect his sister (knowing that she committed the murder to help him, thus repaying his debt to her) and then poisons himself provides a much better interpretation of all the data. (Bayard's hypothesis is not that this ambiguity is an effect of Christie's unconscious mechanisms, but that she was fully aware of this fact and wrote the novel as a trap and a test for really attentive readers.) What Bayard provides is thus again the counter-story to the novel's official story.

In his more recent *L'affaire du chien des Baskerville*, Bayard[92] applies the same method of "critique policière" (detective literary criticism) to Conan Doyle's classic: he demonstrates that, while he fully accepts the entire content of the novel, there is a much better solution to the mystery than the one proposed by Sherlock Holmes at the end: the murderer is not Jack Stapleton but his wife Beryl, and the true murder is that of Jack himself (who disappears on the moor), not those of Charles Baskerville and Selden, which were mere accidents cleverly used by Beryl to avenge herself on her unfaithful husband. Bayard compares *The Hound of the Baskervilles* with Agatha Christie's *Towards Zero*, in which Nevile Strange, a professional tennis player, kills his old aunt, Lady Tressilian, and then plants at the murder scene two series of clues: the first (and rather obvious) implicates him in the murder, while the second (much more subtle) one points toward his ex-wife Audrey, who is then arrested not only for the murder of Lady Tressilian, but also for the attempt to put the blame on her ex-husband. Just prior to her hanging, Superintendent Battle arrives at the truth: Lady Tressilian's murder was in itself without any significance; the real aim of the murderer was to kill his ex-wife Audrey, so he needed the police investigation which would lead to her arrest and hanging. The same goes for *The Hound of the Baskervilles*, although with a double twist: the preceding superfluous murders do not take place at all, the murderer simply manages to impose on Holmes their reading as a murder inculpating her husband; the murderer succeeds in her plan, Holmes is duped. . . . How, precisely, does such a trick work? The (appearance of the) first murder is staged in order to attract the attention of the investigator or the police, and there we find Holmes's fundamental mistake, more serious than his misreading of clues: he forgets to include himself, his own investigative engagement, in the crime, i.e., he does not see that *the appearance of a crime was staged for his gaze*, in order to involve him (so that, as the murderer hopes, he will inculpate and cause the death of the wrong person). Here again we are dealing with a reflexive redoubling: what the detective sees as a reality to be discovered, as a mystery to be explained, is already a story told to him to attract his interest.

This is how, from a proper Hegelian-Lacanian perspective, we should subvert the standard self-enclosed linear narrative: not by means of a postmodern dispersal into a multitude of local narratives, but by means of its redoubling in a hidden counter-narrative. (This is why the classic detective whodunit is so similar to the psychoanalytic process: in it also, the two narrative registers—the visible story of the discovery of a crime and its investigation by the detective, and the hidden story of what really happened—are "at the same time distinct, simultaneous, and antagonistic, and the construction of the narrative itself is supported by the junction between the two stories.") And is not one way to conceptualize class struggle also such a split between the two narratives which are "at the same time distinct, simultaneous, and antagonistic, and the construction of the narrative itself is supported by the junction between the two stories"? If one starts to tell the story from the standpoint of the ruling class, one sooner or later reaches a gap, a point at which something arises which doesn't make sense within the horizon of this story, something which is experienced as meaningless brutality, something akin to the unexpected intrusion of the murdering figure in the shower scene from *Psycho*.

In 1922, the Soviet government organized the forced expulsion of leading anti-Communist intellectuals, from philosophers and theologians to economists and historians. They left Russia for Germany on a boat known as the *Philosophy Steamer*. Prior to his expulsion, Nikolai Lossky, one of those forced into exile, enjoyed with his family the comfortable life of the haute bourgeoisie, supported by servants and nannies. He "simply couldn't understand who would want to destroy his way of life. What had the Losskys and their kind done? His boys and their friends, as they inherited the best of what Russia had to offer, helped fill the world with talk of literature and music and art, and they led gentle lives. What was wrong with that?"[93] In order to account for such a foreign element, we have to go to "story number 2," the story from the standpoint of the exploited. For Marxism, class struggle is not the all-encompassing narrative of our history, it is an irreducible clash of narratives.—And does the same not go for today's Israel? Many peace-loving Israelis confess to their perplexity: they just want peace and a shared life with the Palestinians, they are ready to make concessions, but why do the Palestinians hate them so much, why the brutal suicide bombings that kill innocent wives and children? The thing to do here is, of course, to supplement this story with its counter-story, the story of what it means to be a Palestinian in the occupied territories, subjected to hundreds of regulations of the bureaucratic microphysics of power—for example, a Palestinian farmer is allowed to dig a hole in the earth no deeper than three feet to find a source of water, while a Jewish farmer is allowed to dig as deep as he likes.

A similar clash of narratives is at the very core of Christianity. One of the few remaining truly progressive US publications, the *Weekly World News*, reported on a recent breathtaking discovery:[94] archeologists discovered ten additional commandments, as well as seven "warnings" from Jehovah to his people; they are suppressed by the Jewish and Christian establishment because they clearly give a boost to today's progressive struggle, demonstrating beyond doubt that God took sides in our political struggles. Commandment 11, for instance, is: "Thou shalt tolerate the faith of others as you would have them do unto you." (Originally, this commandment was directed at the Jews who objected to the Egyptian slaves who joined them in their exodus continuing to practice their religion.) Commandment 14 ("Thou shalt not inhale burning leaves in a house of manna where it may affect the breathing of others") clearly supports the prohibition of smoking in public places; Commandment 18 ("Thou shalt not erect a temple of gaming in the desert, where all will become wanton") warns of Las Vegas, although it originally referred to individuals who organized gambling in the desert close to the camp of wandering Jews; Commandment 19 ("Thy body is sacred and thou shalt not permanently alter thy face or bosom. If thy nose offends thee, leave it alone") points toward the vanity of plastic surgery, while the target of Commandment 16 ("Thou shalt not elect a fool to lead thee. If twice elected, thy punishment shall be death by stoning") is clearly the reelection of President Bush. Even more telling are some of the warnings: the second warning ("Seek ye not war in My Holy Lands, for they shall multiply and afflict all of civilization") presciently warns of the global dangers of the Middle East conflict, and the third warning ("Avoid dependence upon the thick black oils of the soil, for they come from the realm of Satan") is a plea for new sources of clean energy. Are we ready to hear and obey God's word?

There is a basic question to be raised here, above the ironic satisfaction provided by such jokes: is the search for supplementary Commandments not another version of the search for the counter-book without which the principal book remains incomplete? And insofar as this Book-to-be-supplemented is ultimately the Old Testament itself, is the counter-Book not simply the New Testament? This would be the way to account for the strange coexistence of two sacred books in Christianity: the Old Testament, the Book shared by all three "religions of the book," and the New Testament, the counter-book that defines Christianity and (within its perspective, of course) completes the Book, so that we can in effect say that "the construction of the Bible itself is supported by the junction between the two Testaments." . . . This ambiguous supplementation-completion is best encapsulated in the lines on the fulfillment of the Law from Jesus' Sermon on the Mount, in which he radicalizes the Commandments (Matthew 5:17–48, quoted from the New International Version):

> Do not think that I have come to abolish the Law or the Prophets; I have not come to abolish them but to fulfill them. I tell you the truth, until heaven and earth disappear, not the smallest letter, not the least stroke of a pen, will by any means disappear from the Law until everything is accomplished. Anyone who breaks one of the least of these commandments and teaches others to do the same will be called least in the kingdom of heaven, but whoever practices and teaches these commands will be called great in the kingdom of heaven. . . .
>
> You have heard that it was said to the people long ago, "Do not murder, and anyone who murders will be subject to judgment." But I tell you that anyone who is angry with his brother will be subject to judgment. . . .

You have heard that it was said, "Do not commit adultery." But I tell you that anyone who looks at a woman lustfully has already committed adultery with her in his heart. If your right eye causes you to sin, gouge it out and throw it away. It is better for you to lose one part of your body than for your whole body to be thrown into hell. And if your right hand causes you to sin, cut it off and throw it away. It is better for you to lose one part of your body than for your whole body to go into hell.

It has been said, "Anyone who divorces his wife must give her a certificate of divorce." But I tell you that anyone who divorces his wife, except for marital unfaithfulness, causes her to become an adulteress, and anyone who marries the divorced woman commits adultery.

Again, you have heard that it was said to the people long ago, "Do not break your oath, but keep the oaths you have made to the Lord." But I tell you, Do not swear at all: either by heaven, for it is God's throne; or by the earth, for it is his footstool; or by Jerusalem, for it is the city of the Great King. And do not swear by your head, for you cannot make even one hair white or black. Simply let your "Yes" be "Yes," and your "No," "No"; anything beyond this comes from the evil one.

You have heard that it was said, "Eye for eye, and tooth for tooth." But I tell you, Do not resist an evil person. If someone strikes you on the right cheek, turn to him the other also. And if someone wants to sue you and take your tunic, let him have your cloak as well. If someone forces you to go one mile, go with him two miles. Give to the one who asks you, and do not turn away from the one who wants to borrow from you.

You have heard that it was said, "Love your neighbor and hate your enemy." But I tell you: Love your enemies and pray for those who persecute you, that you may be sons of your Father in heaven. He causes his sun to rise on the evil and the good, and sends rain on the righteous and the unrighteous. If you love those who love you, what reward will you get? Are not even the tax collectors doing that? And if you greet only your brothers, what are you doing more than others? Do not even pagans do that? Be perfect, therefore, as your heavenly Father is perfect.

The official Catholic way to interpret this series of supplements is the so-called *Double Standard View*, which divides the teachings of the Sermon into general precepts and specific counsels: obedience to the general precepts is essential for salvation, but obedience to the counsels is necessary only for perfection, or, as it was said already in *Didache*: "For if you are able to bear the entire yoke of the Lord, you will be perfect; but if you are not able to do this, do what you are able."[95] In short, the Law is for everyone, while its supplement is for the perfect only. Martin Luther rejected this Catholic approach and proposed a different two-level system, the so-called *Two Realms View*, which divides the world into the religious and secular realms, claiming that the Sermon applies only to the spiritual: in the temporal world, obligations to family, employers, and country force believers to compromise; thus a judge should follow his secular obligations to sentence a criminal, but inwardly, he should mourn for the criminal's fate.

Clearly, both these versions resolve the tension by introducing a split between the two domains and constraining the more severe injunctions to the second domain. As expected, in the case of Catholicism, this split is externalized into two kinds of people, the ordinary ones and the perfect (saints, monks . . .), while in Protestantism it is internalized into the split between how I interact with others in the secular sphere, and how I relate to others inwardly. Are these, however, the only ways to read this? A (perhaps surprising) reference to Richard Wagner might be of some help here: a reference to his draft of the play *Jesus of Nazareth*, written somewhere between late 1848 and early 1849. Together with the libretto *The Saracen Woman* (*Die Sarazenin*, written in 1843 between *The Flying Dutchman* and *Tannhäuser*), these two drafts are key elements in Wagner's development: each of them indicates a path which might have been taken but was abandoned, i.e., it points toward a what-if scenario of an alternate Wagner, and thus reminds us of the open character of history. *The Saracen Woman* is, after Wagner found his voice in the *Dutchman*, the last counterattack of Grand Opera, a repetition of *Rienzi*—if Wagner had set it to music, and if the opera had turned out to be a triumph like *Rienzi*, it is possible that Wagner might have succumbed to this last Meyerbeerian temptation, and developed into a completely different composer. Similarly, a couple of years later, after Wagner exhausted his potential for Romantic operas with *Lohengrin* and was searching for a new way, *Jesus* again stands for a path which differs completely from that of the music-dramas and their "pagan" universe—*Jesus* is something like *Parsifal* written directly, without the long detour through the *Ring*. What, among other things, Wagner attributes there to Jesus is a series of alternate supplementations of the Commandments:

> The commandment saith: Thou shalt not commit adultery! But I say unto you: Ye shall not marry without love. A marriage without love is broken as soon as entered into, and who so hath wooed without love, already hath broken the wedding. If ye follow my commandment, how can ye ever break it, since it bids you to do what your own heart and soul desire?—But where ye marry without love, ye bind yourselves at variance with God's love, and in your wedding ye sin against God; and this sin avengeth itself by your striving next against the law of man, in that ye break the marriage-vow.[96]

The shift from Jesus' actual words is crucial here: Jesus "internalizes" the prohibition, making it much more severe (the Law says no actual adultery, while I say that if you only covet the other's wife in your mind, it is the same as if you have already committed adultery, etc.); Wagner also internalizes it, but in a different way—the inner dimension he evokes is not that of intention, but that of love that should accompany the Law (marriage). The true adultery is not to copulate outside marriage, but to copulate in marriage without love: simple adultery just violates the Law from outside, while marriage without love destroys it from within, turning the letter of the Law against its spirit. So, to paraphrase Brecht yet again: what is a simple adultery compared to (the adultery that is a loveless) marriage! It is not by chance that Wagner's underlying formula "marriage is adultery" recalls Proudhon's "property is theft"— in the stormy events of 1848, Wagner was not only a Feuerbachian celebrating sexual love, but also a Proudhonian revolutionary demanding the abolition of private property; so no wonder that, later on the same page, Wagner attributes to Jesus a Proudhonian supplement to "Thou shalt not steal!":

> This also is a good law: Thou shalt not steal, nor covet another man's goods. Who goeth against it, sinneth: but I preserve you from that sin, inasmuch as I teach you: Love thy neighbour as thyself; which also meaneth: Lay not up for thyself treasures, whereby thou stealest from thy neighbour and makest him to starve: for when thou hast thy goods safeguarded by the law of man, thou provokest thy neighbour to sin against the law.[97]

This is how the Christian "supplement" to the Book should be conceived: as a properly Hegelian "negation of negation," which resides in the decisive shift from the distortion of a notion to a distortion constitutive of this notion, i.e., to this notion as a distortion-in-itself. Recall again Proudhon's old dialectical motto "property is theft": the "negation of negation" here is the shift from theft as a distortion ("negation," violation) of property to the dimension of theft inscribed into the very notion of property (nobody has the right to fully own the means of production, their nature is inherently collective, so every claim "this is mine" is illegitimate). The same goes for crime and Law, for the passage from crime as the distortion ("negation") of the Law to crime as sustaining the Law itself, i.e., to the idea of the Law itself as universalized crime. We should note that, in this notion of the "negation of negation," the encompassing unity of the two opposed terms is the "lowest," "transgressive" one: it is not crime which is a moment of Law's self-mediation (or theft which is a moment of property's self-mediation); the opposition of crime and Law is inherent to crime, Law is a subspecies of crime, crime's self-relating negation (just as property is theft's self-relating negation). And ultimately, does the same not go for nature itself? Here, "negation of negation" is the shift from the idea that we are violating some natural balanced order to the idea that imposing on the Real such a notion of balanced order is in itself the greatest violation . . . which is why the premise, the first axiom even, of every radical ecology is "there is no nature."

These lines cannot but evoke the famous passages from The Communist Manifesto which answer the bourgeois criticism that communists want to abolish freedom, property, and family: it is capitalist freedom itself which is effectively the freedom to buy and sell on the market, and thus the very form of unfreedom for those who have nothing but their labor-power to sell; it is capitalist property itself which means the "abolition" of property for those who own no means of production; it is bourgeois marriage itself which is universalized prostitution . . . in all these cases, the external opposition is internalized, so that one opposite becomes the form of appearance of the other (bourgeois freedom is the form of appearance of the unfreedom of the majority, etc.). However, for Marx, at least in the case of freedom, this means that communism will not abolish freedom but, by abolishing capitalist servitude, bring about actual freedom, the freedom which will no longer be the form of appearance of its opposite. It is thus not freedom itself which is the form of appearance of its opposite, but only false freedom, freedom distorted by the relations of domination. Is it not, then, that, underlying the dialectic of the "negation of negation," a Habermasian "normative" approach imposes itself here immediately: how can we talk about crime if we do not have a preceding notion of legal order violated by criminal transgression? In other words, is the notion of law as universalized / self-negated crime not autodestructive? This, precisely, is what a properly dialectical approach rejects: before transgression there is just a neutral state of things, neither good nor bad (neither property nor theft, neither law nor crime); the balance of this state of things is then violated, and the positive norm (Law, property) arises as a secondary move, an attempt to counteract and contain the transgression. With regard to the dialectic of freedom, this means that it is the very "alienated, bourgeois" freedom which creates the conditions and opens up the space for "actual" freedom.

This Hegelian logic is at work in Wagner's universe up to *Parsifal*, whose final message is a profoundly Hegelian one: The wound can be healed only by the spear that smote it (*Die Wunde schliesst der Speer nur der sie schlug*). Hegel says the same thing, although with the accent shifted in the opposite direction: the Spirit is itself the wound it tries to heal, i.e., the wound is self-inflicted.[98] That is to say, what is "Spirit" at its most elementary? The "wound" of nature: the subject is the immense—absolute—power of negativity, of introducing a gap / cut into the given-immediate substantial unity, the power of *differentiating*, of "abstracting," of tearing apart and treating as self-standing what in reality is part of an organic unity. This is why the notion of the "self-alienation" of Spirit (of Spirit losing itself in its otherness, in its objectivization, in its result) is more paradoxical than it may appear: it should be read together with Hegel's assertion of the thoroughly nonsubstantial character of Spirit: there is no *res cogitans*, no thing which (as its property) also thinks; Spirit is nothing but the process of overcoming natural immediacy, of the cultivation of this immediacy, of withdrawing-into-itself or "taking off" from it, of—why not?—alienating itself from it. The paradox is thus that there is no Self that precedes the Spirit's "self-alienation": the very process of alienation creates / generates the "Self" from which the Spirit is alienated and to which it then returns. (Hegel here turns around the standard notion that a failed version of X presupposes this X as their norm (measure): X is created, its space is outlined, only through repetitive failures to reach it.) Spirit self-alienation is the same as, fully co-incides with, its alienation from its Other (nature), because it constitutes it-self through its "return-to-itself" from its immersion in natural Otherness. In other words, Spirit's return-to-itself creates the very dimension to which it returns. (This holds for all "return to origins": when, from the nineteenth century onward, new nation-states were constituting themselves in Central and Eastern Europe, their discovery and return to "old ethnic roots" generated these roots.) What this means is that the "negation of negation," the "return-to-oneself" from alienation, does not occur where it seems to: in the "nega-tion of negation"; the Spirit's negativity is not relativized, subsumed under an all-encompassing positivity; it is, on the contrary, the "simple negation" which remains attached to the presupposed positivity it negated, the presup-posed Otherness from which it alienates itself, and the "negation of negation" is nothing but the negation of the substantial character of this Otherness itself, the full acceptance of the abyss of the Spirit's self-relating which retroactively posits all its presuppositions. In other words, once we are in negativity, we never quit it and regain the lost innocence of Origins; it is, on the contrary, only in "negation of negation" that the Origins are truly lost, that their very loss is lost, that they are deprived of the substantial status of that which was lost. The Spirit heals its wound not by directly healing it, but by getting rid of the very full and sane Body into which the wound was cut. It is a little like the (rather tasteless version of the) "first-the-bad-news-then-the-good-news" medical joke: "The bad news is that we've discovered you have severe Alzheimer's dis-ease. The good news is the same: you have Alzheimer's, so you will already have forgotten the bad news by the time you get back home."

In Christian theology, Christ's supplement (the repeated "But I tell you . . .") is often designated as the "antithesis" to the Thesis of the Law—the irony here is that, in the proper Hegelian approach, this antithesis is synthesis itself at its purest. In other words, is what Christ does in his "fulfillment" of the Law not the Law's Aufhebung in the strict Hegelian sense of the term? In its supplement, the Commandment is both negated and maintained by being elevated/trans-posed onto another (higher) level. This is why we should reject the common-place criticism which cannot but arise here: from the Hegelian standpoint, is the "second story," this supplement which displaces the "first story," not merely a negation, a split into two, which needs to be negated in its own turn in order to bring about the "synthesis" of the opposites? What happens in the passage from "antithesis" to "synthesis" is not that another story is added, bringing together the first two (or that we return to the first story, which is now rendered more "rich," provided with its background): all that happens is a purely formal shift by means of which we realize that the "antithesis" is already "synthesis." Back to the example of class struggle: there is no need to posit some all-encompassing global narrative which would provide the frame for both opposing narratives: the second narrative (the story told from the standpoint of the oppressed) is already the story from the standpoint of social totality—why? The two stories are not symmetrical: only the second story brings home the antagonism, the gap that separates the two stories, and this antagonism is the "truth" of the entire field.

THE MONSTROSITY OF CHRIST

Although, for Chesterton, Hegel was the worst of modern nihilistic "German philosophers," the proximity of his theological paradoxes to the Hegelian dialectic cannot fail to strike us. Let us approach this proximity from the other (Hegel's) side, by confronting the core question of Hegelian Christology: why the idea of Reconciliation between God and man (the fundamental content of Christianity) has to appear in a single individual, in the guise of an external, contingent, flesh-and-blood person (Christ, the man-God)? Hegel provides the most concise answer in his lectures on the philosophy of religion:

> Cannot the subject bring about this reconciliation by itself, through its own efforts, its own activity—so that through its piety and devotion it makes its inner [life] conform with the divine idea, and express this conformity through its deeds? And further, is this not within the capability [not merely] of a single subject but of all people who genuinely wish to take up the divine law within themselves, so that heaven would exist on earth and the Spirit would be present in reality and dwell in its community?[99]

Note Hegel's precision here: his question is double. First, the individual's divinization, spiritual perfection; then, the collective actualization of the divine community as "heaven on earth," in the guise of a community which lives totally in accordance with the divine law. In other words, the hypothesis that Hegel entertains here is the standard Marxist one: why cannot we conceive a direct passage from In-Itself to For-Itself, from God as full Substance existing in itself, beyond human history, to the Holy Spirit as spiritual-virtual substance, as the substance that exists only insofar as it is "kept alive" by the incessant activity of individuals? Why not such a direct dis-alienation, by means of which individuals recognize in God qua transcendent substance the "reified" result of their own activity?

So why not? Hegel's answer relies on the dialectic of positing and presupposing: if the subject were to be able to do it on its own, through its own agency, then it would have been something merely *posited* by it—however, positing is in itself always one-sided, relying on some presupposition: "The unity of subjectivity and objectivity—this divine unity—must be a presupposition for my positing."[100] And Christ as God-man is the externally presupposed Unity/Reconciliation: first the immediate unity, then the mediate one in the guise of the Holy Spirit—we pass from Christ whose predicate is love to love itself as subject (in the Holy Spirit, "I am where two of you love each other . . .").

But even here it may appear that one can counter Hegel with Hegel himself: is not this circle of positing-presupposing the very circle of substance-subject, of the Holy Spirit as a spiritual substance kept alive, effectively existing, arriving at its actuality, only in the activity of living individuals? The status of the Hegelian spiritual substance is properly virtual: it exists only insofar as subjects act as if it exists. As we have already seen, its status is similar to that of an ideological cause like Communism or My Nation: it is the "spiritual substance" of the individuals who recognize themselves in it, the ground of their entire existence, the point of reference which provides the ultimate horizon of meaning to their lives, something for which these individuals are ready to give their lives, yet the only thing that "really exists" are these individuals and their activity, so this substance is actual only insofar as individuals "believe in it" and act accordingly. So, again, why cannot we pass directly from spiritual Substance as presupposed (the naive notion of Spirit or God as existing in itself, without regard to humanity) to its subjective mediation, to the awareness that its very presupposition is retroactively "posited" by the activity of individuals?

Here we reach Hegel's key insight: Reconciliation cannot be direct, it has first to generate (appear in) a *monster*—twice on the same page Hegel uses this unexpectedly strong word, "monstrosity," to designate the first figure of Reconciliation, the appearance of God in the finite flesh of a human individual: "This is the monstrous [*das Ungeheure*] whose necessity we have seen."[101] The finite fragile human individual is "inappropriate" to stand for God, it is "*die Unangemessenheit ueberhaupt* [the inappropriateness in general, as such]"[102]—are we aware of the properly dialectical paradox of what Hegel claims here? The very attempt at reconciliation, in its first move, produces a monster, a grotesque "inappropriateness as such." So, again, why this weird intrusion, why not a direct passage from the (Jewish) gap between God and man to (Christian) reconciliation, by a simple transformation of "God" from Beyond to the immanent Spirit of Community?

The first problem here is that, in a way, the Jews have already done it: if ever there was a religion of spiritual community, it is Judaism, this religion which does not say a lot about life after death, or even about "inner" belief in God, but focuses on the prescribed way of life, of obeying the communal rules: God "is alive" in the community of believers. The Jewish God is thus both at the same time: a transcendent substantial One and the virtual One of spiritual substance. So how is this Jewish community of believers different from the Christian one, from the Holy Spirit?

In order to answer this crucial question correctly, we should bear in mind here the properly Hegelian relationship between necessity and contingency.

In a first approach, it appears that their encompassing unity is necessity, i.e., that necessity itself posits and mediates contingency as the external field in which it expresses-actualizes itself—contingency itself is necessary, the result of the self-externalization and self-mediation of the notional necessity. However, it is crucial to supplement this unity with the opposite one, with contingency as the encompassing unity of itself and necessity: the very elevation of a necessity into the structuring principle of the contingent field of multiplicity is a contingent act, one can almost say: the outcome of a contingent ("open") struggle for hegemony. This shift corresponds to the shift from S to $, from substance to subject. The starting point is a contingent multitude; through its self-mediation ("spontaneous self-organization"), contingency engenders-posits its immanent necessity, just as Essence is the result of the self-mediation of Being. Once Essence emerges, it retroactively "posits its own presuppositions," i.e., it sublates its presuppositions into subordinated moments of its self-reproduction (Being is transubstantiated into Appearance); however, this positing is retroactive.

The underlying shift here is the one between *positing presuppositions* and *presupposing the positing*:[103] the limit of the Feuerbachian-Marxian logic of dis-alienation is that of positing presuppositions: the subject overcomes its alienation by recognizing itself as the active agent which itself posited what appears to it as its substantial presupposition. In religious terms, this would amount to the direct (re)appropriation of God by humanity: the mystery of God is man, "God" is nothing but the reified/substantialized version of human collective activity, and so on. What is missing here is the properly Christian gesture: in order to posit the presupposition (to "humanize" God, reduce him to an expression/result of human activity), the (human-subjective) *positing itself should be "presupposed," located in God as the substantial ground-presupposition of man, as its own becoming-human/finite*. The reason is the subject's constitutive finitude: the full positing of presuppositions would amount to subject's full retroactive positing/generation of its presuppositions, i.e., the subject would be absolutized into the full self-origin.

This is why the difference between Substance and Subject has to reflect/inscribe itself into subjectivity itself as the irreducible gap that separates human subjects from Christ, the "more than human" monstrous subject. This necessity of Christ, the "absolute" subject which adds itself to the series of finite human subjects as the supplementary a ($+ + + + ... +a$), is what differentiates the Hegelian position from the young Marx–Feuerbachian position of the big Other as the virtual Substance posited by collective subjectivity, as its alienated expression. Christ signals the overlapping of the two kenoses: man's alienation from/in God is simultaneously God's alienation from himself in Christ. So it is not only that humanity becomes conscious of itself in the alienated figure of God, but: in human religion, God becomes conscious of himself. It is not enough to say that people (individuals) organize themselves in the Holy Spirit (Party, community of believers): in humanity, a transsubjective "it" organizes itself. The finitude of humanity, of the human subject (collective or individual), is maintained here: Christ is the excess which prohibits simple recognition of the collective Subject in Substance, the reduction of Spirit to objective/virtual entity (presup)posed by humanity.

These precise distinctions also enable us to account for the passage of what Hegel called "objective spirit" to "absolute spirit": it is through Christ's mediation that OS changes into AS. There is no Holy Spirit without the squashed body of a bird (Christ's mutilated corpse): the two poles, the Universal (the virtual infinity/immortality of the Holy Spirit (OS)) and the Particular (the actual finite/mortal community of believers (SS)) can be mediated only through Christ's monstrous singularity.

We do not pass from OS to AS by way of a simple subjective appropriation of the "reified" OS by the collective human subjectivity (in the well-known Feuerbachian–young Marx pseudo-Hegelian mode: "the subjectivity recognizes in OS its own product, the reified expression of its own creative power")—this would have been a simple reduction of OS to subjective spirit (SS). But neither do we accomplish this passage by positing beyond OS another, even more In-Itself, absolute entity that encompasses both SS and OS. The passage from OS to AS resides in nothing but the dialectical mediation between OS and SS, in the above-indicated inclusion of the gap that separates OS from SS within the SS, so that OS has to appear (be experienced) as such, as an objective "reified" entity, by the SS itself (and in the inverted recognition that, without the subjective reference to an In-Itself of the OS, subjectivity itself disintegrates, collapses into psychotic autism). (In the same way, in Christianity, we overcome the opposition of God as an objective spiritual In-Itself and human (believer's) subjectivity by transposing this gap into God himself: Christianity is "absolute religion" only and precisely insofar as, in it, the distance that separates God from man separates God from himself (and man from man, from the "inhuman" in him).)

One can also put it in the following way: all that happens in the passage from OS to AS is that one takes into account that "there is no big Other." AS is not a "stronger" absolute entity in comparison with OS, but a "less strong" one—to reach AS, we pass from reified Substance to a subjectivized virtual substance. AS thus avoids both pitfalls: in it, neither is SS reduced to a subordinate element of the self-mediation of the OS, nor is the OS subjectivized in Feuerbachian–young Marx style (reduced to a reified expression-projection of SS). We reach AS when we (SS) are no longer the agent of the process, when "it organizes itself" in-through us—not, however, in the mode of perverse self-instrumentalization. This is the pitfall of Stalinism: in Stalinism, the big Other exists, we, Communists, are its instruments. In liberalism, in contrast, there is no big Other, all there really is is just us, individuals (or, as Margaret Thatcher put it, there is no such thing as society). A dialectical analysis shows how both these positions rely on the other: the truth of the Stalinism OS is subjectivism (we—the Party, the Stalinist subject—constitute the big Other, we decide what is the "objective necessity" we pretend to realize); the truth of liberalism is the big Other in the guise of the objective network of rules which sustain the interplay of individuals.

One can also put it in the terms of the dialectics of ontology and episte-mology: if the encompassing unity of necessity and contingency is necessity, then the necessity (gradually discovered by our cognition as the underlying Notion of the phenomenal contingent multiplicity) had to be there all the time waiting to be discovered by our cognition—in short, in this case, Hegel's central idea, first clearly formulated in his Introduction to the *Phenomenology of Spirit*, that our way toward truth is part of the truth itself, is canceled, i.e., we regress to the standard metaphysical notion of Truth as a substantial In-Itself, independent of the subject's approach to it. Only if the encompassing unity is contingency can we claim that the subject's discovery of necessary truth is simultaneously the (contingent) constitution of this truth itself, i.e., that—to paraphrase Hegel—the very return to (rediscovery of) eternal Truth generates this Truth. This is the dialectical reversal of contingency into necessity, i.e., the way the outcome of a contingent process is the appearance of necessity: things retroactively "will have been" necessary. This reversal was nicely described by Jean-Pierre Dupuy:

> The catastrophic event is inscribed into the future as a destiny, for sure, but also as a contingent accident: it could not have taken place, even if, in *futur antérieur*, it appears as necessary. . . . If an outstanding event takes place, a catastrophe, for example, it could not not have taken place; nonetheless, insofar as it did not take place, it is not inevitable. It is thus the event's actualization—the fact that it takes place—which retroactively creates its necessity.[104]

Dupuy provides the example of the French presidential elections in May 1995; here is the January forecast of the main French polling institute: "If, on next May 8, Monsieur Balladur is elected, one can say that the presidential election was decided before it even took place." If—accidentally—an event takes place, it creates the preceding chain which makes it appear inevitable, and this— not clichés about how the underlying necessity expresses itself in and through the accidental play of appearances—is *in nuce* the Hegelian dialectics of con-tingency and necessity. The same goes for the October Revolution (once the Bolsheviks won and stabilized their hold on power, their victory appeared as an outcome and expression of a deeper historical necessity), and even of

Bush's much-contested first US presidential victory (after the contingent and contested Florida majority, his victory retroactively appears as an expression of a deeper US political trend).

The infamous "Krug's pen objection to dialectics" (Krug was a contemporary of Hegel who challenged him to deduce dialectically the very pen he was writing these lines with)—which, according to the empiricist commonsense, Hegel answered with a brisk dismissal that hardly concealed the fact that he had no answer—is thus doubly wrong. Here we are back with the dialectic of necessity and contingency: not only does Hegel (quite consistently with his premises) deduce the *necessity of contingency*, i.e., how the Idea necessarily externalizes itself (acquires reality) in phenomena which are genuinely contingent. Furthermore (and this aspect is often neglected by many of his commentators), he also develops the opposite—and theoretically much more interesting—aspect, that of the *contingency of necessity*. That is to say: when Hegel describes the progress from "external" contingent Being to its "inner" necessary Essence which "appears" in it, the appearance's "self-internalization" through self-reflection, he is thereby describing not the discovery of some preexisting inner Essence, the penetration toward something that was already there (this, precisely, would have been a "reification" of the Essence), but a "performative" process of constructing (forming) that which is "discovered." Or, as Hegel puts it in his *Logic*, in the process of reflection, the very "return" to the lost or hidden Ground produces what it returns to. This means that it is not only the inner necessity that is the unity of itself and contingency as its opposite, necessarily positing contingency as its moment. It is also contingency which is the encompassing unity of itself and its opposite, necessity; that is to say, *the very process through which necessity arises out of necessity is a contingent process*. If Hegel were in effect to "deduce" contingency from necessity, he would have begun his logic with Essence, not with Being, which is the domain of pure contingent multiplicity. The standard counterargument according to which this entire process of dialectical passages is nonetheless necessary, forming a self-enclosed System, also misses the point: yes, it is—but this necessity is not given in advance, it is itself generated, forming itself out of contingency, which is why it can be apprehended only retroactively, after the fact. If we reduce this gradual process of necessity emerging through contingency's self-mediation to a process of penetrating the deceptive appearance of things and discovering the (already-existing) underlying Necessity, then we are back to precritical substantialist metaphysics, i.e., we are ultimately reducing / subordinating Subject to Substance.—One of the culminating points of the dialectic of necessity and contingency is Hegel's infamous deduction of the rational necessity of hereditary monarchy: the bureaucratic chain of knowledge has to be supplemented by the King's decision as the "completely concrete objectivity of the will" which "reabsorbs all particularity into its single self, cuts short the weighing of pros and cons between which it lets itself oscillate perpetually now this way and now that, and by saying 'I will' makes its decision and so inaugurates all activity and actuality."[105] This is why "the conception of the monarch" is "of all conceptions the hardest for ratiocination, i.e. for the method of reflection employed by the Understanding."[106] In the next paragraph, Hegel further elaborates this speculative necessity of the monarch:

> This ultimate self in which the will of the state is concentrated is, when thus taken in abstraction, a single self and therefore is immediate individuality. Hence its "natural" character is implied in its very conception. The monarch, therefore, is essentially characterized as this individual, in abstraction from all his other characteristics, and this individual is raised to the dignity of monarchy in an immediate, natural, fashion, i.e. through his birth in the course of nature.

> *Addition:* It is often alleged against monarchy that it makes the welfare of the state dependent on chance, for, it is urged, the monarch may be ill-educated, he may perhaps be unworthy of the highest position in the state, and it is senseless that such a state of affairs should exist because it is supposed to be rational. But all this rests on a presupposition which is nugatory, namely that everything depends on the monarch's particular character. In a completely organized state, it is only a question of the culminating point of formal decision (and a natural bulwark against passion. It is wrong therefore to demand objective qualities in a monarch); he has only to say "yes" and dot the "i", because the throne should be such that the significant thing in its holder is not his particular make-up. . . . In a well-organized monarchy, the objective aspect belongs to law alone, and the monarch's part is merely to set to the law the subjective "I will."[107]

The speculative moment that Understanding cannot grasp is "the transition of the concept of pure self-determination into the immediacy of being and so into the realm of nature." In other words, while Understanding can well grasp the universal mediation of a living totality, what it cannot grasp is that this *totality, in order to actualize itself, has to acquire actual existence in the guise of an immediate "natural" singularity.*[108] The term "natural" should be given its full weight here: just as, at the end of Logic, the Idea's completed self-mediation releases from itself nature, collapses into the external immediacy of nature, the State's rational self-mediation has to acquire actual existence in a will which is determined as directly natural, unmediated, *stricto sensu* "irrational."

While observing Napoleon on a horse in the streets of Jena after the battle of 1807, Hegel remarked that it was as if he saw there the World Spirit riding a horse. The Christological implications of this remark are obvious: what happened in the case of Christ is that God himself, the creator of our entire universe, was walking out there as a common individual. This mystery of incarnation is discernible at different levels, up to the parent's speculative judgment apropos of a child, "Out there our love is walking!", which stands for the

Hegelian reversal of determinate reflection into reflective determination—as with a king, when his subject sees him walking around: "Out there our state is walking." Marx's evocation of reflective determination (in his famous footnote in chapter 1 of *Capital*)[109] is also inadequate here: individuals think they treat a person as a king because he is a king in himself, while, in effect, he is a king only because they treat him as one. However, the crucial point is that this "reification" of a social relation in a person cannot be dismissed as a simple "fetishist misperception"; what such a dismissal itself misses is something that, perhaps, could be designated the "Hegelian performative": of course a king is "in himself" a miserable individual, of course he is a king only insofar as his subjects treat him like one; the point, however, is that the "fetishist illusion" which sustains our veneration of a king has in itself a performative dimension—*the very unity of our state, that which the king "embodies," actualizes itself only in the person of a king.* That is why it is not enough to insist on the need to avoid the "fetishist trap" and to distinguish between the contingent person of a king and what he stands for: what the king stands for comes into being in his person, just like a couple's love which (at least within a certain traditional perspective) becomes actual only in their offspring.

And, *mutatis mutandis*, that is the monstrosity of Christ: not only the edifice of a state, but no less than the entire edifice of reality hinges on a contingent singularity through which alone it actualizes itself. When Christ, this miserable individual, this ridiculous and derided clown-king, was walking around, it was as if the navel of the world, the knot which holds the texture of reality together (what Lacan in his late work called the *sinthom*), was walking around. All that remains of reality without Christ is the Void of the meaningless multiplicity of the Real. This monstrosity is the price we have to pay in order to render the Absolute in the medium of external re-presentation (*Vorstellung*), which is the medium of religion.

In the triad of art, religion, and science (philosophy), religion is crucial as the site of a gap, of an imbalance between form and content. In art, especially in Ancient Greek art, there is organic unity and harmony between form (the beautiful "plastic individual") and universal content, i.e., the beautiful individual is a model which directly makes present the universal dimension. With religion, this immediate harmony is disturbed, there is a gap between the sensual content (narrative of real-life events) and the true meaning, which is why organic unity is replaced by allegory, i.e., by external re-presentation (*Vorstellung*). (In philosophical science, the unity of form and content is reestablished, since the notional content is directly articulated in its proper (notional) form.)[110] This contradiction proper to the order of re-presentation reaches its extreme in Christ. With regard to Christ, Hegel in effect points forward to some Kierkegaardian themes (the difference between genius and apostle, the singular evental character of Christ), especially with his emphasis on the difference between Socrates and Christ. Christ is not like the Greek "plastic individual" through whose particular features the universal/substantial content directly transpires (as was exemplarily the case with Alexander). This means that although Christ is man-God, the direct identity of the two, this identity also implies absolute contradiction: there is nothing "divine" about Christ, even nothing exceptional—if we observe his features, he is indistinguishable from any other human individual:

> If we consider Christ only in reference to his talents, his character and his morality, as a teacher, etc., we are putting him on the same plane as Socrates and others, even if we place him higher from the moral point of view. . . . If Christ is only taken as an exceptionally fine individual, even as one without sin, then we are ignoring the representation of the speculative idea, its absolute truth.[111]

These lines rely on a very precise conceptual background. It is not that Christ is "more" than other model figures of religious or philosophical or ethical wisdom, real or mythical (Buddha, Socrates, Moses, Mohammed), that he is "divine" in the sense of the absence of any human failings.[112] With Christ, the very relationship between the substantial divine content and its representation changes: Christ does not represent this substantial divine content, God, he directly is God, *which is why he no longer has to resemble God*, to strive to be perfect and "like God." Recall the classic Marx Brothers joke: "You look like Emmanuel Ravelli." "But I am Emmanuel Ravelli." "No wonder, then, that you look like yourself!" The underlying premise of this joke is that such an overlapping of being and resembling is impossible, there is always a gap between the two. Buddha, Socrates, etc., *resemble* gods, while Christ *is* God. So when the Christian God "manifests himself to other men as an individual man, exclusive and single . . . like a man excluding all others,"[113] we are dealing with the singularity of a pure event, with contingency brought to its extreme—only in this mode, excluding all efforts to approach universal perfection, can God incarnate himself. This absence of any positive characteristics, this full identity of God and man at the level of properties, can occur only because another, more radical difference makes any positive differential features irrelevant. This change can be succinctly described as the shift from the upward movement of the becoming-essential of the accident to the downward movement of the becoming-accidental of the essence:[114] the Greek hero, this "exemplary individual," elevates his accidental personal features into a paradigmatic case of the essential universality, while in the Christian logic of Incarnation, the universal Essence embodies itself in an accidental individual.

Or, to make the same point in another way, the Greek gods appear to humans in human form, while the Christian God appears as human to himself. This is the crucial point: for Hegel the Incarnation is not a move by means of which God makes himself accessible/visible to humans, but a move by means of which *Gods looks at himself from the (distorting) human perspective*: "As God manifests himself to his own gaze, the specular presentation divides the divine self from itself, offering the divine the perspectival vision of its own self-presence."[115] Or, to put in Freudian-Lacanian terms: Christ is God's "partial object," an autonomized organ without a body, as if God picked his eye out of his head and turned it on himself from the outside. We can guess, now, why Hegel insisted on the *monstrosity* of Christ.

It is therefore crucial to note how the Christian modality of "God seeing himself" has nothing whatsoever to do with the harmonious closed loop of "seeing myself seeing," of an eye seeing itself and enjoying the sight in this perfect self-mirroring: the turn of the eye toward "its" body presupposes the separation of the eye from the body, and what I see through my externalized/autonomized eye is a perspectival, anamorphically distorted image of myself: Christ is an anamorphosis of God.[116]

It is only in this monstrosity of Christ that human freedom is grounded; and, at its most fundamental, it is neither as payment for our sins nor as legalistic ransom, but by enacting this openness that Christ's sacrifice sets us free. When we are afraid of something (and fear of death is the ultimate fear that makes us slaves), a true friend will say something like: "Don't be afraid, look, I'll do it, what you're so afraid of, and I'll do it for free—not because I have to, but out of my love for you; I'm not afraid!" He does it and in this way sets us free, demonstrating *in actu* that it can be done, that we can do it too, that we are not slaves. . . . Recall, from Ayn Rand's *The Fountainhead*, the description of the momentary impact Howard Roark makes on the members of the audience in the courtroom where he stands on trial:

> Roark stood before them as each man stands in the innocence of his own mind. But Roark stood like that before a hostile crowd—and they knew suddenly that no hatred was possible to him. For the flash of an instant, they grasped the manner of his consciousness. Each asked himself: do I need anyone's approval?—does it matter?—am I tied?—And for that instant, each man was free—free enough to feel benevolence for every other man in the room. It was only a moment; the moment of silence when Roark was about to speak.[117]

This is the way Christ brings freedom: confronting him, we become aware of our own freedom. The ultimate question is thus: in what kind of universe is freedom possible? What ontology does freedom imply?

TOWARD A MATERIALIST THEOLOGY

In September 2006, Pope Benedict XVI caused uproar in Muslim circles when he quoted the infamous lines of a fourteenth-century Byzantine emperor:

"Show me just what Mohammed brought that was new, and there you will find only evil and inhuman, such as his command to spread by the sword the faith he preached." Some commentators defended the Pope's remarks as the beginning of a serious theological dialogue between Christianity and Islam; along these lines, Jeff Israely praised the Pope's "razor-sharp intellect" for shifting

> the terms of a debate that has been dominated by either feel-good truisms, victimization complexes or hateful confrontation. He sought instead to delineate what he sees as a fundamental difference between Christianity's view that God is intrinsically linked to reason (the Greek concept of Logos) and Islam's view that "God is absolutely transcendent."
>
> Benedict said Islam teaches that God's "will is not bound up with any of our categories, even that of rationality." The risk he sees implicit in this concept of the divine is that the irrationality of violence might thereby appear to be justified to someone who believes it is God's will. The essential question, he said, is this: "Is the conviction that acting unreasonably contradicts God's nature . . . always and intrinsically true?"[118]

In the same move, the Pope also condemned Western "godless secularism," in which the divine gift of reason "has been warped into an absolutist doctrine." The conclusion is clear: reason and faith must "come together in a new way," discovering their shared ground in the divine *Logos*, and "it is to this great *Logos*, to this breadth of reason, that we invite our partners in the dialogue of cultures."[119]

Whenever someone proposes such a simplistic Aristotelian middle-of-the-road solution of avoiding the two extremes, everyone acquainted with the Stalinist notion of the Party line as the proper path between the rightist deviation (in the Pope's case: Muslim irrationalism) and the leftist deviation (godless secularism) should react with great suspicion—there are two things at least to add. First, the Pope's remarks which provoked outrage among Muslims should be read together with his remarks, a week earlier, on the "irrationality" of Darwinism. The Pope removed Father George Coyne from his position as director of the Vatican Observatory after the American Jesuit priest repeatedly contradicted the Pope's endorsement of "intelligent design" theory, which essentially backs the "Adam and Eve" idea of creation. The Pope favors intelligent design, which says that God directs the process of evolution, over Charles Darwin's original theory, which holds that species evolve through the random, unplanned processes of genetic mutation and the survival of the fittest. Father Coyne, on the contrary, is an outspoken supporter of Darwin's theory, arguing that it is compatible with Christianity. The Pope wrote in *Truth and Tolerance*:

> The question is whether reality originated on the basis of chance and necessity and, thus, from what is irrational; that is, whether reason, being a chance by-product of irrationality and floating in an ocean of irrationality, is ultimately

just as meaningless; or whether the principle that represents the fundamental conviction of Christian faith and of its philosophy remains true—In principio erat Verbum—at the beginning of all things stands the creative power of reason. Now as then, Christian faith represents the choice in favor of the priority of reason and of rationality.[120]

This, then, is the first qualification one must add: the "reason" of which the Pope speaks is a reason for which Darwin's theory of evolution (and, ultimately, modern science itself, for which the assertion of the contingency of the universe, the break with Aristotelian teleology, is a constitutive axiom) is "irrational." The "reason" of which the Pope speaks is the premodern teleological Reason, the view of the universe as a harmonious Whole in which everything serves a higher purpose. (This is why, paradoxically, the Pope's remarks obfuscate the key role of Christian theology in the birth of modern science: what paved the way for modern science was precisely the "voluntarist" idea elaborated by, among others, Duns Scotus and Descartes, that God is not bound by any eternal rational truths. That is to say: while the illusory perception of scientific discourse is that it is a discourse of the pure description of facticity, the paradox resides in the coincidence of bare facticity and radical voluntarism: facticity can be sustained as meaningless, as something that "just is as it is," only if it is secretly sustained by an arbitrary divine will. This is why Descartes is the founding figure of modern science precisely when he made even the most elementary mathematical facts like $2 + 2 = 4$ dependent on the arbitrary divine will: two and two is four because God willed it so, with no hidden obscure chain of reasons behind it. Even in mathematics, this unconditional voluntarism is discernible in its axiomatic character: one begins by arbitrarily positing a series of axioms, out of which everything else is supposed to follow.) —Second qualification: but is Islam really so "irrational," does it really celebrate a totally transcendent/irrational God above reason? In the same issue of Time magazine in which Israely published his praise of the Pope, there is an interesting interview with the Iranian President Mahmoud Ahmadinejad, who advocates exactly the same unity of reason (logic) and spirituality. To the question what he would ask Bush in the public debate between the two that he proposed, Ahmadinejad replied:

> I would ask him, Are rationalism, spirituality and humanitarianism and logic—are they bad things for human beings? Why more conflict? Why should we go for hostilities? Why should we develop weapons of mass destruction? Everybody can love one another. . . . I have said we can run the world through logic. . . . Problems cannot be solved through bombs. Bombs are of little use today. We need logic.[121]

And, in effect, from the perspective of Islam, it is Christianity as the religion of love which is not "rational" enough: its focus on love makes God all too human, biased, in the figure of Christ who intervenes in creation as an engaged and combative figure, allowing his passion to overrun the logic of the Creator and Master of the universe. The Muslim God, on the contrary, is the true God of Reason; he is wholly transcendent—not in the sense of frivolous irrationality, but in the sense of the supreme Creator who knows and directs everything and thus has no need to get involved in earthly accidents with partial passion. Mohammad Bouyeri, the Islamist who killed the Dutch filmmaker Theo van Gogh, wrote in his letter to Hirshi Ali (a letter stuck with a knife into Van Gogh's body):

> You, as unbelieving fundamentalist, of course don't believe that there is a Higher Power who runs the universe. You don't believe in your heart, with which you repudiate the truth, that you must knock and ask this Higher Power for permission. You don't believe that your tongue with which you repudiate the Direction of this Higher Power is subservient to His laws.[122]

This idea, according to which our very acts of opposing God are directed by God, is unthinkable in Christianity. No wonder, then, that Islam finds it much easier to accept the (to our common sense) paradoxical results of modern physics: the notion of an all-encompassing rational order which runs against our common sense. No wonder that, to many a Western historian of religion, Islam is a problem—how could it have emerged *after* Christianity, the religion to end all religions? Its very geographical site belies the cliché on Orientalism: much more than belonging to the Orient, the location of Islam makes it a fatal obstacle to the true union of East and West—a point made most succinctly by Claude Lévi-Strauss:

> Today, it is behind Islam that I contemplate India; the India of Buddha, prior to Mohammed who—for me as a European and because I am European—arises between our reflection and the teachings which are closest to it . . . the hands of the East and the West, predestined to be joined, were kept apart by it. . . .
>
> The West should return to the sources of its torn condition: by interposing itself between Buddhism and Christianity, Islam Islamized us when, in the course of the Crusades, the West let itself be caught in opposition to it and thus started to resemble it, instead of delivering itself—in the case of the nonexistence of Islam—to the slow osmosis with Buddhism which would Christianize us even more, in a sense which would have been all the more Christian insofar as we were to rise beyond Christianity itself. It was then that the West lost its chance to remain woman.[123]

This passage from the last pages of *Tristes tropiques* articulates the dream of a direct communication and reconciliation between West and East, Christianity and Buddhism, male and female principles. Like a harmonious sexual relationship, this direct contact would have been a chance for Europe to become feminine. Islam served as the screen interposing itself between the two, preventing the rise of a harmonious hermaphroditic world civilization—with its interposition, the West lost its last chance to "remain woman." (What this view fails to note is how Islam itself is grounded on a disavowed femininity, trying to get rid of the umbilical cord that links it to the feminine.) Islam thus functions as what Freud called *Liebesstoerer*: the intruder / obstacle of the harmonious sexual relationship. This harmonious relationship, of course, would have been the one under the predominance of femininity: the male West would have rejoined the feminine East and thus "remain[ed] woman," located itself within femininity.

François Regnault defined the Jews as "our *objet a*"—but is this asexual "partial object" not the Muslims? We usually talk about the Jewish–Christian civilization—perhaps the time has come, especially with regard to the Middle East conflict, to talk about the *Jewish–Muslim civilization* as an axis opposed to Christianity. (Recall a surprising sign of this deeper solidarity: after Freud published his *Moses and Monotheism* in 1939, depriving the Jews of their founding figure, the most ferocious reactions to it came from Muslim intellectuals in Egypt!) Was Hegel not already on the trace of it with his insight into the speculative identity of Judaism and Islam? According to a commonplace notion, Judaism (like Islam) is a "pure" monotheism, while Christianity, with its Trinity, is a compromise with polytheism; Hegel even designates Islam as the "religion of sublimity" at its purest, as the universalization of Jewish monotheism:

> In Mohammedanism the limited principle of the Jews is expanded into universality and thereby overcome. Here, God is no longer, as with the Asiatics, contemplated as existent in immediately sensuous mode but is apprehended as the one infinite sublime Power beyond all the multiplicity of the world. Mohammedanism is, therefore, in the strictest sense of the world, the religion of sublimity.[124]

This, perhaps, explains why there is so much anti-Semitism in Islam: because of the extreme proximity of the two religions. In Hegelese, what Islam encounters in Judaism is itself in its "oppositional determination," in the mode of particularity. The difference between Judaism and Islam is thus ultimately not substantial, but purely formal: they are the same religion in a different formal mode (in the sense in which Spinoza claims that the real dog and the idea of a dog are substantially one and the same thing, just in a different mode).[125]—Against this, we should argue that it is Judaism which is an "abstract negation" of polytheism and, as such, still haunted by it (there is a whole series of clues pointing in this direction: "Jehovah" is a plural substantive; in one of his commandments, God forbids the Jews to celebrate other gods "before" him, not when outside of his gaze; etc.), while Christianity is the only true monotheism, since it includes self-differentiation into the One—its lesson is that, in order truly to have One, you need three.

Perhaps, then, we should propose, in a Hegelian mode, a new triad of monotheisms: first, Judaism, monotheism in its "immediate" (particular, tribal-genealogical) form; then, Islam as its direct abstract negation, the immediate assertion of universality. If Judaism deploys an extraordinary persistence, but in a particularist mode, Islam is universalist, but can sustain only short expansionist outbursts, after which it loses its impetus and collapses into itself, lacking the energy to transpose this impetus into a permanent form. Christianity is then the dialectical "synthesis" of the two, the only true monotheism in contrast with the two abstractions of Judaism and Islam.

The underlying logic of Islam is that of a rationality which can be weird, but allows for no exception, while the underlying logic of Christianity is that of an "irrational" exception (unfathomable divine mystery) which sustains our rationality—or, as G. K. Chesterton put it, the Christian doctrine "not only discovered the law, but it foresaw the exceptions":[126] it is only the exception which allows us to perceive the miracle of the universal rule. And, for Chesterton, the same goes for our rational understanding of the universe:

> The whole secret of mysticism is this: that man can understand everything by the help of what he does not understand. The morbid logician seeks to make everything lucid, and succeeds in making everything mysterious. The mystic allows one thing to be mysterious, and everything else becomes lucid. . . . The one created thing which we cannot look at is the one thing in the light of which we look at everything. Like the sun at noonday, mysticism explains everything else by the blaze of its own victorious invisibility.[127]

Chesterton's aim is thus to *save reason through sticking to its founding exception*: deprived of it, reason degenerates into a blind self-destructive skepticism: in short, into total *irrationalism*—or, as Chesterton liked to repeat: if you do not believe in God, you will soon be ready to believe anything, including the most superstitious nonsense about miracles. . . . This was Chesterton's basic insight and conviction: that the irrationalism of the late nineteenth century was the necessary consequence of the Enlightenment rationalist attack on religion:

> The creeds and the crusades, the hierarchies and the horrible persecutions were not organized, as is ignorantly said, for the suppression of reason. They were organized for the difficult defense of reason. Man, by a blind instinct, knew that if once things were wildly questioned, reason could be questioned first. The authority of priests to absolve, the authority of popes to define the authority, even of inquisitors to terrify: these were all only dark defenses erected round one central authority, more undemonstrable, more supernatural than all—the authority of a man to think. . . . In so far as religion is gone, reason is going.[128]

Here, however, we encounter Chesterton's fateful limitation, a limitation which he himself overcame when, in his wonderful text on the book of Job, he shows why God has to rebuke his own defenders, the "mechanical and supercilious comforters of Job":

> The mechanical optimist endeavors to justify the universe avowedly upon the ground that it is a rational and consecutive pattern. He points out that the fine thing about the world is that it can all be explained. That is the one point, if I may put it so, on which God, in return, is explicit to the point of violence. God says, in effect, that if there is one fine thing about the world, as far as men are concerned, it is that it cannot be explained. He insists on the inexplicableness of everything. "Hath the rain a father? . . . Out of whose womb came the ice?" (38:28f). He goes farther, and insists on the positive and palpable unreason of things; "Hast thou sent the rain upon the desert where no man is, and upon the wilderness wherein there is no man?" (38:26). . . . To startle man, God becomes for an instant a blasphemer; one might almost say that God becomes for an instant an atheist. He unrolls before Job a long panorama of created things, the horse, the eagle, the raven, the wild ass, the peacock, the ostrich, the crocodile. He so describes each of them that it sounds like a monster walking in the sun. The whole is a sort of psalm or rhapsody of the sense of wonder. The maker of all things is astonished at the things he has Himself made.[129]

God is here no longer the miraculous exception that guarantees the normality of the universe, the unexplainable X who enables us to explain everything else; he is, on the contrary, himself overwhelmed by the overflowing miracle of his Creation. Upon a closer look, there is nothing normal in our universe—everything, every small thing that is, is a miraculous exception; viewed from a proper perspective, every normal thing is a monstrosity. For example, we should not take horses as normal and the unicorn as a miraculous exception—even a horse, the most ordinary thing in the world, is a shattering miracle. This blasphemous God is the God of modern science, since modern science is sustained precisely by such an attitude of wondering at the most obvious. In short, modern science is on the side of "believing in anything": is not one of the lessons of the theory of relativity and quantum physics that modern science undermines our most elementary natural attitudes and compels us to believe (accept) the most "nonsensical" things? To clarify this conundrum, Lacan's logic of the non-All can again be of some help.[130] Chesterton obviously relies on the "masculine" side of universality and its constitutive exception: everything obeys natural causality—with the exception of God, the central Mystery. The logic of modern science is, on the contrary, "feminine": first, it is materialist, accepting the axiom that nothing escapes natural causality which can be accounted for by rational explanation; however, the other side of this materialist axiom is that "not all is rational, obeying natural laws"—not in the sense that "there is something irrational, something that escapes rational causality," but in the sense that it is the "totality" of rational causal order itself which is inconsistent, "irrational," non-All. Only this non-All guarantees the proper opening of the scientific discourse to surprises, to the emergence of the "unthinkable": who, in the nineteenth century, could have imagined things like relativity theory or quantum physics?

The Catholic Church was therefore as a rule always on the side of commonsense realism and the universal natural explanation, from Chesterton to Pope John Paul II, who endorsed both evolutionism—with the exception of the unique moment when God imparts to humans the immortal soul—and contemporary cosmology—with the exception of that unfathomable singularity the Big Bang, the point at which natural laws are suspended (this is why he implored scientists to leave the mystery of the Big Bang alone). No wonder many neo-Thomists noted a weird similarity between their own ontology and the ontology of dialectical materialism, both defending a version of naive realism (objects that we perceive really exist out there independently of our perception).[131]

This is why both Catholicism and dialectical materialism had such problems with the "open" ontology of quantum mechanics. That is to say: how are we to interpret its so-called "principle of uncertainty" which prohibits us from attaining full knowledge of particles at the quantum level (to determine the velocity and the position of a particle)? For Einstein, this principle of uncertainty proves that quantum physics does not provide a full description of reality, that there must be some unknown features missed by its conceptual apparatus. Heisenberg, Bohr, and others, on the contrary, insisted that this incompleteness of our knowledge of quantum reality indicates a strange incompleteness of quantum reality itself, a claim which leads to a breathtakingly weird ontology. When we want to simulate reality within an artificial (virtual, digital) medium, we do not have to go to the end: we just have to reproduce features which make the image realistic from the spectator's point of view. If there is a house in the background, for instance, we do not have to construct through a program the house's entire interior, since we expect that the participant will not want to enter the house; or the construction of a virtual person in this space can be limited to his exterior—no need to bother with inner organs, bones, and so on. We just need to install a program which will promptly fill in this gap if the participant's activity necessitates it (if, for example, he plunges a knife deep into the virtual person's body). It is like when we scroll down a long text on a computer screen: earlier and later pages do not preexist our viewing them; in the same way, when we simulate a virtual universe, the microscopic structure of objects can be left blank, and if stars on the horizon appear hazy, we need not bother to construct the way they would appear to a closer look, since nobody will go up there to take such a look at them. The truly interesting idea here is that the quantum indeterminacy which we encounter when we inquire into the tiniest components of our universe can read in exactly the same way, as a feature of the limited resolution of our simulated world, i.e., as the sign of the ontological incompleteness of (what we experience as) reality itself. That is to say: let us imagine a God who is creating the world for us, its human inhabitants, to dwell in—his task

> could be made easier by furnishing it only with those parts that its inhabitants need to know about. For example, the microscopic structure of the Earth's interior could be left blank, at least until someone decides to dig down deep enough, in which case the details could be hastily filled in as required. If the most distant stars are hazy, no one is ever going to get close enough to them to notice that something is amiss.[132]

The idea is that God, who created–programmed our universe, was too lazy (or, rather, he underestimated our—human—intelligence): he thought that we, humans, would not succeed in probing into the structure of nature beyond the level of atoms, so he programmed the matrix of our universe only to the level of its atomic structure—beyond that, he simply left things fuzzy, like a house whose interior is not programmed in a PC game.[133] Is, however, the theologico-digital way the only way to read this paradox? We can read it as a sign that we already live in a simulated universe, but also as a signal of the ontological incompleteness of reality itself. In the first case, the ontological incompleteness is transposed into an epistemological one, i.e., the incompleteness is perceived as the effect of the fact that another (secret, but fully real) agency constructed our reality as a simulated universe. The truly difficult thing is to accept the second case, the ontological incompleteness of reality itself. That is to say: what immediately arises is a massive commonsense objection: but how can this ontological incompleteness hold for reality itself? Is not reality defined by its ontological completeness?[134] If reality "really exists out there," it has to be complete "all the way down," otherwise we are dealing with a fiction which just "hangs in the air," like appearances which are not appearances of a substantial Something. Here, precisely, quantum physics comes in, offering a model of how to think (or imagine, at least) such "open" ontology. Alain Badiou formulated this same idea in his notion of pure multiplicity as the ultimate ontological category: reality is the multiplicity of multiplicities which cannot be generated or constituted from (or reduced to) some form of Ones as its elementary ("atomic") constituents. Multiplicities are not multiplications of One, they are irreducible multiplicities, which is why their opposite is not One but Zero, the ontological void: no matter how far we progress in our analysis of multiplicities, we never reach the zero level of its simple constituents—the only "background" of multiplicities is thus Zero, the void.[135] That is Badiou's ontological breakthrough: the primordial opposition is not that of One and Zero, but that of Zero and multiplicities, and the One emerges later. To put it even more radically: since only Ones fully "really exist," multiplicities and Zero are the same thing (not *one and* the same thing): Zero "is" multiplicities without Ones which would guarantee their ontological consistency.

There is a detail which, perhaps, tells a lot about the difference between Europe and the USA: in Europe, the ground floor in a building is counted as 0, so that the floor above it is the "first floor," while in the USA the "first floor" is at street level. In short, Americans start to count with 1, while Europeans know that 1 is already a stand-in for 0. Or, to put it in more historical terms: Europeans are aware that, before we start counting, there has to be a "ground" of tradition, a ground which is always-already given and, as such, cannot be counted; while the USA, a land with no premodern historical tradition proper, lacks such a "ground"—things begin there directly with self-legislated freedom, the past is erased (transposed onto Europe).[136] So which of these two positions is closer to the truth? Neither—it is only in Poland that they seem to have found the proper solution to this alternative: in hotel elevators, *they skip 1 altogether,* i.e., they start to count floors with 0 and then pass over directly to 2. When, in a Warsaw hotel, I asked the porter how one can jump directly from 0 to 2, I was taken aback by the simple truth of his answer—after a moment of perplexity, he told me: "Well, I guess that the moment one starts to count the floors, the ground floor itself must be counted as one. . . ." He got it right: "one" is originally not the number which follows zero, but zero itself counted as one—only in this way can the series of counted "ones" start (one One, then another One, etc., ad infinitum); the original multiplicity, the correlate of the void, is not to be confused with this series of Ones. This solution is thus based on the correct insight which Badiou developed in his ontology: reality is a multiplicity in which the void and the multiple coincide, i.e., the multiple is not composed of "ones," but is primordial.[137]

We should thus get rid of the fear that, once we ascertain that reality is the infinitely divisible, substanceless void within a void, "matter will disappear." What the digital information revolution, the biogenetic revolution, and the quantum revolution in physics all share is that they mark the reemergence of what, for want of a better term, I am tempted to call *postmetaphysical idealism.* It is as if Chesterton's insight into how the materialist struggle for the full assertion of reality, against its subordination to any "higher" metaphysical order, culminates in the loss of reality itself: what began as the assertion of material reality ended up as the realm of pure formulas of quantum physics. Is this really, however, a form of idealism? Since the radical materialist stance asserts that there is no World, that the World in its Whole is Nothing, materialism has nothing to do with the presence of damp, dense matter—its proper figures are, rather, constellations in which matter seems to "disappear," like the pure oscillations of superstrings or quantum vibrations. On the contrary, if we see in raw, inert matter more than an imaginary screen, we always secretly endorse some kind of spiritualism, as in Tarkovsky's *Solaris,* in which the dense plastic matter of the planet directly embodies Mind. This "spectral materialism" has three different forms: in the information revolution, matter is reduced to the medium of purely digitized information; in biogenetics, the biological body is reduced to the medium of the reproduction of the genetic code; in quantum physics, reality itself, the density of matter, is reduced to the collapse of the virtuality of wave oscillations (or, in the general theory of relativity, matter is reduced to an effect of space's curvature). Here we encounter another crucial aspect of the opposition idealism/materialism: materialism is not the assertion of inert material density in its humid heaviness—such a "materialism" can always serve as a support for gnostic spiritualist obscurantism. In contrast, a true materialism joyously assumes the "disappearance of matter," the fact that there is only void.

In his *Logiques des mondes*, Badiou provides a succinct definition of "democratic materialism" and its opposite, "materialist dialectics": the axiom which condenses the first is *"There is nothing but bodies and languages . . . ,"* to which materialist dialectics adds *". . . with the exception of truths."*[138] There is a more constrained anthropological version of this axiom: for democratic materialism, *"there is nothing but individuals and communities,"* to which materialist dialectics adds: *"Insofar as there is a truth, a subject subtracts itself from all community and destroys all individuation."*[139] The passage from Two to Three is crucial here, and we should bear in mind all its Platonic, properly metaphysical, thrust in the direction of what, prima facie, cannot but appear as a proto-idealist gesture of asserting that material reality is not all that there is, that there is also another level of incorporeal truths.

Here Badiou performs the paradoxical philosophical gesture of defending, as a materialist, the autonomy of the "immaterial" order of the Event. As a materialist, and in order to be thoroughly materialist, Badiou focuses on the idealist topos *par excellence*: How can a human animal forsake its animality and put its life at the service of a transcendent Truth? How can the "transubstantiation" from the pleasure-oriented life of an *individual* to the life of a *subject* dedicated to a Cause occur? In other words, how is a free act possible? How can one break (out of) the network of the causal connections of positive reality and conceive an act that begins by and in itself? In short, Badiou *repeats within the materialist frame the elementary gesture of idealist anti-reductionism*: human Reason cannot be reduced to the result of evolutionary adaptation; art is not just a heightened procedure of providing sensual pleasures, but a medium of Truth; and so on. Additionally, against the false appearance that this gesture is also aimed at psychoanalysis (is not the point of the notion of "sublimation" that the allegedly "higher" human activities are just a roundabout, "sublimated" way to realize a "lower" goal?), this is already the significant achievement of psychoanalysis: its claim is that sexuality itself, sexual drives pertaining to the human animal, cannot be accounted for in evolutionary terms. This is how we should locate the shift from biological instinct to drive: instinct is just part of the physics of animal life, while drive (death drive) introduces a metaphysical dimension. In Marx, we find the analogous implicit distinction between working class and proletariat: "working class" is the empirical social category, accessible to sociological knowledge, while "proletariat" is the subject-agent of revolutionary Truth. Along the same lines, Lacan claims that drive is an ethical category. (From a strictly Freudian viewpoint, there is a problem with this duality of human animal and subject: in order for the Event to inscribe itself into the human animal's body, and thus transform the individual into the subject, this human animal itself has already to be derailed/distorted by drive, by what Eric Santner calls its "too-muchness." To put it even more pointedly: what Badiou misses is the simple fact that there is no human animal (governed by pleasure and reality principle, bent on survival, etc.)—with humanity proper, animality is derailed, instinct is transformed into drive, and it is only into such a distorted animal that an Event can inscribe itself.)

This makes clear the true stakes of Badiou's gesture: in order for materialism to truly win over idealism, it is not enough to succeed in the "reductionist" approach and demonstrate how mind, consciousness, etc., can nonetheless somehow be accounted for within the evolutionary-positivist frame of materialism. On the contrary, the materialist claim should be much stronger: it is only materialism that can accurately explain the very phenomena of mind, consciousness, etc.; and, conversely, it is idealism that is "vulgar," that always-already "reifies" these phenomena.

Today, many orientations claim to be materialist: scientific materialism (Darwinism, brain sciences), "discursive" materialism (ideology as the result of material discursive practices), what Alain Badiou calls "democratic materialism" (spontaneous egalitarian hedonism), etc., up to attempts at "materialist theology." Some of these materialisms are mutually exclusive: for "discursive" materialists, it is scientific materialism which, in its allegedly "naive" direct assertion of external reality, is "idealist" in the sense that it does not take into account the role of "material" symbolic practice in constituting what appears to us as reality; for scientific materialism, "discursive" materialism is an obscurantist muddle not to be taken seriously. I am tempted to suggest that discursive materialism and scientific materialism are, in their very antagonism, the front and the obverse of the same coin, one standing for radical culturalization (everything, including our notions of nature, is a contingent discursive formation), the other for radical naturalization (everything, including our culture, can be accounted for in the terms of natural biological evolution). (We should note here how this duality of naturalist materialism and discursive materialism echoes the duality that, according to Badiou, characterizes "democratic materialism," for which there are only bodies and languages: naturalist materialism covers bodies, and discursive materialism covers languages.)

This multiplicity is matched by the multiplicity of spiritualist tendencies: versions of traditional Christianity, Judaism, and Islam are supplemented by so-called "postsecular" thought (Derrida, Levinas), neo-Bergsonism (Deleuze, for some), not to mention the multiple forms of New Age spirituality, from "Western Buddhism" to neo-paganism. (Peter Hallward was right in unearthing the idealist kernel of Deleuze's thought: Badiou's polemics against Deleuze is arguably one of the latest figures of the eternal struggle of materialism against idealism.)[140] Within this complex picture, relations between the couple materialism/idealism and the political struggle are often "overdetermined"— for example, the recent popularity of scientific materialist direct attacks on religion (the big bestseller "troika" of Sam Harris, Richard Dawkins, Daniel Dennett) is certainly sustained by the ideological need to present the liberal West as the bastion of Reason against the crazy Muslim and other irrational fundamentalists. It is our wager that only the materialism of void and multiplicity, going well beyond the commonsense assertion of "external" material reality as the only thing that "really is," is the materialism that, as Hegel would have put it, reaches the level of its notion.

The difference between multiplicities and the void is thus a pure difference, not the difference between two ontic entities, not even between Something and Nothing (as if there are multiple Somethings surrounded by the void of Nothing, as in ancient atomism), but "ontological." The difference with Heidegger is that Heidegger's ontological difference is the difference between entities and their "world," the historical horizon of their meaning which takes place as the epochal Event of the disclosure of a new world. I am therefore tempted to say that the difference between Badiou's and Heidegger's ontological difference is the one between "pure" and "applied" (or, rather, "schematized" in the Kantian sense of the term) difference: the Heideggerian difference is always-already "schematized" as a particular epochal disclosure of Being. In Badiou's terms, the Heideggerian ontological difference is the one between what appears and its appearing as such, the World within which it appears.

This ontological openness of the oneless multiplicity also allows us to approach in a new way Kant's second antinomy of pure reason, whose thesis is: "Every composite substance in the world consists of simple parts; and there exists nothing that is not either itself simple, or composed of simple parts."[141] Here is Kant's proof:

> For, grant that composite substances do not consist of simple parts; in this case, if all combination or composition were annihilated in thought, no composite part, and (as, by the supposition, there do not exist simple parts) no simple part would exist. Consequently, no substance; consequently, nothing would exist. Either, then, it is impossible to annihilate composition in thought; or, after such annihilation, there must remain something that subsists without composition,

that is, something that is simple. But in the former case the composite could not itself consist of substances, because with substances composition is merely a contingent relation, apart from which they must still exist as self-subsistent beings. Now, as this case contradicts the supposition, the second must contain the truth—that the substantial composite in the world consists of simple parts.

It follows, as an immediate inference, that the things in the world are all, without exception, simple beings—that composition is merely an external condition pertaining to them—and that, although we never can separate and isolate the elementary substances from the state of composition, reason must cogitate these as the primary subjects of all composition, and consequently, as prior thereto—and as simple substances.[142]

What, however, if we accept the conclusion that, ultimately, "nothing exists" (a conclusion which, incidentally, is exactly the same as the conclusion of Plato's *Parmenides*: "Then may we not sum up the argument in a word and say truly: If one is not, then nothing is?")? Such a move, although rejected by Kant as obvious nonsense, is not as un-Kantian as it may appear: it is here that we should apply yet again the Kantian distinction between negative and infinite judgment. The statement "material reality is all there is" can be negated in two ways: in the form of "material reality *isn't all there is*" and the form of "material reality *is non-all*." The first negation (of a predicate) leads to the standard metaphysics: material reality isn't everything, there is another, higher, spiritual reality. . . . As such, this negation is, in accordance with Lacan's formulas of sexuation, inherent to the positive statement "material reality is all there is": as its constitutive exception, it grounds its universality. If, however, we assert a nonpredicate and say "material reality *is non-all*," this merely asserts the non-all of reality without implying any exception—paradoxically, we should thus claim that "material reality *is non-all*," not "material reality is all there is," is the true formula of materialism.

Does this ontological "fuzziness" of reality also not allow us a new approach to modernism in painting? Are the "stains" which blur the transparency of a realist representation, which impose themselves as stains, not precisely indications that the contours of constituted reality are blurred, that we are approaching the preontological level of fuzzy proto-reality? That is the crucial shift a viewer has to accomplish: stains are not obstacles that prevent our direct access to represented reality; they are, on the contrary, "more real than reality," something that undermines from within the ontological consistency of reality—or, to put it in old-fashioned philosophical terms, their status is not epistemological but ontological. Recall again the standard transcendent figure of God as a secret Master who knows the meaning of what appears to us as meaningless catastrophe, the God who sees the entire picture in which what we perceive as a stain contributes to global harmony: we should pass this gap that separates the entire harmonious picture from the stains it is composed of in the opposite direction—not withdrawing from meaningless stains to the wider harmony, but moving forward from the appearance of global harmony to the stains that compose it.

The only true alternative to this ontological fuzziness is the no less paradoxical idea that, at some point, the endless process of dividing reality into its components reaches its end when the division is no longer the division into two (or more) parts/somethings, but the division into a part (something) and nothing. This would be the proof that we have reached the most elementary constituent of reality: when something can be further divided only into a something and a nothing.—Do these two options not refer again to Lacan's "formulas of sexuation," so that the irreducible-multiplicity option is "feminine" and the division of the last term into something and nothing is "masculine"? Furthermore, is it not that, if we can reach the point of last division (and thus the ultimate One, the last constituent of reality), then there is no "creation" proper, nothing really new emerges, merely the (re)combinations of existing elements, while the feminine "fuzziness" of reality opens up the space for creation proper? The underlying problem here is: how do we pass from multitude-that-is-Zero to the emergence of One? Is it that One is a multiple which "stands for nothing," i.e., is it that Ones exist only at the level of symbolic re-presentation, while in the Real there are only multiples?

One can argue that atheism is truly thinkable only within monotheism: it is this reduction of many (gods) to one (God) that enables us to confront directly 1 and 0, i.e., to erase 1 and thus obtain 0.[143] This fact was often noted, but it was as a rule taken as a proof that atheism cannot stand on its own two feet, that it can only vegetate in the shadow of Christian monotheism—or, as John Gray put it:

> Atheists say they want a secular world, but a world defined by the absence of the Christians' god is still a Christian world. Secularism is like chastity, a condition defined by what it denies. If atheism has a future, it can only be in a Christian revival; but in fact Christianity and atheism are declining together.[144]

What, however, if we turn this argument around: what if the affinity between monotheism and atheism demonstrates not that atheism depends on monotheism, but that monotheism itself prefigures atheism within the field of religion—its God is from the very (Jewish) beginning a dead one, in clear contrast with the pagan gods who irradiate cosmic vitality. Insofar as the truly materialist axiom is the assertion of primordial multiplicity, the One which precedes this multiplicity can only be zero itself. No wonder, then, that only in Christianity—as the only truly logical monotheism—does God himself turn momentarily into an atheist. So when Gray claims that "contemporary atheism is a Christian heresy that differs from earlier heresies chiefly in its intellectual crudity,"[145] we should accept this statement, but we should also read it along the lines of the Hegelian reversal between subject and predicate, or between genus and its species: contemporary atheism is a heretical species of Christianity which retroactively redefines its own genus, positing it as its own presupposition. In his *Notes Towards a Definition of Culture*, T. S. Eliot remarked that there are moments when the only choice is the one between heresy and nonbelief, when the only way to keep a religion alive is to perform a sectarian split from its main corpse. Exactly the same happened with Christianity: the "death-of-God theology" marks the moment when the only way to keep its truth alive was through a materialist heresy split from its main corpse.

The resulting materialism has thus nothing to do with the assertion of "fully existing external reality"—on the contrary, its starting premise is the "non-all" of reality, its ontological incompleteness. (Recall Lenin's deadlock when, in *Materialism and Empiriocriticism*, he proposes as a minimal philosophical definition of materialism the assertion of an objective reality which exists independently of the human mind, without any further qualifications: in this sense, Plato himself is a materialist!) Neither does it have anything to do with any positive determination of content, like "matter" versus "spirit," i.e., with the substantialization of Matter into the only Absolute (Hegel's critique is fully justified here: "matter" in its abstraction is a pure *Gedankending*). We should thus not be afraid of the much-decried "dissolution of matter in a field of energies" in modern physics: a true materialist should fully embrace it. Materialism has nothing to do with the assertion of the inert density of matter; it is, on the contrary, a position which accepts the ultimate void of reality— the consequence of its central thesis on the primordial multiplicity is that there is no "substantial reality," that the only "substance" of the multiplicity is void. (The difference between Deleuze and Badiou here is the one between idealism and materialism: in Deleuze, Life is still the answer to "Why is there Something and not Nothing?," while Badiou's answer is a more sober one, closer to Buddhism and Hegel—*there IS only Nothing*, and all processes take place "from Nothing through Nothing to Nothing," as Hegel put it.) This is why the opposite of true materialism is not so much a consequent idealism but, rather, the vulgar-idealist "materialism" of someone like David Chalmers, who proposes to account for the "hard problem of consciousness" by postulating "self-awareness" as an additional fundamental force of nature, together with gravity, magnetism, etc.—as, literally, its "quintessence" (the fifth essence). The temptation to "see" thought as an additional component of natural/ material reality itself is the ultimate vulgarity.

In *Philosophical Arabesques*, one of the most tragic works in the entire history of philosophy (a manuscript written in 1937, when Nikolai Bukharin was in the Lubyanka prison, awaiting execution), Bukharin tries to bring his entire life experience together for the last time into a consistent philosophical edifice.

The first choice, the crucial battle, that he confronts is the one between the materialist assertion of the reality of the external world, and what he calls the "intrigues of solipsism." Once this key battle is won, once the life-asserting reliance on the real world liberates us from the damp prison-house of our fantasies, we can breathe freely, we have only to draw all the consequences of this first key result. The mysterious feature of the book's first chapter, in which Bukharin confronts this dilemma, is its tension between form and content: although, at the level of content, Bukharin adamantly denies that we are dealing here with a choice between two beliefs or primordial existential decisions, the whole chapter is structured like a dialogue between a healthy but naive materialist and Mephistopheles, standing for the "devil of solipsism," a "cunning spirit" which "drapes itself into an enchantingly patterned cloak of iron logic, and it laughs, poking out its tongue."[146] "Curling his lips ironically," Mephistopheles tempts the materialist with the idea that, since all we have direct access to are our subjective sensations, the only way we can pass from here to a belief in some external reality which exists independently of our sensations is by a leap of faith, "a *salto vitale* (as opposed to *salto mortale*)."[147] In short, Mephistopheles' "devil of logic" tries to seduce us into accepting that independent external reality is a matter of faith, that the existence of "holy matter" is the fundamental dogma of the "theology" of dialectical materialism. After a series of arguments (which, I have to admit, although not all totally devoid of philosophical interest, are irredeemably marked by pre-Kantian naivety), Bukharin concludes the chapter with the ironic call (which, nonetheless, cannot conceal the underlying despair): "Hold your tongue, Mephistopheles! Hold your dissolute tongue!"[148] (In spite of this exorcism, the devil continues to reappear throughout the book—see the first sentence of chapter 12: "After a long interval, the demon of irony again makes his appearance.")[149] A radical materialist should, paradoxically, give the devil his due, rejecting naive reliance on external reality as the vulgar-materialist obverse of idealism. In the choice presented by the title of chapter 2 of Bukharin's book—"Acceptance and Nonacceptance of the World"—he does not so much reject the world as, rather, include in its texture its suspension, what the great mystics and Hegel called the "Night of the World," the eclipse of constituted reality.

So, back to Badiou: when he emphasizes the undecidability of the Real of an Event, his position is radically different from the standard deconstructionist notion of undecidability. For Badiou, undecidability means that there are no neutral "objective" criteria for an Event: an Event appears as such only to those who recognize themselves in its call, or, as Badiou puts it, an Event is self-relating; it includes itself—its own nomination—in its components.[150] While this does mean that one has to decide about an Event, such an ultimately groundless decision is not "undecidable" in the standard sense; it is, rather, uncannily similar to the Hegelian dialectical process in which, as Hegel made clear in the Introduction to his *Phenomenology*, a "figure of consciousness" is measured not by any external standard of truth but in an absolutely immanent way, through the gap between itself and its own exemplification / staging. An Event is thus "non-all" in the precise Lacanian sense of the term: it is never fully verified precisely because it is infinite / unlimited, i.e., because there is no external limit to it. And the conclusion to be drawn here is that, for the very same reason, Hegelian "totality" is also "non-all." In other (Badiou's) terms, an Event is nothing but its own inscription into the order of Being, a cut / rupture in the order of Being on account of which Being can never form a consistent All. Of course, Badiou—as a materialist—is aware of the idealist danger that lurks here:

> We must point out that in what concerns its material the event is not a miracle. What I mean is that what composes an event is always extracted from a situation, always related back to a singular multiplicity, to its state, to the language that is connected to it, etc. In fact, so as not to succumb to an obscurantist theory of creation *ex nihilo*, we must accept that an event is nothing but a part of a given situation, nothing but a *fragment of being*.[151]

However, we should go a step further than Badiou is ready to go: there is no Beyond of Being which inscribes itself into the order of Being—there is nothing but the order of Being. We should recall here yet again the paradox of Einstein's general theory of relativity, in which matter does not curve space, but is an effect of space's curvature: an Event does not curve the space of Being through its inscription into it—on the contrary, an Event is *nothing but* this curvature of the space of Being. "All there is" is the interstice, the non-self-coincidence, of Being, i.e., the ontological nonclosure of the order of Being.[152] The "minimal difference" which sustains the parallax gap is thus the difference on account of which the "same" series of real occurrences which, to the eye of a neutral observer, are just part of ordinary reality are, to the eye of an engaged participant, inscriptions of the fidelity to an Event. For example, the "same" occurrences (fights on the streets of St. Petersburg) which are to a neutral historian just violent twists and turns in Russian history are, to an engaged revolutionary, parts of the epochal Event of the October Revolution. This means that, from the Lacanian perspective, the notions of parallax gap and of the "minimal difference" obey the logic of the non-All.[153]

So when David Chalmers proposes that the basis of consciousness will have to be found in a new, additional, fundamental—primordial and irreducible—force of nature, like gravity or electromagnetism, something like an elementary (self-)sentience or awareness,[154] does he not thereby provide a new proof of how idealism coincides with vulgar materialism? Does he not precisely miss the pure ideality of (self-)awareness? It is here that the topic of finitude in the strict Heideggerian sense should be mobilized: if one tries to conceive of consciousness within an ontologically fully realized field of reality, it can only appear as an additional positive moment; but what about linking consciousness to the very finitude, ontological incompleteness, of the human being, to its being originally out-of-joint, thrown-into, exposed to, an overwhelming constellation?

It is here that, in order to specify the meaning of materialism, one should apply Lacan's formulas of sexuation: there is a fundamental difference between the assertion "everything is matter" (which relies on its constitutive exception—in the case of Lenin who, in *Materialism and Empiriocriticism*, falls into this trap, the very position of enunciation of the subject whose mind "reflects" matter) and the assertion "there is nothing which is not matter" (which, with its other side, "non-All is matter," opens up the space for the explanation of immaterial phenomena). This means that a truly radical materialism is by definition nonreductionist: far from claiming that "everything is matter," it confers upon "immaterial" phenomena a specific positive nonbeing.

When, in his argument against the reductive explanation of consciousness, Chalmers writes: "even if we knew every last detail about the physics of the universe—the configuration, causation, and evolution among all the fields and particles in the spatiotemporal manifold—*that* information would not lead us to postulate the existence of conscious experience,"[155] he makes the standard Kantian mistake: such a total knowledge is strictly nonsensical, both epistemologically and ontologically. It is the obverse of the vulgar determinist notion articulated, in Marxism, by Nikolai Bukharin, when he wrote that if we were to know the whole of physical reality, we would also be able to predict precisely the emergence of a revolution. This line of reasoning—consciousness as an excess, a surplus, over the physical totality—is misleading, since it has to evoke a meaningless hyperbole: when we imagine the Whole of reality, there is no longer any place for consciousness (and subjectivity). There are two options here: either subjectivity is an illusion, or reality is in *itself* (not only epistemologically) non-All.[156]

We should thus, from the radically materialist standpoint, fearlessly think through the consequences of rejecting "objective reality": reality dissolves into "subjective" fragments, *but these fragments themselves fall back into anonymous Being, losing their subjective consistency*. Fredric Jameson drew attention to the paradox of the postmodern rejection of a consistent Self—the ultimate result is that we lose its opposite, objective reality, which gets transformed into a set of contingent subjective constructions. A true materialist should do the opposite: refuse to accept "objective reality" in order to undermine consistent subjectivity.

In *The Human Touch*, Michael Frayn pointed out the radical relativity of our notion of the universe: when we talk about the microdimensions of quantum physics, so small that we cannot even imagine their scope, or about the vastness of the universe, ignorant of our lives, so large that we, humans, are an imperceptible speck in it, we always presuppose our gaze, our "normal" measures of greatness: quantum waves are small, the universe is large, with regard to our standards. The lesson is that *every* notion of "objective reality" is bound to a subjective point.

What, then, is the proper atheist stance? Not a continuous desperate struggle against theism, of course—but not a simple indifference to belief either. That is to say: what if, in a kind of negation of negation, true atheism were to return to belief (faith?), asserting it without reference to God—only atheists can truly believe; the only true belief is belief without any support in the authority of some presupposed figure of the "big Other." We can also conceive these three positions (theism, negative atheism, and positive atheism) along the lines of the Kantian triad of positive, negative, and infinite judgment: while the positive statement "I believe in God" can be negated as "I don't believe in God," we can also imagine a kind of "infinite" negation, not so much "I believe in un-God" (which would be closer to negative theology) but, rather, something like "unbelief," the pure form of belief deprived of its substantialization— "unbelief" is still the form of belief, like the undead who, as the living dead, remain dead.

NOTES

1. G. K. Chesterton, *The Complete Father Brown Stories* (Ware: Wordsworth Editions, 2006), pp. 394–395.

2. There is one feature which may appear to make Hegel a pagan: for Hegel, the difference between Christianity and pre-Christian "pagan" religions is not that the latter are "false," that they celebrate illusory gods, while the Christian God "really exists." The development of religions from primitive animism through polytheism to the last triad of Judaism, Christianity, and Islam, is *inherent to divinity itself*, it is God's self-development—a notion which, from within the perspective of a Christian believer, cannot but look like heresy, even blasphemy.

3. See Vladimir Lossky, *In the Image and Likeness of God* (Crestwood: St. Vladimir's Seminary Press, 2001). Is Lossky here not too brief, ignoring the mysticism proper to Catholic spirituality? The God of St. Theresa is definitely not the "God of philosophers."

4. G. W. F. Hegel, *Lectures on the Philosophy of Religion*, vol. 3 (Berkeley: University of California Press, 1987), p. 84.

5. Lossky, *In the Image and Likeness of God*, p. 120.

6. Ibid., p. 109.

7. St. Irenaeus, quoted from ibid., p. 97.

8. Lossky, ibid., p. 97.

9. Ibid., p. 103.

10. Ibid., p. 105.

11. Ibid., p. 104.

12. Ibid., p. 102.

13. St. Basil, quoted in ibid., p. 54.

14. Lossky, ibid., pp. 89–90.

15. Ibid., p. 94.

16. Ibid., p. 92.

17. David Appelbaum, foreword to Reiner Schürmann, *Wandering Joy* (Great Barrington, MA: Lindisfarne Books, 2001), p. ix.

18. Schürmann, *Wandering Joy*, p. 70.

19. Ibid., p. 56.

20. Ibid., p. 215.

21. Ibid., p. 113.

22. Ibid., p. xiii.

23. Ibid., p. 85.

24. Ibid., p. 26.

25. Ibid., p. 80.

26. Ibid.

27. Ibid., p. 214.

28. Ibid., p. 40.

29. Ibid., p. 115.

30. Ibid., p. 117.

31. Ibid., p. 123.

32. Ibid., p. 162.

33. See Jean Laplanche, *New Foundations for Psychoanalysis* (Oxford: Basil Blackwell, 1989).

34. Jean Laplanche, *Essays on Otherness* (London: Routledge, 1999), p. 255.

35. Schürmann, *Wandering Joy*, p. 123.

36. Ibid., p. 156.

37. Ibid., p. 159.

38. This eventality is already there in Aristotle: substance is not a "thing," but that which forever, continuously, persists in time, i.e., the difference between substance (*ousia*) and accident is internal to the event.—There is, from the opposite end of Western history, a further parallel between Eckhart and quantum physics. In the latter, a shift occurs in the relationship between particles and their interactions: in an initial moment, it appears as if first (ontologically, at least) there are particles interacting in the mode of waves, oscillations, etc.; then, in a second moment, we are forced to enact a radical shift of perspective—the primordial ontological fact consists of the waves themselves (trajectories, oscillations), and particles are nothing but the nodal points in which different waves intersect. Analogously, in Eckhart, the Event is first an interaction between entities (God, man . . .); then, there is this process as the only true reality.

39. Schürmann, *Wandering Joy*, pp. 164–165.

40. Ibid., p. 161.

41. Ibid.

42. G. K. Chesterton, *Orthodoxy* (San Francisco: Ignatius, 1995), p. 139.

43. Schürmann, *Wandering Joy*, p. 155.

44. Ibid., p. 87.

45. Ibid., p. 124.

46. Ibid., p. 32.

47. Ibid., p. 220.

48. Ibid., p. 209.

49. Henry Corbin, "Apophatic Theology as Antidote to Nihilism," *Umbr(a)* 2007, p. 71.

50. Ibid., p. 72.

51. Ibid., p. 71.

52. Gershom Sholem, *Kabbalah* (New York: Meridian, 1978), p. 94.

53. Ibid.

54. Ibid., p. 95.

55. Ibid., p. 94.

56. G. K. Chesterton, *The Man Who Was Thursday* (Harmondsworth: Penguin, 1986), pp. 44–45.

57. Ibid., pp. 45–46.

58. Ibid., pp. 48–49.

59. Ibid., pp. 168–170.

60. Ibid., p. 170.

61. Ibid., p. 180.

62. Ibid.

63. Ibid., pp. 182–183.

64. Ibid., p. 183.

65. Chesterton, *Orthodoxy*, p. 145.

66. Ibid.

67. Ibid.

68. For a more detailed analysis of the philosophical implications of Chesterton's *Orthodoxy*, see chapters 2 and 3 of Slavoj Žižek, *The Puppet and the Dwarf* (Cambridge, MA: MIT Press, 2003).

69. See Alain Finkelkraut and Peter Sloterdijk, *Les battements du monde* (Paris: Fayard, 2003), p. 131.

70. "Und alles Draengen, alles Ringen / Ist ewig Ruh' im Gott den Herrn."

71. Along the same lines, it was already Schelling who conceived God's fall into time, his break out of eternity, not as a fall proper, but as the resolution of the supreme contradiction, of the divine madness, the overcoming of the divine claustrophobic self-enclosure into the Openness of time: God created the temporal universe in order to save himself from his own madness. In strict analogy with the inherent universal antagonism of capitalist modernity, with regard to which particular forms of modernity are so many attempts to resolve this antagonism, God prior to creation (prior to *logos*) is a God caught in infinite pain, and all (possible) particular worlds are so many divine attempts to find peace with and in himself, to create an entity that would serve him as a support of his stability. God is not primary Reconciliation but the infinite pain of self-tearing-apart.

72. There is another ironic coincidence of opposites in the casting of Sutler: the dictator Sutler is played by the same John Hurt who, in the last version of 1984, played Winston Smith, the ultimate victim of a dictatorial regime.

73. There is a brief hint in this direction in the middle of the film; however, it remains unexploited.

74. An analogous failure to accomplish the crucial step occurred in the fifth season of 24, which came very close to redeeming itself in the eyes of all leftists: when it became clear that the negative power behind the terrorist plot was none other than the President of the United States himself, many of us were eagerly waiting to see if Jack Bauer would apply also to the President—the "most powerful man on earth, the leader of the free world" (and other Kim-Jong-Il-esque titles that he possesses)—his standard procedure in dealing with terrorists who do not want to divulge a secret that might save thousands . . . in short, would he *torture* the President? Unfortunately, the authors did not risk this redeeming step: when Bauer is on the point of shooting the corrupt President, he cannot do it out of respect for the office of President.

75. G. K. Chesterton, "Introduction to the Book of Job," <www.chesterton.org/gkc/theologian/job.htm>.

76. We should recall here that the story of Job also plays a crucial role in Islam, for which Job is the epitome of a pure believer.

77. John D. Caputo and Gianni Vattimo, *After the Death of God* (New York: Columbia University Press, 2007), p. 66.

78. There is a stupid question which should be raised here: why does God not consider telling Job the truth—that it was all staged to test Job's faith, and that Job won and the Devil is defeated?

79. Catherine Malabou, *The Future of Hegel* (New York: Routledge, 2005), p.109.

80. G. W. F. Hegel, *Faith and Knowledge* (Albany: SUNY Press, 1977), pp. 55–56.

81. Malabou, *The Future of Hegel*, p. 110.

82. Ibid., p. 103.

83. Ibid., p. 111.

84. Ibid., p. 112.

85. Jean-Louis Chrétien, "Le Bien donne ce qu'il n'a pas," *Archives de philosophie* 2 (1980).

86. Malabou, *The Future of Hegel*, p. 107.

87. Hegel, *Lectures on the Philosophy of Religion*, vol. 3, p. 233.

88. In the underrated film *Torn Curtain*, this netherworld is the Communist DDR. The motif of fire (during the credits and in the ballet sequence) signals hell, and the film's narrative stages a journey through the curtain (that divides our reality from the netherworld) into the netherworld. Consequently, is Professor Lindt, the goal of this journey, not a figure of a gentle Devil?

89. Piglia's text, to which Miller refers without providing any references, is "Tesis sobre el cuento," *Revista Brasileira de Literatura Comparada* 1 (1991), pp. 22–25.

90. Jacques-Alain Miller, "Profane Illuminations," *lacanian ink* 28 (2007), pp. 12–13.

91. Pierre Bayard, *Who Killed Roger Ackroyd?* (New York: New Press, 2000).

92. Pierre Bayard, *L'affaire du chien des Baskerville* (Paris: Editions de Minuit, 2008).

93. Lesley Chamberlain, *The Philosophy Steamer* (London: Atlantic Books, 2006), pp. 23–24. To avoid a misunderstanding, let me state clearly that I find this decision to expel the anti-Bolshevik intellectuals totally justified.

94. "The Ten Commandments Were Just the Beginning . . . ," *Weekly World News*, November 6, 2006, pp. 24–26.

95. Available online at <www.earlychristianwritings.com/text/didache-roberts.html>.

96. Richard Wagner, *Jesus of Nazareth and Other Writings* (Lincoln: University of Nebraska Press, 1995), p. 303.

97. Ibid., pp. 303–304.

98. G. W. F. Hegel, *Aesthetics*, vol. 1 (Oxford: Oxford University Press, 1998), p. 98.

99. *G. W. F. Hegel: Theologian of the Spirit*, ed. Peter C. Hodgson (Minneapolis: Fortress Press, 1997), p. 237. Since this translation of some chapters from Hegel's lectures on the philosophy of religion is unreliable and fragmentary, one should always check against the German original.

100. Ibid.

101. Ibid., pp. 238–239.

102. G. W. F. Hegel, *Werke*, vol. 17 (Frankfurt am Main: Suhrkamp, 1969), p. 272.

103. See the last chapter of *The Sublime Object of Ideology* (London: Verso, 1989).

104. Jean-Pierre Dupuy, *Petite métaphysique des tsunami* (Paris: Seuil, 2005), p. 19.

105. G. W. F. Hegel, *Elements of the Philosophy of Right* (Cambridge, UK: Cambridge University Press, 1991), para. 279.

106. Ibid.

107. Ibid., para. 280.

108. Did not the Marxists who mocked Hegel here pay the price for this negligence in the guise of the Leader who, again, not only directly embodied the rational totality, but embodied it fully, as a figure of full Knowledge, not only as the idiotic point of dotting the i's. In other words, a Stalinist Leader is *not* a monarch, which makes him much worse. . . .

109. Karl Marx, *Capital*, vol. 1 (London: Penguin, 1990), p. 144.

110. Another way to express the difference between art and religion is to link it to the opposition between time and space: religion is to art as time is to space, the self-negation

of the immediate representational content which is reduced to a mere re-presentation of meaning. Art directly renders/presents its content in spatial/sensuous presence, while religion re-presents its content in the sequential form of a narrative proceeding in time.

111. G. W. F. Hegel, Lectures on the Philosophy of History (New York: Dover Publications, 1956), p. 325.

112. As for this absence of failures, there is a nice joke about what ensues when Christ, in front of a large crowd, proclaims his famous "Let the one who is without sin throw the first stone!": he is immediately hit with a stone; he then turns in the direction from where the stone came and says reproachfully: "Mother! I told you to stay home!"

113. Hegel, Lectures on the Philosophy of Religion, vol. 3, p. 142.

114. For this distinction, see Malabou, The Future of Hegel, p. 119.

115. Ibid., p. 118.

116. Another indication of this externality of God with regard to himself is pointed out by G. K. Chesterton in "The Meaning of the Crusade," where he quotes with approval the description of the Mount of Olives he got from a child in Jerusalem: "A child from one of the villages said to me, in broken English, that it was the place where God said his prayers. I for one could not ask for a finer or more defiant statement of all that separates the Christian from the Moslem or the Jew." If, in other religions, we pray to God, only in Christianity does God himself pray, that is to say, address an external unfathomable authority.

117. Ayn Rand, The Fountainhead (New York: Signet, 1992), p. 677.

118. Jeff Israely, "The Pontiff Has a Point," Time, September 25, 2006, p. 33.

119. Ibid.

120. Available online at <http://www.ignatiusinsight.com/features/cardratzinger_tt_oct 04.asp>.

121. "We Do Not Need Attacks," Time, September 25, 2006, pp. 24–25.

122. Available at <http://www.militantislammonitor.org/article/id/320>.

123. Claude Lévi-Strauss, Tristes tropiques (Paris: Plon, 1955), pp. 472–473.

124. G. W. F. Hegel, Philosophy of Mind (Oxford: Clarendon Press, 1971), p. 44.

125. Even Hegel's logic of triads seems to get stuck in a deadlock here: the triad that offers itself, but that Hegel cannot admit, of course, is that of Judaism–Christianity–Islam: first the immediate/abstract monotheism which, as the price to be paid for its immediate character, has to be embodied in a particular ethnic group (which is why the Jews renounce all proselytism); then Christianity with its trinity; finally Islam, the truly universal monotheism.

126. Chesterton, Orthodoxy, p. 105.

127. Ibid., p. 33.

128. Ibid., p. 39.

129. Chesterton, "Introduction to the Book of Job."

130. For the logic of non-All, see Jacques Lacan, Seminar, Book XX: Encore (New York: Norton, 1998).

131. Here, even a towering figure like Lenin was not a materialist: as his critics pointed out, in *Materialism and Empiriocriticism* he proposes as a minimal definition of materialism the assertion of an external "objective" reality that exists independently of our minds, leaving open (as relying on scientific progress, not on philosophy) any further determination of this reality. According to this criterion, however, is Plato's idealism not materialist, since ideas definitely exist independently of our minds? It is clear that, for Lenin, the consciousness which "reflects" external reality is the Exception.

132. See Nicholas Fearn, *Philosophy: The Latest Answers to the Oldest Questions* (London: Atlantic Books, 2005), p. 77.

133. See ibid., pp. 77–78.

134. The opposition to this notion of ontological completeness defines Hegel's Idealism: its core resides in the assertion that finite (determinate, positive-substantial) reality is in itself void, inconsistent, self-sublating. From this, however, it does not follow that this reality is just a shadow, a secondary reflection, etc., of some higher reality: there is *nothing but* this reality, and the "suprasensible is appearance qua appearance," i.e., the very movement of the self-sublation of this reality. So we really pass "from nothing through nothing to nothing": the starting point, immediate reality, deploys its nothingness, it cancels itself, negates itself, but there is nothing beyond it. . . . This is why Hegel cannot be situated with regard to the opposition between transcendence and immanence: his position is that of the *absolute immanence of transcendence*. In other words, his position can be grasped only in a temporal shift: first, one asserts transcendence (in an apophatic way)—immanent/immediate positive reality is not all, it has to be negated/overcome, it points beyond itself; then, this overcoming is posited as thoroughly immanent: what is beyond immediate reality is not another higher reality, but the movement of its negation as such.

135. See Alain Badiou, *Being and Event* (London: Continuum, 2006).

136. Perhaps this feature accounts for another weird phenomenon: in (almost) all American hotels housed in buildings of more than twelve floors, there is no thirteenth floor (to avoid bad luck, of course), i.e., one jumps directly from the twelfth floor to the fourteenth floor. For a European, such a procedure is meaningless: whom are we trying to fool? As if God doesn't know that what we designated the fourteenth floor is really the thirteenth floor? Americans can play this game precisely because their God is just a prolongation of our individual egos, not perceived as a true ground of being.

137. In contrast to this 0 which counts as 1, there is the 1 *which counts as 0*: the symptomal torsion of a world, its part of no-part. While the 0 which counts as 1 is the point of a world, its suturing feature, the 1 which counts as 0 is, on the contrary, its eventual site, the site from which one can undermine the world. One should thus distinguish the Zero which is the correlate of ontological multiplicity from the zero which is the part of no-part of a situation, "a (determinate) zero" of a world; the two are related as the pre-symbolic Real and the real of the remainder/inconsistency of a symbolic order.

138. Alain Badiou, *Logiques des mondes* (Paris: Editions du Seuil, 2006), p. 9.

139. Ibid., pp. 9–17.

140. See Peter Hallward, *Out of This World* (London: Verso, 2006).

141. Immanuel Kant, *Critique of Pure Reason* (London: Everyman's Library, 1988), p. 264.

142. Ibid., pp. 264–265.

143. I owe this insight to Stathis Gourgouris, Columbia University.

144. John Gray, *Straw Dogs* (London: Granta, 2003), pp. 126–127.

145. John Gray, *Black Mass* (London: Penguin, 2007), p. 189.

146. Nikolai Bukharin, *Philosophical Arabesques* (London: Pluto Press, 2005), p. 40.

147. Ibid., p. 41.

148. Ibid., p. 46.

149. Ibid., p. 131.

150. See Alain Badiou, *L'être et l'événement* (Paris: Editions du Seuil, 1989). Badiou identifies four possible domains in which a Truth-Event can occur, four domains in which subjects emerge as the "operators" of a truth-procedure: science, art, politics, and love. Do the first three truth-procedures (science, art, and politics) not follow the classic logic of the triad of True–Beautiful–Good—the science of truth, the art of beauty, the politics of the good? So: what about the fourth procedure, love? Does it not stick out from the series, being somehow more fundamental and universal? There are thus not simply four truth-procedures, but *three plus one*—a fact perhaps not emphasized enough by Badiou (although, regarding sexual difference, he does observe that women tend to color all other truth-procedures through love). What is encompassed by this fourth procedure is not just the miracle of love, but also psychoanalysis, theology, and philosophy itself (the *love* of wisdom). Is not love, then, Badiou's "Asiatic mode of production"—the category into which he throws all truth-procedures which do not fit the other three modes? This fourth procedure also serves as a kind of underlying formal principle or matrix of all procedures (which accounts for the fact that, although Badiou denies religion the status of truth-procedure, he nonetheless claims that St. Paul was the first to deploy the very formal matrix of the Truth-Event). Furthermore, is there not another key difference between love and other truth-procedures, in that, in contrast to others which try to force the unnameable, in "true love" one endorses/accepts the loved Other *just because of the unnameable x in him or her?* In other words, "love" designates the lover's respect for what should remain unnameable in the beloved—"whereof one cannot speak, thereof one should remain silent" is perhaps the fundamental proscription of love.

151. Alain Badiou, *Theoretical Writings* (London: Continuum, forthcoming).

152. This is why we should ask the key question: is there a Being without Event, simply external to it, or is every order of Being the disavowal-obliteration of a founding Event, a "perverse" *je sais bien, mais quand même* . . . , a reduction-reinscription of the Event into the causal order of Being?

153. Badiou's counterargument to Lacan (formulated, among others, by Bruno Boostels) is that what really matters is not the Event as such, the encounter with the Real, but its consequences, its inscription, the consistency of the new discourse which emerges from the Event. I am tempted to turn this counterargument against Badiou himself— that is to say, against his "oppositional" stance of advocating the impossible goal of pure presence without the state of representation, I am tempted to claim that we should summon up the strength to "take over" and assume power, no longer just to persist in the safety of the oppositional stance. If we are not ready to do this, then we continue to rely on state power as that against which we define our own position.

154. See David Chalmers, *The Conscious Mind* (Oxford: Oxford University Press, 1996).

155. Ibid., p. 101.

156. Along the same lines, what makes Saul Kripke's argument against classic identity theory (see Saul Kripke, "Identity and Necessity," in *Identity and Individuation*, ed. Milton K. Mu-

nitz [New York: New York University Press, 1971]) so interesting and provocative is the strong claim that, in order to refute the identity between subjective experience and objective brain processes, it suffices for us to be able to *imagine* the possibility of a subjective experience (say, of pain) without its material neuronal correlative.—More generally, it is crucial to note how the entire anti-identity argumentation follows Descartes in resorting to hyperbolic imagination: it is possible to *imagine* that my mind exists without my body (or, in more modern versions: to imagine that, even if I were to know everything about the processes in a person's brain, I would still not know what his subjective experience is).

The Double Glory, or Paradox versus Dialectics: On Not Quite Agreeing with Slavoj Žižek

John Milbank

No one is more rawly exposed than Slavoj Žižek. Somewhat like the tragicomic, clownlike Christ he sometimes invokes, he stands before us without the least vestige of pretense, revealing every last symptom of his quirky subjectivity, while always allowing this to witness to the universal. His seemingly constant descent into trivia and obscenity, his frequent metafictional deviations, consistently perform a vision that is far more serious than that of most of his contemporaries.

In an important sense, he bears a theological witness.[1] First of all, this is to the nature of modernity and postmodernity. He insists that what the latter embodies is merely the extremity of modernity and that it is a tragic, not a superficially joyous prospect. Secondly and correspondingly, he also insists that this ultramodernity is postmetaphysical only insofar as it remains the consummation of metaphysics in a Hegelian rather than a Heideggerian sense. Thirdly, he insists that if modernity is Hegelian, then it is also ineluctably Western, European, and Christian. This modernity he (in some ways rightly) endorses and therefore, in the fourth place, he insists that the universalist project of the West, which we should never abandon, is also a Christian project. In the fifth place he properly links modernity with a specific set of mutations in the Western understanding of Christianity, which have to do with the different but linked legacies of Eckhart, Luther, and Boehme, but also with the quite different legacy of Scotism and nominalism-voluntarism.

But in the sixth place Žižek argues that the legitimacy of the modern age must be one of Christian atheism, and that once this has been grasped one can articulate better a Marxist materialism and the true nature of a critique of the capitalist phase of modernity.

It is here that I wish to register a slight disagreement. What is ironic in Žižek's project is that he insists that Christianity alone articulates a universal logic, but does so in an atheistic mode. This renders him, of course, far nearer to "orthodoxy" (as he acknowledges) than all those craven, weak, sentimental theologians, doused in multiple tinctures of mauvaise foi, who claim to believe in some sort of remote, abstract, transcendent deity and who yet compromise the universal claims of Christianity in favor of mystical relativism, glorification of hypostasized uncertainty, and practical indulgence in the malignly infinite air-shuttle of mindless "dialogue."

For myself, I would wish to defend the idea that this universal logic must be theistic, must endorse a belief in a transcendent deity. What is really at stake in this disagreement? It is a question of a shift of perspective. What matters is not so much that Žižek is endorsing a demythologized, disenchanted Christianity without transcendence, as that he is offering in the end (despite what he sometimes claims) a heterodox version of Christian belief. The atheism, on my reading, is not the upshot of critique, nor of reading the Christian logic through to the end, but rather of accepting too readily, after Hegel, the perspectives of Luther, of Boehme, and of voluntarism-nominalism, whilst misinterpreting those of Meister Eckhart. This means that I am in negative agreement with Žižek concerning Hegel—of whom he is a relentlessly accurate interpreter. Yes, Hegel was already a Christian nihilist and "atheist," and here it is notable that Žižek's tragic (but also comic) reading of Hegel concurs in many ways (much more than most of her supporters are likely to concede) with that of Gillian Rose, while pushing her rendering to a much more consistent "atheistic" conclusion.[2] (This means, however, that the left-Hegelian reading of Hegel is redundant—because, as Žižek argues, the theological element is strangely essential to Hegel's "atheism," which cannot be converted into Feuerbachian or even Marxist humanism without loss of rigor.)

So for me it is the dialectical perspective itself which engenders the nihilistic version of Christian universalism. This is not to say that there is not a lot of truth in the dialectical perspective which is closely linked to the tragic perspective—and in certain ways I agree with Žižek (as with Gillian Rose) that one can reduce postmodern difference to dialectics and point out the tragedy falsely concealed in its celebration of a prevaricating postponement.[3] However, I would propose that both dialectics and the reign of difference remain closely bound up with the same set of modern assumptions. The alternative to both is *paradox*—which one can also name "analogy," "real relation," "realism" (regarding universals), or (after William Desmond) the "metaxological."[4]

But here one can point out an interesting *symptom* in Žižek's writings. Basically, he endorses a Whiggish, Protestant metanarrative. Christianity gradually, if dialectically, posits its own covertly presupposed radicalism. Protestantism negates the Catholic negation of (Eastern) Orthodoxy, Hegel is the fully fledged Protestant consummation of Christian metaphysical logic. However, he reveals a distinct penchant for Catholic thinkers—not just for Eckhart (whose Catholicism he suppresses in an all too clichéd fashion), but more strikingly for modern Catholics (or Anglo-Catholics) such as Claudel, T. S. Eliot, and Chesterton, not to mention the perspectives of the Catholic film director Alfred Hitchcock. To this list one should also add the name of Søren Kierkegaard, given that his linking of faith with reason (and vice versa) restores a basically Catholic perspective (even though Žižek does not recognize this).[5] In the case of Eckhart, Chesterton, and Kierkegaard especially, Žižek tends to celebrate the *paradoxical* character of their thought. Ostensibly, he treats paradox as merely a logical moment to be surpassed: its stasis must advance toward the dynamism of negative dialectics. This applies especially to the logic of incarnation: the paradox of the God who is also man must give way to the dialectical advance toward God only revealed in his absence in humanity—upon which tragic basis the universally just community can at last be founded. And yet, is not

Žižek symptomatically entranced by the figure of the poor stuttering clown who is absurdly God himself? But the dialectical perspective clearly loses and deconstructs this coincidence of opposites, just as it loses this vivid picture itself and its narrative background. Therefore, it is just at the point where Žižek is so obviously entranced (like the nobly childish Chesterton) by picture and narrative, that he gives himself away.

Now, to be sure, he has his own *rationale* for this symptomatic: the images are ultimate in their total contingency and randomness. And this means that they are all reduced to an excreted remainder. But is this really believable—precisely, of Žižek? Does he not love some images more than others, and so for their specific content? Is the Christological clown really attended to *only* because of his spluttering? Wherein then lies detection of his comic nobility, as with Shakespeare's Richard II? But if some images are preferred over others, then we have the issue of a *mediating preference*, of a selective, privileged (even hierarchized) contingency. Unlike the "vanishing mediator" which is the atheistic Christ as God, presupposed for the sake of the universal spiritual community only as "any and every" suffering individual, such that only his sheer contingency is the crucial thing, in this alternative scenario the mediating of mediation, and so of a specifically identified mediator, would remain. And clearly, as will be further expounded below, this is one crucial aspect of paradox.

My case is that there is a different, latent Žižek: a Žižek who does not see Chesterton as sub-Hegel, but Hegel as sub-Chesterton. A Žižek therefore who has remained with paradox, or rather moved back into paradox from dialectic. And this remaining would be sufficient to engender a Catholic Žižek, a Žižek able fully to endorse a transcendent God, in whom creatures analogically participate.

This, however, does not imply a "neomedieval" Žižek in any usual sense. Part of the case which I wish to adumbrate below is that the in certain ways atypical medieval theologian Meister Eckhart—and also by implication Eriugena and Cusanus—is misread by Žižek, in the wake of a host of other commentators, through later Protestant, Behmenist, and Idealist spectacles. This perspective, however, is by no means wholly erroneous, for it is perfectly true that Hegel and Schelling were in some ways building on the theologies of the three medieval thinkers just mentioned. However, their specific development of this slightly more "underground" (though not heterodox) current of medieval Catholic thought is heavily influenced by Protestant, Gnostic, and Kantian outlooks—which are ultimately built upon Scotist and Ockhamist assumptions. There is a strong case for saying that all three outlooks are in fact alien to the notions of Eriugena, Eckhart, and Cusanus. Indeed, in the case of the latter two thinkers, recent research shows that their ideas were adumbrated partly to criticize the "protomodernity" of Franciscan thought (Scotism and nominalism-voluntarism). In rendering this criticism, there is, nevertheless, a certain dialectical debt to the opposition, and furthermore the very defense of traditional "participation metaphysics" required these thinkers to emphasize much more radically than before the ontological all-sufficiency of God and the ontological primacy of the divine intellectual point of view in a way that also newly problematized the creator/creation distinction and all the inherited dualities of nature/grace, reason/faith, essence/persons, generation/creation, creation/deification, and deification/incarnation. Hence the radicalism of these thinkers is in fact the radicalism engendered by a defense of orthodoxy. They were "radically orthodox" in a very specific sense. And my case is that their "paradoxical" outlook does not require to be "completed" by a dialectical one, but would in reality be betrayed by the latter.

The defense of paradox has to be conjoined with a refusal of the Protestant metanarrative to which Žižek is in thrall. In fact, at both the theoretical and the historical level the issue of Catholic versus Protestant is far more fundamental than the question of theism versus atheism—the latter is merely a subplot of the former conflict, which is today notably resurfacing. The key illusion of the Protestant metanarrative is that the mode in which modernity has occurred, and the stages that it has gone through, are the necessary and only possible mode and stages. Once again, Žižek is very close to seeing this, insofar as he refuses the necessitarian and progressivist misreadings of Hegel. For Hegel, as he rightly says, indicates not the logical inevitability of the course of human history, but rather the dependency of even our most abstract, universal assumptions on past contingent events that might have occurred otherwise and retain an unlimited potential for alternative renderings.

However, there is a limit to both Hegel and Žižek's consistency in this regard. And this limit concerns—paradoxically—the absolutization of the contingent as such. If contingencies are only contingent, if no contingency is "to be preferred" or is uniquely revelatory in the specificity of its contingency rather than the mere contingency of its contingency, then, after all, one can tell the story of history (as Hegel does, and Žižek implicitly in his wake) as the contingent dawning of the realization that there "is" only the contingent remainder. Such a realization, while being a mere historical event, still has a uniquely disclosive relationship to eternal truth, and so, after all, uniquely cannot be "gone back upon" save at the price of bad faith—a point on which Žižek frequently insists. Moreover, in relation to the arrival of this insight, previous claims for a universal structure of essential and teleological significance must be shown to be negatively self-defeating, at least in terms of the supremacy of this insight itself.

Perhaps the latter could be a matter of faith—but no, for both Hegel and Žižek the contingent insight into the supremacy of contingency is itself the only way to achieve rational transparency and self-consistency, while not denying the reality either of the objective physical world, or of the free, self-directed subject. For these reasons, while one can agree with Žižek that Hegel does not demonstrate the fated logical necessity of all reality, but rather that *there is only random and aporetic contingent finitude*, and that this is the content of "absolute truth," he does not sufficiently recognize that this very apotheosis of the random involves a claim to perfect insight into the fated logical necessity of the real. If Hegel says the opposite of what most people think (and he does), this opposite is still curiously identical with the caricature. The thinker who really escapes this caricature is not Žižek but Alain Badiou, since Badiou speaks of an allegiance to contingent events in their thick consistency (and not just in terms of their exemplification of Event as such). But Žižek rejects this sort of Badiouian fidelity in the name both of an impersonal Freudian drive to the destruction of the constituted (the "death drive"), and of a stricter Hegelianism which refuses a positive infinite that is more than the indefinite "ever more" of the finite.[6]

Because, after all, modernity necessarily builds toward Hegel's conclusions as far as Žižek is concerned, he tends to read the history of theology in terms of a series of ineluctable advances: Eckhart goes beyond Aquinas, Boehme beyond Eckhart, and Hegel beyond them all, in a way that is also indebted to the voluntarist disenchantment of the cosmos. But should not one take thick historical contingency far more seriously than this? It is easy, for example, to imagine that a more humanist reformation might have taken place (in fifteenth- and sixteenth-century Spain this had at one stage more or less already occurred)[7] such that, while lay life and piety would have moved more center-stage, the specifics of Reformation and Counter-Reformation dogmatics would not have dominated the European future. This could well have entailed less standoff between divine will and human freedom, less dualism of nature and grace in theory and of secular and sacred in practice—with the upshot that economic and political institutions might have remained more ecclesiastically shaped, even though now more lay-directed. For, characteristically, both the Reformation and the Counter-Reformation, albeit in different ways, encouraged a separation of spheres between religious piety and worldly practice. But this had never been the aim of such a clearly "modern" man as Thomas More: rather, he hoped that lay life would be more and more infused by a spirit of "monastic" practice. Overwhelmingly, this is the version of modernity that the Christian East has hoped for—one can think of Dostoyevsky in particular. But for Žižek, such dreaming is to be confined to a sad archaism of an initial "immediacy" as prevailing between ideal content and living community, inherited tradition and current collectivity. The projected move to merge world with monastery (as entertained also in nineteenth-century France by Balzac and Ballanche) cannot for Žižek count as an "alternative" modern strategy because for him, in hock to the Reformation as it happened to occur, there can be but one such strategy.

One can say that the same mode of "pious laicization" was also what was desired in the Middle Ages—with different stresses—by those proto-humanists Dante and Eckhart. In the latter case, one can see clearly extremely "modern" elements of concern for the importance of practical, everyday life, for equal treatment of all human beings, including women, and for the practice of a self-giving love that does not abandon the concerns of justice. Why is it not legitimate to imagine "another" Christian modernity that would be linked to the universal encouragement of mystical openness and productivity, rather than the separation between a forensic faith and an instrumentalizing reason? But as I shall show, such a modernity would persist with the alternative dynamism of paradox and not pass over into the hypocritical sterility of dialectics.

From the point of view of a more Catholic historiography, we really do not need to see the Reformation, the return of gnosticism, the rise of pantheism, and the arrival of enlightenment as in any way inevitabilities, any more than we need so to regard the idea that primary ontology must be derived from natural science. All these tendencies in different ways refuse mediation, by dividing reality between the universal and necessitated on the one hand and the merely contingent on the other. To do so, however, is arbitrarily to select the transcendental dominance of a merely negative, mutually alienating mediation; or, in other words, of dialectics. Yet from the Catholic point of view of trust in specifically disclosive sacramental processes of mediation between the universal and the particular, as between mind and reality, the intellect and the senses, all we have here is the accidental triumph of what T. S. Eliot called the "disassociation of sensibility"—the long-sustained triumph of a particular cultural fashion.

Yet at the same time, this is not to indulge in a historiography of lamented catastrophe, pure and simple. There is no historical deposit of pure Catholic culture, even if there are some more or less exemplary epochs. This is because this culture has always been pregnant with true new developments, including the further release of a sense of freedom and equality, powerfully present in Eckhart. Just because these impulses were later realized in a distorted guise does not mean that the entirety of this realization is inauthentic. Christianity switched the metaphysical focus toward "personality" as the ultimate reality, and the unfolding of this dynamic explodes without stopping from the year 1 *Anno Domini* onward. (I would assume that Žižek would agree with me that to say with political correctness "CE" is ironically to say "AD" all the more emphatically.) However "distorted" the theologian may find modernity to be in Christian terms, the fact remains that the ever-increased emergence of the personal in terms of the search for free expression, sexual liberation, gender equality, and social mobility is ineluctably (as Žižek implies) a Christian phenomenon. But what the theologian critically adds is that this further emergence is crippled by the denial of an ultimate ontological reality open to the personal, or for which personhood could sustain itself infinitely in terms of the arrival at a telos of personal fulfillment. In the absence of the latter, personality degenerates into surface froth which in reality is manipulated by mass constraints, reducing even the apparent freedom of much modern art mostly to variants upon the predictable and preestablished.

It is for this reason that the Catholic theologian is unable simply to say "modern, post-Romantic expressive subjectivity is a mistake, let us return to classical sobriety as a better support for Christian dogma." For she is forced to recognize that modern subjectivity is full of authentically Christian developments which have occurred outside a proper Catholic aegis, even if the lack of such supervision has led to horrendous distortions. In the same way, a Catholic response to a post-Ockham thought-world that has given much more attention to the rigors of logic, the possibilities of freedom, and the unavoidability of linguistic mediation, cannot simply restate a participatory metaphysical vision as if none of this had happened. On the contrary, it rather asks (with logical validity) whether rational rigor, creative freedom, and the linguisticality of thought are incompatible with this vision and do not instead require it, if the appearances of reason and freedom are in the end to be saved. Conversely, the logic of a specifically Christian participatory metaphysics may actually be much better stated in these "postmodern" terms.

So the crucial thing at issue between myself and Žižek is the question of the interpretation of Christianity. I wish to argue that he concludes that atheist Christianity is true Christianity only because he accepts a dialectical (Lutheran, Behmenist, Kantian, Hegelian) version of Christian doctrine as the most coherent. By contrast, I claim that there is a radically Catholic humanist alternative to this, which sustains genuine transcendence only because of its commitment to incarnational paradox. Such a humanism is diversely found in Eckhart, Kierkegaard, Chesterton, and Henri de Lubac.

But what are the real practical stakes here? They are both personal and political. Agreeing with Žižek, I would refuse the postmodern free play of endless difference and never-resolved aporia as in reality still the hell of pointless solitude spoken of so well by Latin American writers and at least one English writer who has visited Latin America. Reality, as these writers suggest, may be as magically playful as one likes, but if it is meaningless then one is still alone and in despair.[8] However, one must nonetheless confront the ambiguity of the Hegelian critique of the postmodern, as found in Gillian Rose as well as Slavoj Žižek. In saying that Hegel is not the gymnast of certainty and identity that the postmoderns have taken him to be, one is inevitably left with a somewhat "postmodern" Hegel who leaves us with sheer contingencies, never-to-be-resolved aporias, middles forever "broken" in time, hopeless failures in love heroically persisted in, and so forth. It is clear that the later Derrida himself moved from the joyfully Nietzschean naturalistic abandonment of the ideal toward a more tragically playful uninterrupted pursuit of the "impossible." At several points Žižek rightly makes fun of this glorification of the never-to-be-reached, inaccessibly mystical goal, and links this to a pseudo-activism indistinguishable from a Buddhistic quietism. But how are the "nihilistic" or "negative" Hegelians (from Adorno onward) themselves to avoid this? How do they differ from the postmodernists other than in tone of voice—either one more relentlessly tragic or else one that opposes genuine humor to Derrida's oh-so-solemn ludicity? It can sound at times in Žižek as if what we share in common is a tragic recognition of the inevitable failure of desire, since it fantasizes ethereal links between subjects that are not really there in a materialist universe.

For according to Jacques Lacan, as with most of the postmodernists, there exists, "besides" the material realm, only the operation of signs which gives rise to subjectivity as an effect of signification. As Lacan puts it, the subject is that which represents one signifier to another in a metonymic chain.[9] But this, of course, simply displaces the older question of how there can be spirit beside matter with the question of how there can be signs beside things.

Here, however, Lacan offers a perhaps more considerable answer than those proffered by later poststructuralists. He points out that the regular procedure of a metonymic chain of signs relies upon a concealed assumed grouping of signs by a meta-signifier which transcendentally determines that signs "of a certain type," but whose number is in principle infinite, are being operated with. It is at this point that Lacan deems that semiotics must be supplemented by mathematical set theory.[10] And it is this conclusion which already opens up the curious link between nihilism and subjectivity that will later be exploited by Alain Badiou and to a degree by Žižek himself. For if a series of signs is more fundamentally a set of numbers, then one can start to comprehend how the phenomenon of language recovers on the surface of the world the anarchic numerical base of all reality involving unrelated "ones" as "unities of multiples," which modern science has always implicitly presupposed. Yet at the same time, the "setting" of a series reveals an ontological space that, while being not exactly governed by subjectivity, is nevertheless one within which subjectivity arises as the moment of wilful decreeing of designated sets (or, one might say, language games) which Lacan sees as being directed by the obscure "real" of bodily desire. It is just at this point that very complex and now hotly debated issues arise as to the relative place of libidinal "energetics" on the one hand (as favored by Deleuze) and para-ontological cultural processes of truth-formation (as favored by Badiou) on the other. But in either case one is dealing with the inscrutable sphere of the "selection" of sets and of cross-fertilization between sets which engenders patterns of relationship and qualitative content that mediate between the mathematical and the linguistic. This sphere can be taken (by materialism) as witnessing at once to an underlying ontological void and yet at the same time to the possibility of subjective existence. For Lacan this existence is especially evidenced by the metaphoric, which symptomatically interrupts the metonymic chains of normal desire to establish specifically characterized personal quirks which both short-circuit the normal links of everyday cause and effect—jumping ahead of the next link to a later one or reaching back beyond a previous link to an archaic one—and also permit the intrusion of one set of links into the sequence of another one.[11]

How, though, is one to interpret this operation of the metaphoric, and so the destiny of human subjectivity? For Deleuze it is a heightening of the more abstract aspect of material desire which is identical with the dynamic process of "life" itself—whose autopoiesis ensures from the outset that there is an excess of "incorporeal" inventive abstraction over solid matter which is yet an essential aspect of material existence (this is clearly very Spinozistic).[12] Such desire is essentially creative and self-fulfilling, if not really relational (and so scarcely to be considered as "love"). For Badiou, on the other hand, something like metaphor forms cultural chains of nonidentical repetition of founding events which ensures a fidelity to those events. Romantic love itself consists in such fidelity, and so not only would fulfillment of desire as relation appear to be possible for Badiou, it would even appear to lie close to defining his paradigm of the truth-process as such. (How exactly this is to be squared with the utter nonrelationality of Badiou's ontology and phenomenology is problematic and is dealt with elsewhere.)[13]

Yet for Lacan, and for Žižek as the more faithful disciple of Lacan, desire is defined by lack and is impossible of fulfillment, even though it can never be renounced in its always quirky specificity. In a way, this is because they remain with the mathematical and the naturally scientific more exclusively than does Badiou. "Reality" (as opposed to "the Real") is for them simply that given material reality which science investigates. Yet if this is an entirely contingent reality, then the immanent infinites which it discloses never point to an actual, simple infinity which would be "God," but rather to the ontological setting of transfinites (as also with Badiou). This suggests, as Žižek argues, that there is no fundamental "totality," but beyond any supposed "all" lies a "not-All," which reappears on the surface of our world as "subjective" interference. However, this "not-All" is something like the anarchic power of the void; it has no content of its own, even if it may negatively reveal itself in the circumstance that physical reality appears at microscopic levels sometimes (according to quantum physics) to conform equally to two incompatible *mathemes* (for example, waves versus particles) both at once. This is tantamount to saying that it conforms equally and undecidably to two transfinite "settings" simultaneously. Žižek refers to this phenomenon as "parallax," and stresses that it permits no possible *mediation* to occur between the two incommensurate sets. Such an emphasis is in line with Lacan's insistence that modern science teaches that "there are only 'ones'" (albeit these ones are sets of multiples) and that any necessary relationality is a religious fiction.

It is this nihilistic mathematization of the semiotic which ensures that desire is both lack and futility. Lacan famously reworked the Saussurian triad of signifier–signified–referent as the Symbolic, the Imaginary, and the Real. But because the diachronic series was for him more fundamentally a synchronic set, any sequence of images was always secretly governed by the chain of abstract symbols. The latter provides the necessary dominance of "law," and the identification of law with "the Father" is merely the result of cultural—and probably biological—contingency. The impersonal "desiring" relay from sign to sign which constitutes the Symbolic is mediated by the subjective desire of an individual, and he must always fix his sense of lack upon a projected image, just as he can have a sense of his own selfhood only by introjection of a mirror image of himself which later becomes his reflective absorption of the ways in which he is addressed and perceived by others. In the case of the male subject, who is for Lacan (again for contingent reasons both cultural and biological) initially the paradigmatic subject, the will to project and be transfixed by an image (the *objet petit a*, substituted for the real subjective *autre*) is obsessively linked with the spontaneous sensations of the male sexual organ. This function is therefore deemed by Lacan to be transcendentally "phallic." But the secret dominance of the image by the impersonal trajectory of the sign and the fact that signs are not intrinsically, relationally connected, but only "setted," ensure that phallic desire is always doomed to disappointment, and that no real sexual relationship can ever be entered into. For the one alone rules, ontologically speaking.[14]

If, therefore, psychoanalysis can never help you to an adult fulfillment of desire (as Freud partially hoped), neither can it truly cure you of desire. For your symptomatic desire is not the sign of a psychic disease—it is rather *sinthom*, what you are, and it is this alone which analysis helps better to reveal. Therefore desire, which cannot be cured, must also be tragically persisted in—regardless of the social chaos thereby caused—because the alternative would be a suicidal abandonment of selfhood.

But what exactly drives the shift from sign to sign, if more fundamentally they are the elements of a static set? What is this force of desire that precedes the subject and yet, in order to operate, must always be quirkily though illusorily subjectified? For Lacan and Žižek it is "the Real." This is never directly accessible outside image and sign, but just as sign constantly subverts image, so also the Real interrupts and reorganizes the work of signs, obscurely converting set into series, short-circuiting every series, and causing the interference of one series with another—in all these cases bringing about the "symptomatic" appearance of subjective personality. What one has here is something neither

Deleuzian nor Badiouian. For the Lacanian/Žižekian "Real" is less a creative force (natural or cultural) than it is the *interruptus* of the absolutely negative which sacrificially refuses the "All" in the name of nothing, yet brings about the short-circuitings and the switches. It is this aspect of the Real which permits Žižek to connect it to Hegelian dialectics.[15]

At the same time, all this tragic male libertinism is heavily qualified by Lacan, and Žižek in his wake. They see the female subject as both empirically and ideally far less phallic than the male subject, and therefore as far less governed by the Imaginary and the *objet petit a*. Women are still, however, like all human subjects, equally governed by the law of the Symbolic, and indeed for this conjoined reason they more obediently submit (albeit often with absolute ironic reserve) to paternal rule in all its guises, rather than embarking on transgenerational and intragenerational rivalries. Yet this is not most fundamentally because law is something alien and heteronomous—even if it happens to be so in nearly all human societies. Instead, for both women and men, the very check of imaginary desire itself is the basis for the giving of the law to oneself as the (Kantian) moral law which both legitimates one's own freedom and recognizes its limit in the freedom of others, which cannot be denied without allowing that they also may inhibit one's own freedom, thereby negating it. Here the paradigmatic instance of "law," which is political law, far from being a disagreeable repression of one's natural desires, liberates one from their aporia, by encouraging one to shift the blame for the disappointment of desire from the structure of desire itself to an alien impeder (the State rulers). But once all law has been derived, after Kant, from the self-giving of the moral law, then this false opposition between subjectivity and legality, freedom and constraint, will and morality, entirely collapses.

Žižek sees this resolution as the fulfillment of St. Paul's exceeding of the law, but in fact the Kantian notion of law as the self-inhibition of freedom which alone releases it in its nonaffective purity (following Rousseau's political ideal) still suggests that morality is legally "over against" our natural desires, and that the will to the good can never be genuinely fulfilled, as it remains ambivalently bound up with such desires: Kant is still stuck in the Old Testament.[16] Hence he lines up law with freedom, but not law with "another" desire, a transfigured natural desire for peace and harmony, as envisaged by St. Paul, which no longer requires either prohibitions or commandments. This is exactly why Lacan realized that the Marquis de Sade was the reverse face of Kant: Sade also taught that enlightenment meant the release of an absolute consensual freedom (including an aporetic consent to coercion) "beyond the pleasure principle." Žižek somewhat obfuscates the point that what really links Kant and Sade here is the fact that they make pain the real measure of the fulfillment of an imperative—toward the moral right in one case, toward perverse pleasure in the other. Yet Žižek is entirely right to say that Sade is not the concealed and subverted truth of Kant—rather, it is a direct implication of the Kantian position. The sadistic and the masochistic can be universally willed—they perversely pass the test of the categorical imperative. Moreover, it can be added that the problem of radical evil in Kant arises from the fact that a universal will to sustain one's freedom cannot really be distinguished from a free will always to bind one's will and so to deny one's own freedom after all, given the way in which ordinary natural desire always clouds our judgment. Therefore a kind of permanent psychic masochism is both aporetically legitimated and rendered indiscernible by Kant's "metaphysics of morals."[17]

But where do Lacan and Žižek themselves stand within this modern moral and sexual entanglement? It seems to me that they are caught between the egotistic imperative of impossible desire on the one hand and an ethical regard for the rights of all on the other. The latter is "feminized" insofar as they both consider that the female subject, as relatively less subject to the Imaginary, is more invaded by the Real. This causes her not to seek possession of the other, but rather to oscillate hysterically between either a total merger with the male other (beyond any "images" of the other) or else holding him at an absolute distance which permits an atomic integrity to be sustained, but also denies desire altogether—though this will then be symptomatically manifest, following Freud's diagnoses. The supposed way out of this hysterical impasse (which of course afflicts all males to some degree also) is that of specifically female *jouissance*, which is a "mystical" unification of self, not with the male, but with the whole of reality and that which negatively exceeds it. Unlike the Catholic Church, therefore, Lacan and Žižek recommend the total abandonment of sex for the cause of religion.

This mystical identification with the whole, or with the "not-All" of the void, entails a kind of detached pointless sacrifice of all for the sake of nothing.[18] But it also seems to permit a certain interpersonal solidarity in the face of the collective defeat of desire to arise. Therefore, alongside the "not giving up on one's desire," Lacan and Žižek also recommend the embracing of "love" rather than desire. "Love" is a willed faithful regard for a specific other whom one elects, beyond the vagaries of desire (now surpassed through mystical *jouissance*), to remain with. Here one should acknowledge Žižek's theoretical and historical correctness in saying that Christianity actually promotes *preferential* love, rather than a generalized respect for all others in their otherness. (For the Augustinian tradition of the *ordo amoris* insists that, as finite creatures, we must love spouse, relations, friends, and guests more than mere strangers and certainly more than enemies.)[19] But otherwise, as with his master Lacan, the entirely accidental character of the elected other, having no regard for *affinity* (which would be dismissed here as either trivially natural or psychically illusory), seems *all too like* the vacuity of the Levinasian respect for the other as other (moralized postmodernism), and in all these cases one detects a continuing sundering of Agape from Eros, combined with a construal of Eros itself in one-way terms of lack and frustration.

And crucially, it is not really clear what criteria can be deployed in order to determine *when* to persist (futilely and probably destructively) with one's desire and *when*, on the other hand, to forbear from this out of loving concern for the other—and so, contradictorily of course, out of concern for the (non) fulfillment of her own sad and futile desiring. This oscillation would appear to be unsatisfactorily arbitrary. It is also the case that, if you can never really decide whether you are truly free as opposed to self-bound, then you can also never really decide whether the other has consented or not to the exercise of your desire. Žižek is highly alert to this—often he reiterates that modernity says both "do what you like, regardless of the other" and yet also "do nothing to the other whatsoever, because any interference overrides her autonomous free decision." Hence the permissive society which "allows sex" is inevitably succeeded by a political correctness which more or less bans the sexual altogether. But Žižek does not fully recognize that his own Lacanian position encourages the same contradictory polarity in a more oscillating, "dialectical" mode.

Moreover, the purely agapeic account of love assumed here is genealogically Franciscan, Protestant, or Jansenist—it is not an account of love which combines reciprocity with generosity, or the erotic with the ecstatic, within the terms of a Catholic metaphysics of participation as expounded by Augustine or Aquinas.[20]

Lacan himself is quite clear: reciprocity in love is impossible within a disenchanted cosmos.[21] Indeed, this is the beginning and the end of his philosophy. Traditionally, prior to Descartes, all knowledge was construed in terms of sexual metaphorics, precisely (as Lacan says) because people imagined there to be an occult reciprocity between knowing and being, mediated by the notion of "form" which can exist both in material things and in the human mind. According to Lacan, Cartesian dualism (which he fundamentally accepts) rendered such a mediation inconceivable, and therefore the traditional sexual metaphorics were gradually abandoned. But Lacan's case is that if sexual relationship as metaphor is now a fantasy, then so too is supposedly *real* sexual relationship. And this is a rigorously precise conclusion, because the reality of sexual relationship *itself* depended upon the knowledge-is-sex metaphor, taken in the inverse sense which renders sex a real knowledge of the other. So the "sublimation" of the sexual, contained in the long tradition of allegorical exegesis of the orientally erotic *Canticles* in the Bible (the "Song of Solomon") which read its rapturous account of a sexual encounter in terms of the love between Christ and the soul or Christ and the Church, by affirming a "spiritual" aspect to sensation (which Jean-Louis Chrétien has now demonstrated *was not metaphor*), actually sustained the idea of sexual relationship in the only way possible, as involving not just the unity of two people but also the "occult" unity of soul with body and soul with soul.[22]

By contrast, without this sublimation, without any intrinsic occult link between what goes on in the mind and what goes on in the material world, including our bodies (the link that was once supplied by "form"), there can be no real experience of the human other through physical touch, while even our own bodily stimulation must be regarded as the "occasion" for the arising of an ethereal mental *jouissance*, which is the very presence of subjectivity itself for Lacan's version of the *cogito*, which, though Freudianized, is really quite close to the authentic Descartes.[23] The mind associates its pleasure with bodily stimulation, but in this respect, as Lacan says, we are *duped* by *jouissance*, and when he speaks of "bodily *jouissance*" he does not mean this literally, as too many of his readers imagine. He also sees the excess of *jouissance* over physical reality, which in one sense is "all there is," as accordingly an excess over being as such.[24] In this respect also he is surprisingly close to Levinas, and it is notable that both thinkers for the most part ignore Merleau-Ponty's critique of Cartesian dualism which regards the body as itself a mediating sphere between the psychic and the material, and therefore permits a truly cognitive and disclosive aspect to the phenomenon of touch and thereby of all sensation, especially the most intimate. (In many ways Merleau-Ponty's perspective is neo-Aristotelian.) Therefore the question of whether sexual relationship is still allowable in modernity is the question of whether it is possible to rework the premodern notion of a mediating threshold between the material and the psychic—a notion which assumes that the psychic is a real aspect of being. Such a question is more silently dismissed than it is discussed by Jacques Lacan.[25]

The issue, then, is whether Protestant and Cartesian disenchantment of the cosmos is cognitively inevitable; it was not for Chesterton. This is the one point about Chesterton that Žižek gets disastrously wrong, as we shall see. If it is not, then perhaps, after all, sexual relationship is possible. D. H. Lawrence showed an identical logical rigor to that of Lacan, but took the opposite side in the same battle by linking (in his novels *Women in Love* and *Lady Chatterley's Lover*) the theme of redemptive sex with a total rejection of the modern technologized divorce between body and spirit and between feeling and reflection. The Lacanian view might lead one either to the cliché that "sex is really in the head" or (if one did not favor his moralizing "love" alternative) to the view that one should avoid the despair of desire by abandoning oneself to the unconscious vagaries of sheer sensory stimulus. And both positions are exactly of the kind entertained by Lawrence's villains and villainesses, representative either of modern indifference to the sexual or of modern metropolitan sexual permissiveness— of which he was a severe if fascinated critic.[26] Both attitudes, and especially the former, he already saw as tending to disconnect procreation from the sexual act since, for modernity, the sexual act concerns a merely passing pleasure, while it considers that procreation should be rationally planned and detached from the vagaries of interpersonal romantic love. (Our entire mode of supposed "sexual liberation" is secretly our succumbing to neo-Malthusian elite manipulation.)

In all these ways Lawrence was oddly near to a Catholic perspective, and perhaps most worried about Christianity because it appeared to him illogically (and differently from Islam in this respect) to exclude sexual relationship from the life of the resurrected body. But in general the pre-Cartesian Catholic metaphysical vision permits a much more literally sexy account of the universal possibility of love. It is only atheists who are stuck with the dreary moralizing puritanism of saying that sexual desire is both narcissistic and impossible of realization, while true love involves a resigned devotion to the any-old contingency of the one with whom one happens to be stuck—this any-old contingency being that person's only inviolable identity.

Here one can claim that the Catholic perspective achieves a materialism in a joyful, positive sense—whereas Žižek's atheism achieves only a sad, resigned materialism which appears to suppose that matter is quite as boring as the most extreme of idealists might suppose. By contrast, for matter to "matter" there must be a recognition of a mediating link between matter and spirit which allows us to recognize, in a neo-Aristotelian manner, that the human being is an integrally "eroto-linguistic" animal. Likewise, for desire to mean an aching lack of the other (as opposed to Deleuzian vitalist solipsism) and yet not to be doomed to entire disappointment, the infinite relay of signs must mediate to us in some measure an actual plenitudinous infinite of realization. Such a mediation will ensure that our "imaginations" of the finally signified (the infinite) are not just illusions, so that the "setting" of reality into series of signifying chains by our "real" corporeal desires can be something more than arbitrary.

Bringing the mediations between spirit and matter, the (actual, positive) infinite and the finite together, such that the first mediation always mediates the second, it then becomes possible to understand how the "imagining" of the other is not always and necessarily idolatry (not always a matter of *objet petit a*) but rather respects at once her given presence and her withheld distance. The "veil" (literal and metaphoric) through which the other appears to me is not necessarily a substitute for the other herself; rather, it is her own more willed corporeal emanation through which she expresses herself as a distinctive and therefore impenetrable enigma, and therefore at the same time reserves herself. And if, in publicly clothing or veiling herself, she thereby presents herself for public negotiation, then it is also the case that my poetic imagining of the other, while being a great risk, may also provide for the other a further expressive habitation which she can appropriate as authentic. And all the same in reverse, naturally.

For here the similarities between man and woman vastly outweigh the differences, while at the same time Lacan's account of sexual difference is by no means entirely wrong. In general a male concern with "artistic" imaginary mediation (*poiesis*) is balanced by a female "social" sense (*praxis*) that mediation itself paradoxically combines in an absolute unity two genders that remain nevertheless integrally distinct in a way that can never be fully expressible. This is the truly positive aspect of the "hysterical," and it is an instance of the paradoxical accentuation of the analogical—which will be explained further below. And in terms of this paradoxical and analogical mediation, the humanly erotic is not obliterated by the relationship to "the divine" but is, rather, able to participate in it, since this relationship also analogically and paradoxically conserves the personhood of the one who is in mystical ecstasy. Just as we must imagine the other in order to be united to her and yet conserve mutual distance, so also we must analogically imagine the infinite God to the same ends. Since the latter relationship may be taken as the ultimate ontological scenario, the interplay between real corporeal desire, the signifying, and the imaginary can be taken as more than the site of perennial human illusion. Inversely, this interplay which composes human generation and human society can be taken as a pathway to God without any ultrahysterical baroque ruptures of the kind favored by Lacan. (But again, this theological dimension will be further elaborated in sections 5 and 6 below.)

2. CATHOLIC VERSUS PROTESTANT METANARRATIVES

The political stakes in my disagreement with Žižek are just as important as the personal. I wish to raise the question of how far all the usual "left" historical narratives are in fact biased toward Protestantism, thereby disguising from themselves the way in which a secular "progressivist" approach to history is in reality secretly committed to a Protestant reading of Christianity—rather than it being the case, as the left often assumes, that Protestantism is a more "progressivist" rendering of the latter. Indeed, even to think in terms of the categories of "traditionalist" versus "progressivist" may be to be held captive by a Protestant religious perspective, which has no real meaning either in purely secular terms, or in genuinely Catholic ones. All this applies especially to the Marxist tendency to see capitalism as a necessary and clearly progressive phase in human development.

However, Žižek himself has on occasion drawn attention to Marx's own ambivalence here: when Marx speaks of capitalism as destroying all tender and patriarchal values, it is clear that he thinks that something good has been lost, even if this loss was inevitable, and even if this tenderness was only a relative good. For what has replaced it is manifestly something worse, and if utopia is ever to arrive, then some new equivalent of the lost tenderness will have to be invented. But the destruction of paternalist concern is clearly, still in our own time, an ongoing process. Therefore today one must ask: if paternalism is often something relatively good, in comparison with the egalitarian ruthlessness of liberal individualism, should the left then accept that for the moment it must be replaced with something worse—namely the indifferent manipulative rule of the market and of the "new political class," whose disciplinary deployment of *surveillance* has now usurped the paternalist ruling idioms of the old establishment?

But it is just here that the dialectical vision strains all credulity and Žižek, to his credit, often recognizes this, just as he adopts Etienne Balibar's revisionist view that not all political violence is retrospectively redeemed as part of an inevitable learning curve (as Hegel as well as Marx supposed).[27] The extreme totalitarian violence of the twentieth century was not obviously productive of any good whatsoever, and the current state of China, along with international complacency toward it, suggests that there is not even any inevitability about the ending of totalitarian abuse. And so one must correspondingly contest the idea that the road to the better always lies temporarily through the worse, or a fortiori through catastrophe. Would it not be more plausible to suppose that one needs to modify paternalism with a greater humility and attentiveness to populist feedback rather than to remove it altogether? Especially as it is clear that, since we are always "educated" animals (even in order to become language users), the role of the parental *in principle cannot be elided*. Žižek has rightly observed that feminists are wrong if they today suppose "patriarchalism" to be the main enemy.[28] And this goes along with the fact that certain modes of liberal feminism are clearly playing the game of capital—of course to the ultimate detriment of women themselves, both as human beings and as women specifically.

All the same, Žižek himself sustains a Marxist inevitablism by arguing (for Hegelian reasons) that alienated bourgeois abstract freedom is the only means by which we can invoke the idea of true freedom, just as the constitutive fetishism of capital (which is not "ideological," as Žižek rightly points out) appears to concur with the symptomatic fetishism that the human subject requires (according to Lacan, as we have just seen in the previous section) in order to be a subject at all. Here the disenchanted denial of the fulfillment of desire suggests that the capitalist market does indeed reveal desire's true vacuity, albeit also indicating, despite itself, how we might move beyond desire toward the haven of love. But is not this all too like that *Buddhistic* mode of resistance which Žižek purportedly abhors?

If the supposed inevitability of the disenchantment of the cosmos and the impossibility of sexual relationship go together, then clearly the commodity and spectacular substitute for these things constitute in an important sense "the truth." But in that case we can see just how, if capitalism is a religion, as Walter Benjamin taught, it is definitely a mode of Protestant religion. Furthermore, one can argue that it is also a species of specifically *Anglo-Saxon* Protestant religion: "all things begin and end in Albion's ancient ruined Druid rocky shore," as William Blake wrote in *Jerusalem*.[29]

According to the American, heterodoxly Marxist historian Robert Brenner, without the purely contingent dispossession of the English peasantry at the end of the Middle Ages and the unique growth of an agricultural wage-relation, market competition and agricultural innovation, and the spread of enclosure which this allowed, fully fledged capitalism (based upon systematic primary accumulation, removal of the means of subsistence leading to enforced market competition and the extortion of surplus value from labor) might never have arisen at all.[30] Moreover, one can add to Brenner that it arguably required for its secure triumph the massive boost provided by the dissolution of the monasteries and the adoption by the economically benefiting gentry of a Calvinism able to assuage their guilt and justify their material windfall. It is then easy to show that the spread of the capitalist system everywhere was mainly to do with the need to adopt it in order to compete and survive—and indeed, this even applies to the incursion of neoliberalism into mainland Europe today.

Even though Brenner has been accused of exaggerating the differences between a bound English and a free French peasantry, of downplaying the role of urban industrial production in the gestation of capitalism, and of projecting backward an English eighteenth-century mass dispossession of land from small-scale owners, none of these qualifications really affects the overall weight of the evidence which he marshals.[31] Thus from a far earlier point, and in much greater numbers, the English peasantry lost their independence, and even if the French peasantry often suffered just as much hardship, this is beside Brenner's precise point. Although dispossession vastly quickened its pace in the eighteenth century, the preference for "sheep over men," and the consequent rise of vagabondage and landless rural laborers (which largely motivated the emergence of the new, more disciplinarian Elizabethan poor laws) was a pattern well established from the late Middle Ages onward. The continued economic primacy of agriculture in this entire period meant that only the rising dominance of a wage-relation and technical innovation in this sector, combined with an ever-increasing release of dispossessed men into the towns, and so into industry, could really bring about a capitalist takeoff, as opposed to the situation pertaining in the Middle Ages, whereby there were already isolated pockets, urban and rural, of wage exploitation, lending money at interest, and the speculative production of goods purely for ever-increasing profit in alien foreign markets.

But as I have indicated, what is lacking from Brenner's account is a recognition that capitalism in England was massively encouraged and driven forward by the justification granted to it by Calvinist theology, and by the association in the minds of the English gentry between their Protestant religion and their landed fortune.[32]

If, however, we combine Brenner with contemporary vindications and reworkings of the Weber–Tawney thesis, then we can claim that Protestantism was not a necessary stage on the way toward enlightened liberal market freedom—rather, the latter emerges only through a set of accidental material circumstances, and through the strange theological legitimation of a new sort of "amoral" economic practice. Indeed, if one follows successively the attitudes of Montesquieu and Voltaire and then Hegel and Fichte toward Britain, one could readily argue that, despite the supposed difference of continental thought from British thought, the former has in reality tended to assume the exemplarity of the English Protestant narration of its own history. Therefore, far from it being true that Britain has always been locked into its own sheltered sociopolitical tranquillity, it is rather the case, as Blake surmised, that it is the island of unique traumas—iconoclasm, industrialization, urbanization, and now deindustrialization—which it promotes, undergoes, resists, survives, and then exports.

This perhaps explains why it is that British defenses of modernity like those of Hume and Bentham and Herbert Spencer tend to be brutally positivistic, while French defenses tend to seek to integrate the modern with a greater autonomy for the subjective, regarded as the site for the preservation of more traditional "feminine" values. The truth of this contrast is in the end psychogeographical: even today, the French landscape allows one (apparently) to have one's modernity and yet still to bask in traditional rural space and produce—whereas the British landscape does not. Either lowland Britain is too often manifestly scarred by the modern, which itself takes the form of a more unconcealed ugliness, unglossed by French technocrats, or else Highland Britain still clings in certain creative ways to premodern sources of inspiration. But this is arguably why Britain has also produced more searching and radical (and therefore less materialistic)[33] critiques of capitalism as a process of enclosure, primary accumulation, and dehumanization linked to the disenchantment of nature: from Cobbett through Carlyle, Pugin, and Ruskin to D. H. Lawrence, Eric Gill, and H. L. Massingham.

But today this partially "anti-Protestant" literature is joined by a notable resurgence in neo-Catholic historiography among British professional historians.[34] What their work tends to do is to unlock the supposedly necessary connections made by the "Protestant Whig" narrative between individualizing religion and nationalism on the one hand, and constitutionalism and lay participation on the other. The latter are confirmed as being of medieval origin, but not as counter-movements to either papal internationalism or ecclesiastical influence—rather as being mainly the products of the latter phenomena themselves.

Here again, then, burgeoning "modern" aspects of the Middle Ages, emerging both within and against "feudalism," can be returned to as having a different

potential from the one which liberal democracy has emphasized—a more plu-
ralist, more corporatist, more distributist, more lay-religious potential which
refuses the modern duality of the economic and the political as much as the
modern duality of secular and sacred. Just this potential was what Chesterton
the political thinker stressed, and his Catholic perspective permitted him to
think of the importance of mediating institutions (cooperatives, guilds, and
corporations) in a way not unlike that of Hegel, but more emphatic than the
latter's far more capitalist "vanishing mediation" would allow.

Now the core of Žižek's Lacanian Marxism lies in the thesis that a psychoanalytic curing from the illusions of desire will encourage us also to refuse the
fetishistic spectacle of the capitalist marketplace.[35] But if capitalism is deemed
an inevitable phase of development and yet capitalism, as I have suggested, is
in many ways Protestant, then this tends to lock us into a Protestant pessimism
about desire and the possibility of human good works. Accordingly—rather
like René Girard, as has been pointed out—Žižek proposes more of a refusal
of desire altogether than a different mode of desiring.[36]

The upshot is that he scarcely moves very far beyond the precise homol-
ogy between late capitalism and postmodern philosophy which he correctly
diagnoses. In what sense for him can capitalism be any more than refused in an
empty subjective gesture? The alternative would indeed appear to be an austere
socialist dictatorship in which the forbidding of futile desire by law benignly
releases us for the privacy of chastened love according to the dictates of the
autonomous law of morality. This really does reek of nostalgia for life within
the tenements of communist Eastern Europe. On the other hand, the insistence upon desire as lack, impossible of fulfillment, also clearly perpetuates a
Kundera-like assault upon that kitsch which tends to be the product of facile
or hypocritical utopianism. In reading capitalism also as (fascinating) kitsch,
Žižek would seem to read it as another promised utopia, and in addition to
be saying that utopia must always and everywhere be falsely promised and yet
must be truly refused in the name of the bleakness of the Lacanian Real. This
tragicomic mode of resignation can, after all, be guaranteed only by a system
of formal rights, if we stress (implicitly siding with Heidegger's reading of
Kant against Cassirer's humanist one) that rights belong to the "inhuman"
of the noumenal which can survive any definitions of the "human" that are
sure to be civic ones, and therefore allow, after all, the abuse of those reduced
to "pure nature" outside any legal code, as with secret American and British
detention centers for terrorist suspects today.[37] But the problem with this "de-
biologizing" of rights is that it still falls foul of the biopolitical aporia (rights
are natural, and yet inaugurated only through the artifice of contract), because
(as Gillian Rose would have pointed out, and Žižek as a Hegelian should realize) the model for the "sublime" character of the noumenal law of freedom
can only be a political one, since it is a metaphysically accentuated projection

of the mere formality of law. This means that it is perfectly possible to abuse a person's body and empirical mind *in the very name* of his noumenal freedom which he is taken to have denied through his terroristic actions. After all, this is precisely the logic of Kant's retributory theory of punishment and justification of the death penalty. By contrast to the idea of rights, only the Thomistic idea of respect for the human person as an animal *by nature* teleologically directed both to a political end and to a supernatural end of unity with an entirely just God can possibly in the future prevent any more Guantánamos.

And yet for Žižek, Kantian rights as a sign of promise can be curiously sustained beyond Hegelian *Sittlichkeit* just at that point where the individual remains autonomously resigned to his own quirky but self-sustaining symptom. However, given this irreducible loneliness and the consequent impossibility of a relational reconciling of one to one, one to another, it would seem that only the most systematic and tortuous bureaucracy could possibly patrol and defend all the urban nests of singularity within which we might be able to make the unilateral gesture of love.

Must we be confined within this Protestant, Jansenist, and totalitarian gloom? Or can an alternative Catholic metanarrative be sustained by both the metaphysical plausibility of the Catholic outlook and its fidelity to the core of Christian doctrine? In the following three sections I will try to adjudicate the question of the true nature and credibility of Christianity, which both Žižek and I take to be "the absolute truth."

3. UNIVOCITY, DIFFERENCE, AND DIALECTIC

Initially, I will try to set out the difference between the three perspectives of Hegelian dialectic, postmodern difference, and Catholic paradox in formal terms.

William Desmond has suggested that one can classify the various historical modes of metaphysics in terms of different onto-logics: a relative stress upon the equivocal, the univocal, the dialectical, and what he calls the "metaxological."[38] By the latter term he means to indicate what has traditionally been described as an "analogical" outlook. For reasons which will emerge, this can also be considered to be a "paradoxical" perspective.

Desmond's approach is ecumenical insofar as he wishes to stress that each mode captures something of phenomenal reality.[39] The latter comes to us only as numbered, as involving a series of items (always as some "thing": the scholastic transcendental *res*), while it further presents itself to us as a series of "somethings" that cannot be substituted for each other (the scholastic transcendental *aliquid*, which later becomes the basis for Leibniz's principle of the identity of indiscernibles).[40] Even in terms of quantitative position in a series, the ineffable uniqueness of "position" and "perspective" emerges, such that while every abstract "one" is formally substitutable for every other one (like the "ones" in set theory, where each "one" indifferently instantiates a certain kind of abstract item, such that one can posit, after P. J. Cohen and in despite of Leibniz, an item identifiable only by its absolutely representative typicality, which is nonetheless discernibly different from all other items of the same "kind"), the ones in a countable series, or the points in a geometric space, are not so intersubstitutable—for here it is phenomenal relationality and directionality which establishes identity (as according to the canons of category theory).[41] Hence phenomenological ratio depends upon sheer equivocal and "incommunicable" difference of situation, established through comparative relation. And quantity as such is further incommensurable with quality; even if quantitative difference shades over imperceptibly into qualitative difference, the meta-difference between the two is betrayed by the fact that we always miss the exact point of the break and the character of this transition, however ardently we may lie in wait for it. Then, within the qualitative field itself, there is no exoteric common measure between texture, sound, and color. And finally, there is still less common measure between sensory qualities and those deemed aesthetic or moral. The very exercises of common sense and reason depend upon our not confusing one thing with another, nor one of these several categories with another. So reality includes the equivocal.

On the other hand, phenomenal reality also exhibits to us the univocal. We would inhabit a chaos without possibility of regular, nonproblematic, interpersonal communication, were it not for the fact that our finite reality is such that we can take it as organized into regular categorial frameworks (which we have no warrant for taking to be *merely* our perspective upon this reality, in a Kantian fashion). The various *aliqua* are recognizable or comparable only because they are really shadowed by a ghostly grid of regularly organized space which is nothing other than the shadow cast by their own interrelations. For we cannot truly imagine an empty space, yet the space which things together compose can be occupied by other, initially alien presences. (The site of my house is a site only as the site of my house and its coordinates, but it might be the site of another house.) Similarly, the uniqueness of events within the flow of time is recognizable and comparable only because they are really and truly shadowed by an ontological clock upon the wall. Again, time passes only as the succession of events, but events project a shadow of other possible events, and it is indeed this very shadow which they traverse and which alone allows them to shine forth in their actual occurrence. Even in the case of the sun and the moon we can imagine other moving celestial bodies, or a day when the sun is totally eclipsed and a night that is entirely irradiated.

The sameness or univocity of the shadows of space and time is therefore an important part of our experience. And while one can speak of separate things only because of their relational difference from each other in time and space (this is how Aquinas construed *aliquid*), nevertheless the "thingness" of their *res* is always in a certain sense the same: a thing, in order to be a thing at all, must sustain a certain consistency and relative completeness, like a town that retains roughly the same centripetal configuration and defensible boundaries over many centuries. This consistency can be termed "substance," however loosely this may be conceived, and without insisting on any priority of substance over event; indeed, for "event" as a category to be ontologically fundamental there must be an oscillating balance between the two, since an event is defined by its fusing of transformation with the establishment of a new relative habitual stability and the modification of preceding stabilities.

The concomitant to a recognition of substance is an equal recognition that in the case of "anything" there is always the "same" presence of more or less "accidental" features, not necessary to recognition of its substantial sameness, and so diversely equivocal in relation to this sameness—even though there can be more or less "necessary" accidents, and even though the distinction between substance and accident is in the end always a problematic one, just because identity is itself a problematic matter of judgment. But this circumstance does not negate the truth that reality always presents itself to us in terms that include more or less stable, if shifting, identities.

In addition, however, reality also presents itself to us in terms of relations that can themselves be relatively constitutive (of one or both of its substantive poles) or relatively accidental. There are some relations without which an individual substantive thing could not remain at all, like that of a tree to the ground, a plant to generative life, a son as son to a father, or a sign to something indicated. There are other relations which are temporarily and non-necessarily fallen-into or entertained, like the proximity of one tree to another, the adoption of a child, or the determination of an arbitrary sign to indicate this rather than that. But both "constitutive" and "accidental" relations are univocally definable. Constitutive relations, it should be added, have a multiple and hierarchical aspect. As Alain Badiou has argued, deploying category theory, reality appears to us always in terms of dominating realities and relatively strong or weak foci, while there is no justifiable reason (*contra* Husserl) to think of these appearances as merely subjective.[42] The relationship of the tree to the ground, for example, is given to us only in the wider phenomenal context of the relationship of the tree also to the light of the sun and then the entire relationship of the sun to the earth in terms of the economy of night and day, the succession of the seasons, and so forth. If space and time are locally "transcendental" for our finite experience, then so are night and day and the bioclimatic cycle for our finite life on planet earth, which is the only finitude we can truly imagine.

Indeed, one aspect of the *poetic* is univocalist: the glory of the constant return of the same, the aesthetic requirement of finite being always to fall within stable essences. Gerard Manley Hopkins's poem "Duns Scotus's Oxford" calls tragic attention to precisely this phenomenon, in lamenting the disintegration of the integrity of a specific place, even if he makes (also poetically?) the Scotist mistake of prioritizing essence over the openness of being, and recognizing only a formal distinction between the two, thereby tending to preclude the possibilities of an abstractive ascent from the particular, or of the temporal preservation of integrity despite transformation—for has not the "base and brickish skirt" of North Oxford, built to house dons newly permitted to marry (significantly enough for the exegesis of the poem's lament for integrity), come to seem to be in new continuity with its more ancient charms? (One can worry about an overhasty dismissal of the new, while retaining Hopkins's suspicion in general of the effects of modern urbanization.) In this way Hopkins is arguably unable to advance to Mallarmé's modernist realization of the poetic centrality of the "absent flower"—which is a kind of point of mediation between the "philosophical" form of flower in general and the empirically sensuous flower in particular.[43] This perhaps leads, in his later poems, to his terrible metaphysical despair when, in Irish urban exile from North Wales, the immediate and particular ceases to seem to him so disclosive of the good and the beautiful.

Yet in true Deleuzian fashion, as the poet of the univocal Hopkins was also the poet of the equivocally different—and again, this is a genuine poetic moment, which he brought to supreme perfection. But the question as to whether individual identity needs to be hypostasized as *haeccitas* remains open both philosophically and poetically: for what a Scotist poetics celebrates is too much a "thisness" thought of apart from a transcendentally necessary relationship to everything else and to *esse* as infinite source. This is the reverse face of a Scotistic tendency to regard such relationships as a fixed "framework," ultimately reduced to an epistemological rather than ontological transcendental supposition within which things are seen to occur—which led eventually to the Kantian idea of the subjective *schemata* of space and time, divorced from their contents.[44] For alternatively, relationality may be seen as abiding in the very poles related, just as one may see the cycles of the seasons as the rhythm of a love affair between sun and earth, light and roots, rather than as some "law" to which they are subjected and which holds outside the pattern of their interaction. (It is apparent that the perspectives of modern science more permit this romantic perspective than do the older Newtonian ones.)

There is, nevertheless, clearly a univocal as well as an equivocal aspect to finite being, and this opens upon beauty as well as upon boredom. But as to whether being itself, or the other transcendental aspects of being (according to medieval philosophy)—thingness, somethingness, unity, goodness, truth, and beauty—are univocal, that is of course more controversial. To say that they are, indeed, univocal is to erect univocity itself into the overriding transcendental principle, and in consequence to put forward a univocalist metaphysics. Similarly, to say that there are no such transcendental unities, that they are rather human fictions, *except* in the case of the univocity of being and of *aliquid* (this being the position of "postmodern" thought, as most exemplarily adumbrated by Gilles Deleuze), is to erect equivocity or "difference" into the supreme transcendental principle, and to have an equivocalist metaphysics. (Heidegger also provides an example of this, despite the "postmetaphysical" jargon.) Here being always occurs differently, within a priority of process (instead of an interplay between substance and becoming, as envisaged by Aquinas himself (though not by neo-Thomism),[45] such that there are only the illusions of substances and stable entities.

However, it must be reiterated that, if being is not transcendentally univocal, this does not mean that it contains no "regional" aspects of univocity, no relative stabilities whatsoever. The very notion of analogy of being depends upon the existence of regional spheres of univocity and equivocity, just as metaphor depends upon the existence of literal speech which constantly locates both identity and difference. If all were metaphor, nothing would be metaphor, and similarly, if all were analogy, there would be no analogies. One can say this without for the present adjudicating as to whether there is any "absolute" identity or difference, as both a univocalist and an equivocalist metaphysics would hold. Thus the fact that finite being presents itself to us in relatively stable categorial terms (as Aristotle argued) shows that finite being can at least to an extent be taken "generically"—as *ens commune*, as Aquinas put it.[46] Just as we require for existential and practical purposes to see qualitative space as shadowed by a regular spatial grid of *mathesis*, and qualitative time as shadowed by an "ontological sundial," so also we necessarily have to think of finite things in terms of a certain univocal democracy of being: all things, either great or small, quantitative or qualitative, material, organic, or personal, are equally either there or not there, since these essences are really distinct from their existential instances. So far, Aquinas and Kant are at one, but this relative necessity for *ens commune* concludes nothing as regards being as such and the relationship of finite to infinite being, any more than the need for spatial measurement or for clock time proves that these aspects have transcendental priority over qualitative and relationally "ecstatic" space and time. Here Aquinas parts company with Kant over being, just as Leibniz or Maine de Biran parts company with Descartes and Kant over space and Bergson and Heidegger part company with Newton and Kant over time.

If, Desmond argues, there are both univocal and equivocal aspects to reality, then, equally, there are dialectical aspects to reality. Here his project intends to accord to Hegel a certain truth, but to regionalize this truth in terms of the more overarching framework of the metaxological.[47]

Of course this raises the question as to whether his logical route to this conclusion is itself disguisedly dialectical—which is no doubt what Žižek would conclude regarding his work. For the moment that issue will be left to one side. But in agreement with Desmond we can say that the phenomenological-ontological region of the dialectical concerns certain implications of relationality. First of all I shall briefly sketch what is questionable in Hegel's reading of all relationality as dialectical, before trying to indicate the proper bounds of dialectics.

Hegel rightly recognized that some relations were constitutional, rather in the way that I have described above. But he further drew from this the more dubious conclusion that *res* were constituted in a "contradictory" fashion. If something is necessarily definable only in relation to what it is not, then it *is*, both in meaning and in reality, what it is not: north is positioned as not south, so it *is* in a sense the south, which is needed in order to situate it. Likewise, if something is definable only in terms of something else, thereby exhibiting a certain "preestablished" or at least long-term, transhistorical relationality to something else (substance compared to accident for the first instance, organic compared to inorganic for the second), then again it "is" also what it is not; it is somehow identified with its own contradiction. [48] Yet since the denied "is" in all these cases is an "is" of predication and not an existential qualifier, then this conclusion does not seem necessarily to follow. Something being "also" what it is not—that thing with which it is in an essential relation—may appear paradoxically to involve a certain coincidence of an "is" with an "is not": for instance, the tree "is" also the ground, even though it is distinguished from the ground and therefore "is not" the ground. But it does not have the outright force of an "antagonistic" contradiction—as if the ground's not being the tree were a denial of the tree's very being, its existentiality. Yet Hegel constantly writes in this sort of metaphoric register as if it clearly had ontological force.

One can also say, following Hegel, that if the most particular thing can be indicated only by general terms like "this" or "is," then yet again one has a certain coincidence of opposites—"thisness" is the most general thing imaginable, as the medieval transcendental doctrine already indicates. [49] In its temporal mode, "this" means "now," and yet when we say—to use Hegel's own example—that "Now is Night," we discover that "now" belongs to an "ontological clock time" apart from night, as has already been discussed. [50] Similarly, if we say "this tree is here," we can turn round in a circle and find that "No tree is here, but a house instead." [51] Yet to say, like Hegel, that the now is "a *negative* in general," in a negative relationship to both day and night, rather than something that is *positively* mediated by both, is surely to misread the "is not" of predicating difference—"now is not night" or even, in one sense, "now is never night," as the "is not" of error and denial. The same goes for Hegel's understanding of "here" as also a negation which sublates the vanishing empirical object.

In either case one misreads him if one takes these observations to be contributing to any genuine metaphysical realism. For what they imply, according to Hegel, is an "empty or indifferent Now and Here"[52] that becomes the paradigm for an equally empty and abstracted "being," all three being initially categories of my knowing and not ontological categories. This contrasts with the realism of Aquinas, for whom the reality of such "universals" in our mind did not imply any such real "indifference," based upon negation, but rather an intentional relation to particulars more primary than any fiction of a merely abstracted universality which the mind might reflectively contrive. The "indifference" of essence is much more in a Scotistic and baroque scholastic tradition, and in the same lineage it involves a closed univocity for abstract terms, rather than an analogical openness. And given that the abstracted "now" and "here" fade for Hegel into the purity of an epistemologically abstract transcendental "is"[53] (which for us has always to be related to both time and space), the universality of "this" is perfectly compatible with nominalism regarding empirical particulars, since William of Ockham also admitted the transcendental univocity of being, besides the general transcendental scope of "substance" and even "quality."

Finally, the distinction between essence and being (in either its Thomistic or its Kantian version) from a Hegelian point of view conceals a latent contradiction. Nothing in a finite determined existence is the ground of its being, says Hegel, just as nothing in the Kantian categorial determination of thought grounds the truth of this thought. Real being and real truth must be infinite— and this is one of Hegel's most genuinely Christian conclusions! But in that case the finite is of itself nothing; is in itself negation. Not merely is the infinite (as for Eckhart and Spinoza) the negation of that negation which is the finite, also the finite itself is the negation of the negation because, as after all manifestly existing, it negates that infinite negation which it essentially is and thereby is neither nothing nor being but "becoming"—which "resolves the contradiction" only through the ceaseless (nihilistic) oscillation established through this strictly negative logic of mutual abolition.[54] It is partly for this reason that for Hegel the finite as such is itself the infinite and also itself "divine."

Now in the long term Hegel is indeed here drawing on certain nominalist considerations, as found for example in William of Ockham, which accused the realist notion of universals and constitutive relations of tending to violate the principles of identity and of noncontradiction. Like Eckhart and Nicholas of Cusa, he responds to this by making the novel move of ontologizing the contradictory itself. Later I shall suggest, however, that the medieval thinkers did so in a Catholic, paradoxical, and still analogical (or metaxological) rather than dialectical manner. This means that they did not on the whole take the violation of identity to mean "contradiction" (capable only of a ceaselessly conflictual "resolution," as any careful reading of Hegel will demonstrate) but, rather, "coincidence." They did not, then, take it to imply the agonistic, but rather an eschatological peace so extreme that even the incompatible are now at one, like the lion lying down with the lamb.

Hegel, by contrast, remains in a stronger negative agreement with Ockham, which reflects his Lutheran inheritance: if something is also that to which it is related and so is not, then this is a source of continuous tension. The particular thing must seek to displace, and yet to coincide with, the universal. The organic as the principle of holistic unification must emerge as the result of a constitutive struggle with the inorganic as the principle of equivocal externality. Masters and slaves must be necessarily struggling against each other, since mastery is a refusal of potential slavery and thereby a fatal blindness about the slave's work and expertise, while slavery is always an attempt to usurp the defining condition of its existence. In each of these instances, that which is finite, since it is a ceasing to be which also denies this ceasing to be, must be in a continuous state of becoming. But this view also defines becoming as intrinsically conflictual: each finite thing at once rejects and upholds the finite status of each preceding finite thing.

And for Hegel this agonism is inscribed at the most ultimate ontological level. Being as such is taken to have no content and so to be identical with nothing, despite the fact that it is the most rarefied abstraction from everything. It is crucial to note here that Hegel comes to this conclusion only because, along with almost the whole of modern philosophy, he assumes, as I have already intimated, a Scotist univocity or quasi-genericity for being. He does not dismiss, because he does not even consider, the Thomistic alternative: namely that being qua being might be an embodied plenitude, identical with the infinite realization of all actual and possible essentialities. In other words, that it might be everything in its absolute fullness, as HCF rather than LCM, while further taking this realized fullness to be (to put this deliberately in rather Hegelian terms) itself paradoxically all along at one with the original source. This perspective gives no ontological weight to nothingness, or at least not in Hegel's nihilistic mode. It therefore avoids the most drastic of all contradictions: speaking of nothing qua nothing as something.

Hegel, however, does not avoid this, because, in a post-Kantian fashion, he can restore a dogmatic metaphysics only on the basis of an absolutization of what is thinkable for human beings. Hence the fact that we are forced, within our modus cognoscendi, to think of being itself as abstractly empty of content, is taken as coinciding with the real ontological situation. Furthermore, since this scheme involves, as we have just seen, ontological contradiction, the real necessity of "illusory being," it is taken by Hegel that the outworking of contradiction in time will also require that certain historical epochs of humanity are mired in practical and theoretical delusion, albeit that this delusion is also a necessary moment of the unfolding of truth. Hence the contradictoriness of supposing there to be an original being in itself at first—in the course of human history—took the alienated form of positing a metaphysical deity "up there," and treating abstraction as though it were an ontic content. (Hegel had no real grasp of the fact that for Augustine and Aquinas, and even in a way Scotus, God was ontological and not ontic.)

So despite Žižek's strictures against the notion that Hegel submits history to a necessarily unfolding logic, it is hard to see that he does not do so in this case—and indeed, Žižek himself speaks as though Christian theology inevitably grasped its own truth at first only in an alienated form. One can agree with Žižek: Hegel's concealed point is the absoluteness of equivocal contingency, yet since he conceives this truth as mired in real contradiction, he also speaks of it as historically emerging by a series of graspably necessary stages for the outworking (at once ontological, cultural, and intellectual) of contradiction.

Once more, it is crucial to note that, as we shall see, Hegel does not speak of a benign "coincidence" of being with nullity (in the manner of Meister Eckhart). Instead, in a truly nihilistic fashion (as he explicitly concedes), he sees nothingness as always undermining being from within and being as always struggling to be born from this dark womb—it is here that, via Boehme, Hegel corrupts Christianity with just that Gnostic-neopagan legacy of which Žižek is so anxious that Christianity be purged! It is this agonistic (and therefore neopagan) ontology which ensures that, for Hegel, the dialectical is the most fundamental onto-logical aspect of finite existence. Just as much as for Hobbes and political economy (to which Hegel was massively indebted)[55] plus Darwin (as Žižek implicitly concedes), nature and history are for him fundamentally a struggle between beings and egos who have equal but incompatible natural rights which can become political rights only at the price of tragic loss and a certain positive legal arbitrariness, as well as the gain of civil peace and order. (Nothing in Hegel, in other words, transcends the biopolitical.)

On the other hand, to return to Desmond's more concessive point, this is not to deny that there are any dialectical phenomena whatsoever. Both in the suborganic and the organic world, it is clear that the stakes of survival often require attention to a double exigency, and that this involves inherent tension. The forces that sustain the upthrust of mountains may also blow them apart, requiring the ambiguous synthesis that is the volcano. The animal evolved to secure its genetic makeup against its environment may also thereby reduce its mobility in the face of that environment's hostility in the shape of predators: the synthesis is the semiotic doubling of real protection as camouflage. How, indeed, as Job asks in his own book, are we to view the conflictual monstrosity of nature theologically? Is this the evidence of the demonic rule of a fallen reality, as St. Paul clearly implies? To some degree, where this monstrosity impinges as natural evil upon human life, this must be the Christian answer, if the goodness of the Creator is to be vindicated.[56] But at the same time, we must resist a limited anthropomorphic perspective upon all natural conflict, which, as the book of Job implies, seems to belong to a sublime game that only God can appreciate, or is part of his own self-amazement (as Chesterton suggested, to the current admiration of Žižek). By analogy, the spectacle of competitive sport and the competitions in intellectual or practical excellence and (to a degree) erotic love that humans engage in are modes of sublimated struggle that are cruel only if we fail to recognize the glory in loss or the need to see that ultimate personal well-being and ethical flourishing must not be entirely indexed to success or failure in these pursuits.

Likewise, in the field of discourse, we often do not identify a mediating position all at once, and must pass through the intellectual struggle between position and counterposition. The upshot here may be the emergence of a "synthesis"—though the question of the nature of a synthesis must remain for now in abeyance. Or it may not—certain questions may remain obstinately aporetic, either because of our cultural limitations or because we can, in the nature of things, catch only an imperfect glimpse of a final resolution, "the absolute truth." It would seem that novels continue to be written in their millions mainly because it is impossible to grasp sexual difference or sexual relationship. Abstract discourse rarely speaks of it save with embarrassment or implausible dogmatism. So interactions between the two generic enigmas that are the two sexes can only be narrated and not understood—and with every novel we read (even the great ones) we almost always have the sense that the real turning points in the plot have been glossed over, that character has only been thinly described and not at all explained in depth, while the course of events narrated has but little application to the course of events in other instances, especially our own. We gain perhaps something of an answer—but still have to continue to read, as we continue to live, in order to find out more. Human beings tend in this way, perhaps inevitably, to take male and female as opposites, and to be perplexed by the obscure conflicts which this opposition entails and the elusiveness of any synthetic harmony between them.

More fundamentally, however, a dialectical region of existence is an upshot of the presence of relatively irreducible difference and identity. That which tends to be sheerly different, "contradictorily" depends for this difference, as Hegel taught, upon its relationship to other things, and therefore must be comparable with them in some respects. The more one stresses the difference of something, or the more something seeks to exhibit its difference, then the more elusive it becomes. As Deleuze realized, a "something" can be established at all only through the repetition of its singularity, but this very repetition compromises its singularity.[57] Inversely, unity is entirely abstract and without effect unless it involves repetition, and repetition always introduces difference because of the identity of indiscernibles. Similarly, as Badiou shows in set-theoretical terms, any *actual* unity is a collection, and therefore presumes multiplicity in order that unity may be posited. For these reasons it was not difficult for Gillian Rose and later Slavoj Žižek to show that Gilles Deleuze was scarcely free of Hegelian dialectic after all. Even if pure difference transcendentally rules, its transcendentality can never appear in all its purity without self-destruction. So it is always merely insisting—always caught back in a play between identity and difference.

This ensures also that, while the transcendental principle may be multiplicity, differences always arrive in pairs and therefore always to some degree in "pairs of opposites." The difference of sensing, for example, is known in relation to the various contrasting "opposite" qualities of "insensate" or of "sensed" or of "understood," and so forth. We have to run through a series of pairings in order to define "sensing," as Socrates and Plato already realized, in the case of any definition of anything whatsoever.

Finally, as Deleuze taught, absolute difference must itself be paired with absolute univocity—and Alain Badiou also is unable to struggle free from this conjunction, even if he indicates that he would like to be able to do so.[58] Thus if being, for Deleuze, occurs always differently, it is still the same being that always occurs, the same life that is expressed in the variegation of non-hierarchized and so indifferent difference. Hence, as Badiou correctly suggests, Deleuze's philosophy is after all poised in a *dialectical* shuttle between absolute governing unity and unmediable difference. And his vitalism, which favors the priority of a virtual force, actually tilts the balance toward unity.

To this degree I am with Žižek: any play between the equivocal and the univocal does not escape dialectics, as people tend to claim—on account of the default of any apparent achieved synthesis and in ignorance of what Hegel actually wrote. Differences cannot occur purely in a series, else one would register only a blur. Instead, even if a difference is different from a multitude of other different things, one can register this multitude only pair by pair, in terms of a series of *specific differences*. "Hotness," for example, belongs in many different differential series, but we can locate its difference only if we begin by noting its difference from cold. This difference is obviously oppositional, but it is precisely through oppositional differences that we make our initial determinations: abstract not concrete, animal not mineral, and so forth. Indeed, every discrete difference tends to have a polar aspect, so that even if we were to take a more incommensurable pair like "hard" and "comely," or "prejudiced" and "lively," or "rock" and "emotion," the mind still tends to place the two terms in some sort of oppositionally contrastive scheme: "comely" then takes on the aspect of "pliable," "prejudiced" of "stiff," "emotion" of fluidity.

In narratological terms, as Žižek correctly argues, even the metonymic flow of a story (including a historical story) is possible, not because it contains an infinite plenitude of meanings—this would undo story, as *Finnegans Wake* tends to indicate but not demonstrate, since it remains a story—but rather because it always contains two stories which always have to do with a metonymic inter-play of cause with effect: something "happens" because one person's story gets entangled with another's; because one person's story is ambivalently linked to another story that occurred before she was born; because the story is the story of how the original story got uncovered; because the time of recall is in tension with the time of original occurrence; because the story that the authorial voice self-narrates is in tension with the fictional events that he is narrating—and so forth. As Žižek implies, this is why novels are so often about the hunter and the hunted, the criminal and the detective, or the betrayer and the betrayed, and why more self-conscious novels are often about twins or doubles.

But does this really show that every narrative (including every historical narrative) is dialectical rather than differential? Not entirely, though insofar as every plot is composed of conflicts, it tends indeed to have a dialectical ele-ment. But in two respects narrative structure refuses dialectics in the Hegelian sense. First of all, it is not governed by determinate negation, since this would undo contingency. In Hegel's case, the posited originality of the *nihil* means that nothingness must always move against itself in order to produce something. This requires the entirely implausible view that negation itself does all the work, such that to negate is also automatically to posit in a particular direction the "next" stage. Such a perspective could apply only if each thing "had only one opposite"—for example, if leaving the North Pole meant that I was head-ing off for the South Pole. Of course it does mean this if my voyage is terrestrial, but it does not mean that I will arrive at the latter destination, unless these are the relevant oppositional coordinates which I have programmed into my Sat-Nav. However, if I am leaving the North Pole in order to go to sea or to return to Britain, then I am operating with the oppositional coordinates ice/sea or away/home, which in either case involves also the coordinate north/south, but not that of North Pole/South Pole. Furthermore, my journey might not be terrestrial, in which case I might leave the North Pole by helicopter or space-ship and therefore would not be heading for the South at all.

In other words, physically "negating" the North Pole implies of itself no entirely determinate direction, even if it implies one vaguely—such as going south or leaving earth for the air or the planet for space. In Hegel's case the situation is worse than this, in that the negation of an entire given situation (as it were, leaving our entire universe) seems to generate its own destination which both is and is not one's starting point. He appears not to face up to the problem of "multiple opposites," the truth that anything is the opposite of something else only in one of its respects. Even in geometrical terms, any point of a square, for example, is "opposite" both to the two points to which it is vertically or horizontally related and at the same time to the point to which it can be internally, diagonally related. A fortiori no real physical position is, for example, purely "on the left": it is also "to the side" or "west" or "peripheral," and so forth.

This question of plural opposition is the second respect in which narrative structures do not conform to a dialectical logic. In narratological terms a story, including even the relatively simple structure of the folktale, is typically composed of a multiple series of overlapping pairs (of stories, persons, places, etc.), whose ramifications implicitly go on for ever, beyond the confines of the story itself, as poststructuralism taught.

Thus, for example, in Diane Setterfield's excellent and hyperbolically gothic novel The Thirteenth Tale, one has a "detective" plot, which concerns the solving of a mystery concerning an elderly female author, Vida Winter, by the young female heroine.[59] However, this "opposition" is complicated by a likeness between the two protagonists insofar as both happen to be twins, thereby indicating that their individual stories can be taken as allegories of each other; this suggests the "between" register of the metaxological, insofar as there is no dialectical synthesis of the two plots, nor a final conclusion which would leave the two plots to go their own separate equivocal ways. The allegorical dimension renders it further unclear as to whether the polarity of the two plots is the decisive polarity in the novel, for the mutual echo directs our attention to the geminal opposition internal to both of the plots: in the case of the detecting heroine her haunting by her sister twin, dead at birth, and in the case of the aged authoress her apparently criminal childhood substitution of herself for her own twin, Adeline, an original lie which has doomed her to a career of dazzling but rather vacuous fiction.

This, of course, permits us to read the initial plot-contrast in further "dialectical" terms of that between the lost twin on the one hand and the suppressed twin on the other. However, this symmetry is broken by the later revelation that the authoress Vida Winter is not a genuine twin after all, but a third hidden vagrant usurping child (the result of a rape committed by a mad uncle of the twins) who has not only displaced one twin but also confused their identities, appearing to substitute for Adeline, but in reality substituting for Emmeline, since Emmeline had already murdered Adeline for removing from her proximity her own secret illegitimate child. Emmeline herself is now a lunatic secretly confined by the authoress in a recess of her rambling Yorkshire house.

This "thirdness" violently resolves a play of opposition by introducing the problematic of multiple opposites, and so of difference, that partially escapes the dialectical stranglehold. The detecting heroine uncovers this dimension only when she escapes from an obsession with her fiction of doubles and laterally invokes to herself the plot of Jane Eyre, which is not about intrafamilial rivalry but about madness and concealment consequent upon sexual hysteria. To see the truth, the heroine must escape the confines of an incestuous paradigm and recall the exogamous logic which more fundamentally rules the human race.

Therefore, more opposite to a twin than her twin is the alien child of another blood, who is able to exploit pure dialectics by confounding the two oppositions in masquerade. Now it no longer appears that suppressed absence and absence caused by active suppression psychoanalytically interpret each other, such that the heroine secretly rejoices in her loss, while the author has secretly preempted the terrible threat of loss of half of oneself contained in the destiny of twinship—as a dialectical reading might be tempted to think. Instead the heroine, in the face of the loss from the outset of her identical other, is able to infer an alterity and a missing factor beyond the simple play of dual belonging and rivalry. By furthermore seeing herself in the mirror of her detection of the other, she is able finally to escape her duality of loss and to form a sexual relationship with a man, Aurelius, who himself turns out to be Emmeline's lost child, and so is involved in a *third basic story* which is that of his search for his mother. Having finally uncovered the famously missing "thirteenth tale" of the authoress, which turns out to be the authoress's own true story, the heroine is able to complete her own story as another, more internalized version of the story of Cinderella (as is made explicit—namely, the story of the sister threatened by her sisters who escapes into a sexual relationship).

So here the dialectical play between two stories is finally subordinated to a third story of the relationship between the opposition of twins on the one hand and the opposition of one bloodline to a totally other bloodline—without traceable links—on the other: whether in the case of the usurping third child, or in the case of the relationship of the story of the heroine to the story of the hero. The latter opposition is, of course, the sphere of marriage. Hence the entire novel turns upon the possibility of multiple opposites, even if these must be taken "pair by pair": of original narrative and uncovering narrative which is doubled by the parallel situation of twins within both narratives that intensifies a rivalry between detector and detected; of the displacement of the opposition of the heroine's story to the authoress's story by the opposition of the heroine's story to the hero's story; of the opposition of twin to twin which is doubled by the opposition of twin in one family to twin in another; of twin to alien intruder and of familial pairing to exogamous pairing. Even the initial opposition of detecting story to original narrative is doubled by the contrast between the author's fictions and what really happened to her—so much so that one is not quite sure whether the "true" thirteenth tale is true after all, but merely another fiction. Finally, the heroine's own story stands as much in contrast to the fairytale story of Cinderella as to the "historical" stories of the authoress and the hero.

And because of this intrusion of sheer difference, along with the role of mediating allegory, salvation here does not lie "psychoanalytically" in the (dialectical) replay of origins, but rather in the (Kierkegaardian) "reduplication" of origin as the contingent arrival of otherness now renewed as a new alterity. This newness, nevertheless, beyond the differential perspective, connects allegorically (or by "nonidentical repetition") to the original loss, permitting the heroine at once to find a husband and to be reconciled to her lost twin in her original otherness (her positive ontological "lostness") that always lay alongside the lost twin's parallel identity.

Therefore love here arrives as what Richard of St. Victor described as *condilectio*, in the course of his explanation of why a loving God is a three-personed God: the authentic love between two is never an exclusive love, but an encountering or generating ecstasy beyond duality and beyond what is dialectically at play between two poles.[60] Thus Setterfield's novel reveals that "thirdness" is a purely positive "arriving" difference (rendered possible by the openness of any oppositional pole to a new oppositional tangent) which supplies, as C. S. Peirce saw, a moment of free subjective interpretation which may be the usurpation of masquerade (the author's history) or may equally be the offer of a loving relationship, advancing from difference to mediating unity (the "comic" conclusion of the novel in expected marriage).

Already, with this analysis, I am trying to suggest how Christian Trinitarian logic has a mediating structure which is *not* dialectical. The key point here (simply to state things baldly for the present, without argument) is that that which lies "between" two poles is paradoxically "extra" to those two poles, an irreducibly hypostatic third. In the case of the infinite Trinity, this extra is itself indeed the procession of the love that lies between Father and Son (as Augustine put it)—yet the arriving externality of this thirdness is still guaranteed by the fact that Father and Son (according to the logic of substantive relation, perfected by Aquinas after Augustine) *are* in their mutually constitutive relationship only through this additional constitutive relationship to the Holy Spirit—which is not so much their "child" as the very womb of desire of truth in which the Father has originally conceived the Word of reason. If, to speak by geometrical analogy, Father and Son are points only because they are the two ends of one line, then this line is a line only because it is the base of a square whose remaining space is the Holy Spirit.

In this way (qualifying Richard of St. Victor's perspective with a more fully Augustinian one), the third loved person is present from the outset as the very "unfinishedness" of desire, within which truth is generated but never interpretively exhausted. In the case of finite echoes of the Trinitarian structure, the extra third may be either emergent from duality (like a child or a shared project or desire), or may alternatively arrive from elsewhere like a third subject. The infinite divine unity of person and hypostasized love is thus divided in terms of finite participated likenesses.

Both narratology and the Trinitarian paradigm therefore suggest how difference exceeds dialectics. Running ahead of myself, I have already suggested, by invoking Setterfield's novel, Augustine, and Richard of St. Victor, how this can be read metaxologically or paradoxically as the logic of love. But of course it can also be read nihilistically (as by Deleuze, Derrida, Lyotard, etc.), so as to say that the third as outdoing the dialectical interplay of sameness and difference is thereby sheerly indeterminate, as much violent intrusion as offer of a free loving gift. (The later Derrida arbitrarily tempered this in Levinasian terms in favor of the view that the intrusion of difference is always the promise of "impossible" gift, but this still leaves every actual deed within indeterminability and moral ambiguity, as he ceaselessly reiterated.)

But on either reading, dialectics is itself reduced to a "moment," to an ontological regionality. Either analogy or equivocity appears to be more logically and ontologically fundamental. Does this then mean that Hegel's overarching dialectical perspective is clearly a piece of outdated metaphysics?

Here I can concede to Žižek that this is not so obviously the case as one might think, because Hegel does not simply conclude to a unifying synthesis. William Desmond's argument with Hegel is that his professed "philosophy of love" is too one-sidedly "erotic" and insufficiently "agapeic," because in the end it suppresses the equivocal in the name of the univocal.[61] This conclusion is quite true to the extent that Hegel reads the nonlogic of the coincidence of opposites in terms of contradiction or conflict in a manner that negatively assumes the absolute primacy of a univocalist logic of identity where a, being a, cannot also be b. If, contradictorily, a is also b, then this contradiction must eventually be worked out to produce a bastard form of self-identical conclusion which is "the Notion," or Absolute Truth.

However, Desmond does not sufficiently recognize the point that Hegelian dialectics just as much reduces the univocal to equivocation. Here one should split the interpretive difference between Desmond and Žižek: in *formal* terms Hegel reduces all to unity, but in *substantive* terms he reduces all to difference. Formally he is hypererotic, swallowing the other in desire for the same, but substantively he is hyperagapeic, finally rendering the divine as the absolute kenosis of contingent unilateral gift. But this perhaps means that, more fundamentally, Hegel favors equivocation and a Lutheran account of Agape. (Desmond himself at his best unites Eros and Agape in the metaxological; but sometimes he seems to tilt the balance toward Agape and a Levinasian disinterested self-giving to the other, with the consequent problem that the metaxological would then reduce to a weak, open dialectic favoring-on-balance of the equivocal—this is just why I am suggesting that the metaxological must also be conceived as the paradoxical.)[62]

How is this the case? Crucially, Hegel's ignoring of the problematic of diverse possible opposites applies only to the outworking of the transcendental categories of being and thinking, just as it applies only to the most general logic of the historical process. For Hegel, as Žižek argues, in real historical, material reality there is only the occurrence and performance of contingent differences, obeying no inexorable dialectical logic whatsoever. Premodern human history and philosophical thought hitherto are both nothing but a working through and beyond the inevitable illusion that there is more to reality than merely this contingency. Therefore the "end of history" means an entering upon human history proper for the first time—the sheer interplay of purely accidental natural and human forces, albeit within rational structures for the sustaining of liberty.

However, Žižek admits a crucial difference between Hegel and post-Hegelian thought, and remains interestingly ambivalent about where his own loyalties here lie. His case is that Hegel was a "vanishing mediator" who, in bringing metaphysics to a conclusion, also opened up a path beyond the metaphysical. Žižek's modification of Heidegger would seem to be that the step beyond metaphysics is in reality indistinguishable from the finishing of metaphysics and the further outworking of this conclusion.

For Žižek, the postmetaphysical means Schelling's "positive" philosophy, Kierkegaard's suprarational subjectivism, scientific and sociological positivism, and Marxist materialism, besides psychologism and psychoanalysis which both, in different ways, tend to refer thought to biological processes. Here a decipherable reigning cosmic reason is displaced either by representation of the sheer givenness of material processes, or by assertion of the excess of personality to impartial reason. It is clear that Žižek himself seeks to articulate a form of Lacanian Marxism which allows for the excess of personality, but finds space for this within a materialist ontology.

If Žižek appeals to Hegel, this is in part because he considers that such a hybrid can only be Hegelian—that only Hegel provides us with something like a materialist philosophy of spirit. This is presumably on account of Hegel's nihilism: if what is original is the nihil, then the only somethings are definite material somethings, yet they are shadowed by the work of negativity which eventually resurfaces as a kind of return to itself of contingency that engenders subjective consciousness. (I am wildly glossing here, but it is heuristically necessary in order to shine a light through the obscurantist fog which Hegel's gnosis tends—logically—to generate.) As with the philosophy of Alain Badiou, it is the nihilism that must be implied by materialism which also throws up aporias and radical contingencies in which subjectivity can somehow take refuge.

But why Žižek's preference for Hegel over Heidegger's nihilistic radicalization of Schelling's outlook? Why not declare that Being itself, as identical with nothing, only "is" ontically in self-denial of pure Being, in a series of positively engendered epochs of being, akin to Schelling's "ages of the world"? One possible answer would be that Heidegger is in fact himself caught in an oscillation between Schelling and Hegel—which may indeed rework Schelling's own oscillation between positivity and dialectics. For Schelling, the historical age of the Father, of obscure mythical determination of possibility, is succeeded by the rational age of the Son, of logical, limited determinations of the will which remain shadowed by the threat of the irruption of latent virtual possibility now dialectically exposed in its radical indeterminacy. Pure dynamic possibility unleashed on the surface of actuality as inchoate force is, for Schelling, the nature of evil as something positive (not negatively privated), as Žižek frequently mentions and endorses. To this age there may eschatologically succeed, for Schelling's Joachite outlook, the age of the Spirit, in which the freedom of possibility is radically invoked, but fully determined as self-giving love. The play between possibility and actuality here is essentially a dialectical play, as with Hegel, except that the entire content, including the formal content, of the actual is provided by an act of positive willing which is eventually fully released as the work of the Spirit. Here the finally resultant positive equivocity is directly traced back to a willing divine source which therefore has to remain actual and existential.[63]

It is for this reason that Schelling was genuinely theistic, where Hegel arguably was not. For the elder and outliving scion of the Tübingerstift, the three human historical ages were grounded in a real transcendent divine metahistory, through which concept Schelling—interestingly—attempted to give a Trinitarian gloss to theology as metaphysics. For this metahistorical scheme, the Holy Spirit is the eternal future synthesis through positive freedom of the open "being" of the Paternal past, which is also the principle of particularity and ego-identity, the source of an outgoing, personal, "present" principle of filial love, which nonetheless rationally and legally "contracts" original being and "posits" being as other to itself, since all conscious personality must, according to Schelling, "restrictively" define itself as other than that of which it is conscious. The Holy Spirit exceeds the character of a Hegelian logical principle for Schelling, because it is the final "personal" expression of a positive and contingent energy that represents the divine "essence" of traditional Trinitarian theology—a "fourth" not subsumable by the play of negations between the three persons, as with Hegel.[64] (It was this energetic "pre-personal" account of the divine essence which was reworked in later Russian theology in terms of the biblical figure of "Sophia.")

Heidegger, of course, was much more obviously atheistic than Hegel. But just for this reason, one could argue that the ontology of *Sein und Zeit* is in reality more negatively dialectical than one might imagine. The ontic ages are here not willed, and onticity itself results "automatically" from the necessary self-negation of being which is identical with nothing if it is to be at all. This simply is Hegel's *Logic*! Moreover, Heidegger also repeats Hegel's conclusion that, since the finite (now the ontic, as Heidegger realizes, to his credit) both is and is not, and exists only in becoming, then being is in fact time. I am tempted to note here, with Chestertonian flippancy, that all the most famous Teutonic professors are indeed in reality Thomas Carlyle's Teufelsdroch, telling us that there "is" but the passing parade of phenomenal garbs of fashion. The Emperor has *only* clothes.

Moreover, for Heidegger, history unfolds through the play of the necessary self-concealment of the ontological in the ontic, moving toward a final unconcealment of the ontological in *Dasein* as heralded by his own philosophy. The logic here is impeccably dialectical. On the other hand, Heidegger wishes to speak of his eschatological epoch in much more vatically disclosive terms than Hegel: being is shown not in the rational organization of the everyday, but in the poetic apprehension of craft and cosmos, which does not so much identify nothingness with contingency, as deploy the typical circumstances of human culture to point back to the inexhaustible mystery of nothingness as being. For this reason, the later Heidegger speaks more and more like Schelling and eventually speaks of "The Last God," implying after all that a certain blind will was always at work in positively establishing every ontic epoch.[65]

But this same oscillation between dialectics and positivity, between Hegel and Schelling, is also found in Žižek. Is it that he thinks Hegel logically points toward Schelling, or that Schellingian insights can be pulled back within a Hegelian framework? A bit of both, perhaps, but perhaps more emphatically the latter. Yet what is really at issue here?

Perhaps what matters to Žižek is that, compared with Schelling, and even with Heidegger, Hegel points toward a more consistent nihilistic materialism, since he dispenses with all voluntarism and vitalism. If, for Hegel, both thought and reality really begin with nothing, then it is this very "atheism" which requires the dialectical principle of determinate negation. Hegel explicitly radicalizes the Christian *creatio ex nihilo* by God into a spontaneous generation of something from nothing, in opposition both to the traditional metaphysical principle *ex nihilo nihil fit* and to the literal Christian understanding of "creation out of nothing," which does not contradict this principle but, rather, hyperbolically confirms it by claiming that an infinite actuality can radically originate the finite, without any preexisting finite principle, such as the Greek *hyle*, unformed matter.[66] If, however, something really comes from nothing alone, then this can only be because nothingness negates itself and therefore a self-negation, without positive supplement, determines the entire way in which things "are." This general principle is then repeated by Hegel for every stage of the logic of reality.

So one reason for Žižek's insistence upon Hegel's more metaphysical edition of modernity would seem to be that negative dialectics is the tone of a more rigorous atheism. Equally, however, Žižek would appear to argue that it is the upshot of this dialectics which alone guarantees that any positivity that exists is the sheerly finite contingent in its actuality, without any subservience to an *élan vital*, crowned virtuality, or mysteriously divine *Sein*. (There is some resemblance here to both Badiou and François Laruelle's also somewhat Hegelian search for a materialism of the purely actual, that does not posit a kind of deity in the form of a transcendent force of possibility or virtuality.)[67]

But it is exactly at this juncture that I need to make the all-important point that atheism is stuck with just as many metaphysical dilemmas as is theology (the traditional theology of transcendence) and, indeed, with remarkably *similar* dilemmas. On the one hand, a strictly atheistic perspective might wish to dispense with all tincture of vitalism, all suggestions of a primordially "forceful" reality, however impersonal. Here the Hegelian nihilistic idea of an original negativity (the heart of his thought, as Žižek notes that Chesterton noted, with his usual bluff precision) indeed offers the prospect of a more relentless godlessness. Yet it is not an accident, as Žižek well realizes, that Hegel had to present his "atheism" in such a Christian metaphysical disguise that it remains unapparent to most readers. For if negativity is the driving force of reality, then a process of formally inevitable unfolding through the strictures of negative logic must also prevail—this being the factor that Žižek tends to play down. And worse: the problem of multiple possible opposites at any given strategic logical juncture has to be dogmatically overridden.

It is here not good enough to say, with Žižek, that sheer equivocal difference is for Hegel the only true positive reality, in a way that half-anticipates the mature Schelling. It is not good enough because it ignores the way in which Hegel operates with an unjustified *duality* of negative logical process on the one hand and sheerly arbitrary positive content on the other. The latter is in fact *too much* screened-off from the always limited logical possibilities offered by any particular circumstance—in theological terms, the problem is that Hegel places all positive reality *outside* the sway of providence, contrary to the way in which he is usually read.[68] But logical process is conversely and symmetrically too screened-off from contingency, and specifically from the problematic of "alternative opposites." So, rather than saying with Desmond that Hegel is in the end univocalist, or with Desmond that he is in the end equivocalist, one should argue that he is in the end (too) formally the former and (too) substantively the latter. He exaggerates both formal consistency and substantive isolation. As Alain Badiou puts it, at the end of an essay on Hegel: "From the red of the vine set upon the wall, one will never draw—even as its law— the autumnal shadow upon the hills, which envelops the transcendental reverse of this vine."[69]

Thus Hegel's logic traces a path of inevitable generation of more and more complex blends of same and different, presupposition and positing, which sketch out an eternal structure in the "preexistent" ("immanent") Trinity of abiding possibility (the subject matter of both the *Science of Logic* and the *Encyclopaedia Logic*) that is "later" bodied forth in the actuality of nature and history—which is the only actuality there truly is: the Idea "freely releases itself in its absolute self-assurance and inner poise . . . [as] the *externality of space and time* existing absolutely on its own account without the moment of subjectivity."[70] The self-standing positivity can be falsely observed by the empirical consciousness as separate from itself, but a speculative intellect will grasp that its own unreserved identity with this sheerly material reality permits an ironic withdrawal into itself from externality, completing "self-liberation" at the point where the science of logic circles back to its commencement with original nullity.[71]

Between this starting point and the final identification of the notional and the real which is the self-externalizing "Idea," the determinate succession of negated negations ensures a hierarchy that runs from inorganic through organic to conscious being. In a philosophical lineage that ultimately runs back to Avicenna's anti-Aristotelian doctrine of the plurality of forms within one substance and the Scotist "formal distinction," Hegel regards "the object" as "the absolute contradiction between a complete independence of the multiplicity, and the equally complete non-independence of the different pieces."[72] Given this contradictoriness of the object as such, qua ontic, the initial "mechanical" object which is "immediate and undifferentiated," comprising "pieces" with only "extraneous" relations to each other and no "affinity," negates itself to give rise to the chemical object where the latent original unity of the object as object is expressed in intrinsic relationships of affinity, such that the objects are what they are only in relation to each other. Yet significantly, the third stage in this scheme of the logic of physical nature, namely "design" or "the teleological relation," does not simply intensify the "affinate" or analogical and realist character of the chemical stage, since for Hegel this is not to do with an inherent ultimate ontological ruling of the metaxological, but with the regional, momentary negative promotion of the unified aspect of the object. Hence the third stage of the teleological, instead of increasing a sense of holding together through affinity, negates the negation that is the chemical, by reinvoking a "mechanical" sense of immediate unity. In this way the motile fluidity of the chemical world is overcome in favor of "design," which is a "self-contained totality." With design we have the point of transition to "the idea" which contains the sphere of biological life and human subjectivity.[73]

And so it is important to see that in Hegel there is a link between the self-contained character of the sheerly material object on the one hand, and the unity of the living organism and still more of the thinking mind on the other.

The more one advances from extrinsic design in inorganic nature to life and then to consciousness, the more the reserve of the ideal over and against the objective which it shapes is removed, and the more the original immediacy of the physical object and the mediated immediacy (synthesizing parts into a stable unity) of subjectivity start to coincide. Usually, the exegesis of Hegel stresses his anti-Spinozistic rhetoric, according to which "Objectivity . . . is only a covering under which the notion lies concealed."[74] But Žižek is right to say that this illusion works for Hegel more fundamentally the other way around—rendering him Spinozistic after all, even though he resists the nomenclature. For the absolute truth of the Notion is arrived at *not* when one sees that the entire content of objectivity is shaped by its striving for the horizon of the Idea which always transcends it, but precisely when one realizes that the Idea is *exhaustively* fulfilled in the facts as we already apprehend them: "Within the range of the finite we can never see or experience that the End has been really secured. The consummation of the infinite End, therefore, consists merely in removing the illusion which makes it seem unaccomplished."[75] If truth is what "makes itself its own result," then this is not because the personal judgment of the truth-making artist which is Spirit remains in charge of being as such, but rather because (as Žižek indicates) the initial moment of "alienation" of nothingness in finite, "nominalist," mechanical particularity is finally revealed to be all there is—whereas the defining human illusion (as Hegel repeats after Fichte) is that there is an original concealment, an original alienation from a substantive, separate deity.[76] All that is in excess of this sheer materiality is the conscious awareness that this is all there is: a certain coming to the surface of the original nullity, which ensures that in the absolute identification of the subjective with the objective, an absolute distinction also persists.

An objection to this reading of Hegel could be based upon the fact that the model for the romantic notion that "truth is its own result," common to all the German idealists, is that of genuine works of art which, if "true," as Hegel says, are not true in the sense of representational correctness, but rather in the sense of being "as they ought to be, i.e. if their reality corresponds to their notion."[77] This statement appears to appeal to a wholly inscrutable sense of unity between ideal form and material specificity, such as a painting or a sculpture might body forth. However, Hegel's philosophy is not content, like that of Hamann, Herder, Novalis, or Schelling (at times and in some degree), to stop with the finality of the aesthetic. If it were, then there could be no final, absolute work of art, because the inscrutable power to synthesize idea with expression would always remain in "ideal" surplus of unknown future artistic horizons to any actual artistic achievement, and it is precisely this surplus which the Hegelian concept of "the Notion" refuses. For this reason, the work of art is for him a mere illustration of the unity of the Notion with reality which is more fundamentally attained by philosophy, because it is *demonstrated* by philosophy. This demonstration consists in the "deduction and development" of the truth of the idea in the sense of its coincidence with the real.[78] Such a deduction is possible only because an aesthetic unity of form with content is in fact sundered: the formal aspect is strictly deduced as a series of unfolding natural and historical stages—albeit that this retrospective deduction is possible only at a particular stage of history (the modern), after nature and humanity have passed through logically necessary stages of illusion which prevented them from grasping concrete logical inevitability.[79] As for the substantive content, this is sheer contingency: not the entelechic circumstances of art, but the random circumstances of the everyday in a disenchanted universe and polity. The mediation of Spirit through the various phases of objectivity proves in the end to coincide with immediacy—not only because mediation is, after all, its "own" work, but also because it is *only* this work, and the positive content of this work is finally the mere residue of immediate objectivity: "The Notion is the interfusion of these moments, namely, qualitative and original being is such only as a positing, only as a return-into-self, and this pure reflection-into-self is a sheer *becoming-other* or *determinateness*, which, consequently, is no less an infinite, self-relating *determinateness*."[80] Hence the perfect unity of Hegel's philosophico-political "work of art" is simply that of absolute freedom of spirit with absolutely aleatory objectivity—a unity which is equally an absolute opposition and mutual diremption. Here the "philosophical" State of realized deed is identical with the ideal and illusorily alienated horizon of the Church, only on account of its unhealed conflict with the latter's falsely imaginative point of view which is yet necessary to the State's own emergence and even continuance. The *broken* middle. Yes indeed.[81]

However, Žižek underplays the fact that the very purity of Hegel's nihilism ironically generates a kind of parody of a neoplatonic chain of being, in the way that I have just explained. Like the plenitudinous Catholic God, Hegel's being-nothing is supremely simple and generates all complexity out of itself in a fashion that requires a certain order and a certain return. Atheism that wishes to purge itself of even this "counterfeit" theology (as Desmond rightly calls it) can do so only by toying with the rival parody of Catholic truth which is positive vitalism—this, as I have already suggested, delivers less hierarchy, but only at the price of something uncomfortably more akin to substantive transcendence. Of course this does not "disprove" atheism—but it serves to point out how it is just as much a difficult-to-argue and problematic view as is the theological one, rather than being a kind of unproblematic default position, once one has dispensed with theological illusion. Moreover, it is perhaps impossible to synthesize strictly nihilistic (mathematical, ideal) atheism with virtualistic atheism in the way that theology can synthesize a primacy of the intellectually "empty" and generative on the one hand, with the primacy of being on the other. (See my discussion of Eckhart in section 5 below.) This is because theology is able to think an infinite, plenitudinous act which, as infinite, coincides with and does not cancel virtual power, which can be conceived as hypereminently the power of the will and the intellect.

If Hegel's very nihilism, and synthesis on the ground of the equivocal, requires an account of the generation of a scale of being, it also requires a retrospective theoretical recapitulation of a historical process which develops toward truth through the necessary overcoming of illusion: "In the course of its process the Idea creates that illusion, by setting an antithesis to confront it; and its action consists in getting rid of that illusion which it has created. Only out of this error does the truth arise. In this fact lies the reconciliation of error with finitude. Error or other-being, when superseded, is still a necessary dynamic element of truth: for truth can only be where it makes itself its own result."[82]

In the final moment of human grasp of the "subjective" truth of "the Notion," it is seen that actual differences which arrive logically as "secondary" are not just "posited" by a comprehending will after the manner of Fichte, negating through "illusion" original indeterminate being which remains in reserved excess (so engendering the philosophical problem of skepticism) but, rather, are naturally given as paradoxically the "original" presupposition of both being and consciousness. So although the universal remains "undisturbed" by becoming, "it does not merely *show*, or have an *illusory being* [*Schein*] in its other, like the determination of reflection [the merely 'Fichtean' stage of 'Essence'] . . . [but] on the contrary, is posited as the *essential being* of its determination, as the latter's *own positive nature*. For the determination that constituted its negative is, in the Notion, simply and solely a *positedness*; in other words, it is, at the same time, essentially only the negative of the negative, and is [i.e., exists] only as this identity of the negative with itself which is the universal."[83] Nothing could be clearer: reality is at once a nullity which negates itself and so remains itself and, at the same time, *only* the sheer equivocity of pure positing.

Through our implicit and explicit grasp of this state of affairs, our conscious minds arrive at the actuality of freedom, so that freedom, as it were, feeds upon the void: "the universal is therefore *free* power; it is itself and takes its other within its embrace but without *doing violence* to it"—that is, by distinguishing itself in alien fashion from the contingent, or questioning the legitimacy of that which happens to be the case.[84] Therefore, as Žižek constantly if obliquely suggests (in the wake of Sartre and Badiou as well as Hegel), materialism rigorously thought through as nihilism also discovers a fundamental emptiness which may obscurely account for subjective freedom.

We are left nonetheless with the mystery of consciousness and the mystery of why the void should somehow be able to come to conscious self-expression. Again, in the face of this conundrum, the atheistic can seem curiously akin to the theological, and, in the case of Hegel, Badiou, Laruelle, and Žižek, it is forced to take even a Christological shape—Christ is the final, divine man, precisely because he elevates free personality beyond essence or even existence (also beyond the law, physical and political, and beyond even the concealed founding axioms of philosophy that require a prior determination of the determinate) into an absolute, and exhibits this as fully present in his finite existence alone.[85] Here we are bound to acknowledge the *seriousness* of "death-of-God theology."

However, in the case of Hegel, as we have seen, it is also clear that a strict nihilism—rather like a strict insistence upon divine simplicity—requires one to see the general structures of reality as conforming to a pyramidal ontological hierarchy, however much the contingent content of natural and especially human history may remain purely undetermined. To escape from this hierarchy may well be to enter the postmetaphysical positivist era of which Žižek speaks, yet in certain crucial ways, of which he is aware, it is also to step *more* into the traditional theological realm than is truly the case with Hegel. It is here, as we have seen, that one can locate the aporetic *double bind* of modernity as well as atheism, which already emerged to view with the crucial work of Comte (who has been every bit as influential a thinker as Hegel). What is more modern and atheistic in one sense (positivist anarchy, beyond Deistic enlightenment and metaphysical striated order) is less so in another (on account of the affinity between the personalism of Christian theology and any positive philosophy which subordinates logic to occasion and contingency— an affinity manifest in the positions of Donoso Cortes, Charles Maurras, and Carl Schmitt). This is why the modern is always torn between "enlightened" and "positivist" versions of its own agenda.

But this applies even to Hegel's own critical version of modernity. For once one admits the narratalogical principle of alternative opposites and multiple dualities, one can deconstruct Hegel's duality between the formal and substantive levels, after the manner of Schelling. Every logical conjuncture now becomes purely aporetic, such that no negation on its own determines the next upshot, and therefore something like a positive "willing" enters the picture even at the formal level. Now the original nullity of God becomes more like a semi-actual chaos of virtual insistence, and the determination of this nullity less a self-determination on the part of nothingness itself and more an emergence of a primordial will which both resists the sheerly inchoate and establishes certain chosen "local" transcendental logics of actual appearing (to echo Badiou's formulations).[86]

Hence to retreat from the pyramidal metaphysics of sheer negativity is also to suggest something much more like traditional theological transcendence. This is why, as Žižek indicates, the post-Hegelian "positive" era in philosophy contains not just Comte and Mach but also Schelling and Kierkegaard and Bergson.

Yet Žižek himself seems to hesitate here: his account of the ethical and of evil sounds more Kantian-Schellingian than Hegelian. To be ethical is autonomously to impose the law of freedom upon oneself, more than it is to play one's preappointed *sittlich* role within the political structures that conserve freedom (even if this can be seen as merely a matter of relative emphasis). And evil is not a factor of finitude, as it is for Hegel, but rather the inappropriate unleashing of untamed infinite virtuality upon the realm of the actual, as it is for Schelling. The antidote to evil for Žižek, also in a somewhat Schellingian idiom, is a certain willed fixing of love upon an arbitrarily selected finite object, rather than the more "loving" reconciliation of the absolute with the freedom of the entirely contingent, as with Hegel. He frequently admires Schelling's view that God is good because he freely and contingently—albeit infinitely—chooses the good, whereas he might (logically speaking) choose evil.[87]

Hence the more Žižek stresses the role of "love," the more he appears to invoke a transcendental positive force, after the fashion of Schelling. Therefore he at times shows some sympathy for Schelling's metahistorical schema. For Schelling, as we have already seen, the "age of the Father," the age of the primordially indeterminate, is also the human historical era of myth, in which the divine is invoked as the monstrous. The "age of the Son" is at once the divine moment of decision for a particular good, and the moment of historical incarnation of God in Christ, in which a particular image of love becomes crystallized. The third age, of the Spirit, is the positive synthesis which reawakens infinite potentiality, but in the direction of the infinitely diverse possibilities of loving action.

While Schelling's schema is Joachite and heterodox, it remains closer than Hegel to an orthodox Christian sense that, since love is a matter of contingent willing and acting, the *pattern* of love in Christ and fidelity to the spirit of that pattern in the "Church" (the true human community) is indispensable to our understanding of love. In this respect Badiou's insistence that every truth-process concerns a fidelity to a founding Event has a definitely Schellingian aspect—and in fact one that is more precisely Kierkegaardian and so less "Joachite" than Schelling, since here fidelity less "spiritually" exceeds the founding event. However, Žižek explicitly rejects Badiou's optimism about truth-processes as positive projects and insists, rather, upon the inevitable disappointment of desire and the need to recognize impossibilities of synthesis or amorous conjunction in the face of the primacy of the negative. His "love" is finally Hegelian and not Schellingian after all, because it is no positive, seeking desire (as with Deleuze and Guattari), but rather, as we have already seen, the disillusioned free embrace of the contingent as the contingent in admission of the impossibility of discovering any general amorous truth or any reality to erotic union.

By the same token, his metahistory is also really more Hegelian than Schellingian. The latter scheme gives a decisive place to the mythical, poetic, and prepolitical era of humanity. In Schelling's final vision, the specificity of the age of the Son indeed retrospectively reconceives the mythical in terms of the realm of abstract possibilities, yet it also by contrast reshapes the poetic as the specifically elected and as symbolically conveying of transcendent reality. The mythical accounts of the generation of gods and of the cosmos are for Schelling stories of how a higher but later "principle" overcomes a prior "nonprinciple"—chaos, the Saturnian gods, and so forth. As such they typologically prefigure Christian Trinitarian doctrine, but in the Christian account God the Father in the Son overcomes his own now abstract initial indeterminacy and, through the Son's Incarnation, human redemption through the self-overcoming of a negative refusal of God becomes possible, in place of a pagan struggle with alien forces extrinsic to the self. Christ's mediation is necessary and more than merely exemplary, because the fallen human refusal of divine love means that human beings really do receive the indeterminate paternal reserve as "wrath," and so as alien pagan monstrosity. But through the Incarnation the Father manifests the age of the Son as his own decision for the Good, and "hands over" the created realm to filial rule until the eschaton. The specifically shaped "glory" of the incarnate Son therefore constitutes the only human access to the notion of a self-overcoming higher principle.[88]

In this way the aesthetic, artistic moment is not surpassed but philosophically elevated. In the third age of the "Johannine Church"—still to come, which will unite Jews, Christians, and pagans—it is generalized, when all become capable of an unmediated self-overcoming, all become "sons of God," and thus the world is restored through the Spirit to the rule of the Father.[89]

For this romantic reworking of Christian philosophy of history (whatever its heterodox shortcomings) there is significantly no necessary incorporation of the recent stage of enlightenment—which rather (as much earlier for Vico) is regarded as the aberrant contingent possibility of reworking the pagan anarchy of myth as the abstract anarchy of pure reason, limited by its purity to sheerly "negative" formal possibility, and unable to attend to the "positive" priority of the existentially concrete, which extends also to God himself, who is once more for the late Schelling, as for Thomas Aquinas, primarily actus purus.[90] By contrast, for Hegel, there most emphatically is such a necessary reckoning with enlightenment as an inevitable and necessary moment. Here the mythical-poetic contains no permanent reserve of value, but instead represents in itself the moment of contingent finite positing that must be surpassed in its initial fetishized immediacy. And the Incarnation is not an event whose symbolic shape is, at least initially (for Schelling) unsurpassable, but rather the elevation of contingency as sheer contingency that does not point sacramentally beyond itself and whose heart is therefore a crucified nullity. The subsequent "age of the Spirit" means for Hegel a generalization of the latter awareness that must be embodied in the structures of modern science, politics, and economics.[91]

It is abundantly clear that Žižek is in the end not a Schellingian romantic but a Hegelian rationalist. He has no truck whatsoever with the disclosive reserve of the symbol or the revelatory power of poetry that is surplus to reason. This renders the archaic merely archaic and over and done with, ensuring that "pure reason" must be the final word of history, and crucially that the *essence* of the historical process must be the negative and counternegative process of the unleashing of reason, including (to be sure) the aporias attendant upon reason and even the "beyond reason" which only reason can disclose to view—in particular the inscrutable absurdity of reality taken as a whole.

However, I have already more than once indicated the problems with this modernist pure atheism. By beginning with a sheer unadulterated nothingness, one curiously echoes theology, by deriving all subsequent reality in an ordered series from pure nullity—as from pure divine simplicity—in such a way that all reality can be logically situated with respect to this *nihil*, in terms of its dialectical self-relating. And just as an entirely rational metaphysical theology, without taint of faith, always proves to be exercising some kind of arbitrary subjective preference, so likewise the idea that determinate negation rules in reality can readily be shown to be an unwarranted act of subjective belief, as Kierkegaard argued (if, indeed, it makes any rational sense whatsoever.) By contrast, the "yet more modern" antimetaphysical insistence upon the problem of alternative opposites, and of aporetic either/or between two given opposites, undoes the pure nihilism of sheer negation and actually may favor again the invocation of a more substantive, actual, and forceful transcendence. At this point the issue becomes once more one of choosing between a Spinozistically influenced vitalist immanentism as against a traditional theological metaphysics of a transcendent creator God. This is the *postmodern* crux that Žižek tries to evade in the name of a continuing Hegelian modernity. But I have just tried to indicate why this endeavor is impossible.

The problem for Žižek is that clearly he resists the former option by rightly arguing that any such mystical celebration of impersonal fated force lines up all too neatly with a celebration of the abstract power of capital. This then leaves him essentially with the choice of Hegel versus Schelling/Kierkegaard as theorists of the Christian revelation of the absolute value of love, the subjective and the personal, a choice between immanentist nihilistic dialectics on the one hand and a postmodern version of Christian orthodox belief in transcendence on the other. The latter is apparently ruled out by Žižek because it is somehow unbelievable, and also because it is negated by the inner logic of Christianity itself (on which claim see below in section 5). But what he is altogether ignoring here is the fact that a legitimate "postmodern" critique of negative dialectics as dogmatically metaphysical newly legitimates a belief in transcendence along with a new primacy for the "positive." (In general one can say that the "positivist," postmetaphysical era in the broadest sense should be equated with "postmodernism." Comte had already lost faith in the Enlightenment, and so was already "postmodern.")

So although Žižek may well be correct in saying that Kierkegaard failed to grasp that Hegel's absolute truth was more the finality of the equivocal than of the univocal, this still does not falsify the Dane's critique of determinate negation in favor of the view that the logic which establishes reality is that of "nonidentical repetition," as setting up an ungrounded *habitus*. Here it is positive persistence which both establishes the "next thing" and secures the reality of the "initial thing" in the first place. Beyond dialectics, the co-belonging of change and persistence as mutually both other and yet the same enters the realm of irreducible paradox. Only the unfathomable discriminations of nature and the decisions of our own ungrounded judgment here permit any distinctions to be made between substance and alteration, *stasis* and *kinesis*. Again, as between dialectics and repetition Žižek is somewhat ambivalent, yet in the end his psychoanalytic view that repetition always undoes itself or is compelled to repeat that which is purely self-grounded, and therefore does not symbolically point beyond itself, suggests the foreclosure of paradox by dialectical witness to a governing absurdity.

The crucial question now is whether one can identify a fourth, paradoxical perspective which cannot be reduced to the dialectical and which supports a Catholic Christian metaphysical, theological, and historical vision not obviously subject to rationalist disproof, dialectical immanent critique, or postmodern deconstruction. As I have already indicated, I shall argue that there is a close belonging of paradoxical with analogical and real-relational aspects of reality. One can refer to this entire phenomenological-logical domain, following William Desmond, as the "metaxological."

What I shall now endeavor to establish, therefore, is that a metaxological or paradoxical, not a dialectical, philosophy gives a true account of mediation. By comparison, what Hegel offers is a kind of *counterfeit* mediation, in which the middle is always exhaustively fractured between the univocal and the equivocal. This is essentially because he travestied, and so misunderstood, the problematic with which Jacobi had confronted Kant and his idealist successors.[92] Hegel declares that the Jacobian suggestion that all knowledge involves an ungrounded faith in the prior existence of the body, and in the trustworthiness of the given which fades imperceptibly into a faith in the divine, is an exaltation of cognitive "immediacy." To this he contrasts the "mediation" offered by his logical philosophy, which will "prove" the link between thought and objective existence which Jacobi merely takes on trust.[93] Yet any exhaustively "proven" mediation must collapse into the twin poles of pregiven univocal formality on the one hand and endlessly arriving, newly given equivocal fact on the other.

By contrast, Jacobi's "faith" implies that thinking always arrives on the scene too late to provide its own foundations, and therefore is *radically* mediated by an intentional link to existence and to other people which it always-already assumes, along with patterns of linguistic use which enshrine this circumstance. Idealism, in response to Jacobi (as much or more than in response to Kant), tried to argue that reason, through a process of self-generation or historical development, could finally catch up with this precognitive existential origin, or demonstrate that the origin was one and the same with this development. But, as we have seen in the case of Hegel, this attempt always involves unwarranted assumptions about that uncertain existential horizon which thought can only assume or have trust in, and cannot in principle ever round upon or master in its own terms. Schelling's final "existential" perspective was close to conceding this point, even if it still tried to comprehend existence as primarily will, whose very arbitrariness can be rationally comprehended. But with Kierkegaard, in effect, Jacobi triumphs after all, because the logic of repetition is nothing other than the admission that thought can only "think after" and interpret by "repeating differently" that which thought has always-already assumed.

This implies that truly one begins not with alienating negation but with mediation, and that one is bound to remain with mediation, such that truth (if it be possible at all) can arrive only as trust in the possibility of subjective discernment of the participation of the finite in the infinite through "momentary" disclosures. And the "consistent" identity of a repetition with that which went before, and of the coincidence of a moment of time with eternity, requires a faith in the absolute "paradoxical" unity of same with different in either case, as Kierkegaard taught.

It is the notion of the metaxological as the paradoxical which must now be expounded.

4. Paradox: A Misty Conceit

Suppose that I am driving my car one cold and misty morning southward toward the River Trent close to my home, along roads which constantly twist and pass up and down hills on their tortuous ways to the eventual descent to the river valley. Everything is univocally bathed in a beautiful, faintly luminous vagueness, tinged at its heart with silver. The mist tends to render contours continuous with each other, as likewise the earth with the sky and both with the distant water of the river, visible only as a slightly intensified inner light. Likewise the near has been rendered somewhat obscure and impenetrable, while the distant has been brought relatively close by its equal shade to that which lies close at hand, as well as by breaks in the mist which may happen to lie far off rather than nearby. Because of the mist, I do not really seem to be going from one place to another. On the other hand, because of the bends and contours, the land seems unstable, to be tossing me about like bedclothes for a restless dreamer. Everything merges into everything else.

On the other hand, against the background of the mist, differences stand out all the more sharply. I see that the land is not its usual brown wash, but consists of trees, houses, churches, roads, and the distant river. In their faint beginnings I distinguish different colors all the more distinctly, and observe all the more strongly how their being associated with different shapes and different entities is an entirely contingent matter—especially when the light of the sun beneath the mist can render the pastures oddly ocher, or the blue of the river oddly turquoise, or the trees oddly purple. The aesthetic drama here is one of suppressed and emergent equivocation. As I drive along, my thoughts likewise may be lulled into a misty wandering, or gradually stirred as roofs and spires emerge into view.

Is there a dialectic also at work here? Yes, in multiple ways. I am driving south only because I know that I am leaving the relatively north, but thereby affirming its northness and so not leaving it behind at all—on the contrary, I am in a sense establishing the constitutive topographical position of the place where I live far more by leaving it than by merely dwelling there. So in negating my place of departure I am also affirming it. Likewise the trees and roofs and spires can emerge as distinct only in relation to the obscure misty background which they thereby continue to affirm and acquire for themselves. Without any opaque density whatsoever, without the shared "mist" of the material, their individuality of form would not be apparent. Nor, inversely, would we see the mist in its luminous whiteness if nothing else were visible whatsoever. So the univocal and the equivocal are indeed always in a dialectical relationship. And this applies also to my thinking process: without the unclarity of the mist, I would not be inspired to look for things in the mist and so beyond its opacity. Furthermore, without the "misty" density of things themselves, their formal shapes would proffer to us no definite items. It is therefore material "mistiness" which at once hides and then reveals—and then reveals only through concealing. Correspondingly, if my thought is to be realistically intentional, if it is to be thought of something, then the very shapes of things which are disclosive for thought return thought to the mystery of the density of background and the density of particular content. Although the mist appears (annoyingly for a dismal functionalist outlook) merely to conceal, in fact it also foregrounds the usual background and renders opaquely transparent the generally local, materially transcendental conditions of our being able-to-know from within our embodiment.

On the other hand, I experience the foggy morning as an anomaly. Overwhelmingly, the dominant element is the mist itself: a continuous white density. The ruling factor here is the univocal, whereas normally ontological univocity assumes the utterly self-denying mode of light. Sameness is here entirely transparent, asserts nothing of its own and therefore yields the stage always to the equivocally different. Nevertheless, on an average morning, the equivocal does not dominate either—I register the respective shapes of spires and roofs and trees only as variations on a continuous space of light brown and as the variegations of a wavering line, traced through the amber consistency of the dawn. If sheer anarchic creativity is the ultimate principle of nature, as for Deleuze, then it may be that it is pure difference which most ultimately insists—but it can never be perfectly realized or fully present, as Deleuze recognized. Any thesis concerning the dominance of the equivocal, therefore, must relativize the stability of any actual given scenario, rendering it somewhat illusory in status. Here material density is downgraded in value just as much as for any thesis which celebrates transcendental unity and the secondary character of perceived differences.

So that which "transcendentally dominates" the local scene before my eyes is, rather, the interplay between the univocal and the equivocal—it is the weaving of things in and out of the mist. The misty foreground/background is the precarious setting for gray jewels, but without these jewels it would not be present to me as a setting at all. Similarly, I would not be traveling physically south were I not mentally leaving my home in the north, and I would not be registering things at all were I not also seeking to know those things hidden by material "mistiness" and yet also disclosed to me through this very same density.

Is it, then, the case that that which "transcendentally dominates," in a topographical sense, is not a differential, but rather a dialectical process? Were that so, then one would have to argue that the gray jewels are the vague setting, and vice versa. Likewise, on the more psychogeographic plane, one would have to argue that the south is the north and vice versa, while formal understanding is material ignorance as well as the other way about.[94] The instability of these impossible, contradictory identifications would explain why we perceive the interplay between the journey and the blinded yet searching gaze as always caught up within a dynamic tension. But from a dialectical perspective, this tension concerns a double movement toward mutual abolition in which the mist constantly denies yet establishes itself by dispersing; the shadowy shapes propose themselves and yet show forth a dense content which is only that of an ontic miasma; while eschatologically, either the mist presses to envelop and include all, and so ceases to be either vague or determined, or else the shapes press to emerge once and for all from the mist into the nothingness of light, so preserving but sublating the ordered logic of the process of this emergence (including the tracing of the shared line that outlines things to the gaze) but revealing the final, absolute truth to be the mere contingent diversity of the various shapes of things. One could argue that the absolute univocity of light and the absolute equivocity of shapes here coincides—or that formally there is only the one, substantively only the many. This, I have already suggested, is in reality the upshot of Hegel's dialectic. And the same upshot would apply if we advert to the more psychogeographic aspects which are ineliminable from any topography: the journey south would have to be the journey toward the abolition of south in the name of the universal north of every new starting point, when traveling southward, or else rather of the equal north/south polarity of any position whatsoever. Alternatively, it would have to be a journey whose only point was the journey, and therefore the scattering promenade of dispersal of all centers and all claims to spatial distinction.[95] Similarly, my precise knowing of anything would have to be an unknowing of its density as being at one with universal density, or else density itself would finally fade in the dawn of sheerly diverse equivocal form, fully disclosed with the manifestness of surface geometry.

But the problem with this perspective is that, just as with the idea that the univocal mist or the equivocal gray jewels dominate the misty landscape, it in reality abolishes that which is synchronically present before us. Granted that the mist and the shapes are in a mutually constitutive tension, we surely experience them as mutually affirming as much or more than as working to abolish each other for a world of pure whiteness on the one hand, or a world of final geometry on the other. If to be hidden is to be shown (against the background of "mist," as including a misty density proper to the thing itself), and therefore to be shown is to be hidden, then this implies not an impossible contradiction that must be overcome (dialectics) but rather an outright impossible *coincidence of opposites* that can (somehow, but we know not how) be persisted with. This is the Catholic logic of *paradox*—of an "overwhelming glory" (*para-doxa*) which nonetheless saturates our everyday reality.

The logic of paradox can, as I have already said, be described also as the analogical, the constitutively relational, or the metaxological. The crucial principle here is that of William Desmond: neither the one nor the many transcendentally rule, nor yet an agonistic play between them (dialectics), even if all these logics have their local part to play and may, through historical distortion, at times and in places appear to usurp the genuinely transcendental function. But this belongs rather to the *metaxu*, the *zwischen*, or the between—to the interweaving of things in and out of the mist.[96] It belongs also to the *relative* dominance of the latter as foreground/background; also to the contrasting relation between the various shapes themselves; to the constitutive tension between directions like north and south; to the reliance of knowing upon unknowing and vice versa. In all these cases, the "metaxological" is irreducible because that which is "shared" and lies "between" cannot be reduced (save at the un-Aristotelian price of destroying the appearances) to a division between aspects that are univocally shared on the one hand and other aspects that are cleanly differentiated on the other. Instead, within this range of phenomenality, what is like the other is like the other precisely in *respect of its difference*; while that which is different is different from the other in *respect of its likeness*. This is precisely why the traditional notion of "analogy," if it means anything at all, and cannot be reduced to a confused mixture of the univocal and the equivocal, must involve a paradoxical dimension. Eckhart and Cusanus, in defending analogy against the Scotist charge that it violated the principle of noncontradiction, conceded the point while arguing that the logic of infinity and of infinite/finite relations requires this violation. In doing so they in effect admitted that an analogical logic is also a paradoxical logic.

The overwhelming double glory, the paradoxical character of the scene through which I am driving, is also its beauty. This beauty resides in the *belonging together* of the mist with the trees and the river, the church spires and the rooftops. Within the scene as it appears to me, the distinctness of these things concerns their resemblance to, and yet difference from, each other. But when I see them as belonging together, as composing a certain pleasing harmony (and the aspect of pleasure or displeasure is never absent from seeing), in a way that is irreducible to any mathematical formula (since it is *just this* specific belonging-together), then I realize that it is precisely with respect to its difference that the church spire "goes with" and so in some sense "is like" (in beauty, and so in "being" in its aspect of beauty) the trees and the roofs. Inversely, the unity of the entire scene before me is a unity that is achieved *through* all the differences that I behold, and so *coincides* with these differences. Moreover, this unity does not simply equalize all the differences: no, the mist itself frames uniquely and three-dimensionally, the far spire discretely dominates the near roofs, the mere hint of a river in the distance orientates the eye in a way that the scattered trees nearby do not.

If one writes off beauty as the merely subjective, the paradoxical dimension does not simply vanish, for the shapes stand out only in relation to each other, whether in reality or for our thought. In this way the *aliquid* is also paradoxically the *alter aliquid*, the thing that it is not, but that it is constitutively related to. In denial of the aesthetic dimension, one can read this circumstance after Hegel (who denied the ontological ultimacy of the aesthetic) dialectically, such that the two contradictorily conjoined poles move thereby toward mutual abolition. But this is merely an elective existential option which tends to deny the immediate givenness of the scene, which, like any given scene, is directly shown to our sight as pleasurable, and as displeasurable (to some degree or other) only in terms of an experienced anomaly.

As concerns the interplay of the shapes in general with the mist, I have already explained how we have here another constitutive relationship which involves paradoxical implications: the distinct is seen only with and so *as* the obscure, and vice versa. Once more this can indeed be read as the dynamics of mutual obliteration, but this destroys the immediate integrity of the scene itself. It may be logically unstable upon reflection, but for the unreflective gaze its beauty is tranquil and undisturbed. And this beauty concerns the way in which the trees, like dryads, escape fleetingly from the mist only by seeming at once to draw back into it, or the way in which the mist is perceived as a glorious veil that hides only to reveal through an extra, diaphanous covering (like the veil of a woman), and by rendering what is secreted all the more present and significant. Thus the mist hides and distances the near, but promotes and brings near the wolds that lie on the opposite bank of the river. Nor is this beauty only a matter of the regard. Because of the all-enveloping character of the mist, my movement up and down the hills and round the bends has become phenomenologically the movement of the landscape itself. If appearances faithfully disclose to us an ontology that includes both matter and spirit (as perhaps both materialists and theologians agree), then within the mist my movement has become my stasis, just as the fixity of the landscape has become its dynamic. And in moving me the landscape also thinks the course of my journey, while by remaining lost in the mist my mental journey must surrender to the entire enduring of the earth and the sky and the river—it must circumscribe the local globe which I am sustaining through my north to south passage, even while it appears to travel diagonally through this new but ancient locality.

This is the case, because the coincidence of north and south, in reality and in my mind, creates between my home and my destination a beautiful single suspended world, whose coherence is specific and unique—at once it is a distinct area with its own unique set of belonging inhabitants, long traditions, and open horizon for the future. Only I, perhaps, so far know this, and yet I can know this only because it is already faintly true. In the psychogeographic dimension we invent new terrains that yet remain purely discoveries.

Finally, when my mind is inclined to get to know the unknown, it is less prompted by curiosity than it is lured by beauty. For what I see within the mist is incomplete for me only because the beautiful as such is suggestive in its surface of something shown and yet withheld: this "vertical" circumstance is at one with its "horizontal" inscrutability whereby we cannot generalize into a formula the belonging-together of the disparate. Because the beautiful is seen as utterly particular and yet as the wider generative significance of the particular, it is perceived as partially disclosive of a hidden depth within the specific which is at the same time a road into the far wolds that form the background to all of reality. So Beauty as such is like the veil of the mist. The mist is both insidiously spreading and impenetrably dense, but since the spread is specified by its suspension across the branches of the trees, it acquires here an invisible "specific density" which is, as it were, the diagonal unity between proportion and disclosure which are both proper to beauty. Beauty lies in this way "on the diagonal" between surface harmony and tantalizing (withheld yet apparent) mystery, and exceeds in its implications even the three-dimensional sphere which contains them both. The harmony can always be further, and nonidentically, extended; what is hidden can be further shown and so yet more deeply concealed. But esoterically and yet discernibly, that which can be further elaborated as surface development is also a further insight into the reserved secret. Or, to put it another way: to construct is also further to notice; to compose is to listen better; to create is to contemplate more deeply. And the reverse, naturally.

To accept that all truth is mediated by beauty is once more to remain with immediately given paradox. In this instance the paradox is that we can know only the unknowable—that only the vague density of things grants them at once their specificity and their external knowability, so freeing our claims to understand from the taint of solipsistic self-reflection. To deny this mediation is to embrace the merely *spectral* mediation of dialectics, which is the tribute exacted from a rigidly univocal/equivocal logic by the shadow of beauty herself. Dialectical mediation is spectral because it finally pulls up the drawbridge of the between—but less to lock all into the plenitudinous castle of pleasures (as Desmond would have it) than to leave all behind for ever in the surrounding marshlands of diversity. Here mediation is only a ghostly train which fulfilled reality points back to as her inevitable wake that once (necessarily) appeared to be the road to her majestic presence.

But genuine mediation, by contrast, *remains to the end*—even in God and as God. Beauty is the true name of the *metaxu*, because it vanishes like the fay—if that which exists only as lying between something and an other something as harmony, or between appearance and being as disclosure, or between objective and subjective as aesthetic judgment, is denied.

The argument, therefore, against Žižek and following Desmond, is that not the dialectical but the metaxological is the framing transcendental reality for any given scenario apparent to human beings. If the univocal is dominant, then the equivocal is ultimately denied. The same applies in reverse if the equivocal is dominant. But if the dialectical is dominant, then (as with ultimate equivocation) the univocal and the equivocal move toward mutually assured destruction. Only a metaxological framing allows all three other logical aspects to remain and not to be overruled. There is the same and the different, and a continuously creative (or contingently disruptive) tension between the two, because what holds sway without holding sway (kenotically, as it were) at the ultimate level is the analogical, which is itself nothing other than the interplay between the one and the many, and the interplay between their peaceful coexistence and their creative conflict.

Nevertheless, two major questions arise in relation to my version of Desmond's thesis. The first concerns the implications of claiming that the logical level which transcendentally governs all being-knowing violates the principle of noncontradiction. Can we really accept that we all the time see (or sense with all the senses) what we cannot possibly think? Yes, we can, if we reflexively think through the difference between the finite and the infinite, and yet the inter-involvement of the two. One finite thing cannot be its opposite, nor can one finite thing both be and not be another finite thing at the same time, in the same place, and in the same respect. If, however, we suppose that there "is" an infinite, then this logic no longer applies. For it is a logic which transcendentally supposes the notion of "limit," of "delimitation," else it cannot operate. But in the infinite there is no presupposed limit—therefore one way to speak of the infinite is to say that here all opposites coincide, all differences are also similarities, and vice versa. One can think the absolute simple infinite only as paradox, yet one is bound to think the infinite as ontologically first (whether one is a theist or an atheist). So beyond the bounds of sense lies—something else.

However, paradox cannot be neatly corralled, if one can so grotesquely speak, into the realm of the infinite. If the infinite is ontologically primary, then the finite must somehow stand in relation to the infinite. Moreover, we know that the finite thing itself bears witness to this primacy, because we cannot conceive of any bounds to the finite as such: we must assume that the finite "goes on for ever" and, moreover, that it does so as much microscopically as macroscopically. This leads us to question whether there truly are any strictly finite things without qualification, outside the sphere of logical supposition. Hegel was right (and merely echoing Augustine): the finite is of itself nothing whatsoever. And Nicholas of Cusa was also right: the infinite identities of the maximum and the minimum reveal that the paradoxicality of the infinite invades the finite realm also.[97] By extension from the merely mathematical example, every finite quality must be supposed to tend to an extreme degree of itself, but at this extremity it is identical to all other qualities. The entirely courageous man, for example, would have the courage not to fear doing justice and would also have the courage to be patient and to cultivate also the other virtues whose lack (according to Aristotle and rightly in extremis) is not compatible with genuine courage—for the unjust man really fears his victims; the rash foolhardy man has not realized the meaning of true bravery, while the liar is fearful of the truth, and so forth. Perhaps this is why, as Chesterton noted, Christ's ethical teaching consisted mainly of a series of ridiculously extreme and at times incompatible imperatives—don't work, don't own anything, carefully cultivate all your talents, never resist, be deliberately feckless, make a long-term investment in the eternally lasting, take the law violently into your own hands in the face of abuses of its spirit, be ruthlessly cunning, be naively innocent, return to childhood, be wiser than all your ancestors, and so on and so forth. As Chesterton further suggested, Christian ethics therefore seems to involve a redefinition of the Aristotelian mean less as a half-and-half balance between different qualities of action and as, rather, a seemingly impossible "both at once."[98] The logic of this would seem to be that an extreme degree of a quality, tending to the infinite, flips over into its opposite—thus, as Paul Claudel noted, turning the other cheek is actually an act of strategic aggression within an ongoing war (unlike responding verbally, or just turning away).[99]

So at its exemplary extreme, ethical action, for Christianity, exceeds finite characterization because infinite courage, for example, is all the virtues and so no longer specifically courage. This is one reason why, for Christian teaching, the ethical belongs beyond the law. As Kierkegaard suggested, the good now lies for Christianity in the utterly singular and so not generalizable (and only problematically communicable), decisively eventful and self-defining action (or series of actions) of the individual person. Here the finite has taken on the weight of an infinitely disclosive significance, such that the personhood or "personality" of the human being breaks entirely, as Jacques Maritain and Emmanuel Mounier taught, the bounds of her "individuality"—she becomes distinct precisely at that point where her action cannot be seen as a mere example of a general principle and, rather, becomes "equal" in significance to humanity taken as a whole.

If the soil of the finite, within our experience, in this way paradoxically "runs out" into the sands of the infinite, then paradoxes also arise when we consider the infinite in relation to the finite. One can agree with Badiou that Hegel's finitized infinite is really but a pseudo-infinite, because the idea of an unended finite becoming reduces to notions of "yet one more" within a posited possibility of the infinite, whereas the idea of the infinite which ineluctably arises within our minds (as Descartes taught) is of something positively actual and in no series with any indefinite finite progression (even if, in modification of Descartes, we can *conceive* the in-finite only according to a *via negativa*.) Nor can one decide by reason alone (as Badiou concedes) whether this infinite is an empty void or a plenitude—in the former case one can deny that there is an infinite set of all the sets, and so that opposites ultimately coincide, since the only infinites with any content are then in consequence the transfinites which actually assume a certain finite setting or qualification. But in the latter—theological—case one must admit, after Cusa, the principle of the *coniunctio oppositorum*.[100]

But whether as void or plenitude, the actual infinite is related paradoxically to the finite. Meister Eckhart saw this most acutely (and in terms whose scope *exceeds* any Hegelian analysis) when he argued that the infinite as "indistinct" is thereby "indistinguishable" from the finite, even though as "uniquely" indistinct it must be in itself the most distinguished thing of all and the most distinguished from the distinct, which is the finite. He therefore concluded that, in the infinite, absolute indistinction and absolute distinction coincide.[101] Hence whereas Hegel enunciated only one side of this paradox—the non-otherness of the infinite to the finite—and was accordingly able to speak of a kind of mutual sublation between finite and infinite, Eckhart also drew attention to the absolute actual otherness of the infinite from the finite, an otherness more extreme than any that pertains between one finite thing and another. This double aspect to the paradox allowed him to remain with the paradoxically analogous, and not (despite what many commentators say) to reduce analogy to the dialectical.[102] Hence for Eckhart the infinite as an actual plenitude is at once indeterminate and entirely determinate, and is entirely the same as the finite only because (in its indistinctness from it) it is more absolutely the finite than the finite is itself the finite, by being its "indistinct" ground which is also inconceivably other to the finite. For Hegel the mist evaporates into the pure mist of nothingness, leaving the stark, bare, wintry trees behind in their isolation. For Eckhart the mist is the related trees of the wood which it wreathes about. Thereby the mist is the beauty of the mist—the beauty of the infinite, as David Bentley Hart has it.[103]

Here we are getting very near the nub of the issue between myself and Žižek. Is it more radical and Christian to say, in heterodox fashion (with Hegel), that the infinite "is only" the absurdly self-grounding finite, or is it more radical and Christian to say, in a kind of hyperorthodox fashion with Eckhart, that the infinite and the finite both coincide and do not coincide—that the infinite is more absolutely finite (determined) than the finite in its very infinitude (indefiniteness), and that the infinite is still the giving source of the finite, even though this is in a sense the self-giving of the finite to itself—granted that the finite as finite has no real self-standing? In the first case we have the tediously mysterious abolition of mystery; in the second case we have the fascinatingly mysterious exposition of mystery in all its simplicity.

It is just another variant on this crucial simplicity of Christian orthodoxy (an orthodoxy as much philosophical as it is theological) that one finds in Kierkegaard. In essential agreement with Plato, he proposed that the truth could only be the stability of the eternal.[104] Yet in both accentuating and reversing Plato's account of our finite access to this truth as "recollection backward," in terms of a "repetition forward" that remains with temporality, Kierkegaard was able to identify truth with paradox and reasoning with negotiation of the paradoxical. Hence it was not for him simply faith that believed the absurd, but rather reason, whose ungrounded presupposition was the paradoxical coincidence of eternity and time as "the truth." For if the eternal is "true," its absolute coincidence of truth and being renders truth no longer recognizable for us and no longer just itself. The only serious location of truth for us must, rather, lie in the coincidence of the temporal with the eternal. Here the realized consistency of an ethico-religious process of nonidentical repetition is taken to be akin to God in its very finite yet open singularity. This process is a series of "moments" in which the dissolution of the present—every present—into the ecstatic flow of time (as for Heidegger) is prevented only by allowing that the abiding character of the present is a partial presence of eternity as such. Through this religious rendering alone can our ordinary perception of life as a series of significant moments be metaphysically accounted for. Kierkegaard realizes in this way that the most immediate things of all have to be read paradoxically, on pain of denouncing the immediate as illusion.

It is crucial to realize here that if paradox is mediation, then it is only mediation which rescues immediacy—or only relationality which secures the irreducible positionality which is individuation.[105]

Yet because of our fallen anxious lack of trust in the mediating distance-yet-unity between infinite and finite, we are humanly unable to realize such perfect kinship through everyday ritual performance. Instead, paradox must be infinitely accentuated in the Incarnation, such that here a specific finite human pattern becomes exhaustively identified with the expressed personality (the *Logos*) of God himself. In this way alone for Kierkegaard can we have truth— because truth has been given back to us from the side of the infinite, potentially healing our most inexorable anxiety. Here once again one has the contrast with Hegelian dialectics: instead of the merely particular disclosing the truth as only the particular, one has this extraordinary yet ordinary particularity coinciding with a truth that is still an infinite universal plenitude. The former rendering suggests that the divine is "only humanity," as if we could ever know what this was, but the latter rendering suggests that true humanity is paradoxically more than humanity. As Chesterton suggests in *The Everlasting Man*, this is one of those instances where the bizarre shape of Christianity can be compared to a key that turns out, for reflection and application, to fit the lock of reality. The idea of the God-Man may be an absurd mystery, but it strangely seems to clarify that mystery (which no Darwinian can even begin to argue away) of the huge gulf between human beings and mere animals, and the way in which human beings are at once weak, oddly unfinished, and indeterminate on the one hand and yet capable of seemingly endless creativity, self-mutation, and new accessions of power on the other.[106]

All of the foregoing suggests that we must think of the infinite and the finite as not concerned with each other at all, and yet as more intimately concerned with each other than any two finite realities might be. Given this reflection, we can make more sense of our phenomenological, psychogeographic experience, and not be tempted dialectically to deny its integrity. When we see things as identical with their opposites, when we see things as like each other in terms of their very differences from each other, then we are sensing the involvement of the finite with the infinite. What we cannot at all understand, we comprehend easily in a single glimpse, just as only our feet, or our artificial vehicles, have ever resolved Zeno's famous paradox.

The second question that may be raised concerning my version of Desmond's logical topology is the issue as to whether the metaxological (analogical, real relational, paradoxical) elevates the static over the dynamic, as compared with the dialectic. This can appear to be the case, insofar as paradox holds together the mist and the trees in a stable embrace. Once more, it must be stressed that this is not ludicrously to deny the endless tensional conflicts in nature—which we cannot of course anthropomorphize as by and large sinister (even if the possibility of an evil element in fallen nature must be seriously entertained, as by Schelling in his novella *Clara*).[107] The sea and the sky do indeed sometimes "wage war" with each other, and there are also those long-term struggles which we never see but which eventually shift continents. However, what is at issue here is whether the more benign appearance of paradoxical beauty is the more transcendentally fundamental circumstance—and I have already given arguments for supposing it to be so. If this is the case, then it is the "between" which ontologically (and so most really and truly, beyond what experimental science is able to discern) holds both mist and trees in place, such that they are in no way struggling against each other. However, this does not rule out the reality of that playful pastoral tension that once reigned everywhere, according to Christian theology, in the (unreachable and untraceable) prelapsarian golden age, and in which human beings took full part. This tension can still be fleetingly glimpsed—and yet glimpsed all the time by the observant. The "both/and" of analogical paradox is in no way static, because the likeness to the other shown through the different identity of the first thing acts to ensure that the first thing reaches further out toward that alterity, yet only by further realizing its own distinctness. Because of the impossibility of truly thinking the paradoxical, this dynamic tension will even be conceived by thought in somewhat dialectical terms—the oscillation of affirmation with denial—as the likeness of the trees to the mist in contrast with their unlikeness. Yet at the same time, a nondialectical attempt is made truly to hold onto both affirmation and denial at once, and this is most of all realized through the deployment of metaphor—the mist becomes the trees' own white, wintry foliage; the trees become the mist's own thickening.

Compared with dialectic, paradox does indeed allow more for the truth of passing stability. Yet at the same time it *also* more genuinely allows for change. This is because any conflict is seeking to abolish by means of victory the processes of alteration which it for the moment sustains; hence where alteration is viewed as inherently agonistic, alteration itself is regarded as merely provisional. Moreover, since dialectic tends to concern a formally determinate process leading to the foregrounding of univocity-in-general together with equivocity-in-general as the absolute truth, it ascribes no ultimate significance to contingent change, nor to an unpredictable process which is as much substantive as it formal. By contrast, only through peaceful Arcadian tension, or its remote echo, can the creatively new, which will be treasured by all, genuinely arise.

The vision in the mist is a transgeneric vision. In this respect there is a direct link between the immediately sensory and phenomenological on the one hand and the ontological or the metaphysical on the other, which is also concerned with the transgeneric. If one ignores this link, then one will endeavor to construct an immanent phenomenology (after the fashion of most "Phenomenology" as a modern philosophical doctrine) as a supposedly final philosophy, by trying ideationally to define the exact categories within which phenomena are given to us, including irreducibly obscure phenomena. Inevitably, this retreat to the a priori subjective is also a retreat to the merely generic and univocal. For it has already been explained how the analogical is something that we "see" rather than understand, and can understand only in terms of the *real* interinvolvement of the finite with the infinite. Any "phenomenological" bracketing of this reality must inevitably favor the finite limits of an entirely comprehending reason, which will acknowledge the reality of the infinite only as an indeterminate "sublime" beyond, essentially apart from finite definition, even if its presence is registered as a "saturation." By contrast, the sensory registering of the analogical (and thereby paradoxical) can be supported not by a Cartesian reason which accepts only the clear and distinct but, rather, by a speculative reason which can "grammatically" envisage that which it can but partially grasp or can scarcely grasp at all.

Given this insight, we can start to understand in a new way how in Aristotle a realist insistence on the importance of sensing for knowing is connected to his analogical ontology (as it would later be described). When we regard a complex scene, we are able to unify all kinds of disparate realities, both individual and collective: the "substance" of a tree is taken together with its "accidental" shape and color; substance and accident are further linked to the relations in which the tree stands (for example, its being blown about by the wind); different generic realities of mineral, vegetable, and animal are integrated with each other by our gaze. What we most directly see is being, but being materialized, precisely because we see first of all the links between things that lie in the "impossible" realm of the simultaneously like and unlike. What we ordinarily see, then, is being as analogical.

But this experience is also psychogeographic, because we first of all see a landscape that calls forth certain emotions and gives rise to certain emotions. Our gaze is primordially apostrophic,[108] because we not only see a world affectively colored, but also discover in landscape and its changes a language for our passions that in part gives birth to these very passions themselves—the greatest philosophical exposition of this is Emily Brontë's novel *Wuthering Heights*. In trying to comprehend this mystery, Aristotle is once more a better guide than modern thought. The density of things which alone composes them is elusive, since it only ever arises along with the shapes of things, their "forms" (*eide* in Greek), which are entirely abstract and abstractable, and can thereby "become" the thoughts of those things themselves in the realm of mind or *psyche* in which our individual minds—mysteriously arising from our brain/body interaction with the world—participate. That these forms are irreducible to mere sensory evidence (as for Locke and Hume) is shown by the synesthetic phenomenon of "common sensing" to which Aristotle, after Plato, also drew attention. The fact that whenever we imagine a flower, we at once link its appearance with its sound and feel and smell, and that this associative capacity affects even our sensory sight of a flower, reveals that sense is always shadowed and enabled by the imagination (Coleridge's "primary imagination"), such that sensations "make sense" only because together they convey to us integral forms which only mind and sense can comprehend together—through imaginative mediation.[109]

Therefore, in perceiving the analogical structure of external reality we also reflexively grasp the analogical or "convenient" (as Aquinas put it) relationship that pertains between intellect and being as mediated by the twilight threshold of the imagination, a faculty especially attuned to the sense of "the between." But this "higher" aspect of analogy concerns the "transcendental" diversity of being as such—whereby it is also the good, the true, and the beautiful, and in its most elevated originating source (God) also the intelligent and the desiring and the discerning. As Eckhart argued, if being as such is also the intellectual, then in a sense, as the highest aspect of being, the intellectual stands "before" being itself. (If God is through and through thought, then his existence is not formally prior to his understanding, as Scotus argued.) But thought, as Eckhart also pointed out, is a kind of nullity precisely because (after Augustine) it is intentional. To think something is kenotic—it is to let that thing be and not to try to be that thing, even not to try to be oneself when thinking oneself. Hence we can see color only if our eye is colorless, come to know something only if our mind goes blank and receptive; it follows, therefore, that if God contains all beings within his simplicity, he must be hyperintellectual and therefore the most empty—such that "if God is to become known to the soul, it must be blind."[110] In this way, for Eckhart, God is not so much being as "purity of being"; this is why he often claimed that a "nothingness" lies even before being. According to his hyper-Thomistic formulation, *esse est Deus*; but one cannot equally say *Deus est esse*, since all of the divine being must be identified with intellectual receptivity and creativity which, at the apex of being, is in a sense more than being.[111]

Later (developing away from his earlier, sometimes rather one-sided antivol-untarism), Eckhart sometimes declared that the nullity of the divine ground is equally a pure willing, or that it lies beyond either knowing and willing in an absolute simplicity that is nonetheless crucially hypergenerative of all determinations in its very indetermination.[112]

This, however, is not at all like Hegel's original nullity. For the latter is a nul-lity identical with being, given that Hegel thought of being as a univocal abstrac-tion. This "null being" exists only by determining itself, and thought arises only through rehearsing this process of self-determination. Hence it becomes clear that actually Hegel perpetuates Duns Scotus's malign "existentialism" that renders pure infinite being a prior logical "moment" in the Godhead. By contrast, Eckhart is far more genuinely intellectualist than Hegel, the "idealist." This is because, for the Rhenish master, intellect was an absolutely primordial reality whose nullity was not the "contradictory" nullity of being as such, which must therefore be overcome, but rather the "donating" nullity of intellect itself, which always kenotically "lets being be." This is why, for Eckhart, thinking is primar-ily creative, primarily a matter of "giving birth," and why also for him the intelligence of the Father is present only in its giving rise to infinite "words" in the Son, whereas for Scotus (reducing the import of the Trinity) the Father's understanding is complete in itself, and is merely "expressed" in the filial im-age which is thereby reduced to instrumentality.[113]

It is nonetheless true that Eckhart links apophasis regarding God with the "nothingness" of thought, whereby the intentionality of thinking, say, an "ap-ple" is so exhaustive that the form of apple in thought is entirely an absence of apple that points back to an actual apple. Developing Aquinas here, Eckhart declares that the entire "image aspect" of a thought, as of any image whatso-ever, derives entirely from that which it images—an image of itself is a nullity. (In effect this glosses an Aristotelian theory of knowledge with a neoplatonic doctrine of participation, itself radicalized by the notion of creation ex nihilo.) Hence God as more primarily intelligence than being is, for Eckhart, also a God whose essence is a kind of nothingness. However, in contrast to Hegel, this nullity applies "from the outset" equally to the Father as understanding and to the Son as conceptual Verbum. Yet it might still seem that what one has here, as Olivier Boulnois suggests, is the bare reflexive self-identification of divine being-as-pure-intellect, such that the void absence of thinking names itself as such. In one sense this is true, yet this must be entirely qualified by Eckhart's comprehension of the emanation of the Verbum as being at one with the emanation of the positive diverse fullness of the Creation—an emanation that "expresses" and does not negate the Paternal creative emptiness, rendering it, also, an intentional plenitude.[114]

In this way, for Eckhart's deepest perspective, intelligence and being are co-primordial. (In the next section I shall deny Žižek's contention that the ontology of unity is more ultimate in Eckhart than the ontology of birth.) Yet by raising intellect to co-primacy with being as a nullity "beyond being," Eckhart was able to allow that there is a kind of infinite "coming-to-be" expressed by the idea of the divine Trinity, without attributing to the passionless God any real change. God, as it were, echoing Eriugena, eternally creates himself.

In terms of Eckhart's Trinitarian metaphysics, it can be seen that the "para-transcendental" relationship between being as a transcendental and intellect as a partial and yet "higher" transcendental, convertible with being as infinite source (but not with being as finite, since not all finite things are capable of thought, though they are all true), is the most primordial circumstance imaginable. Hence when our minds either contemplate the divine creation or shape human products in a "detached," maximally intellectual mode, we participate in the infinite original "letting be," which is the very essence of goodness, the "spiritual" co-product of paternal intelligence and filial existence: "to the extent that I am close to God, so to that extent God utters himself in me. The more that all rational creatures in their works go out of themselves, the more they go into themselves."[115]

So not only do we immediately "see" the analogy of being when we gaze at the trees in the mist, we also immediately experience as emotional delight the "convenient" infinite proportion that pertains between intellect and being, and is yet more fundamental than being itself. In this *ratio* lies the most ultimate *metaxu*. And this "between" constitutes also the most ultimate Trinitarian paradox, since here the original nullity of understanding "is" only through exhausting itself in the provision of being, while inversely, being is being only through being given, through being creatively understood and permitted to be.

And if the divine self-understanding is simple and intuitive, then it makes perfect sense that we most of all participate in this through sensory intuition.[116] Via the senses we intuit being; via sensory–mental coordination we intuit the infinite connection between being and understanding. This is the natural situation which prevails especially for children. Yet we take the world to be like this only through the operation of right desire; hence, even in the primordially given, a secret judgment is already at work. Because a judgment has already been made implicitly, it is possible for us to judge otherwise—and perversely, according to the assumed veracity of the original, paradoxical vision. It is possible to favor the dominance of the univocal, equivocal, or dialectical, and thereby to abolish reality as it appears to us. And because of the inevitable onset of increasing adult reflection, one more and more requires an explicit judgment to be made in favor of the analogical. This judgment can be made only by a metaphysical speculation that is prepared to concede an external reality exceeding what we can grasp and an ineffable analogical proportion within being, as also between being and the intellect and between finite and infinite which we see and feel but cannot comprehend. It is in just this way that, as Chesterton discerned, a Catholic metaphysics is the guardian of the most ordinary, which includes the most poetic, experience.

5. CHRISTIANITY, PARADOX, AND DIALECTICS

So far, I have argued that our ordinary experience is paradoxical, and that this can be denied only at the cost of denying its reality.

This is a very Chestertonian argument, defending the extraordinariness of the ordinary. It is quite different from Žižek's materialist Hegelian argument which wishes to denature the ordinary by rendering it merely ordinary and then claiming that there is only the ordinary—with the exception of subjectivity, but we will come to that later. His attempts to enlist Chesterton to this cause—as if paradox tended toward dialectics—are not convincing. For Chesterton, like Augustine, was so astonished by the oddity of everyday reality that he found it very easy to believe in the existence of ghosts and fairies, magic and miracles, as he indicates in several places. Indeed, he considered these realities to be a matter of *popular* record, and their denial to be a product of undemocratic elitist skepticism and intellectual snobbery: "As a common-sense conclusion, such as those which we come to about sex or about midnight (well knowing that many details must in their own nature be concealed) I conclude that miracles do happen. I am forced to it by a conspiracy of facts: the fact that the men who encounter elves or angels are not the mystics and the morbid dreamers, but fishermen, farmers, and all men at once coarse and cautious; the fact that we all know men who testify to spiritualist incidents but are not spiritualists. . . ."[117] Chesterton's argument here that certain things can be plausibly supposed to occur which are nonetheless inaccessible to generally surveyable evidence (or predictability) is concise, witty, and brilliant—indeed, it is clear that if Lacan and Žižek have stopped believing in miracles, they have equally stopped believing in sex and midnight.

This is the only point where Žižek is in substantive exegetical error concerning Chesterton, but his error is nonetheless understandable. For Chesterton indeed considered that modern nonreligious people were too *hasty* in invoking the supernatural, simply because they had not long enough pondered the bizarre character of the everyday world and had ceased to think of it as the divine creation, and so worthy of wonder. Similarly, he thought that they were liable to believe in any old novel superstition, whereas the older folk beliefs, while recognizing unknown forces, also placed them within a logical and religious worldview. So he was well disposed toward elves, but dismissive of spiritualists whose account of the afterlife was sentimental and incoherent, and incompatible with Christian orthodoxy. He was also suspicious of spiritualism's pseudo-scientific character and attempts to summon spirits at will through absurdly domestic mechanical procedures. But this does not at all mean that he denied the reality of the genuinely interruptive and surprising miracle, nor even the reality of certain "magical" communications (never simply reducible to technique) between mind and matter. The point is, rather, that he thought these to be scarcely more astonishing that what occurs all the time.[118]

But is the claimed truth of Christian revelation better presented in terms of a paradoxical or a dialectical logic? Does it announce the coincidence of the ordinary with the extraordinary, or rather a necessary journey through extraordinary illusion, which finally leaves us in an ordinary forever alienated from the extraordinary—even if we can console ourselves, as Žižek does, with the thought that this is the most extraordinary thing of all? Let us examine this issue with respect to the theological topoi mainly considered by Žižek—those of Trinity, Creation, and Christology.

The theological authors whom Žižek cites are in particular Eckhart, Kierkegaard, and Chesterton. In all three cases one can say that these authors tended to search for the overall *logic* of Christian belief, and were "radically orthodox" in the sense that they tended to accentuate its aporetic features and come to terms with them by suggesting that this overall logic is a paradoxical logic. The same can be said of Eriugena and Nicholas of Cusa, and in the twentieth century of Henri de Lubac. All these thinkers appear to push Christian teaching to its problematic limits. Yet their radicalism is essential for orthodoxy in the face of probing critiques—especially those of Scotists, nominalists, and rationalists, who fail to reckon with the idea that there might be a peculiar Catholic logic with its own specific but justifiable assumptions. One can well say that the writings of Maximus the Confessor, St. Augustine, and Thomas Aquinas represent more balanced and diverse syntheses which can continue to correct the sometimes one-sided or too narrowly focused emphases of these "radicals." And yet the radicals are today essential insofar as they push to required extremes certain themes already clearly adumbrated by the three great "synthesizers." Their attempt to find a common logic throughout Christian belief ensures that doctrine is not reduced to a random series of revealed declarations, and that a Christian understanding of reason can be presented in continuity with a rational comprehension of the role of revelation. Following Žižek, accordingly, I will pay special attention to Eckhart, Kierkegaard, and Chesterton.

With respect to the Trinity, Žižek's historical perspective is eccentric and inadequate. He considers the history of this doctrine in terms of three moments which are: 1. The Eastern Orthodox account (according to the twentieth-century lay Russian theologian Vladimir Lossky); 2. Meister Eckhart; and 3. Jacob Boehme / G. W. F. Hegel.

These three Trinitarian moments correspond, according to Žižek, to three historically ecclesiological moments, just as Hegel's unfolding Trinitarian logic corresponds phenomenologically to certain secular historical moments. Hence Orthodoxy stands for the mediation of organic tradition which permits a hazy unity between the individual believer, the Church, and God. This would seem to be a bit like the initial stages of the "logic of essence" in Hegel, or in phenomenological-historical equivalence the time of paganism (which Orthodoxy for Žižek still echoes). A sleepily assumed "becoming" blends particularity with transcendence. The Roman Catholic phase, on Žižek's account, sounds by contrast more like the later "reflective" stage of the logic of essence, in which transcendent source and "posited" particularity are at once more distinguished from each other and yet linked in terms of origin and how that origin expresses itself. This corresponds historically to Hegel's account of medieval Latin Catholicism: a phase (supposedly) of more extreme alienation of the transcendent deity and yet more codified and institutionalized understanding of mediation. Again roughly in accordance with Hegel's understanding of how reflection unfolds, this alienation, according to Žižek, reaches a much greater extreme with the Protestant Reformation, since God now becomes remote and inscrutable and at the same time *only* qualitatively expressed in terms of what he has ordained via revelation. (An earlier sense of participation in the inner life of God is here lost to view.) Žižek considers that this extremity of alienation is necessary, because it finally allows one to see that the divine source is void and "is" only in what is "created"—though this is really not created at all; it is, rather, self-emergent from nothing. It was Hegel who finally saw this and brought reformation to completion. Hence, as we have already noted, in the *Science of Logic* Hegel says that "creation *ex nihilo*" is only pictorial language for the philosophical truth of the emergence of beings from Being-which-is-nothingness. So the conclusion of the dialectical process is here the absolute separation of the one from the many which favors mainly an equivocal outcome—each and every believer (for Luther) or citizen (for Hegel) is in "immediate touch" with God, and finally *is* God in respect of the believer's or citizen's symptomatically incurable subjectivity—to intrude Žižek's Lacanian note.

This final stage of atheistic Protestantism regarded as true Christianity corresponds to Hegel's "logic of the Notion" and historically to the modern State and economic market—in fact to the liberal "end of history." One might object here that Hegel speaks of both the Church and the State as the realized "Notion" which embodies an absolute coincidence of idea with reality, free at last of any ideal alienation. Yet once again, as we have already seen, Žižek is an astute reader of Hegel: this is not really organicism, because the logic of the Notion, whereby the divine source "is" only in that to which he has given rise, such that there is no longer any "reflective" tension between source and product, is echoed in the relation between a Church and its members or a State and its subjects/citizens. The State ensures the coincidence of idea with reality *not* because it is, as a whole entity, a mysterious ideal-thing to be worshiped but, rather, because it is *nothing but* its citizens who ascribe to laws, just as the economic market is *nothing but* the players of an economic game which they have invented. Just as, within the logic of essence, it seems that God has "posited" beings, so likewise within an alienated politics it seems that it is the sovereign which accords "subjecthood." And it is remarkable, as Žižek notes, that so many standard renderings of Hegel speak as if he remained at the level of this logic. But according to the third and conclusive logical stage, the logic of the Notion, beings themselves are self-posited in a pure positivity, and it is they themselves who have "presupposed" God as their original source—though at the nonalienated end of the process they come to see that the most ultimate presupposition is really just their own self-positing. In a similar fashion, it appears at first to human beings that they are legitimated by the State as a mystical, divine reality, but in the long term they come to see that the State is something which they themselves presuppose in the very act of positing: the State, like the capitalist commodity, is a fiction—yet as Žižek rightly notes, it is not thereby an *illusion concealing a deeper truth*: rather, it is a fiction necessary to human civil existence. The only collective house which humans can and must inhabit is a pretend one.

It is here that Žižek is at his most perceptive—and in a way which relates to the heart of his project of a saving of the subject through a nihilistic version of materialism, to which I have already referred. It is at this point also that his theory of religion embodies a Hegelian modification of Marxism: religion is not so much, as for Marx, a meta-illusion which disguises the necessary illusions of the State and the commodity as, rather, a primarily necessary human illusion which allows human subjectivity to come into being at all, and then further permits the necessary illusions of State and market to be realized.[119] Since, Žižek argues, in materialist fashion, "all there is" is materially determined processes, such that the human being "is" only body and brain, the human subjective sense of a free exception to this state of affairs is an invocation of the "not-All" which signifies the contingency of the material totality itself—an excess over its determinate logic which, Žižek argues, is now detected by physical science at the macro and micro margins of physical reality—and which I (like Hegel) have already argued can also be registered by everyday experience. Referring to the way in which, for quantum physics, the same reality can be indeterminately described in two different and mutually incompatible registers, Žižek speaks, as already mentioned, of a "parallax" logic governing all of reality, beyond mediation.[120] This clearly corresponds to his reading of Hegel in terms of a final total rupture between the one void and the many positive instances of reality, besides the equivocal incompatibility between instances of the latter.

All that he can empirically appeal to here, however, is the *immanence* of this phenomenon and the impossibility for *science as a properly univocal discourse* to imagine any mediation in a seemingly impossible situation. Yet it remains possible for poetry to claim to discern and elaborate paradoxical mediations and so to "save" reality, which is the aim of science, in a way no longer possible for science itself . . . perhaps raising the question of whether we now need a new sort of "poetic science."[121] It also remains possible for theology to construe parallax phenomena as the mark of the relative nonreality of finitude and the way in which it is sustained in its depths by the infinite. A finite thing may be at once impossibly both a wave and a particle because at its deepest point of interiority, where it ceases to be merely itself, it is both and neither—just as for Nicholas of Cusa the minimum finite thing coincides with the maximum finite thing.

In this way, Žižek's atheistic reading of the "not-All" remains arbitrary and preferential, as he might possibly concede. Yet it is indeed a kind of parody of the theological view that human beings are in the image of God—and herein lies the relative seriousness of nihilistic materialism as against Anglo-Saxon materialist materialism. For both views, theological and nihilistic, human subjectivity, which wanders the earth as an even more detached, vagrant surface, recovers on the surface of reality itself something of its ontological depths, and brings this to bear beyond, and sometimes against, any merely material fastnesses. For the atheistic variant, as expounded by Žižek, the idea of free, rational subjectivity as lying "beyond the All" cannot be first of all merely imagined and inhabited, because even such imagination and inhabitation already assumes its reality. Humanity simply is this fiction; therefore it cannot knowingly commence this fiction, but must have always-already *presupposed* it. It must initially erect (and not project, as with Feuerbach) this subjective reality as God, as something real because it is more original than phenomenal appearances. Only with the passage of time can it reappropriate this necessary illusion, by coming to see how subjectivity is merely humanity's *own* rendering of the "not-All," by which self-fictioning it alone exists as humanity.

Hegel, and then Žižek in his wake, had the further insight to realize that initial alienation is repeated in immanent terms in the case of Christology. Human beings cannot first of all generically reclaim subjectivity or personality for themselves. Just as they must first of all (and fully so in the case of Christianity alone, which is why this religion is the final absolute truth of religion for Hegel, Lacan, and Žižek) see God as personal, so also they must first see a single revered individual as fully personal with an exceptional excess of (natural, aesthetic, ethical, and religious) life over the law, in the case of Jesus Christ. (Though whether this requires Christ's real as opposed to supposed historicity, Hegel may not be entirely clear.) Even the pure immanence of subjectivity as only human must first be presupposed, because subjectivity as self-directing and exceptional cannot be, by definition, a general theory, but only an experience, only the specific affirmation by someone which others later repeat, differently. There has to be a first real human subject, and the theory and reality of subjectivity can only be a recounting of the beginnings of this subjectivity and of continued intersubjective fidelity to this origin. This is why the supposition of naive atheists that the West can leave behind either Christology or ecclesiology is worthy to be greeted only with ironic laughter. Žižek is right to intimate that in this regard Kierkegaard (in *Philosophical Fragments*) to a considerable degree merely builds upon Hegel, though he fails to ask (unlike Badiou) just why one should prefer a nihilistic fidelity to any old subject (Christ as the pathetic failed clown, etc.) over a positive fidelity to Christ's specificity which was, bizarrely, both tragicomically absurd and triumphantly glorious. If one specific person is required in order to commence subjectivity in general as the necessary illusion of the subjective (in order that there might be the subjective), then why should it not be the case that this commencement was possible only as true, paradigmatic subjectivity which conjoined nature to the imagination of something supernatural? This question, as the discerning reader will realize, connects obliquely with my earlier one about how a nihilistic materialism can really account for the phenomenon of consciousness.

Finally, Žižek sees that this pattern of supposed-positing-reversed-into-presupposition occurs for a third time in the case of Church and State. It is first imagined that through the Church Christ's personality is mediated to us, but later we come to see that we are all, in our own immediate right, "sons of God." Yet once more the presupposition in its illusory form could not have been avoided. However, in this case the priorities of individual and general are reversed. Subjectivity had to commence with one single subject, but we all later become subjects by assuming that subjectivity is also a general human norm. Since, nonetheless, subjectivity stems from the grace of God mediated by Christ, this generality must be conserved by an institution and by its legal-sacramental norms. And even once it is seen that we are all "sons of God," and that the Church implies through its pictorial visions the real community of free persons, this "notion" must itself be first presupposed and, in fact, must always be presupposed in the institution of the State, whose laws alone accord and sustain a natural human freedom for all. (Once more, Hegel does not escape the biopolitical, because this immanent presupposition remains with the aporia of a nature that is real and effective only when accorded a legal status.)

From the above we can see how Žižek's metanarrative of denominational progression fits into the Hegelian metanarrative of the necessarily presupposed development of Christianity into its own "atheistic" truth. However, Žižek's account of denominational progression is not very historically convincing, and the facts really do not fit any dialectical mold. (In some ways I am a British empiricist. . . .) Eastern Orthodoxy was not a stage before Latin Catholicism, but from quite early on a parallel phenomenon. In many ways both can be described in terms of an organic immanentism of tradition, but the strong survival in the East of imperial structures led at once to a less sharp division of secular from sacred matters, and at the same time to a more purely mystical and liturgical understanding of the life of the Church. In the West, by contrast, the occupation of a barbarian vacuum encouraged a much-accentuated legal and practical role for the life of the Church itself, and it was this (perhaps more than any supposed "Roman temperament," though this cannot be discounted) which encouraged in the West the sense of a socially reformist project exceeding the bounds of the legal State. Yet these features do not amount to any "essence" of alienated papal authority, since the latter emerged gradually and for contingent reasons. Conflicts in the West between imperial or kingly powers (often invoking Byzantine models) and the papacy led eventually to a strong distinction of sacred and secular, broadly equated with clerical and lay realms. This tended eventually to pervert ecclesiastical legalism into a defense of clerical privileges and a legalistic approach to the mediation of grace itself.

And these practical tendencies of Latin Christendom were compounded by a voluntarist theology, which thought in terms of an inscrutable God mediating his decrees through absolute earthly powers. But there was nothing "inevitable" about this shift, since the construal of divine subjectivity as sheer free will, unconstrained by reason, is by no means incontestably a "purer" realization of the personal. Certain statements by Žižek show that he assumes this to be the case—that somehow Christianity points ineluctably to Descartes's extreme voluntarism for which even the laws of arithmetic are a matter of divine reflection. Within the same matrix lies his scorn for the traditional theological idea that freedom lies only in willing what one should will—namely, the good and the true; and that the genuinely free will, willing the good, is a reality entirely determined by the divine will. Yet scorn is out of place here—since one can argue, to the contrary, that a will not guided by a true rational end is unable to distinguish the spontaneous from a hidden blind constraint (whether in the case of the divine or the human will). Only the blend of desiring and reasoning provides a sense of personal "character," whereas reasoning alone allows only for an impersonal logic, and willing alone only for a forceful imposition whose arbitrariness is always transcendentally prior to a decreed pattern, which patterning then conveys nothing of what is proper to the willing person herself. To be free, therefore, for an earlier theology, means to participate remotely in the divinely infinite fusion of thought with desire, the divinely infinite personifying power. And this participation can be at one level "entirely" the work of divine determining freedom precisely because God as the ontological and the human as the ontic are not competing on the same ontic plane.[122] But all these subtleties were lost sight of by voluntarism, which had abandoned the sense that reason is the highest kind of living appetition, esoterically linked to being itself, and therefore saw willing as an ungrounded act of choice, sundered from the reasoning process. Voluntarism is always the reverse face of rationalism—and the thought that the rational as a closed system may itself be an arbitrary product, transcended by a nihilistic "not-All," is an inevitably perverse consequence of rationalist presuppositions themselves.

There is therefore no reason to suppose that earlier Orthodox or Catholic models of immanent self-government by tradition were inherently unstable or bound to dissolve—even if they might gradually have developed a stronger sense of the free play of innovation and the capacities of the individual personality. One cannot ascribe this sense solely to the Protestant model, in Žižek's fashion, since it was here dialectically tied to the relationship to a voluntarist God and to an absolutely authoritative, unmediated biblical text. In no sense does this link represent a third, final moment in Christian development because, as Michel de Certeau argued, an alien, extrinsic papal authority and an alien, extrinsic biblical authority are rival versions of the same modern religious paradigm which is consequent upon the loss of the sense that, through the Eucharist, the Church as a whole participates in the historical body of Christ, and so in the divine.[123] Nicholas of Cusa's more pluralistic, dispersed, and democratic sense of ecclesial authority was in fact a humanist reworking of this *ancient* model in contrast to the modern, "alienated" and extrinsicist assumptions of both Reformation and Counter-Reformation.[124] One should ascribe the historical triumph of the modern rather than the ancient model not to any outworking of a material logic but, rather, to contingent processes of ideological and political struggle.

By not seeing any of this, Žižek remains captive to the myth that modernity is bound to be Protestant, and so in effect always recommends a Protestant version of modernity. And his ecclesial "phenomenology" is paralleled by his unfolding of its shadow, a Trinitarian "logic." Here, eccentrically enough, his three reference points are Lossky, Eckhart, and Boehme/Hegel. Once again, the contrast between Christian East and Christian West is overdrawn, because he accepts uncritically Lossky's account of Orthodox Trinitarian theology, to which few experts would now assent. Basically, the point at issue is that a much later rendering of the refusal of the *filioque* (after Photius), as denying any procession of the Spirit *per filium* whatsoever, is read back by Lossky (as by many modern Orthodox) into the thinking of the Cappadocians and of Maximus the Confessor. Yet in reality they accepted a *per filium* account, and did not think of the two processions of Son and Spirit as simply given, unconnected "mysteries." Already they distinguished the persons of the Trinity by relational position, and came near to the idea of "substantive relation" later fully defined by Aquinas. This means that the Christian Orthodox account of the Trinity was concerned with a rational logic all along—this is no mere later Western affair, as Žižek implies.[125]

This mistake is highly significant, because it tends to gloss over the point that this rational logic is not necessarily a dialectical logic—Žižek hastens onward through Eckhart and Boehme to Hegel as if the Western relational understanding of the Trinity were bound to lead to this dialectical upshot. Here, indeed, he is in negative agreement with Lossky, and many of the modern Orthodox, but the perspective is completely erroneous. For the logic of the Trinity is not dialectical but paradoxical. It is not, as for Hegel, that the Father taken as origin is an indeterminate being-nothingness who must "become" by alienating and denying himself in the Son, and then recovering himself as original source in the Spirit—first in the "essential" or "reflective" sense that the posited realm of Sonship is that of "illusory being," but finally in the "notional" sense that there is only alien positing, which commences with the Son and is then universalized in the realm of the Spirit (which, historically, is the realm of Church-State). Instead, for the most classical Christian perspective, as developed from Gregory of Nyssa through Augustine to Aquinas, the Father in his absolute plenitude as arche nevertheless can never even be considered "in himself" as a first "moment," since this origin is entirely exhausted in the filial image which it expresses. This does not, however, mean that it is abolished or negated in what it expresses, since the paradoxical logic of substantive relation also operates with absolute symmetry the other way around: the Son, as expressed image, is only that which he images or expresses. It is perhaps no accident that it was an orthodox Anglican clergyman who invented looking-glass logic: for the logic of the Trinity suggests that the Father is only his image in a mirror, and yet that this image is indeed a "mirror image"—in itself entirely transparent and containing only its reflected source. "My dear one is mine as mirrors are lonely," as another Anglican, W. H. Auden, wrote in his poetic commentary on The Tempest.[126]

It might seem, accordingly, as if there is really no original person (the Father) and no person as mirrored image (the Son), but only an impersonal passage of light. However, Trinitarian theology suggests instead that there is still a source and still a mirror because there is indeed a "looking-glass world" behind the mirror, a world in which light from the original source continues to travel impossibly through and beyond the mirror's reflective surface, such that there is a strange hidden realm of meta-reflection, born of both the original source and the image of this source. Since their pure relationship can be in turn related to through a further pure relationship (to the Holy Spirit), the poles of the first relationship are reaffirmed—just as the drawing of a square from a base ensures that the line of the base does actually have termini and is not a mere indefinite line that would not be a relation at all. The "looking-glass world" of the Spirit is a creative, latently "multiple" world, because it concerns a reinvocation of the Paternal expressive source along with interpretive attention to the expressed image of the Son. Yet in keeping with paradox, the image in the mirror that images only what is shown in the mirror *is* only the world behind the mirror, while the latter *is* only the source and its insepa-rable mirror image—just as the world of dreams, which for Lewis Carroll it represented, in turn *is* only everyday reality and its accompanying "mirrored" self-consciousness.

But—to ask a question which Christian tradition has admittedly failed to ask—could this imply that there is then only an "impersonal square" of light, which, like the mere passage of light invoked above, would be after all without relation? Does substantive relation always collapse into Laruelle's unilateral passage—the indefinite line, or the sides of an open square going on and on for ever? . . . Here, once more, one must recognize the implicit "multiplicity" of the person of the Holy Spirit, which the tradition has indeed always recog-nized by linking it with the giving of grace and with the Church. The "squaring" that is the Spirit requires that the two points of the base and the projection of the square from the base (Father, Son, and Spirit) be reaffirmed through the cubing of the square, and so on ad infinitum into inexpressible dimensions. The Spirit is not just the square, but also all these dimensions. All of them together express only the original relation between the two points that is a line, yet the infinity of this expression in the infinite world behind the looking glass ensures the reality of the first relation despite its substantive absolute degree that threatens to abolish relationality altogether.

For this paradoxical, nondialectical logic, there is never any contradiction, conflict, or tension. The origin rather *coincides* with its opposite, which is that which the origin generates, while the reverse also applies. As Eckhart puts it: "the Father is a speaking work and the Son is speech working. Whatever is in me proceeds from me; if I only think it, my word manifests it, and still it remains in me. So does the Father speak the unspoken Son and yet the Son remains in him."[127] Likewise, the "third," which is the Spirit, is not a synthesis, neither one that favors the univocal source, nor one that favors the equivocal difference of the effect (as, Žižek rightly argues, is the correct rendering of Hegel). Rather, it is the confirmation (according to the logic of the *condilectio*, invoked earlier) that the ecstatic passage between Father and Son is indeed a love between two and not simply an impersonal "flash" of passage or fusion.[128] But this means that love between two can be confirmed *only* by seeing that love is contagious be-yond the mere claustrophobia of the dyad. For this paradoxical logic, the third *is only* the two, but the two *is only* the passage to the third. Therefore the third is *a remaining and not a vanishing mediator.* The third is the between that always allowed the passage from the one to the two, or the same to the different, even though it is the "product" of the one and the two, the same and the different. The third, the Holy Spirit, is therefore the principle of analogy, which "transcendentally" governs the Trinity, and is in a sense the personal expression of the personifying power of the "essential" interplay between all three persons which, as I said above, several modern Russian theologians have identified, after the Bible, as "Sophia."[129] The Spirit lies analogically between identity and difference, yet it allows the univocal and the equivocal their place, since it is itself entirely the upshot of the interplay between them. Yet in the Godhead specifically, because of the presence of substantive relation, there is no dialectical *agon* whatsoever, not even of the "playful" variety. The tensional play here is rather that of the dance—*perichoresis*, as the Greek Fathers said—and not of the sports field. No more Olympus, no more Olympiad; but Parnassus persists, now the Muses peacefully triumph over the gods themselves.

The logic of the Trinity does not then favor a solemn, serious, and tragic Teutonic shadowing of real history. Instead, it frivolously invokes a lost or hidden realm of fantastic pure play—which interrupts history only at one point, when somehow this light of the fantastic, as the light of the Nativity Star, manages to break through the natural-historical darkness that has demonically concealed it from our view.

Žižek, however, fails to be aware of this. He does not realize that the idea that the Father is the Father only in generating the Son through the procession of the Spirit is not first and foremost concerned with the "seriousness" of a divine relationship to history. Nor that it is much more lightheartedly concerned with God's self-joying and the human joy that arises to think that there is indeed first of all and finally such joy, even if it is for us now in time almost totally concealed. He assumes, wrongly, that the real meaning of substantive relation must be that the Father is the Father only as the Father of the incarnate Jesus Christ. Yet the more genuine and yet lighter meaning of this idea is that God in himself is relationship, and therefore is love conceived of as an infinite exchange—as Eros as well as Agape, and therefore in a very un-Lacanian fashion as the infinite transcendental *possibility* of sexual relationship. It might appear weightier, but is in reality more boring, to suppose that the Son first becomes the Son only in the Incarnation. This suggests a serious dialectical becoming of God as he descends into time. But with far greater levity, St. John's Gospel and St. Paul (at least) proclaim that the identity of one human being with God is in fact the disclosure of the Father's eternal paternity of the divine personality of the Son which alone humanizes this particular human being, Jesus Christ. What is lightly and joyfully disclosed here is not the dialectical identity of God but the eternally paradoxical existence of God as pure relationship, and as thereby able to enter into an absolute personal identity with finite createdness.

Yet this levity is more serious than seriousness. For, according to Meister Eckhart, in the infinite play between Father and Son lies the paradigm for human justice. He compares the Father to justice and the Son to the just man: "if the Father and the Son, justice and the just man, are one and the same in nature, it follows . . . that the just man is equal to, not less than, justice, and similarly with the Son in relation to the Father."[130] Without the just man, says

Eckhart here, there would be no justice at all, since justice must be done. All justice must be expressed justice, performed justice, since justice as a mere idea would not be existing justice at all. In this way he advances beyond Plato, putting forward a kind of pragmatism. On the other hand (and here we see the seriousness of the lonely mirror), he also insists that unless the just man was expressing the idea of justice, he would not be just. Justice must be particular, and so exceptional and distinctive, yet this performed justice must also be recognizable by all, and so universal and reapplicable in its bearing (the communication of the Son to the Spirit). This might portend a Derridean aporia (justice must be an exception to itself, but then it is not universal and just, and so on), but that is but deconstructed dialectic, whereas Eckhart expounds a paradox: in the unique and even exceptional instance, we really do glimpse the ineffable universal pattern of justice. Inversely, this pattern is only its ceaseless expression in particular acts of justice: "the just man is the 'word' of justice, by means of which justice manifests and declares itself. For if justice did not justify anyone, no one would know it."[131]

It follows from this that when we see the perfectly just man on earth, namely Christ, we see at once the *infinite* particular, the concrete universal (in a sense more radical than Hegel's), and also the infinitely abstract source of this infinite particularity. For Eckhart does *not* fully expound the Trinity in terms of the ethically and politically just man, but rather deploys the idea of the just man as an imperfect figure for the Trinity. Even in the case of the perfectly just man, Christ, the idea of justice is not canceled and fulfilled in its performance, as for Hegel—for then we should have only the elevation of the individual will and its specific decision, without exemplarity, permitting in consequence only a literal notion of community as the formal coordination of individual wills (for all Hegel's talk of *Sittlichkeit*—which in reality reduces to the market's election of specific roles for freely willing individuals and the reflexive individual celebration of this coordination which serves as the basis for a certain "corporatist" tempering of the effects of outright competition).[132] Instead, when we see that justice has been perfectly done in the particular, the idea of justice is all the more affirmed as "source" in its open and mysterious horizon, even though we now see that all this idea consists in is the "generation" of actual deeds of justice. (This is like Hegel insofar as the source is the generation, but unlike Hegel insofar as the generation remains identical with a fully actual source.) Hence a Platonism concerning justice is not denied, as with Hegel, but rather redoubled with the Trinitarian notion by a kind of "Platonic pragmatism." If justice lies only in the deed of justice, yet the deed of justice must express not just itself but also justice, then there must be an infinite deed of justice . . . prior to Christ this could be dimly intimated in Schelling's notion of later higher powers in myth that overcome earlier more sinister powers, or more strongly in biblical traditions concerning a hypostasized wisdom that was "with" God at the beginning of creation. But with Christ's life this infinite reality is "proved," since—by a further paradox—the infinite deed of justice here coincides with a finite deed of justice that is finally enacted upon the Cross (paradoxical justice, in which the innocent criminal judges all his judges).

Liberalism (and Marxism, which is but a variant upon liberalism) knows of no justice—only mutual agreement to agree or, more likely, to differ. But justice involves an objectively right proportionate distribution, as Aristotle taught, and beyond this a will to encourage all in their infinite fulfillment within their appropriate social roles, as St. Paul taught. Therefore justice is identical with objective social harmony. But this requires that every individual moment of justice reflect universal abstract justice in its infinite potential of will to further fulfillment of persons, even though this is exhausted by (infinite) practical distribution. As Eckhart began to see, the logic of justice, if it be a reality, is paradoxical after a Trinitarian fashion: "For all the virtue of the just and every work that is wrought by the virtue of the just is nothing but this, that the Son is begotten of the Father."[133] If, however, as for Hegel and Žižek, the perfectly just man is sundered from a transcendent Father supposed to be "alien" (since what is refused here is, basically, the voluntarist and hyperontic "Nobodaddy"), then we do not have any showing forth of justice but, rather, the first epiphany of the modern, alienated, and nonexemplary subjective individual.

It is for this radical reason that the eternal, "immanent" Trinity should have priority, as Christian orthodoxy declares, over the "economic" Trinity, or the Trinity as mediated to the Creation in space and time. Yet Žižek in point of fact takes the immanent Trinity less seriously even than Hegel who, as Emil Fackenheim rightly argued, still takes account of the economic/immanent difference, even if he reduces the immanent Trinity to a kind of shadowy eternal logic of the nihil, which in reality operates only insofar as the nihil self-exits into the world of nature, as Hegel declares at the end of the Logic.[134] Žižek simply states, without argument, that what the doctrine that the Father is Father only in generating the Son must "really" mean is that God is God only in becoming incarnate. Thus he briskly suggests that it is in Eckhart that one first locates the real implication of the Latin position on the Trinity.

However, this is not an accurate exegesis of Eckhart, who by no means reduces the immanent to the economic Trinity.[135] Once more Žižek reduces paradox to dialectic. But if one does so, is one not left with something relatively banal? Namely, that the immanent "is only" the economic Trinity, and so God "is only" the creation itself, or "is only" a man. Behind the inflated rhetoric of such statements lies mere atheism, for which there is no creation but only nature (or worse) and no man as a creature in the image of God, but only a rather weird, crippled, but dangerously complex animal (which is Žižek's reduction of Chesterton's famously paradoxical anthropology).

But if, instead, the workings of the Trinity in time *are also* the immanent Trinity, then one has paradox and something much more interesting, because then one has declared, not that the ordinary and disappointing is after all the All, but rather that the ordinary is after all not ordinary, and so is not after all disappointing, if one will but look again. This is tantamount to saying—yes, in one sense atheism is correct, "there is only this world," but on the other hand, if that is correct, then one needs to take in a much more serious and nonrhetorical sense the idea that this world—or the exceptional person within this world—is then God. Hence "there is only this world" can also be logically read as "there is only God."

Now one way to read Eckhart's "radicalization of orthodoxy" would be to take him as saying that *both* pantheism and acosmism are true: or that it is true both that "there is only the world" (but including worlds of which we may not know) and that "there is only God"—hence his many extreme statements to the effect both that (1) God "needs me"; I myself can judge God or see all that God sees; and that (2) in its innermost ground, the created soul (and, indeed, the Augustinian "seminal reason" of every created thing)[136] is identical with the uncreated deity. However, Eckhart does not leave this as aporia in postmodern terms, or as a vision of dialectical "parallax" in those of Žižek. He does not say that either God must be nothing or the world must be nothing, and therefore that they both abolish each other (the essence of all postmodern philosophical nihilism, which Žižek scarcely challenges). Rather, he says—paradoxically, with hyper double-gloriousness—that both "alls" coexist, even though each of the two is all—since the quasi-all of finitude and the more-than-all of simple infinitude are on different planes and do not compete, but are somehow able to coexist according to the creative power of the "all" that is the simply infinite.

Consequently, in Trinitarian terms, Eckhart does not say *only* that the generation of the Son from the Father is the same act as the act by which the Father creates the world: "when God speaks the word it is God and here it is a creature";[137] he *also* says that the creation of the world is entirely included within the generation of the Son from the Father: "God always spoke only once. His word is only one. In this one word He speaks His Son and the Holy Spirit and all creatures, and yet there is only one word in God."[138] His point is that God *is* the God who freely chooses to go outside himself, and by going outside himself returns to himself, since he is replete: "the more He is in things, the more he is outside things."[139] This means, then, that (1) God simply *is* the going outside himself; that creation, in its coming to be, *is* the divine Son, just as, through perfect detachment, we become God giving birth to God within ourselves: "the Father begets His Son in the innermost of the Soul."[140] Likewise, in its immanent desire, Creation is God returning to himself. But it also means that (2)

God from eternity within himself and "before" Creation is the God who goes outside himself and returns to himself: hence he is Father, Son, and Holy Spirit. Likewise, when we give birth to God in our souls, it is also God giving birth to ourselves as his sons by grace within his Son who is his Son by nature: "[the Father] begets you with His only-begotten Son as not less than Him."[141]

This is why Eckhart could insist before his accusers at Cologne that he retained the distinction between the Son as the pure "image" of God and human beings as being created "to the image" of God[142]—our identity with divine generation is accorded by grace, and results from the "nullity" of the image of God in us insofar as it resides in an alien vessel. The total donatedness and dependency of the *imago dei* requires that in its heart as image it is one with that perfect *imago* which is the divine Son. For this reason Eckhart, following here Dietrich of Freibourg, saw the image of God in us as residing paradoxically in the "imageless" depth of the soul beyond the actual distinguished operations of intellect and will—where Augustine and Aquinas had located a *vestigium trinitatis*. Yet rather than thereby detaching the theme of the *imago dei* from the echo of the Trinity, Dietrich and Eckhart linked it more firmly back to the specific function of the second person of the Trinity as expressed image, always linked to a desiring return to the Paternal source in the Holy Spirit.

As Olivier Boulnois notes, with great insight, this is subtly linked with Eckhart's reinvocation of a more Dionysian and Eriugenian as opposed to Augustinian view that all access to God, even that of reason, is via a theophanic mediating work of imaging that escapes full rational comprehension. But one could argue that Eckhart reconciles this view with the Western Christian insistence, in fidelity to St. Paul's words, on an immediate and complete grasp of the divine essence in the beatific vision, by suggesting that God in his Trinitarian being is infinite mediation, infinite "dense" theophany, infinite mystery even to himself. Therefore "to see as we are seen" is to see entirely through that *imago* which is the divine Son, whom we experience beyond imagining, reasoning, and desiring.[143]

So although Eckhart expresses himself in extreme terms, none of all this is alien to orthodox Catholic tradition. The notion of the mystical birth of the Son in our souls ultimately derives from Origen, while Aquinas in his *Sentence Commentary* had already said that the procession of the Trinitarian persons and the act of divine creation are essentially the same, and that the "temporal procession" only adds a "sort of relation to the temporal effect."[144] What he meant was that God, being simple, possesses only one eternal act, such that his decision to create and performance of creation are included in the outgoing of the Son and the Spirit. Thomas was therefore already aware that the distinction between God and not-God is aporetic, and can be thought only paradoxically. This is indeed implied by his key doctrine that God is *esse* and that finite existence is, qua existence, a participation in being which involves a division between *esse* and *essentia*, which coincide in God alone. Eckhart simply pushes the implication of this doctrine to the far limit: only God "is" in a sense, though he also "is not" since he does not "exist," but is "to be" (again in agreement with Aquinas), and as the intellectual power to be he is in a sense a "nullity" in excess even of *esse* (this in addition to Aquinas). In another sense only creatures exist, only they possess "mere being," and cannot by themselves originate being as such. God is all in all, therefore there can be nothing besides God, and it is for this reason that Eckhart declares that the existence even of "God" in the usual sense, as "over against us," must be denied: "all things added to God are not more than God alone."[145] If, nevertheless, something besides God impossibly exists, then this is because God in himself is an ecstatic, generating God who goes beyond God. The doctrine of the Trinity can then be taken as the paradoxical (non) resolution of the aporia of God's omnipresence—namely, that this renders him all in all and yet all in something that is finitely "besides" this infinite all. In a non-Žižekian sense, God himself is for Eckhart the "not-All."

In the case of the inherited tradition up till Aquinas, however, it would certainly seem that the infinity of the divine generation and procession is in excess of the divine creation and return, even though it happens also in virtue of the latter, according to the eternal divine decree which cannot be separated from God's very being. (This means that many modern Christian theological accounts of the "contingency" of the divine decision to create are a bit simplistic, and fail to be aware of the ontological difference between God as *esse* and mere existences whose being is not their essence and whose contingent decisions are not entirely at one with their power to will or the integrity of their personalities.) For Eckhart, however, it sounds more as if creation (with return) and generation (with procession) are indeed entirely coterminous, but differentiated in terms of entirely incommensurable infinite and finite perspectives. For this not to involve a limiting of God, one seems to require the later Cusan and Pascalian idea of the entirely indefinite character of the finite creation itself, which, because it is not self-bounded, "runs out" at its aporetic limits into identity with the simple divine infinite.[146]

And I think that this radicalism is required by a more rigorous Trinitarian orthodoxy since God, as simple, gives only "once." His self-expression and return, that is his entire self, cannot be in real excess of his expression beyond himself and return from this, else God would hold something back from us and therefore would not, of his very nature, be entirely generous. Aquinas already insisted that God is more, not less, omnipotent in his capacity to share everything to the maximum possible degree, including being itself, which means that God paradoxically gives creatures a share in existentiality, which is itself the power of "self-standing." It is on this basis that God can further paradoxically share with spirits the power of spontaneous free intellection. Eckhart simply takes this perspective to its logical conclusion: nothing that God internally gives does he externally withhold, since one gives reflexively to oneself only by ecstatically risking all one's resources. Only through such outgoing can one of oneself existentially increase. As Chesterton taught, every finite act is a kind of limiting self-sacrifice.[147] In the divine case, God's infinite self-limiting is inherently paradoxical and is like a kind of sacrifice that forgoes nothing through choice, since it is the choice of everything, yet still forgoes this nothing because it leaves behind its null security[148] to take the risk of everything: that everything which, as Chesterton so acutely realized, is still in a way like "one country with its own flag," since if we cannot choose the country of our birth, it is all the more the case that we cannot choose the structured everything that is divinely ordained being.[149] This absurd, ineluctable loyalty is, all the same, the most imperative loyalty, since we cannot defect from it and yet—by a further impossibility—we nonetheless try to. And this endeavor is evil itself—but we will come to that matter presently.

But God's infinite self-loyalty is his continual commitment to giving all away. Traditional Trinitarian doctrine contrasted infinite generation with finite creation. Modern theology and philosophy, grounded in late scholasticism, has either, in its conservative version, accentuated our finitude in terms of an impassable "transcendental" boundary (Kant), or usurped infinity for the finite world itself (Spinoza and then Hegel, in a different version of the same thing). But in Eriugena, Eckhart, and Cusanus, we catch a glimpse of a road not yet taken: a radicalization of Trinitarian orthodoxy, which is still more faithful to this orthodoxy. Certainly it is true that Christianity, like Judaism and Islam, posits a God who is transcendent to the cosmos in a way that even Platonism only dimly intimated.[150] This God is no longer the highest aspect of a whole, but inconceivably beyond any whole. To say this, however, is immediately to invoke aporia: the God entirely beyond the totality cannot be merely other to this totality; as hyper-other he must also be "not-other," as Nicholas of Cusa put it.[151] The God who is the giving source of everything must be the inner reality of everything—more each thing than each thing is itself: more stone in the stone than the stone, and more man in the man than the man, as Eckhart realized (following Augustine and Aquinas).[152] Since God is simple, one can even dare to say that in a sense he is no "more" than a stone that we see by the wayside in its verity, which itself is no less eloquent according to Eckhart than a speaking human being—even though the true stone is the comprehended stone, and the stone cannot (at least fully) comprehend itself.

Along the lines of such considerations, an "alternative Trinitarian modernity" would affirm that there is an infinite God in his replete immanence, and yet that there is also an infinite finitude—a boundless mystery within and beyond things which denies any possibility of projecting à la Kant just how far our knowledge may extend. If it does not (for an act of faith, as Jacobi suggested against Kant) extend participatively to the simple infinite, then nothing finite can be known either. The indefiniteness of finite things "fades out" (as Pascal taught, beyond Descartes) to an actual infinity in which things are divinely themselves, beyond themselves. But inversely, as Maximus the Confessor already suggested, God from his uttermost depths is the God who points all the way back to the reality of the stone by the wayside and the man making his joyful or weary way along the way itself.[153]

From all this one can see indeed how Hegel and Žižek are "nearly" right. Yet this proximity is also a chasm: it turns the images in the mirror that is the world into freestanding images, so shattering the mirror, or pretending to deny that the world is ontologically self-giving or phenomenal and "reflecting back to us" all the way down, even if we can never see into these depths. But the lonely mirror of the world remains a mirror, and only a partial mirror, which still, on pain of sterile and meaningless self-reference, sees itself through conscious spirit as reflecting an infinite source of creation that is nonetheless self-constituted in the very act of creation (or of self-imaging in the mirror). Because it is aware that the source is mysteriously exhausted in its giving of the creature, and yet that this creaturehood is partial, it also intimates an "infinite mirror" which is the divine *Logos*. Paradox alone sustains both God and the reality of the world, so permitting us to search and hope for a meaningful world.

At the center of the paradoxical link between Trinity and Creation, as we have seen, stands the notion that the self-remaining is also that which ecstatically goes forth. This is perhaps stressed better by Eckhart than by any other Christian theologian, and Žižek indeed sees the importance of Eckhart's consistent emphasis that the Christian God is the God who gives birth. At the same time, he follows Rainer Schürmann in arguing that Eckhart is in the end somewhat (for Žižek, too) "Buddhistic," since he speaks of a "ground" of deity that lies beyond the Trinitarian persons. However, this is to ignore the details of Eckhart's statements, as more careful exegetes like Alain de Libera are aware.[154] For Eckhart says that the simple ground is beyond *both* the persons *and* the essence: "this light [the 'spark in the soul'] is not content with the divine nature's generative or fruitful qualities . . . this same light is not content with the simple divine essence [*götlich wesen*] in its repose, as it neither gives nor receives, but it wants to know the source of this essence, it wants to go into the simple ground, into the quiet desert, into which distinction never gazed, not the Father, nor the Son, nor the Holy Spirit. In the innermost part . . . there it is more inward than it can be to itself, for this ground is a simple silence and by this immovability all things are moved, all life is received by those who in themselves have rational being."[155] Once more, this is only to radicalize what one can already find in Thomas Aquinas, who declared that the distinction of persons and essence is only a matter of our mode of signification, since God is absolutely one and simple.[156] Eckhart is therefore speaking of the way in which we can mystically experience the transcendental simple unity of God, which we cannot rationally think. And in the passage just quoted, he continues to maintain that the most still and unmoving is also the most hypergenerative, just as he also explains that transcendental unity is "difference beyond difference," hyperbolic difference which does not inhibit but enables difference: "the difference comes from the oneness, that is, the difference in the Trinity. The oneness is the difference and the difference is the oneness. The greater the difference, the greater the unity, because this is difference beyond difference. Even if there were a thousand persons, there would be nothing but oneness."[157] Elsewhere he explicitly affirms that God in his very ground is the God who gives birth—implying that the *arche* of the Father is in one sense this ground: "for whatever is in God moves him to beget; indeed from His ground, from His being and His nature the Father is moved to beget."[158] Eckhart remains in this way true to the ontological implications of the linguistic *triplex via* of Dionysius the Areopagite and Aquinas: attributively or eminently speaking, God is absolutely personal, and is perfected essence; negatively speaking he is neither, but "causally" or "mystically" speaking, beyond both he is a hypereminent generative unity.[159]

Now there is a concealed but crucial reason why it is convenient for Žižek to deny that "birth" is ultimate for Eckhart. For it permits him to intimate that this cannot really be a Catholic thought, and is only really available to the seventeenth-century Protestant artisan and heresiarch Jacob Boehme. I have tried to show, to the contrary, how the ultimacy of birth can be thought through paradoxically—as the coincidence of giver and recipient in the case of generation and creation, and the coincidence of infinite and finite in the case of the Incarnation. However, since Žižek wishes to argue that it can be thought through only dialectically, he favors essentially gnostic thinkers (Boehme, Hegel, and Schelling) for whom birth implies alienation and the involvement of evil, thinkers for whom birth must be painful, through ontological circumstance and not mere ontological lapse. But it is just such metaphysical misogyny which Catholic orthodoxy alone has always challenged—and Eckhart notably argued (beyond the Patristic perspective) that the later emergence of Eve's from Adam's side was not a sign of secondary inequality but, rather, mirrored the equal birth of the Son from the Father in the Trinity: "[The Just] live eternally with God [or at the home of God, Bî gote] not beneath or above. They perform all their works with God, and God with them. Saint John says, 'The Word was with God.' It was wholly equal, and it was close beside, not beneath there or above there, but just equal. When God made man, he made woman from man's side, so that she might be equal to him. He did not make her out of man's head or his feet, so that she would be neither woman nor man for him, but so that she might be equal. So should the just soul be equal with God and close beside God, equal beside him, not beneath or above."[160]

Since birth is now infinite and painless, and also male as well as female, the female human body destined physically to give birth is raised to equality and to eschatological hope of birth without painful trauma. This is also the hope of equality with the divine source, and so of justice, an infinitely full receiving of the good in an abiding plenitude before and for us (who are the redeemed from a contingent lapse), again beyond trauma.

In Boehme, the theses that creation is alienation and that evil has its origin in God belong together. Once Luther had expelled any notion of erotic, preferential love from his thoroughly unbiblical account of Agape, Eros could return within Protestantism only in a dark guise.[161] Hence the relational connection of Father and Son is seen by Boehme in terms of agonistic tension, of an unbearable burning. Originally there was the Paternal freedom of the nothing, which is now something like a pure original void, completely unlike Eckhart's productive nullity of knowing and desiring. So that when a will (somehow) arises in Boehme's void, it emerges as a hunger of unappeasable desire for something other than itself, a desire that is already inherently a tragic lack, as for Lacan. The will seeking to find something in the nothing finds only nothing, and so is driven to manifest something out of itself as will, which is at once the Son and "nature," or the external creation. The purity of Agape is attained (echoing themes of the Lurianic Kabbala) only through a further movement of withdrawal of the Paternal through the clarified light and pure love of the Holy Spirit, back into the freedom and stillness of its original being.[162] The external creation reflects both the evil of filial burning and the spiritual desire for return to original void purity—and this is manifest in the double violence and harmony of chemical, biological, and meteorological processes, which Boehme describes in terms of a Hermetic and alchemical vocabulary.[163] The process whereby the Son endures and finally exceeds in the Spirit the Paternal wrath is both manifested and accomplished in the Incarnation and Crucifixion.

Through all this heterodoxy runs the simple thought that light derives from fire—thus by analogy the clarity of Agape can emerge only by resisting the wrath of Eros.[164] It should be noted that this schema is in fact modified by Schelling—who sees God as always refusing evil as the mere possibility of rejection latent in the divine ground—and much more followed through in its implications by Hegel, who indeed renders the Creation an alienated "fall."[165]

What lies behind this strange preference of one strand of modern thought for gnosticism—all the way from Boehme to Žižek?[166] Why is creation now thought of as in itself a fall—albeit a fall that is already curative of an original divine evil?[167] One reason, as Cyril O'Regan suggests, is that already in Boehme, for all the Hermetic dress, there is a new modern drive to theological explanation clearly present. In this sense also, besides the ontologizing of the agonistic, Boehme is gnostic, but his exaggeration, after Luria, of gnostic tropes—pushing the origin of evil right back into the original Godhead itself, whereas for Valentinus and other early Christian gnostics, this was always reserved—has to do with a kind of *rationalizing of gnosis*, whereby the known "secrets" of theosophy get more and more explicitly expounded.[168] Boehme wants to fully account for both diverse manifestation beyond the original One and the reality of evil. He concludes that the fullest explanation of the former can be given in terms of the latter—because he supposedly discovers "objective" reasons for evil as fundamentally struggle, and he explains manifestation in terms of this conflict.[169] (This is why his work fully belongs to the century of the "New Science" and of Thomas Hobbes, and is anything but a quaint archaism.) By comparison, as O'Regan rightly says, neoplatonism, Eriugena, and Eckhart spoke of manifestation in terms of the superabundance of good, and this is really not to theoretically explain manifestation or the ground of manifestation in God, but rather to narrate a process of giving, grounded in unfathomable mystery.[170] However, if evil is now thought to be accountable for, then that notion itself derives from a more general modern shift toward the possibility of theodicy and the felt need for such an idiom. Theodicy is a specifically modern project, mostly unknown to the Middle Ages—hard as this may be for us to believe, this period knew of no "problem of evil." For that epoch, as for the earlier Patristic one, evil was the "impossible" denial of one's loyalty to the all, to being as such. It was an act of privation and of self-deprivation—a matter of trying absurdly to be less than one really is. Evil therefore had no ontological status, and in consequence did not need to be explained. It was the irrational, by definition inexplicable, since less than the real, which is convertible with the rational.[171] The new outlook of theodicy, by contrast, was boosted by univocal ontologies in the wake of Duns Scotus. In the era when being remained analogical, then a thing could be held to possess different intensities of existence. Existence was not, as yet, defined (after Scotus) merely by double negation as "that which is not nothing"—a circumstance which illustrates the proximity of dialectics to univocity. To exist in a lesser fashion—as stones, plants, humans, and angels all do, according to Aquinas—can still be to exist in a proper fashion, to the proper degree. But the participatory framework also allows for the "impossible possibility" that a creature may perversely lack even the degree of being which it is supposed to possess. Hence the thesis that evil is privation, an absence which distorts the positive, is naturally linked to the analogia entis.

But in terms of a univocal ontology, to say that evil in a certain sense "is not," seems to run foul of its presumptive existential either/or. If evil is a reality, on the univocal view, then it becomes natural to see it as a positive reality—for example, as an act that infringes the divine law, but has of itself a specific determinate content. This is like seeing robbery, for example, as merely anarchic, without reflecting, like Chesterton, that the robber in fact seeks his own, albeit improper, share in moneyed order. But to take the more traditional, privation view of evil is to recognize, with Chesterton, that if anyone at all is to be locked up for public safety (apart from those who threaten our lives and bodies, or else themselves), it should surely be dangerously naive atheists like Richard Dawkins and Christopher Hitchens, not mere criminals, since the latter are not questioning the sources of order and nobility as such, and often can proffer the plea of poverty or emotional abuse.[172]

Žižek considers that Chesterton could not take the further step of seeing all law as itself the supreme (but necessary) crime. However, Chesterton was well able to see the criminality of much of modern law as protective of economic injustice and excessive central power—he was simply defending the popular belief as upheld even by most criminals that there is "order as such," which marks the difference, as Rowan Williams has recently suggested, between political critique that is nihilistic and political critique that can become newly constructive.[173] Žižek's denial of this would ensure that, after all, the elitist nihilist should get off scot-free, while the pathetic small-time criminal is (as Kant, the theorist of positive "radical evil," indeed taught) *absolutely* guilty, since his crime is not slightly to mistake the good, but entirely to negate, through a counterpositive deed, the "right" of political law which is backed by the moral law. Hence Žižek fails to see that in demanding a "further extreme" from Chesterton, he does not really agree with him at all; he is *not*, like the populist Catholic Edwardian, humanistically on the side of the sad little defaulting man, since to be on his side demands acceptance of the privation theory of evil.

And if law as such (the very idea of law, "eternal" and "natural" law) is also crime, then wherein lies the good for Žižek? Not in an order beyond order, the New Testament counterlaw of love, but rather in the self-legislating of the free subject which commands only freedom. This may indeed result in the consensus of all to sustain the freedom of each by respecting the freedom of all, but this—as Lacan recognized, and Žižek agrees—is indistinguishable from the free will of all to bind all, to limit all, including a binding and limiting of oneself. Not de Sade *against* Kant, as an equally possible logic of Enlightenment autonomy, but Kant as *also* de Sade, as Žižek rightly concludes. So what Žižek appears to be saying (and this is consonant with the entire structure of his thought) is that all law must be crime, because an arbitrary collective self-binding belongs to the ethical sphere as such, just as evil is part of the dialectic of divine goodness. But, as much as postmodernism, this confines us to aporia without hope of real political change. By contrast, the Catholic privation theory of evil offers hope because it sustains belief in a hidden absolute order "beyond and against order."

If evil is a positive reality within finite being, then one theoretical option is to trace it back to God himself, and this is just what was undertaken by Boehme. But it should be crystal-clear from the above analysis that this move does not represent, as Žižek suggests, simply a further progressive unveiling of the implications of Trinitarian belief. To the contrary, it represents a loss of the

Trinitarian sense that God is paradoxically a self-giving, and that divine love is as much peaceful erotic exchange as it is one-way agapeic donation. We are dealing here with drastically different theological conceptions, not with a situation where there is an evolution to a clearer grasp of the Christian "essence."

It is for this reason that one cannot see Hegel, the legatee of Boehme, as enunciating the best possible account of the logic of Christian belief. On the contrary, it is clear that it is a heterodox account which actually *ignores* the possibility of a radicalization of orthodoxy. It also represents something *far more conservative* than this possibility, because it presents the tragedy of the liberal and politically economic compromise as the best possible human reality. Since Hegel was unable to think the double glory of the paradoxical, his stage of "reflection," in which the human mind entertains the idea both of the divine source and of that which this source posits, can only for him result in a skeptical suspicion of the phenomenal world whose existence, by determining the source which is being / nothingness, also gnostically betrays it and conceals it, thereby ensuring that real finite being is also "illusory being." Yet this is *not*, as certain "soft" readings of Hegel suppose, a matter of mere cognitive illusion. To the contrary: several passages make it clear that philosophical skepticism authentically corresponds to the "illusory" character of dialectical contradiction itself. The process of real "becoming" (which is all that there is for Hegel) is the outworking of the initial contradiction according to which abstract original (because univocal) being is identical with its opposite, which is nothing. Thus in becoming, one thing succeeds another, because the existence of a particular thing always dissolves into its inherent nothingness, which in turn must assert its "being" by engendering another particular existence, and so forth. Yet if contradiction is the motive force of real becoming, it remains—for the strictly *rationalist and nonparadoxical Hegel*—all the same a violation of the logic of identity, and so, in a sense, illusory—even though this illusion is really existent, rather like the way in which capitalism and the State are fictions right down to the bottom of their actual reality. What we have here is a kind of *parody* ("counterfeit," as Desmond says) of the orthodox Catholic idea that Creation really exists even though it is impossible. Paradox affirms the full reality of the impossible and the contradictory, whereas dialectics declares that an existing contradiction, because it is a contradiction, must be destroyed even though it exists. Dialectics is like a civic bureaucrat who says that a bizarre building put up in the town without permission cannot really be there at all because it stands upright without legal warrant, and therefore must be discreetly pulled down at dead of night, to ensure that a bright dawn will reveal that it had only ever appeared to be there, on an earlier day of mists and mirages.

In the final Hegelian unraveling of contradiction, what remains is univocal formal absence alongside substantive equivocal differences—a purer positing that is but a self-positing of the posited, as he indicates. This final abolition of mediation bypasses the (non-)possibility of paradox, and travesties the Christian legacy. So it was not Kierkegaard but, rather, Hegel who left *either/or* as the last word. Certainly Kierkegaard believed that the subjective election of paradox is the nondialectical choice which we should make for both faith and reason: *either* this choice, or the choice of nihilism, including the choice of dialectics. But what one properly chooses here is the authentic *both-and* of his paradoxical logic, for which utter sacrificial abandonment of everything whatsoever is also "absurd" return—given that, as with Eckhart, we give up all for the sake of the inexhaustible giver. (Lacan and Žižek seek to preserve only the abandonment without the return—thereby perverting the meanings of Claudel in *L'otage* and Evelyn Waugh in *Brideshead Revisited*, besides that of Kierkegaard in *Fear and Trembling*.)

I have already considered the paradoxical status of Creation to some degree. But what is most crucial here is the recognition that this paradox is that of a pure gift. The purest gift gives the recipient herself to herself. This is completely realized only with the idea of creation *ex nihilo*, which ensures that finite existence is gift without remainder, gift without contrast to something other than gift. Univocalist and voluntarist renderings of this doctrine, by trying to rid it of supposedly alien Greek traces of ideas of participation and emanation, ironically end up by putting forward a new variant of pagan dualism. For if finite being fully is (since it is not nothing) on its own account, without *methexis*, then even though it is fully caused by God, its existence, formally speaking, is not created by God, but preexists God as an a priori possibility. For Augustine and Aquinas, by contrast, finite being was possible even in its very existence, only through a participation in infinite actuality. The newer view instead grants a certain independent receptive status to the creature, such that, as the possibility of finite existence, fully comprehensible as to its makeup in its own terms without reference to God (according to Duns Scotus) it, as it were, receives from God simply an efficiently causal bringing of this possibility into existence. Its actual existence then accrues to it as something belonging to it in its own right once "handed over." As nonparticipative it does not continue to be held as a gift and held on trust as a gift.[174]

This permits later scholasticism to conclude that what belongs to the purely natural order belongs to it by necessity or external decree or a combination of both, whereas what belongs to the order of grace is received by or attributed to human creatures purely gratuitously and extrinsically.[175] The assumption now is that "gift requires a contrast" because it is implicitly assumed that for a gift to be received, the recipient must stand on an autonomous basis that does not depend upon any generosity—thus in the instance of the Creation, univocal self-standing of finite being permits a possessive appropriation of the initial gift of creation, which then allows the human creature to receive grace as a gift which she does not really need according to nature. Not accidentally, the assumed model here is of the property owner as the one who can alone receive gifts, because he already has all that he needs. The landless pauper, by contrast, can only receive "charity," now reduced to modern "benevolence," which is but the pseudo-gift of the guilty trying to render a belated justice in meager form under the guise of a dutiful generosity. Applied theologically, this gives us the notion that all human creatures are replete as regards nature, yet like indigent paupers as regards grace—since while the divine gift is "not needed" by nature, it is needed according to an inscrutable supernatural justice. Divine charity is now therefore reduced to something which "justifies," in an extrinsic, imputed sense (whether we are talking about the Reformation or much of the Counter-Reformation), in such a way as to present God as being at once a benefactor to which we are beholden and yet also a landlord who must grudgingly "render justice" to the evicted.

The older, participatory theological metaphysic was by contrast based implicitly on the idea that gift can be original, "without contrast." Here it is necessary, for a radicalized orthodoxy, to try to enter into the collapsed density of Catholic logic, and to see several things at once in panscopic vision, which are normally kept separate. The idea of the Trinity ensures that God is pure giver, pure gift, and pure renewal of gift, without remainder. The notion implied here of personhood and pure gift as substantive relation involves a kind of degree maximum of participation. God the Father shares himself entirely, beyond sharing. As the great seventeenth-century French theologian (who stood in certain ways in an Eckhartian lineage) Cardinal Pierre de Bérulle put it, the Son is *entirely independent*, like the Father, and so, by implication, *of the Father*, precisely because of substantive relationality.[176] For if the Son is only a derivation from the Father, who is in turn only the deriving of the Son, then the Son in no way depends upon him. In this way substantive relationality thinks paradoxically beyond the opposites of autonomy and heteronomy, while showing how both notions presuppose a kind of latent struggle for ontological terrain which Trinitarian doctrine refuses. As Jean-Luc Marion astutely comments, Bérulle has here seen that the idea of emanation gives us the notion of a productivity without dependence[177]—and it is surely for just this reason that the neoplatonists sometimes described emanation as *dosis*, gift. What "goes forth" from itself gives itself, and so, in providing rather than "causing," actually sets free in relation to a source, even while sharing something which remains the source—just as we can render a gift our own *as gift* only if it conserves for us the memorial of the giver.

Hence while creation does not involve the absolute degrees of both receptivity and initiatory autonomy which are exemplified by the *Logos* within the Trinity, it still involves in some measure an autonomy that is engendered precisely through heteronomous receptivity, and so sustains in due measure the same Trinitarian paradox. Creation can exist as "self-sustaining" only because God gives everything to finitude insofar as finitude can receive it. The finite, like the Son and the Spirit, is only emanated participation, because this is a strict implication of creation *ex nihilo*—any denial of this denies also the omnipotence and omnipresence of God. But emanated participation is also absolute relationality—not reversible absolute relationality, as within the Trinity, but asymmetrical absolute relationality, in which God is not "really related" to his creation (as Aquinas says) but the creation is only its relatedness to God, its creative source, in its very independence from God and even its native capacity for spontaneity.

Such participation or asymmetrical absolute relationality is also pure, since the creature is only a "share" of the divine being. This share is not, however, a real part, but, as Aquinas says, a "quasi-part," since the share here is an independent mirrored copy, and yet the image in the created mirror is entirely given by God, who gives freestanding being itself.[178] The model of gift is extremely apt here, since a genuine giver gives something of himself, and yet something that he "has" only in the act of giving. The true giver, therefore, both causes to participate and establishes a relationship which is initially asymmetrical. In the case of God it remains absolutely so, and yet by this very circumstance it is paradoxically the case that the recipient, dependent even for her very self upon the giver, must be in herself all gratitude without remainder, on pain of ceasing to be, and therefore makes a ceaseless return to the giver (which he nonetheless does not "need"—because this return is only the return that he makes to himself) to the maximum degree conceivable. In giving a gift to something which is that gift, God ensures that the most fundamental property of the creature is latently reflexive—only the giving of this gift to oneself establishes any substance. This does indeed mean (so that Hegel is half-right here) that the Christian paradigm for substance is the self-reflective subject, and therefore that the created gift can be fully given only to spirits who thereby mediate the divine gift to inert things and govern the whole created order—whether we are speaking of angels, the world soul, or human beings. The cosmos, since it exists only as gratitude, must render its return to God as a conscious return. Therefore spiritual creatures crown the creation not by arbitrary *fiat*, but as a necessary part of the logical (paradoxically logical) structure of creation itself.[179]

So as created gifts, creatures also render the return of gratitude. Yet since they are entirely gift, entirely a sharing, entirely an asymmetrical relation, this gratitude is also given to them by God. Although it is consequent upon the initial gift from the finite point of view, from the infinite, divine point of view, the reverse applies. Creatures are given to be in order to return to God, in order to return to God through gratitude. Herein lies the greater glory. And if the paradoxical double glory of God is that creatures are also glorified, also justified, then the paradoxical double glory of the creation is that it is not only glorious in its own beauty, but all the more glorious as glorifying its maker. This means that it is less the case that the deification of human beings gratuitously ensues upon the first gift of creation than that the gift of creation exists only for, and exists only in, and through, the spiritual return to God made through the liturgical praise of God, the finite act of gratitude.

The traditional participatory view (as summed up in Aquinas) understood that, if creatures are not self-standing, then there is nothing complete and autonomous in finite nature, including especially human nature, which is unaware of its origin. To be grateful for one's creation is to long to know and to be united with the source of this creation, not merely to exercise a polite rational curiosity about where one came from, as baroque scholasticism had it. In this way, the creature of his very nature paradoxically longs for and somehow intimates what he cannot know by nature and cannot even intimate by nature alone—namely, his supernatural raising to the vision of God and the status of participated sonship. The created human creature strives to be completed by an end which she can receive only as a further gift. But after this "natural orientation to the supernatural" was half called into question by Scotism and nominalism, its defense by thinkers like Eckhart, Pico della Mirandola, Cusanus, and later Pierre Bérulle, tended to radicalize the entire notion.[180]

In the case of Eckhart, any separation of nature and grace, reason and faith, the Bible and metaphysics, Christ and reason, is more explicitly avoided than in the earlier case of Aquinas, and this is surely significant. As with the more orthodox of the Renaissance thinkers later on, this is not the mark of his rationalization of faith, nor of his relative indifference to revealed specificity, but rather of his attempt to recover an older integralism by intensifying it. Hence Eckhart carries the Thomist vision of analogy and the natural orientation to the supernatural to a new excess of paradox: creation exists as "first grace" only through the further gratuitously given impulse of "second grace," whereby the whole cosmos (as for Maximus the Confessor) returns to God in a process that is consummated only through human deification. Thus Eckhart declares that "in the work of nature and creation the work of recreation and grace shine out."[181]

And for all Eckhart's intellectualism, which he shares with the Rhineland mystical-scholastic tradition, from Albert the Great onward, and for all the derivation of his radical doctrine of the *imago dei* from Dietrich of Freibourg within this tradition, it is clear that other radical elements in his thinking derive less from this perspective than from a drastic thinking through of Aquinas's metaphysics. This is shown by the fact that, whereas Dietrich adopted an Averroistic position which denied any real distinction between being and essence, so effectively seeing existence as entailed by essential definition, Eckhart followed Aquinas's version of the Avicennian distinction between the two, which sees essence as being in potential to the "higher form" of being. He added to this a distinction and noncoincidence in finite creatures between being and intelligence, which ensures that the nonintellectual being of human creatures cannot simply be regarded as de facto subordinate, even if it is so de jure.[182] Accordingly, there are hints in Eckhart that, like Aquinas (and, indeed, Augustine as opposed to "Augustinians"), he still thinks that the human intelligence can achieve reflexivity only via the detour of sensory understanding, whereas this view was rejected by the far more Plotinian Dietrich.[183] It is the latter, and not Eckhart, who would seem to be the grandfather of the German idealists, and indeed of Heidegger, who does not in reality depart far from their assumptions.

Eckhart's radicalism is, in a fundamental respect, more in continuity with Aquinas than with Dietrich's intellectualism, because it depends upon the view that all finite existence really derives participatively from God. Possibly in the face of a Franciscan favoring of univocity, the Rhineland Dominican insisted that primordial, univocal being belongs to divine infinite being alone, not, as with Duns Scotus, to both infinite and finite, although in a secondary sense it can also be found within certain patterns of consistency and preestablished relationship in the finite which underlie and allow causality of all kinds to operate—he cites the mutual ordering between form and matter, and agent and passive recipient, which ensures an overwhelming dominance of the communication of like to like. (As in the case of Desmond, Eckhart allows for "regional univocity.") In particular, Eckhart argues that the Trinitarian relations exceed relations of mere causal dependence because the divine being is univocal, and all true causal relations are hierarchical and analogical.[184] Thereby he outmaneuvered Scotus by strictly lining up the Franciscan's preferred concept for distinguishing God, namely infinity, with the preferred Thomist marks of recognition, namely *esse ipsum* and simplicity—though one might well ask here whether Eckhart's paradoxical account of the Trinity should not qualify what univocity means, when seen in infinite terms, with the idea of infinitely perfect image as a kind of hyperbolic analogical exactitude.

If an admitted primacy for the univocal now lies in the infinite, then finite being as hierarchically causal, analogical being can in fact be seen as still more strictly dependent and, in fact, as paradoxically borrowed from God, in whose possession it always really remains.[185] However, Eckhart also states that when we are justified by Christ, we become one with divine justice in a univocal sense.[186] This, though, is not a Scotist univocity between the infinite and the finite, but a univocity which results from our absolute conjoining to the infinite through grace.

One can certainly say that, for Eckhart, a finite thing equally is and is not, and inversely that God, as Eckhart already declares, is "the negation of negation"— in a sense he is more truly nothing than the nothingness of the *ex nihilo*. God must be understood in these terms because he is "One," a term which, while it does not qualify "Being" in the way that the transcendentals "True" and "Good" do, is not only, for this reason, closer to being, but also "the purity and core and height" of being, insofar as any relative nonbeing entails negation and thereby diversity, and therefore being, in refusing any such negation, can be understood at its "height" to be the negation of negation which is transcendental unity. Being, in knowing no exception to itself, knows no diversity; therefore it is Unity, and it is Unity which holds Being to be Being rather than vice versa, even though Unity "adds nothing" to Being and is not therefore "beyond being" in a neoplatonic sense.[187]

But this is not really a turn away from analogy to dialectics, as we have already seen. For in maintaining a certain conjunction of being and nullity both for creatures and for God, Eckhart is accentuating the paradox of coinciding opposition that was always latent in the notion of analogy which recognizes a phase "between" identity and difference, yet not as something which could be shared out, section by section, between the univocal and the equivocal. Hence, in speaking mainly of the "vertical" analogy between God and creatures, Eckhart claims not merely that the pivotal exemplary pole of analogical comparison is in God, but also that all the true ontological "modes" of finite things which are remotely like this pole are in God also, and that here, moreover, they are all ineffably equal with each other: relation at one with substance, the gnat at one with the soul.[188] Yet it is possible to find near-equivalents of these statements in Aquinas, as we have already seen. The logic of the angelic doctor's own account of divine naming requires that God is "more like" creatures than they are like themselves, and therefore that they of themselves contribute nothing whatsoever to their own ontological identity.[189] If God is nonetheless, as both Aquinas and Eckhart agree, infinitely more unlike creatures than he is like them, then this dimension arises because eminence is always negatively qualified "hypereminence" (see note 159 above).

Eckhart merely brings the analogical tradition of the Dionysian triplex via to its implied paradoxical conclusion by asserting that the modes of the things said to be "like" God lie in God as esse, and yet that God as openly receptive and generative intellectus is a "nullity" that exceeds all our affirmations.

In one sense this affirms an "acosmism." Yet as we have already seen, this is equally balanced by a "pantheism" allowed for by the ultimacy of the principle of inner divine birth. Between the two poles lies no dialectical shuttle of mutual abolition, but rather a positive paradoxical tension wherein the "pantheistic" is always the "acosmic" and vice versa. A natality that is neither infanticidal nor parricidal governs this para-ontology, refusing the tragic principle of intergenerational hatred unto death (the theme of much, if not most, tragic drama—King Lear, The Seagull, and so forth). The ruling principle of this philosophy or theology, which is derived directly from the Thomist real distinction, is the paradoxical "superaddition of the most inward and essential," in continuity with the ideas of the neoplatonist Proclus, who proclaimed (in passages cited by Thomas) that the highest cause always works within things "more inwardly" than lower causes.[190] Thus the *esse* of God gives existence to everything and is the existence of everything, even though "existence" is the enigma most proper to each separate reality. Again following Aquinas, but with more accentuated paradox, Eckhart sees this principle as operating also within ontic reality, and also in terms of the logic of supervening grace.

Accordingly, Eckhart declares (implicitly against the Avicennian tradition and Duns Scotus) that within ontic reality the entire substantive reality of the matter/form compound derives from the higher reality which is form, such that matter is not a kind of "quasi-form" which could potentially exist on its own, *propter potentia absoluta dei*. Similarly, within any substance, its unity, coherence, and holding-together derive entirely from the whole and in nowise from the parts. The latter are parts at all only by "participating" in the whole. This means that the form of even a finite substance is always single, and there are no latent multiple subforms, as for Scotus, which would always permit the absolute power of God to break up the integrity of any finite substantive reality, inorganic or organic.[191] Moreover, for Eckhart both quantities and qualities are superadded to things—"a mixed body is quantified by quantity alone" and also "qualified by quality alone," such that "a white shield receives its white existence, insofar as it is white, from whiteness; it has absolutely no whiteness of itself. And insofar as it is a shield it returns nothing to whiteness itself."[192] This "insofar" is an important qualification, since Eckhart is not suggesting that there is a property of whiteness floating about in the finitely metaphysical ether. Rather, this is implicitly a participated reflex of the Trinitarian paradox: just as there is Paternal justice only in the just Son, so there is whiteness only in white things like the shield—yet this whiteness all arrives from a mysterious invisible palette that is "elsewhere," since nothing in a shield as such gives rise to whiteness, and there is nothing about whiteness that confines it to tincturing the surface of a shield.

In this manner Eckhart, in a remarkable fashion (but one that is anticipated by Aquinas), sees the principle that all existence is "borrowed" as a gift from God as distributed downward along an entire series of existences by the borrowing of forms, qualities, quantities, and wholes throughout the entire structure of finite reality: "a thing as a whole, with all its parts and properties, holds the same existence totally from its end alone as from a final cause alone, from its form as from a formal cause and from its matter passively or receptively."[193]

It is important to stress these hierarchical, antimaterialist, and "non-Darwinian" aspects of Eckhart's ontology, because they show how he cannot be easily recruited for any lineage that leads straight to the modernity which we happen to have.

It is, rather, Scotus who suggested a univocal "democracy" between infinite and finite, form and matter, whole and parts. On the other hand, as with the modern political process itself, the dethroning of the old metaphysical establishment by Scotus merely ushers in new class of more wilful hierarchs, and ensures the ontological dominance of sheer size (the infinite) and might (the power to sunder and rearrange any apparent integrity).

By contrast, Eckhart is in a way the "Red Tory" who radicalizes the old establishment itself, by elevating the divine monarch out of sight and so into kenotic proximity. And surely this (not Hegel's mystical and mystified liberalism) is what the nativity of Christ proclaims! Since all derives from a topmost source that is above any conceivable ontic height (and so deeper than any ontic depths), everything is equal in relation to this ontological summit, thereby relativizing all merely ontic degrees. In a sense, as Eckhart declares, a stone proclaims as much of God as does a man; it simply cannot articulate this. And even within the ontic degrees, the same conservative radicalism is at work: *all* the parts of a thing are equal, since all contribute to a holistic unity—our toenails as much as our hearts and brain, for example. And matter, by existing only through form, exists uniformly through this borrowed dignity, through a kind of kenosis of form which permits matter to retain her negative mystery (after Aristotle) and not to be denatured into a "quasi-form." For the latter idea, while appearing to allow matter to exist in its own right, in reality turns matter into "lesser form" and thereby idealizes it. Hence Eckhart's stricter dualistic hylomorphism is in reality *more materialist* than Scotus's pressing toward a leveling of matter with form that really tends toward a formalist monism. And surely this is the most materialist one can be? If matter is "held up" by form, which is itself held up by the divine *esse*, then one has the sacramental glorification of matter instead of the reduction of all to "mere matter" which turns out always to mean some sort of vitalist doctrine of rarefied ideal force, like Philip Pullman's "dust." Materialist materialism is simply not as materialist as theological materialism.

Eckhart, therefore, put forward a metaphysical democracy of an alternative kind to that of the Franciscans, whose ideas in this respect have also shaped modern political thinking.[194] It follows, then, that an Eckhartian political agenda would also be different from our inherited norms. Here we have only fragmentary indications from Eckhart himself. We know, however, that he refused the extreme proto-individualism of the Franciscan-inspired "spirituals" of his time, who rejected any necessity for order or hierarchy in the ecclesial or secular realms. This, one could say, was tantamount to refusing a burgeoning contractualist version of democracy, since the contract is the only thing that can distill order out of an individualist anarchy. Yet at the same time, Eckhart in effect proposed an alternative kind of democratic leveling that is linked with his mystical sense of the equality of everything in relation to God, even though an ontic inequality remains. As with the New Testament itself, this combination implies more than a merely formal or interior equality. Hence, perhaps in qualification rather than rebuttal of the Augustinian *ordo amoris* (according to which there is hierarchy in the loving imperative, based on the Gospel principle of loving most the closest, who is "the neighbor"), Eckhart suggests that, from the mystical perspective of identity with God, one should love all equally.[195] Such a principle of equal concern for all—which can only be socially realized, since it is unattainable for the isolated individual working by himself—implies a radical extension of social welfare. And this implication accords with Eckhart's double stress on the practical and on justice.

In the first case we find confirmation in the ethical register of the ultimacy of birth in Eckhart's ontology. Going "inward" to attain contemplative unity is not, for Eckhart, the final goal—as it never is, for all authentic Christian mystics.[196] To the contrary, the attainment of perfect detachment, or a kind of refusal to let contingent circumstances alter one's fundamental abiding mood of openness to God, is a way of allowing the divine love to come to constant new birth in one's soul, and so of proceeding ecstatically outward toward others. The "emptied" soul is also the fertile soul, the soul open to performing God's will as its own and so of acting creatively, which means precisely to act without egotism, although still with personal distinctness—in fact for the first time with personal distinctness (see below): "therefore, if God is to make anything in you or with you, you must beforehand have become nothing."[197]

Eckhart's stress upon "detachment" as the supreme human virtue meant that he repudiated any specific spiritual "ways" or "paths." No discipline or routine or method is ever recommended by him—and in this respect he can be sharply distinguished from the late-medieval devotees of the *imitatio Christi* and so forth. If Eckhart clearly sought to close the gap between the laity and the religious elite, then he did *not* do so in the name of a new, proudly but lightly read pious bourgeois humanist elite, because more than once he insists that the highest mystical knowledge of Christ can be attained while working at an ordinary job or enjoying oneself in an ordinary sensuous sort of way.[198]

For detachment is a practical *via negativa*. And yet Eckhart is not even recommending a negative path as *the* way, albeit a trackless one. To the contrary, he famously insisted that one was more likely to be closer to God by getting on with one's business or pleasure at the board or by the hearthside: "when people think that they are acquiring more of God in inwardness, in devotion, in sweetness and in various approaches than they do by the fireside or in the stable, you are acting just as if you took God and muffled his head up in a cloak and pushed him under a bench. Whoever is seeking God by ways is finding ways and losing God, who in ways is hidden."[199] Even detachment is not a specific counterpractice but simply an existential stance. And this stance is not for its own sake, but for the sake of creative unity with the divine Father who brings to birth infinite rational acts in the Son through the Spirit's power of love. Thus Eckhart notoriously contradicted an entire history of exegesis by suggesting that Martha had no need to envy Mary, because her "better" part was not the final, integral human role of loving service, which instead was being performed by Martha.[200]

The democratic implications are obvious. Not that there should be no more contemplative ladies and serving girls (the alternative is really what we have today—women who shop and women who work in degrading impersonal labor till they drop), but that the latter group represent the dignity of labor, which is the highest dignity of all, and therefore worthy of honor and proper reward and good treatment by others. (By contrast, the theorists of "no hierarchy in principle" always end up promoting systems in which the "lowlier" social roles are accorded no dignity *as* roles, since dignity has been alienated to the abstraction of "the individual as such," and therefore the treatment of people in such roles—cleaners, waitresses, etc.—always degenerates in reality, as has duly occurred.) And the idea of "detachment" as such also had for Eckhart a directly democratic bearing. For it is in and through detachment that we attain an attitude of "justice" which is one of equal concern for all: "thus it is that along with any perfect good 'all good things together' come from the act of giving birth. Justice is begotten and born in the just person from the Unbegotten Justice as the Son, the Father's brightness."[201]

This is not the modern fiction of such concern, as though this were really attainable for a single human being. Rather, it is the "impossible" and paradoxical adoption of the divine point of view, for since God is the infinite creator, he can genuinely identify himself with the imperative "love all," since he alone can realize this imperative. For a finite person to identify with this "impossible" imperative is tantamount to *a commitment to change in anticipation of the eschaton*. It means never being satisfied with existing practices of charity, and remaining constantly open to further helping those to whom one is close, and endlessly extending one's own circle of proximity (though not so widely that we betray those with whom we are most intimate).

In so doing we participate in the life of the Trinity, which Eckhart notably and unusually tried to explicate in terms of the paradigm of justice—as has already been discussed. The Father is abstract justice, but this is a reality only because the Son is like the realized just man. If God is just, then this is because he is internally an infinite *realization* of justice. For such "pragmatism," as we have already seen, there is no justice before it is enacted, but on the other hand justice can be enacted only because it expresses an open, infinite horizon of justice which even an infinite fulfillment does not foreclose, because this horizon is itself infinite. Hence the infinite "spirit" of justice both remains and reemerges in paradoxical excess of even the "infinitely all" of the infinitely just *logos*.

Hence to become mystically one with God is to become caught up into the infinite rhythm of detachment and fertility. Even to "see" justice, we must have already started to perform it. And yet in performing it we must continue to see it, and even to see it in excess of our performance in order that we be spurred to further realizations of the just. This is Eckhart's account of "justification by faith"—it can only be by faith, and yet it must make us really just—which is much more simply, profoundly, and consistently Catholic than most of Luther's renderings of this doctrine (even if, at his best, he came close to Eckhart's understanding of the matter). Before and beyond Luther, Eckhart had managed to bring justification center stage, but in the (genuinely Pauline) sense of real social justice, and yet at the same time in a way that insisted (more drastically than Aquinas) that we can be just only by a faithfully detached openness to receiving Christ within our souls—which must, of course, be by grace (see further below). The politics implied here is ceaselessly revisionary, but it does not make the "ontologizing" mistake of imagining that the divine perspective can be utopically put into practice all at once, or can ever be entirely displayed within finite structures.

To understand how we can read Eckhart as proffering "an alternative modernity" and "a road not taken," we need to dwell further upon the ways in which his promotion of an individual will toward equal love and justice is both like and unlike the recommendations and practices of the modernity which we actually have. I have already said that for Eckhart the imperative toward justice as equality requires a relationship with (and even an identity with) God, in a way that is not exactly true for Kant, and even less true for the way in which Kant has been read by secular thinkers. For if we simply submit to this imperative as human beings, then either it remains a merely formal regulative ideal which we can never realize, such that the consequent practical vacuum is in reality filled up with utilitarian calculations and brutal power relationships, or else one has the utopian endeavor to realize the divine imperative here on earth in the name of some human group: an attempt which will always result in a terroristic attempt to realize the impossible through infinitely detailed enforcement of an ever-expanding blueprint which must necessarily substitute for divinity.

Similar considerations apply to Eckhart's extreme statement of identity with God—according to which we can judge God, exercise power over God, and so forth, as much as the other way around.[202] Again, this is not a modern Kantian or Hegelian doctrine of human autonomy, according to which man is *substituted* for God. Rather, it is a *paradoxical* doctrine of divine-human identity which cuts both ways. We are identical with God only because God (following Augustine) is our own deepest identity. For Kant (and even Hegel in his wake) we are autonomous because the finite will is univocally equal with the infinite divine will. (This view is already established in Descartes's *Meditations*.)[203] But for Eckhart the individual human capacity to judge in one's own right is attained only through analogical and paradoxical identity with the divine infinite will, which alone is fully free because it infinitely, and therefore securely, chooses always the Good.

That human autonomy is for Eckhart also always (paradoxically) heteronomous is shown most clearly in the Christological aspect of his account of human selfhood. When I was discussing the paradoxical logic of the "superadded as the essential" in Eckhart above, I mentioned that it applied also to his account of supervening grace, as well as his account of the ontological/ontic proportion and the inner structures of the ontic (form and matter, whole and parts). This is shown most importantly in his Christology, where, in logical accordance with his embracing of the Thomist real distinction, he also espouses the (final) view of Aquinas that there is only one divine *esse* in the incarnate Son, not two existences—infinite and finite. (The latter was the position of Duns Scotus, among many others.)[204] Just as all finite existence is borrowed from God, the existence of matter is borrowed from form, the existence of the parts qua parts is borrowed from the whole, and the existence of particularized quality from quality as such (white shield from whiteness), so also Christ's human existence is entirely derived from the divine person of the *Logos* by which he is enhypostasized. And in this instance the borrowing is more than participation, but amounts to full identity: "I grant that in the man assumed by the Word there is the one personal hypostatic *esse* of the Word itself, and yet Christ was truly a man in exactly the same sense as other men." [205]

This means that Christ was a fully integral human being (the first since the Fall) only by virtue of the fact that he was a divine person, and that the goodness of divinity completely accrued by grace to his human nature. Eckhart states clearly that it is only by the extension of this grace (through ecclesial, sacramental means) to other human beings that they attain to real personhood, and to the "rebirth" of Christ within themselves, when they *abandon* their individual human personhood and themselves put on (by grace) the personhood of the divine Son: "God assumed human nature and united it with his Person. At this point human nature became God because he took on human nature and not a human being [human personhood and human *esse*]. Therefore, if you want to be this same Christ and God, abandon all that which the eternal Word did not assume. The eternal Word did not assume *a* man. Therefore, leave whatever is *a* man in you and whatever you are, and take yourself purely according to human nature. Then you are the same in the eternal Word as human nature is in him; for your human nature and his are without difference. Thus I said in Paris that in the just man is fulfilled whatever the holy scriptures and the prophets had ever said [of Christ]."[206] Hence perfect human autonomy is attained only through a sharing in the most absolute degree of heteronomy imaginable—namely, the paradoxical circumstance that the only true human being who ever lived was not in fact a human person at all, but a divine one.

Thus in Eckhart what can appear to be the substitution of man for God is in reality predicated upon a drastic substitution of God for man. This is Kierkegaardian paradox, not Hegelian dialectic, for both autonomy and heteronomy equally hold true. It also follows that, while Eckhart's talk of the birth of God in the soul can appear to have little to do with the historical Incarnation, this is far from being the case. For because this birth is always by grace, it is somewhat akin to Kierkegaard's notion of "reduplication" of Christ's life. Since, as Kierkegaard pointed out, the incarnation of God involves a paradoxical coincidence of infinite with finite, this is not a truth that can "directly" appear in nonparadoxical finite terms. So much so is this the case that, in reality, God can appear only incognito, in a kind of playful disguise. Yet clearly, were this incognito absolute (as Žižek appears to imply, since his Christ is but a stuttering madman), no recognition could take place. So even if the upshot of the Incarnation is that we now see God as fully there in ordinary life, unqualified by law, this can first *appear to view* only through an event which combines the extraordinary with the ordinary. This is exactly what Žižek fails to see. Thus Kierkegaard says that indeed miracles were necessary in order to indicate the extraordinary, and Chesterton points out how Christ is presented as behaving in a superhuman and very ethereal way in the Gospels, even though this is interwoven with sudden switches into another mode where he appears as utterly human—and even as subject to quite childish tantrums. As Chesterton—prodigiously for his time—suggested, this fits with the way the New Testament fuses the *Roman*, Latinate sense of domestic welcome and respect for childhood (and for women) with the Hebrew sense of the sublimely apocalyptic.

But Kierkegaard rightly says (echoing Augustine) that a miracle is only a sign that has to be interpreted, and therefore that it remains a merely ambiguous indication which is still "indirect," like the seemingly "direct" statement "Christ was God" itself, which inverts into indirection since it has no plain sense that we can comprehend, but rather indicates the "impossible." Every indirect statement requires interpretation; therefore for Kierkegaard we can acknowledge Christ in theory only by "reduplicating" the Incarnation in a practice which itself retains a certain indirection in its linguistic dimension. In his later recognition of this dimension of apostleship, Kierkegaard starts to see how even our pointing to Christ remains enigmatically self-referential after the habit of Christ's own discourse, and so he begins to grasp the ecclesial aspect which remained hitherto more or less denied within his thinking.[207]

The idea of the repetition of Christ in our own lives as sustaining indirection helps in the interpretation of the Eckhartian link between the Incarnation and the birth of Christ in the soul. This birth is by grace and by virtue of a sacramental transmission, and yet because of the inexpressible paradox of the Incarnation, its representation must be through a repetition that is nonidentical, and therefore also springs from the unique personality of the Christian follower, which the grace of Christ's divine personhood transmitted through his humanity allows to arise in its fullness. And this new personal manifestation of Christ itself expresses more the enigma of one's own true personality than it communicates any representable truth.

With respect to this issue of Christological redemption, Žižek is right to say that nothing like a penal substitution theory of atonement is to be found in Eckhart, but then such theories arose only from Luther onward in any case. Previous Catholic theories, including that of Anselm, never (if one reads carefully) suggested that an infinite God could receive any finite tribute, since this would have negated Christ's aseity, and pre-Reformed theology was governed by principles of metaphysical rigor.[208] Rather, they all insisted that sin, as necessarily finite by definition, locks one into finitude, and so further into structures of death and sinfulness. This can be overcome only by the entry of the infinite into the finite and the paradoxical identification of the infinite with the finite. Žižek suggests that a revelation that there is only the finite, and that this is somehow infinite, permits the finite of itself to overcome (or somewhat quixotically to overcome) evil. But traditional doctrines of the atonement held together and in tension the view that finitude must indeed extract itself from its contingent self-binding and yet that it cannot do so by definition, once it has denied its ontologically constitutive relationship to the infinite—and so also denied itself. The practical paradoxical solution to this aporia is the Incarnation, wherein the finite, through perfect action in time and through suffering perfectly its own fault by dint of personification through the infinite (by the eternal Son), at last overcomes that fault.

Eckhart indeed says little specifically regarding the atonement. But traditional theories, as just explained, saw not just the action on the Cross but the Incarnation itself as resolving the aporia of sin. Here the "perfect suffering" of the Cross is but one aspect of an entire action whereby the finite is restored to full existence in time through its paradoxical conjunction with the infinite. And it is this entire mysterious *dynamis* which is then sacramentally communicated through the Church's offices. (But already, before the Reformation, much later medieval theology tended to reduce the saving aspect of Christ's life to the action upon the Cross.) Eckhart's derivation of all proper human personality from Christ's divine personality, as just described, implies precisely a radical version of the traditional view that the Incarnation as such is an atoning work, since for Eckhart human beings can be restored to their true selves only through Christic grace.

At the same time, grace is not for Eckhart merely a contingently added topmost layer to reality. If it exemplifies the principle that the superadded is paradoxically the essential, then this is because it most of all exemplifies the following principle: as supremely unnecessary gift ("you shouldn't have . . ."), it is also the most absolutely necessary thing of all ("but in retrospect, without this, what would I have done?"). These statements hold true for Aquinas as well as for Eckhart, yet in Eckhart's case they are established with more Christological directness. As with Aquinas, humans were created for Eckhart in order to be deified; therefore creation exists for the sake of deification (which is by grace), since the higher cannot serve the lesser. In this sense, for both thinkers, grace is also cosmological, since the cosmos is created for the existence of intelligence, and it is only immanent intelligence that holds the cosmos together.[209] But for Aquinas, the Incarnation (at least in the historical form in which it occurred)[210] is an emergency remedy for sin, even if it was decreed and enacted eternally, on account of God's foreknowledge, and even if the upshot of the glory of the divine humanity far exceeds the circumstance that occasioned it. For Eckhart, on the other hand, as for Scotus, the Incarnation would have occurred even without the contingent interruption of sin. But Eckhart's reasoning to this conclusion is not Scotistic in the slightest. For the Franciscan, by an Anselmian argument, only God can offer adequate glory to God, since he refuses the paradox of deification (failing to see that there is no true Christianity without this).[211] The German Dominican, on the other hand, acknowledges that infinite glory can be given back to God through deification that achieves paradoxical identity with God, through Christ. If, unlike Aquinas, he considers that this grace would always have been the grace of Christ, even without the Fall, then this is because he thinks that even the return to God that is deification, although it can occur (ontologically, assuming there had been no Fall) without Incarnation, should not be lacking to God in his very nature, rather than as mere tribute to God, if God is, in Pauline terms, to be "all in all" and, as God, should be all in all.[212]

For this reason, in words preserved for us from his lost *quaestio* on the metaphysics of the Incarnation only by his accusers, Eckhart writes: "from the first intention the word assumed human nature, that is, this nature in Christ, for the sake of the whole human race. By assuming that nature in him and through him, he bestowed the grace of sonship on all men."[213] Sermon 5b makes it clear that our participation in the eternal birth of the Son from the Father is from all eternity by way of the descent into Mary's womb. Moreover, because the latter birth, which is an emergency measure in the face of sin, fulfills the "universal" process of incarnation which would have occurred anyway without the Fall, the Incarnation of God in Christ is identical (by grace) with the birth of the Son in the soul. Eckhart gives an example which belongs to the world of Grimm's fairy tales: "Suppose that there were a mighty king who had a fair daughter whom he gave to the son of a poor man. All who were of that man's family would be ennobled and honored by this." (The example shows that Eckhart still clearly distinguishes between birth by nature and birth by grace.) He goes on in the same sermon to declare: "that is what the text means with which I began: 'God has sent His Only-Begotten Son into the world.' You [in practical, personal terms] must not by this understand the external world in which the Son ate and drank with us, but understand it to apply to the inner world. As truly as the Father in his simple nature gives his Son birth naturally, so truly does he give him birth in the most inward parts of the spirit, and that is the inner world. Here God's ground is my ground and my ground is God's ground. Here I live from what is my own, as God lives from what is his own."[214]

One can infer from this that Eckhart's view that there would always have been an incarnation process even without the incursion of sin is tantamount to a practical resolution of the aporia of the "impossibility" of the existence of the Creation as "only God" and yet also as "not God." As we have seen, this implies that God in himself is "more than himself," and even that he is what he is not—namely, the Creation. This could well suggest a dialectical tension that needed a univocalist resolution after all. But incarnation, on Eckhart's reasoning, far from confirming dialectic, decisively rejects dialectic in favor of paradox: God is eternally within himself also what he is not, namely the finite, since at one point, which by grace is every point, the finite has been eternally conjoined to his *Logos* in terms of its character, the elusive shape of its enigma, or in other words its "personality"—which is not, after all, its own personhood, but instead that of the divine Son. In the end, according to the strict logic of a hyperbolic orthodoxy, creation, deification, and incarnation are all identical.

The Eckhartian view that the Incarnation is an eternal reality, regardless of sin, doubly confirms that the cosmos exists in its perfection (as manifesting the perfection of God as "all in all") only through "second" grace. The natural and necessary therefore exists by virtue of the supernatural and gratuitous. And in consequence, as Henri de Lubac realized, the creation is incomprehensibly paradoxical, since it is constituted by the fact that what need not be constantly outweighs and proves more essential and necessary than what must be—more necessary than necessity itself.[215]

The same view also moves still further away from any "mythological" notions, rightly despised by Žižek, that God responds to the emergency of sin by coming up with a cunning plan—the kind of theology that appeals to second-rate Anglo-Saxon athletes. For it can now be seen that evil is also a sin against the remedy against sin which is always-already there. In rejecting the absolute dependence (to echo Schleiermacher's fine phrase) of the finite upon the infinite, it also rejects the secret ("hidden from before all worlds," as the New Testament teaches) personal unification of the finite with the infinite. This ensures that evil is not simply tragic, requiring the sacrifice of the God-Man himself (in order to suffer evil perfectly, and so surpass it) but also comic—in a way that should be to Žižek's taste. It is comic because, in impossibly denying the constitutive dependence of the finite upon the infinite, it fails to see that the infinite as infinite does not exclude the finite and so, simply *as* infinite, will be bound to conjoin to itself the finite—which it can do in only *one specific instance*, else it will not have resumed the real experience of the finite, given that the finite most of all exists as conscious experience of itself. In this respect Žižek is precisely right—to be all in all God must also be, beyond even Hebraic sublime otherness, the specifically exceptional in time, thereby establishing, against the old law which is "the law of sin," the law of true human life paradoxically based upon exception to human law and upon fidelity to the criminal death of the one who first identified himself as this exception. Monotheism as such demands this—which is why both Judaism and Islam are simply not monotheistic enough and (when they do not temper their legalism with mysticism) dangerously confine God to the abstract universality of law elevated above all specific instances of the application of law. (This significantly falls foul of Eckhart's Trinitarian justice paradox as enunciated above.)

Hence even the impossible attempt to forgo the infinite has always-already been undone even in its very character of "illusory being." Since the infinite has from eternity subsumed also the finite, it does not let the finite go when the finite tries to let the infinite go. Instead, the infinite, through its personification of the finite, suffers infinitely finitude's evil illusion. In a specific place and time, of course, because there is no other way finitely to suffer, just as there is no other way for finitude to be subsumed.

Finally, this view doubly confirms that evil is merely privative. For now we can see that evil is not merely a partial concealment of the plenitude of the Good. We can also see that it is an almost complete concealment of the remedy for evil (namely, divine–human forgiveness) from the very outset.

Žižek rightly sees that for justice and truth to be possible, it was necessary that first of all one man be recognized as God. He sees this far more clearly than most contemporary theologians. However, he should further accept the full *scandalon* of the New Testament: namely, that this necessity, in its actuality, really is conjoined to the infinite in its own actuality. Exactly why? Because according to his present view, Christianity really means that all we have is "only the finite," which means "any old finite"; therefore any old vagary of the human will is justified. But on the orthodox reading, Christianity means that one specific finite moment really is of absolute infinite significance, beyond all human imaginings. In consequence, because there is "also the actual infinite," one particular finite can assume a value that it could not were it "only the finite." And then all other finites can also assume this value through "reduplication." But by this token they cease to be "any old finites," as with the non-principles of an anarchic democracy. Instead, for a more paradoxical but hopeful democracy, they assume infinite value to the hierarchical degree that they pedagogically resume the personality of Christ, differently, but analogically. This very pattern of resuming is a harmony, and therefore justice, since it repeats a life in whom has always been recognized not simply "any old finite human life" but the very pattern of justice for both time and eternity.

6. ON THE PHILOSOPHY OF HISTORY

The logic of Christianity is therefore paradoxical rather than dialectical. Analogy, paradox, real-relationality, the realist recognition of universals that are more than generalizations—all these things can be said to comprise the "metaxological." A rational metaphysical discourse that foregrounds this mode bends abstraction back toward the lifeworld, as I tried to explain in section 4. It also bends reflective language back toward the metaphorical and poetic. And it is this observation that should guide a Catholic approach to the philosophy of history, as was seen in seventeenth- and eighteenth-century Naples by the enigmatic Giambattista Vico. The prehistorical is not by Catholic thought despised (all the way from Vico to Christopher Dawson) in the way in which it tends to be by Protestant reflection (although we have seen how Schelling is an important exception to this). Instead, it is rather seen that both Christianity and a viable reason require a kind of balance between the prehistorical and the historical. For the overabstraction of reason leads to nihilism and skepticism about reason itself, leaving no basis for a genuine social consensus. This is why Joseph Ratzinger indeed does not want to defend modern scientistic reasoning, as Žižek points out—but the latter fails to reckon with the Pope's argument to the effect that pure reason, left entirely to its own resources, always destroys reason. This is why "progress" is ambiguous, and if it is inevitable, as Žižek's Protestant metanarrative assumes, then we are doomed.

But a Catholic philosophy of history, as Vico again suggested, rescues us from just that sort of essentially pagan (or gnostic) fatalism with which Hegel's account of history is still imbued—even on Žižek's reading, as I have tried to show.[216] For Vico showed how the "idolatry" of pagan religion was essentially bound up with *a too limited* version of the poetic, as compared with Hebrew "sublimity"—a Longinian insight which he shared with many contemporaries, but developed more radically. Paganism tends to be confined to certain tropes which always operate in the same way and whose mode of comparison is subject to a fully logical grasp (especially reduced metonymy and synecdoche), thereby insinuating a possible manipulation of the divine and the joint manipulation of the human and the divine by faith. Only monotheism allows, by comparison, an openly metaphorical invocation of God, which truly retains the mysterious paradoxical tension of both / and, and so invites endlessly further exploration and does not permit degeneration into the idea of capture of the divine by univocal technique which often translates into a calculus of blood. For as Chesterton suggested, where polytheistic myth was taken overseriously (where usually, as he rightly said, it was a kind of "dream," half-believed in against a background of a dimly intimated and yet more seriously true monotheism) its fatalistic and amoral plot lines tended to encourage both human sacrifice to remorseless deities (as in ancient Carthage) and practices of sinister magic.[217]

Yet neither does "the rule of metaphor" (to use Paul Ricoeur's phrase) inversely imply that outside the range of technique there is only the equivocal caprice of the deities or the inscrutable equivocation of faith. Metaphor is instead somewhat like "covenant"—a definite but open bond that binds both God and the Creation, since its mode of comparison cannot be rendered as univocal likeness. Yet abstract reason, as Vico also suggested, in a very Platonic mode, is not the enemy of the poetic but rather its ally, insofar as it is the very vagueness of the abstract concept that keeps alive the sense of metaphoric ambiguity and prevents a mere "paganism" of poetic language, which insists upon a conventional sense and order of tropical equivalents. (One can compare and contrast this with Lacan's categorization of linguistic erotics in terms of metonymy and metaphor, as discussed in section 1.)

In this way, reason as "metaxological" promotes the metaphorical. A reflective refusal of the idolatrous (accomplished in different idioms by both the prophets and by Socrates) actually encourages the more idiosyncratically creative, just as Eckhart's "detachment" permits the greater spontaneity of reason. Yet inversely, as Plato's practice shows, only the qualification of reason by myth and poetry ensures that reason will not degenerate into a pure abstraction that recognizes only univocal and equivocal (plus dialectical) truths. Vico suggested that such pure reason is another mode of paganism, since the chains of ineluctable proof which it alone celebrates (the Stoic *sorites*) are all too like the chains of dogmatic narration which sought to bind the powers of the gods.

The entire Bible, but more especially the New Testament, is, like Plato, counterprogressive insofar as it resists the advance to pure abstraction by reinvoking the poetic, yet in a nonpagan way which seeks a positive relationship to the properly vague abstraction of a nondogmatic reason (as reflected in the wisdom literature and the New Testament's post-Philonian engagement with Greek philosophy). The balance is proclaimed with the most paradoxical extremity in the idea that reason itself has become incarnate, which means that the rational is now fully accessible only by the "indirectness" of a poetic discourse concerning this event. (Kierkegaard is the most hyperrational of all Western philosophers, in realizing that reason exists, if it exists at all, only as this paradox.) Catholicity is in one sense this balance—which is also the balance between the democracy of reason on the one hand and the esoteric hierarchy of the poetic on the other. Without this balance one gets instead the hidden complicity of the apparent openness of reason with the much more hidden and impenetrable (because senseless) secrecy of wilful power.

Thus from the Catholic point of view the history of Christendom is not, as for some Protestant perspectives, the gradual distillation of a Christian essence or the recovery of an essence after backsliding. Nor is anything whatsoever about Christian history inevitable—and both Protestant and Enlightenment historiography have underestimated the "romantic" role of character, symbol, and event, especially for premodern ages which thought, and so acted, in far more concrete and psychogeographic terms.[218] Again, Chesterton pointed this out—arguing that we lack a history which would tell us, for example, the real mass-psychological reasons why the Romans won, and the Carthaginians lost, a struggle that logically should have terminated, after Hannibal's heroic endeavor, in the victory of the far more pragmatic and mercantile Carthaginians—who for Chesterton were a supreme example of a (Vichian) evolution of a sinister sacrificial paganism into a protomodern inaesthetic rationalism.[219]

Instead, for a Catholic historiography, the narrative of Christendom is the contingent story of whether or not the balance of reason with poetry has held. This balance renders reason more realistically rational as disclosing a rational though mysterious universe, and poetry more poetic as nonclassically subjective. Where it fails, therefore, both reason and imagination go equally astray. And this is exactly why, as Žižek mentions, Chesterton rightly says that the entire apparatus of the Catholic magisterium was necessary most of all for the "difficult defence of reason."[220]

But this balance cannot merely have held, here and there. Its "holding" has to be ceaselessly re-created, and once it has been challenged (more seriously from within than from without—as in the case of nominalism, which began very early, as Chesterton pointed out, in the course of stressing that the hold of Christianity has *always* been precarious, though it has also been oddly resilient),[221] then the balance has to be somewhat reconceived. The work of Eckhart in the face of univocalist and voluntarist thought is a good case in point.

For all the above reasons I reject Žižek's defense of Hegel's reading of Christianity and of Christian history. From a Catholic and radically orthodox perspective we have not passed definitively into a postmedieval fuller realization of Christianity. Instead we are still living out a "certain" Middle Ages that is univocalist, voluntarist, nominalistically equivocal, and arcanely gnostic.

It is time that we abandoned the paganism of progress and recovered a more authentic Middle Epoch—as exemplified by Eckhart's reworking of the Catholic balance in the face of a later Middle Ages that was already thoroughly modern.

But the term "middle" would then be more truly justified by the new creative holding of the balance, which is nothing other than the metaxological to-and-fro of the absolutely paradoxical.

NOTES

1.   This chapter is primarily a response to Žižek's text "The Monstrosity of Christ: A Modest Plea for the Hegelian Reading of Christianity" in the present volume, which gives perhaps the most direct summary so far of his own philosophy. Also addressed to some degree is his essay "Building Blocks for a Materialist Theology," which is chapter 2 of his book *The Parallax View* (Cambridge, MA: MIT Press, 2006).

2.   See Gillian Rose, *Hegel contra Sociology* (London: Athlone, 1981).

3.   See Gillian Rose, *Dialectic of Nihilism* (Oxford: Basil Blackwell, 1984).

4.   See William Desmond, *Being and the Between* (Albany: State University of New York Press, 1995); William Desmond, *God and the Between* (Oxford: Blackwell, 1987).

5.   Kierkegaard also criticized Luther for exalting faith at the expense of works, and insisted—in an extremely "Catholic" fashion—on the inseparability of the two.

6.   Žižek, *The Parallax View*, p. 112.

7.   See Marcel Bataillon's classic treatise *Érasme et l'Espagne: Recherches sur l'histoire spirituelle du XVIe siècle* (Paris: E. Droz, 1937).

8.   See Octavio Paz, *The Labyrinth of Solitude*, trans. Lysander Kemp et al. (New York: Grove Press, 1985); Gabriel García Márquez, *One Hundred Years of Solitude*, trans. Gregory Rabassa (London: Penguin, 2000); Malcolm Lowry, *Under the Volcano* (London: Penguin, 2000).

9.   Jacques Lacan, *On Feminine Sexuality: The Limits of Love and Knowledge (Seminar XX: Encore 1972–1973)*, trans. Bruce Fink (New York: W. W. Norton, 1998), p. 49. For a brilliant and nuanced theological critique of Lacan, see Marcus Pound, *Theology, Psychoanalysis and Trauma* (London: SCM, 2007).

10.   Lacan, *On Feminine Sexuality*, pp. 46–49.

11.   Jacques Lacan, "The Agency of the Letter in the Unconscious or Reason since Freud," in *Écrits: A Selection*, trans. Alan Sheridan (New York: W. W. Norton, 1977), pp. 146–178; *On Feminine Sexuality*, pp. 126–129.

12.   See Gilles Deleuze, *Pure Immanence: Essays on a Life*, trans. Anne Boyman (New York: Zone, 2001).

13.   See John Milbank, "The Return of Mediation, or the Ambivalence of Alain Badiou," *Angelaki* 12, no. 1 (April 2007), pp. 127–143.

14.   See Lacan, "The Mirror Stage as Formative of the Function of the I as Revealed in Psychoanalytic Experience," "The Signification of the Phallus," and "The Subversion of the Subject and the Dialectic of Desire in the Freudian Unconscious," in *Écrits: A Selection*, pp. 1–7, 281–291, 292–325.

15.   See Lacan, *On Feminine Sexuality*, passim; Žižek, "Building Blocks for a Materialist Theology."

16.   See my essay "Evil: Darkness and Silence," in *Being Reconciled: Ontology and Pardon* (London: Routledge, 2003), pp. 1–25.

17.   See Milbank, "Evil: Darkness and Silence"; Jacques Lacan, "Kant with Sade," trans. James Swenson, *October* 51 (Winter 1989); Žižek, "Building Blocks for a Materialist Theology."

18.   Žižek, "Building Blocks for a Materialist Theology."

19.   On the *ordo amoris*, see Robert Spaemann, *Happiness and Benevolence* (Notre Dame, Ind.: Notre Dame University Press, 2000), pp. 106–118.

20. See Pierre Rousselot, The Problem of Love in the Middle Ages: A Historical Contribution, trans. Alan Vincelette (Milwaukee: Marquette University Press, 2001). This work was mentioned along with other prewar discussions of love and the Western legacy by Jacques Lacan in his famous Seminar XX. See Lacan, On Feminine Sexuality, p. 75.

21. Lacan, On Feminine Sexuality, pp. 96, 128.

22. Jean-Louis Chrétien, Symbolique du corps: La tradition chrétienne du Cantique des Cantiques (Paris: Presses Universitaires de France, 2005), pp. 15–44.

23. See Michel Henry, "The Critique of the Subject," in Who Comes after the Subject?, ed. Eduardo Cadova et al. (London: Routledge, 1991), pp. 157–166.

24. Lacan, On Feminine Sexuality, p. 70.

25. On Merleau-Ponty and Aristotle, see my article "The Soul of Reciprocity," in Modern Theology, July 2001, pp. 335–391; October 2001, pp. 485–509.

26. D. H. Lawrence, The First Women in Love [earlier version] (London: One World Classics, 2007); Lady Chatterley's Lover (London: Penguin, 1961).

27. Žižek, The Parallax View, pp. 337–340.

28. I heard Žižek make this statement at Birkbeck College, London, in September 2007.

29. William Blake, Jerusalem, the Emanation of the Giant Albion, in The Complete Poems, ed. W. H. Stevenson (London: Longman, 2007), p. 712.

30. Robert Brenner, "Agrarian Class Structure and Economic Development in Pre-Industrial Europe," Past and Present, February 1976; Merchants and Revolution: Commercial Change, Political Conflict, and London's Overseas Traders 1550–1653 (London: Verso, 2003). See also Ellen Meiksins Wood, The Origins of Capitalism (London: Monthly Review Press, 1999).

31. See T. H. Aston and C. H. E. Philpin, eds., The Brenner Debate: Agrarian Class-Structure and Economic Development in Pre-Industrial England (Cambridge, UK: Cambridge University Press, 1985).

32. See R. H. Tawney, Religion and the Rise of Capitalism (Harmondsworth: Penguin, 1980); Marcel Hénaff, Le prix de la vérité: Le don, l'argent, la philosophie (Paris: Seuil, 2002), pp. 351–380.

33. Because the assumptions of philosophical materialism lie all too close to those of capitalism itself.

34. For an overall statement of "British Catholic Historical Revisionism," see the book by the Welsh Catholic Edwin Morgan, The English Nation: The Great Myth (Stroud: Sutton Publishing, 1998).

35. Žižek, The Parallax View, pp. 271–387.

36. See Frederiek Depoortere, "The End of God's Transcendence? On Incarnation in the Work of Slavoj Žižek," Modern Theology 23, no. 4 (October 2007), pp. 497–523. This is an insightful article, but it goes wrong in seeing the objet petit a as positive and associated with the drive to love rather than the desire of something as a thing.

37. Žižek, The Parallax View, pp. 337–342.

38. Desmond, Being and the Between.

39. In what follows I am putting my own gloss on Desmond's schema, to which I am nonetheless enormously indebted.

40. See Philipp W. Rosemann, Omne ens est aliquid: Introduction à la lecture du "système philosophique" de saint Thomas d'Aquin (Louvain and Paris: Éditions Peeters, 1996).

41. See Alain Badiou, *Being and Event*, trans. Oliver Feltham (London: Continuum, 2005), pp. 327–387; Alain Badiou, *Logiques des mondes: L'être et l'événement, 2* (Paris: Seuil, 2006); Peter Hallward, *Badiou: A Subject to Truth* (Minneapolis: University of Minnesota Press, 2002), pp. 293–315.

42. Badiou, *Logiques des mondes*, passim.

43. Gerard Manley Hopkins, *Poems and Prose*, ed. W. H. Gardner (Harmondsworth: Penguin, 1963), p. 21; "Duns Scotus's Oxford," p. 40; Badiou, *Logiques des mondes*, pp. 25–29.

44. See Ludger Honnefelder, *La métaphysique comme science transcendentale* (Paris: Presses Universitaires de France, 2002).

45. See Rosemann, *Omne ens es aliquid*; John Milbank and Catherine Pickstock, *Truth in Aquinas* (London: Routledge, 2001).

46. Milbank and Pickstock, *Truth in Aquinas*, p. 40.

47. Desmond, *Being and the Between*, pp. 131–175.

48. G. W. F. Hegel, *Science of Logic*, trans. A. V. Miller (New York: Prometheus, 1999), Volume One, Book One, Section One, Chapter 2, B (a) p. 119; 3, p. 120; (b) 2, p. 125: "Thus something through its own nature relates itself to the other, because otherness is posited in it as its own moment; its being-within-self includes the negation within it, by means of which alone it now has its affirmative determinate being."

49. G. W. F. Hegel, *Phenomenology of Spirit*, trans. A. V. Miller (Oxford: Oxford University Press, 1977), §92: "An actual sense-certainty is not merely this pure immediacy, but an instance of it"; and §§90–99, pp. 58–61.

50. Ibid., §96, p. 60.

51. Quoting ibid., §98, pp. 60–61.

52. Ibid., §99, p. 61.

53. Ibid.: "Pure Being remains, therefore, as the essence of this sense-certainty."

54. Hegel, *Science of Logic*, Volume One, Book One, Section One, Chapter 2, B (c)(α) p. 131, (γ) pp. 136–137. For a brilliant demonstration that such a logic informs *all* nihilisms, see Conor Cunningham, *Genealogy of Nihilism* (London: Routledge, 2002), especially on Hegel, pp. 100–131.

55. See Lawrence Dickey, *Hegel: Religion, Economics and the Politics of Spirit 1770–1807* (Cambridge: Cambridge University Press, 1989).

56. For a fine defense of this perspective, see David Bentley Hart, *The Doors of the Sea: Where Was God in the Tsunami?* (Grand Rapids: Eerdmans, 2005).

57. Gilles Deleuze, *Difference and Repetition*, trans. Paul Patton (London: Athlone, 1994), pp. 1–27.

58. Alain Badiou, *Deleuze: The Clamor of Being*, trans. Louis Burchill (Minneapolis: University of Minnesota Press, 1994), pp. 23–26, 43–44, 51–53, 58–59. But both Deleuze and Badiou are wrong to think that Heidegger viewed the Being/beings relation analogically; in reality he also (as Gillian Rose pointed out) viewed it univocally.

59. Diane Setterfield, *The Thirteenth Tale* (London: Orion, 2006).

60. Richard of St. Victor, *De Trinitate*, Book III, Chapter XV, in *Richard of St. Victor: The Twelve Patriarchs; The Mystical Ark; Book Three of the Trinity*, trans. Grover A. Zinn (New York: Paulist Press, 1979), p. 389: "as long as the second does not have a *condilectus* [someone who shares in love for a third], he lacks the sharing of excellent joy."

61. Desmond, *Being and the Between*, pp. 395–406. The talk of "disinterest" here is perhaps too extreme, along with talk of a "ruination" of the erotic self and a stress on a unilateral "going out" that is not always clearly enough also a "returning" to self, which would be the real logic of ecstasy. See also Desmond, *God and the Between*, p. 143.

62. Ibid., pp. 406–417.

63. F. W. J. Schelling, *Philosophie der Offenbarung 1841 / 42*, selected and introduced by Manfred Frank (Frankfurt am Main: Suhrkamp, 1977), XXIII–XXXV, pp. 250–325.

64. F. W. J. Schelling, *The Ages of the World*, trans. Jason M. Wirth (Albany: State University of New York Press, 2000).

65. Martin Heidegger, "Der Letzte Gott," in *Beiträge zur Philosophie (vom Ereignis)* (Frankfurt am Main: Vittorio Klostermann, 1989), pp. 405–421.

66. Hegel, *Science of Logic*, Volume One, Book One, Section One, Chapter 1, C.1, p. 84: "Becoming implies that nothing does not remain nothing but passes into its other, into being. Later, especially Christian metaphysics, while rejecting the proposition that out of nothing comes nothing, asserted a transition from nothing into being: although it understood this proposition synthetically or merely imaginatively, yet even in the most imperfect union there is contained a point in which being and nothing coincide and their disinterestedness vanishes." Hegel goes on to claim that those who stand by this traditional principle that nothing comes out of nothing are subscribing to Eleatic monism or Spinozistic pantheism, for which all becoming is really the abiding actuality of an immanent unity. But in reality Hegel is not defending but abandoning a realist understanding of *creatio ex nihilo* and only supplying an acosmic moment for his own pantheistic outlook, which, as Jacobi rightly saw, is but one more variant on Spinozism. If all immanent being is only a "preceding" nothing, then in a sense "there is only" a void God—but in a more fundamental sense this void "is" only in the succession of finite becoming. And finally, it is possible to read Spinoza as saying the same thing, and his "Absolute" as also "in itself" nothing, and so as an acosmic totality that does not exist of itself—even if it is only a Deleuzian development of Spinozism that makes this fully apparent. See Cunningham, *Genealogy of Nihilism*, pp. 59–68.

67. See John Mullarkey, *Post-Continental Philosophy: An Outline* (London: Continuum, 2006), pp. 83–156.

68. See John Milbank, *Theology and Social Theory: Beyond Secular Reason* (Oxford: Blackwell, 2006), pp. 147–176.

69. Alain Badiou, "Hegel and the Whole," in *Theoretical Writings*, trans. Ray Brassier and Alberto Toscano (London: Continuum, 2006), p. 238.

70. Hegel, *Science of Logic*, Volume Two, Section Three, Chapter 3, p. 843.

71. This is my exegesis of the concluding words of the *Science of Logic*. See ibid., pp. 843–844.

72. G. W. F. Hegel, *Hegel's Logic, Being Part One of the Encyclopaedia of the Philosophical Sciences* (1830), trans. William Wallace (Oxford: Oxford University Press, 1989), IX, §194, p. 260.

73. Ibid., §194, p. 261.

74. Ibid., §212, p. 274.

75. Ibid.

76. Ibid., §194, p. 260.

77. Ibid., §213, p. 276.

78. Ibid.

79. Hegel, *Science of Logic*, Volume Two, Section Three, Chapter 3, p. 841: "the method [of logic], which thus winds itself into a circle, cannot anticipate in a development in time that the beginning is, as such, already something derived; it is sufficient for the beginning in its immediacy that it is simple universality."

80. Hegel, *Science of Logic*, Volume Two, Section One, Chapter 1, A, p. 601.

81. Gillian Rose made much of the fact that Hegel at times described his philosophy as "speculative" rather than as "dialectical." However, he seems to have meant the latter term in the sense of the Kantian antinomies which supposedly for Kant left one in an impassable aporia, and so confined theoretical philosophy to the "critical," forbidding any full development of an ontology. Certainly Hegel envisaged by the "speculative" a coincidence of contradictory notions like the universal and the particular, but that this was not a perfect, paradoxical coincidence, but rather a dialectical one which sustained an antagonism, is clearly shown by multiple passages, some of which are discussed in my main text. Moreover, by insisting strongly on the broken, diremptive character of mediation, Rose herself emphasized the dialectical character of the speculative and, in consequence, the violence that supposedly remains at the heart of loving unity. The truth is that, in terms of a sheerly negative dialectics, Adorno is more like Hegel than he himself realized, while his compensating Jewish sense of a surplus of the real over cognition, allied to his account of a mediating nonconceptual approach to the real through "constellations" of mutually enhancing, emotionally experienced, and imagined "ideas," in reality breaks *far more* with dialectics than Rose ever did! See Gillian Rose, "From Speculative to Dialectical Thinking—Hegel and Adorno," in *Judaism and Modernity* (Oxford: Blackwell, 1993), pp. 53–63.

82. *Hegel's Logic*, §212, p. 274.

83. Hegel, *Science of Logic*, Volume Two, Section One, Chapter 1, A, pp. 602–603. See also, for the doctrine of illusory being, Volume One, Book Two, Section One, Chapter 1, pp. 394–408.

84. Ibid., p. 603.

85. See François Laruelle, "Qu'est-ce que la non-philosophie?", in Juan Diego Blanco, *Initiation à la pensée de François Laruelle* (Paris: L'Harmattan, 1997), pp. 13–64; François Laruelle, *Le Christ futur: Une leçon d'hérésie* (Paris: Exils Éditeur, 2002), esp. pp. 40–44.

86. Badiou, *Logiques des mondes*.

87. For a critique of Schelling's positive view of evil and of Kantian "radical evil," see Milbank, *Being Reconciled*, pp. 1–25.

88. Schelling, *Philosophie der Offenbarung*, XXVII–XXVIII, pp. 278–299.

89. Ibid., XXXIV–XXXV, pp. 312–325.

90. Ibid., V–XII, pp. 121–176.

91. See Milbank, *Theology and Social Theory*.

92. See Friedrich Heinrich Jacobi, *The Main Philosophical Writings and the Novel Allwill*, trans. George di Giovanni (Montreal/Kingston: McGill/Queen's University Press, 1994).

93. *Hegel's Logic*, §§63–64, pp. 97–101. Hegel also makes the bad mistake of aligning Jacobi's sense of the limits of reason with that of Kant. In reality they have opposite implications. Kant thinks he can found the legitimacy of finite theoretical reason, and therefore rule any applications of this reason to the infinite out of bounds. Jacobi

thinks that reason cannot legitimately be self-founded even as finite, and that the extrarational assumptions that reason is forced to make even in order "to get going" disallow any discernment of whether we can think only the finite. Indeed, for Jacobi we have to trust the infinite in order reliably to think the finite, and so can think the finite only as some measure of participation in the infinite, which we must therefore also think in some degree.

94. See Merlin Coverley, *Psychogeography* (London: Pocket Essentials, 2006).

95. "Scatter Promenade" is the name of a traditional English round dance.

96. Heidegger already developed an ontology of the *zwischen*, but for a critique of its inadequacy, see John Milbank, "The Thing that Is Given," *Archivio di Filosofia* 74, nos. 1–3, *Le tiers*, ed. Marco M. Olivetti (2006), pp. 503–509.

97. Nicholas of Cusa, *On Learned Ignorance*, in *Selected Spiritual Writings*, trans. H. Lawrence Bond (New York: Paulist Press, 1997), pp. 87–206.

98. G. K. Chesterton, *The Everlasting Man* (San Francisco: Ignatius, 1993), pp. 169–213.

99. Paul Claudel, *Ways and Crossways*, trans. John O'Connor (New York: Sheed and Ward, 1933), pp. 129–134.

100. See Badiou, *Being and Event*, pp. 161–170; Milbank, "The Return of Mediation."

101. Meister Eckhart, *Commentary on the Book of Wisdom*, 144–157, in *Meister Eckhart: Teacher and Preacher*, ed. Bernard McGinn (New York: Paulist Press, 1986), pp. 161–171. Eckhart is here commenting on Wisdom 7:27a: "And since it is one, it can do all things."

102. This includes Bernard McGinn, who is nonetheless a good interpreter of Eckhart on many points. See his introduction to *Meister Eckhart: Teacher and Preacher*, pp. 25–26. McGinn suggests that Eckhart, unlike Aquinas, sunders the link between eminence and attribution, and "dialectically" claims that "what can be affirmed of God must be denied of creatures and vice-versa"—except in the case of the terms *esse* and *unum*, which belong properly to God in an eminent degree. He actually admits that in many texts Eckhart treats *verum* and *bonum* in an eminent manner, but still cites Eckhart's *Sermons and Lectures on Ecclesiasticus* in support of his "dialectical" reading: "Analogates have nothing of the form according to which they are analogically ordered rooted in positive fashion in themselves." But this is only to agree with Aquinas's already radical *imago* doctrine, rather than with later neoscholasticism—*nothing* of a created excellence (any *vestigium* or *imago Dei*) which shows some resemblance to God really derives from the creature itself, since it is an entirely "borrowed," participated quality. (See Aquinas, ST III Q.25 a.3; Olivier Boulnois, *Au-delà de l'image: Une archéologie du visuel au Moyen Âge, Ve–XVIe siècle* [Paris: Seuil, 2008], pp. 263–330, and further below in the main text.) Eckhart is simply underscoring this point more strongly, in order possibly to head off Scotistic univocalist understandings of analogy which would allow that the finite can possess some excellence such as goodness qua finite. On this see Alain de Libera, whom McGinn mentions but does not seem to have fully pondered: *Le problème de l'être chez Maître Eckhart: Logique et métaphysique de l'analogie* (Geneva: Revue de théologie et de philosophie, 1980). McGinn rightly says that Eckhart's position on analogy is similar to that of John Scotus Eriugena, but again the latter is not denying, in the passage cited by McGinn, the Dionysian link between eminence and attribution (to use a later terminology). Where Eriugena innovates, and sees something that Aquinas perhaps does not see, is in saying that God is not in continuity with any finite term insofar as the latter always implies an opposite—a circumstance that is incompatible with divine simplicity. Hence being implies nonbeing, good wickedness, truth falsehood, sight blindness, and running slowness. Therefore God is not "strictly speaking" being, goodness, truth, or even God taken as "sight" or "running" (*theos* being supposedly derived from the Greek words for "sight" or "to run," since God in the Bible

sees all of reality and is said to "run through all things"), but is rather *hyperousias, hyper agathos, hyperalēthēs*, and even *hypertheos*. The "hyper" attached to excellence terms shows that, despite the extreme negation, eminence is still linked to attribution—whether because (this is not completely clear in Dionysius; see note 159 below) attribution is itself negatively qualified as eminence, or because there is a "supereminence" that synthesizes the attributive with the negative. Eriugena, in a Proclean vein, shows that the logic of analogy itself indicates that God lies beyond the logical sphere in which "opposition" or "contradictoriness" can any longer have any bearing (*Periphyseon* I, 495B10–460B 22). This insight is then recovered and developed further by Eckhart and Nicholas of Cusa in the face of Scotistic and nominalistic critiques of analogy as violating the principle of noncontradiction. ("Quite" and "So what?", they respond, in effect.) The insight is *not* identical, as McGinn asserts, with Maimonides' far greater apophaticism, typical of the Jewish refusal of any taint of idolatry (and yet paradoxically saving of a literal reading of biblical anthropormorphism), according to which it is no truer to say that God is loving or merciful than to say that he hates or is angry. For here we do not have Eriugena's articulation of the *hyperagathos*, and so forth. For Maimonides, the positive predications concern only the divine economy, not his essence. This is manifestly not the case with Eckhart, and when he cites Maimonides' view, this is just reportage of a non-Christian position; he never says he agrees with it, as McGinn claims. Having summarized also prior Christian positions on naming God, Eckhart proceeds to give his own views, which substantively concur with those of Aquinas: we name perfections imperfectly according to our sensorily limited *modus cognoscendi* and experience of perfections in creatures as "imperfect, divided and scattered"; all perfections are precontained in God, and are simply and substantially at one with him; these perfections include power, wisdom, and goodness as well as being and unity. Moreover, and still more emphatically, God as supremely existing, good, and true is the donating source of those perfections as they are found in a limited form within the created order, but he is *not* the source of evil, nor of anything else negative. Indeed, all that can be *entirely* denied of God is negation itself. Eckhart here adds (as he indicates) to the Dionysian tradition the notion of the "negation of negation," but this accentuates and does not diminish the idea of analogy as eminence or supereminence! Eckhart is consistently clear that there is analogical continuity of perfection between Creator and Creation, but that the fullness and reality of perfections derive from God alone. This insistence he then pushes in a paradoxical direction that is not dialectical in a Hegelian sense, nor even, *pace* McGinn, in a neoplatonic sense—if by that one means that neoplatonism generally did not see an analogical continuum as reaching into the One itself (though this is qualifed by Proclus). See Eckhart, *Commentary on Exodus*, 37–78, in *Meister Eckhart: Teacher and Preacher*, pp. 54–70.

103. David Bentley Hart, *The Beauty of the Infinite: The Aesthetics of Christian Truth* (Grand Rapids: Eerdmans, 2003).

104. For an expansion of the following account of Kierkegaard, see John Milbank, "The Sublime in Kierkegaard," in *Post-Secular Philosophy: Between Philosophy and Theology*, ed. Phillip Blond (London: Routledge, 1998), pp. 131–156.

105. A relational and participatory account of individuation—in both the metaphysical and the political sphere—has been well developed by Adrian Pabst in his as yet unpublished Cambridge doctoral thesis.

106. Chesterton, *The Everlasting Man*, p. 36: "Man is at once a creator moving miraculous hands and fingers and a kind of cripple." In this book Chesterton also pointed out (pp. 23–55) how the discovery of paleolithic cave painting had confounded all the evolutionary notions current in his period of a supposed "primitive" *Homo sapiens*. The man in the cave was clearly just like you or me—an observer, artist, player, and worshiper as well as a hunter and a gatherer.

107. F. W. J. Schelling, *Clara, or, On Nature's Connection to the Spirit World*, trans. Fiona Steinkamp (Albany: State University of New York Press, 2002).

108. On the trope of apostrophe, see supremely Catherine Pickstock, *After Writing: On the Liturgical Consummation of Philosophy* (Oxford: Blackwell, 1998), pp. 192–198. Also the unpublished Oxford doctoral thesis of Gavin Hopps, now of St. Andrew's, on romantic poetry.

109. See Milbank and Pickstock, *Truth in Aquinas*.

110. Eckhart, Sermon 71, in *Meister Eckhart: Teacher and Preacher*, p. 324.

111. Master Eckhart, *Parisian Questions*, Q. 1, "Are Existence and Understanding the Same in God," in *Parisian Questions and Prologues*, ed. Armand A. Maurer (Toronto: Pontifical Institute of Medieval Studies, 1974), pp. 43–50; Sermon XXIX, in *Meister Eckhart: Selected Treatises and Sermons*, trans. James M. Clark and John V. Skinner (London: Fontana, 1963), pp. 201–205. See p. 204: "God alone brings things into being through the intellect, because in him alone being is understanding." (Latin numerals for Eckhart's sermons denote the Latin sermons; Arabic numerals the German ones.)

112. See Sermon 52 in *Meister Eckhart: The Essential Sermons, Commentaries, Treatises and Defense*, trans. Edmund Colledge O.S.A. and Bernard McGinn (New York: Paulist Press, 1981), p. 201. Here Eckhart says that blessedness consists in both knowing and loving, or rather in something beyond both. He does not seem entirely to have abandoned intellectualism, however, declaring in Sermon 71, p. 324 (see note 110 above), that in unity with God "the soul feels neither love nor perturbation nor fear. Knowledge is a sound foundation and bedrock for all being. Love has no place to inhere except in knowledge." The last sentence makes it clear that love is equally present in the ultimate stage of human existence, but that knowledge still has a certain priority precisely because of its "terminal" and yet receptive character. Love is guided by the knowledge of the loved object or person, and seeks a full knowledge of it/him. But love *remains* in this full knowledge, precisely because knowledge, as an intentional "null" receptivity, has to sustain a distance between knower and known in order to remain knowledge. The problem with voluntarism, by comparison, as Pierre Rousselot saw at the beginning of the last century, is that it tends to reduce the distance of the other from me purely to my interior response to the other, which is compatible with solipsism. Equally, one could add to Rousselot, it tends to reduce the presence of the other to a heteronomous force or lure into which we have no sympathetic insight. See Pierre Rousselot S.J., *The Intellectualism of St Thomas* (London: Sheed and Ward, 1935), pp. 17–60.

113. See Catherine Pickstock, "Duns Scotus: His Historical and Contemporary Significance," in *Modern Theology* 1, no. 4 (2005), pp. 543–574.

114. See Boulnois's important exposition of Eckhart's *imago* theory in *Au-delà de l'image*, pp. 289–330.

115. Eckhart, Sermon 53, in *Meister Eckhart: The Essential Sermons*, p. 204. See also "On Detachment," in *Meister Eckhart: Selected Treatises and Sermons*, pp. 156–167; Sermon XXIX, p. 205.

116. See Milbank and Pickstock, *Truth in Aquinas*, pp. 60–111.

117. G. K. Chesterton, *Orthodoxy* (London: Bodley Head, 1957), p. 262.

118. See further G. K. Chesterton's successful stageplay, *Magic; a Fantastic Comedy* (Seattle: Inkling Books, 2006).

119. See Slavoj Žižek, *The Fragile Absolute—or, Why Is the Christian Legacy Worth Fighting For?* (London: Verso, 2000); Slavoj Žižek, *On Belief* (London: Routledge, 2002); Slavoj Žižek, *The Puppet and the Dwarf: The Perverse Core of Christianity* (Cambridge, MA: MIT Press, 2003).

120. Žižek, *The Parallax View*, passim.

121. See C. S. Lewis, *The Abolition of Man* (London: Geoffrey Bles, 1947), pp. 39–55.

122. See John Milbank, *The Suspended Middle: Henri de Lubac and the Debate Concerning the Supernatural* (Grand Rapids: Eerdmans, 2005), pp. 88–103.

123. Michel de Certeau, *The Mystic Fable*, trans. Michael B. Smith (Chicago: University of Chicago Press, 1995), pp. 79–112.

124. Nicholas of Cusa, *The Catholic Concordance*, trans. Paul E. Sigmund (Cambridge, UK: Cambridge University Press, 1995); Milbank, *Being Reconciled*, pp. 105–137.

125. See John Milbank, *The Word Made Strange* (Oxford: Blackwell, 1997), pp. 171–193.

126. W. H. Auden, "The Sea and the Mirror; a Commentary on Shakespeare's *The Tempest*," in *Collected Poems*, ed. Edward Mendelson (New York: Vintage, 1991), p. 421.

127. Eckhart, Sermon 53, in *Meister Eckhart: The Essential Sermons*, p. 204.

128. On *condilectio*, see further Emmanuel Falque, "La condilection ou le tiers de l'amour," *Archivio di Filosofia* 74, nos. 1–3, *Le tiers*, ed. Marco M. Olivetti (2006), pp. 459–474.

129. See Sergei Bulgakov, *Sophia, the Wisdom of God: An Outline of Sophiology*, trans. Patrick Thompson et al. (New York: Lindisfarne Press, 1993).

130. Meister Eckhart, "Commentary on the Gospel According to St. John," in *Meister Eckhart: Selected Treatises and Sermons*, p. 228.

131. Ibid.

132. Again see Milbank, *Theology and Social Theory*, pp. 147–176.

133. Eckhart, Sermon 39, "A Sermon on the Just Man and on Justice," in *Meister Eckhart: Selected Treatises and Sermons*, p. 50.

134. Emil Fackenheim, *The Religious Dimension in Hegel's Thought* (Boston: Beacon Press, 1967), pp. 149–154.

135. He clearly distinguished between creation *ex nihilo* and inner-Trinitarian generation/procession, for example in *The Book of the Parables of Genesis*, Chapter One, 9, commenting on Genesis 1:1, "In the beginning God created heaven and earth," in *Meister Eckhart: The Essential Sermons*, p. 96.

136. Eckhart, "Commentary on the Gospel According to St. John," in *Meister Eckhart: Selected Treatises and Sermons*, p. 244; Sermon 22, in *Meister Eckhart: The Essential Sermons*, p. 194. At the first locus Eckhart follows Augustine in speaking of "a certain virtual being" that things have in God, beyond nothingness, before they are created out of nothing; in the second one he makes it clear that his "spark" is indeed nothing other than the Augustinian "seminal reason," and that all created things, not just souls, have uncreated/created sparks. This is also akin to Maximus's teaching about the *logoi* (which may just possibly derive indirectly from Augustine) and the modern Russian theory of the uncreated/created Sophia.

137. Eckhart, Sermon 30, in *Meister Eckhart: Selected Treatises and Sermons*, p. 55.

138. Ibid.

139. Ibid., p. 54.

140. Ibid., p. 55.

141. Ibid.

142. Meister Eckhart, "Response to Article 4," in Gabriel Théry O.P., "Édition critique des pièces relatives au procès d'Eckhart contenues dans le manuscrit 33b de la bibliothèque de Soest," in Archives d'histoire doctrinale et littéraire du Moyen Âge, 1926, p. 188.

143. See Boulnois, Au-delà de l'image, pp. 133–171, 289–330. But it might be argued that Boulnois is wrong to indicate that, because Dionysius thinks that the vision of God is always mediated by an image that exceeds the merely mental image or concept—so that it includes for us also the bodily—he therefore implicitly ascribes something like Gregory of Nyssa's epectasis, or unending advance, even in eternity, to the divine essence that can never be fully grasped. The latter concept was rather introduced into a Dionysian schema by Eriugena, after reading Gregory's writings (John Scotus Eriugena, Periphyseon I, 447A–450C; V, 919A–D). Instead, Dionysius seems to have thought of the beatific "vision" in more personally holistic and radically identitarian terms, after the manner that I have suggested in the main text: "Moses . . . plunges into the truly mysterious darkness of unknowing. Here, renouncing all that the mind may conceive, wrapped up entirely in the intangible and the invisible, he belongs completely to him who is beyond everything. Here, being neither oneself nor someone else, one is supremely united by a completely unknowing inactivity of all knowledge and knows beyond the mind by knowing nothing" (Mystical Theology, 1001A). This "mystical" knowledge of God contains no suggestion of the "incomplete" and is surely more than a nominal vision of the invisible as the invisible, as Boulnois says, thereby perhaps assimilating it to something like the post-Kantian sublime. And it may be that precisely because Gregory thinks of the mystical state as a higher "looking," the gaze can never be complete, while because Dionysius thinks of it as active "liturgical" being swallowed up in the dark sanctuary (Moses "plunges"), beyond both corporeal imagination and reasoning, he regards it as "finished." See Ysabel de Andia, Henosis: L'union à Dieu chez Denys l'Aréopagite (Leiden: E. J. Brill, 1996), esp. pp. 355–367. Hence the contrasts do not here run so clearly between East and West as Boulnois claims, and it could be that the Dionysian tradition can already resolve in a Trinitarian manner the very important tension that Boulnois so ably disinters between "Western" rational comprehension of a God who is in himself rational mediation and "Eastern" insistence on the need for suprarational mediation, while tending to see God as in himself the supreme "One" beyond any mediation whatsoever, including a rational one.

144. Thomas Aquinas, Sententiarum I, dist. 16, q.1 a.1 c.

145. Eckhart, Sermon 30, p. 56.

146. Nicholas of Cusa, On Learned Ignorance, Chapter Twenty-Three, 70–73, in Selected Spiritual Writings, pp. 119–120; Blaise Pascal, Pensées, trans. A. J. Krailsheimer (London: Penguin, 1972), 418, p. 149.

147. Chesterton, Orthodoxy, pp. 66 ff.

148. This would be a more orthodox version of Schelling's idea that there is an "overcoming" or "victory" eternally proper to God.

149. Chesterton, Orthodoxy, pp. 103–130.

150. See Romano Guardini, The End of the Modern World (Wilmington: ISI Books, 1998), pp. 1–27.

151. Nicholas of Cusa, De li non aliud, in Complete Philosophical and Theological Treatises of Nicholas of Cusa, trans. Jasper Hopkins (Minneapolis: Banning, 1988), vol. 2, pp. 1108–1178.

152. Eckhart, Sermon 53, in Meister Eckhart: The Essential Sermons, p. 25: "the Father speaks the Son out of his power and he speaks him in all things . . . the being of a stone speaks

and manifests the same as does my mouth about God; and people understand more by what is done than by what is said." Thomas Aquinas, ST Q.18 a.4 ad 3: "absolutely speaking [*simpliciter*] natural things have their being in the divine spirit more truly than in themselves."

153. Maximus the Confessor, *The Church's Mystagogy*, in *Maximus Confessor: Selected Writings*, trans. George C. Berthold (New York: Paulist Press, 1985), Chapter Two, p. 189.

154. Alain de Libera, *La mystique rhénane: D'Albert le Grand à Maître Eckhart* (Paris: Seuil, 1994), pp. 253–254. De Libera stresses that Eckhart is speaking of the mysterious absolute unity of the three persons, and not of an essence beyond the personal. He cites Sermon 67, which declares that, while the image of God in us concerns only the divine operation, the uncreated/created *scintilla* in the soul is united at once with the divine Trinitarian operation and the "immanence of being from which they have never gone forth." Eckhart does not displace Trinitarian theology with Proclusean henology—rather, he innovates by trying to think them both together. And this novelty seems to be demanded by the paradoxical insistence of traditional Trinitarin doctrine that triadicity does not qualify unity but, rather, accentuates it.

155. Eckhart, Sermon 48, in *Meister Eckhart: The Essential Sermons*, p. 198.

156. Aquinas, ST I Q.39 a.1.

157. Eckhart, Sermon 10, in *Meister Eckhart: Teacher and Preacher*, p. 265.

158. Eckhart, Sermon 39, in *Meister Eckhart: The Essential Treatises*, p. 52.

159. The identification of attribution and eminence made here is not, however, entirely clear in either Dionysius or Aquinas. The former speaks of a *triplex via* for speaking of God, comprising cause (*aitia*), eminence (*hyperoxes*), and remotion (*aphageos*) (*The Divine Names*, 872A). He suggests that eminence is identical with the cataphatic way, and that causal invocation of God would involve a hypereminence—in much the way that a form of a thing in Plato is like yet also unlike the things that copy it. On the other hand, Dionysius speaks elsewhere of causal invocation as qualifying affirmation (*theseis*, or "standing"), and of eminence as qualifying negation (*The Mystical Theology*, 1048B). In this fourfold scheme, eminence itself seems to be the synthesizing term, and to unite attribution with negation such as to suggest that if, for example, one says that God is "good but in an eminent degree," this qualifies both cataphasis and apophasis. Perhaps more commonly, Aquinas speaks in the latter terms, and he frequently sees the causal way as linked with the attributive way: see ST I Q.12 a.8 ad 2; SCG 3.49. However, he also sometimes says that attribution adds eminence to a mere indication that God is the causal source of a finite quality like goodness (ST I Q.13 a.6), and distinguishes knowledge of God "by cause" from knowledge of God "by likeness" (In Boeth. Super de Trin. 6.3). Because, for Aquinas, however, God as cause is formal/final as well as efficient cause, the distinctness of causality from eminence would surely tend to imply, within the terms of his own metaphysics, a hypereminence and not an absence of eminence. That is to say, God as the uttermost height of excellence manifests that excellence also in an unknown "different" manner. Without this "hyper" qualification of eminence, it could be reduced merely to the infinite degree of a quality univocally known about, as with Scotus. I am indebted to discussions about this exegetical problem with Aaron Riches of the universities of Virginia and Nottingham.

160. Eckhart, Sermon 6, in *Meister Eckhart: The Essential Sermons*, p. 187.

161. Luther's thought is often described as paradoxical, but in reality it is proto-dialectical, because it tends to postulate that God as God in his divine essence goes over "momentarily" to finitude, death, and the consequences of sin, thereby enduring a contradiction, even a disguise, but not perfecting a coincidence of opposites.

162. Jacob Boehme, *The Signature of All Things* (Cambridge, UK: James Clarke, 1969), Chapter II, pp. 13–21.

163. Ibid., Chapter III, pp. 22–31.

164. Ibid., Chapter XI, pp. 129–151.

165. See Cyril O'Regan, *The Heterodox Hegel* (Albany: State University of New York Press, 1994), esp. pp. 11–169. Essentially the same line on Hegel as primarily Behmenist was already taken (with far less scholarly support) in my 1990 book *Theology and Social Theory*.

166. See, classically, Eric Voegelin, *Science, Politics and Gnosticism: Two Essays* (Washington, DC: Gateway, 1997); and, for a much more detailed development and modification of "the Voegelin thesis," Cyril O'Regan, *Gnostic Return in Modernity* (Albany: State University of New York Press, 2001).

167. Many otherwise orthodox theologians today do not escape from a gnostic contamination in the shape of suggestions that the real good is a "tested" good that can emerge only through a trial with evil. But orthodoxy proclaims the absolute untroubled innocence of God: it is this that the God-Man manifested to us even through his tribulations—this lesson of experience being for us the only way in which innocence can be regained.

168. See Simone Pétrement, *A Separate God: The Origins and Teachings of Gnosticism*, trans. Carol Harrison (San Fra ncisco: Harper, 1984), esp. pp. 351–387.

169. Boehme, *The Signature of All Things*, esp. Chapters XIV–XVI, pp. 176–223.

170. See Cyril O'Regan, *Gnostic Apocalypse: Jacob Boehme's Haunted Narrative* (Albany: State University of New York Press, 2002), esp. pp. 74, 80.

171. See Milbank, *Being Reconciled*, pp. 1–25.

172. G. K. Chesterton, *The Man Who Was Thursday* (London: Penguin, 1986), p. 46. While Žižek is right to say, after Chesterton himself, that this is a pre-Christian text, it is still a prolegomenon to Christianity, because if "Sunday" is the source of both law and anarchy, he is to be identified not with God (as Žižek supposes, despite Chesterton's explicit denial of this in a newspaper article: see p. 185) but with something like nature in her fallen condition. He is akin to a kind of "fallen Sophia." Were the latter to be taken as the deity himself, or his fallenness to be seen as both inevitable and comically redemptive, then one would have a kind of gnosticism—which Chesterton here toys with, perhaps to indicate its counterfeit closeness to orthodoxy.

173. Rowan Williams, "Archbishop's Liverpool Lecture: Europe, Faith and Reason," at <www.archbishopof canterbury.org.1547>.

174. See Pickstock, "Duns Scotus: His Historical and Contemporary Significance"; John Milbank, "Only Theology Saves Metaphysics," in *Belief and Metaphysics*, ed. Peter M. Candler Jr. and Conor Cunningham (London: SCM Press, 2007), pp. 452–500.

175. See Milbank, *The Suspended Middle*, passim.

176. Pierre Bérulle, *Grandeurs de Jésus*, VI, 7, [1], in *Oeuvres complètes* (Paris: Cerf, 1997).

177. Jean-Luc Marion, *Sur la théologie blanche de Descartes* (Paris: Presses Universitaires de France, 1981), p. 147.

178. See Milbank and Pickstock, *Truth in Aquinas*, pp. 19–59.

179. See Claude Bruaire, *L'être et l'esprit* (Paris: Presses Universitaires de France, 1983); John Milbank, "The Gift and the Mirror: On the Philosophy of Love," in *Counter-Experiences:*

Reading Jean-Luc Marion, ed. Kevin Hart (Notre Dame, Ind.: Notre Dame University Press, 2007), pp. 253–317.

180. See Milbank, *The Suspended Middle*, passim.

181. Théry, "Édition critique des pièces relatives au procès d'Eckhart," pp. 230–231.

182. Eckhart, *Commentary on the Book of Exodus*, Exodus 3:14: *Ego sum qui sum*, and Sermon XXIX, both in *Meister Eckhart: Selected Treatises and Sermons*, pp. 218, 204; Dietrich of Freibourg, *De ente et essentia*, in *Thomas d'Aquin/Dietrich of Freibourg: L'Être et l'essence: Le vocabulaire médiéval de l'ontologie* (Paris: Seuil, 1996), trans. Alain de Libera and Cyrille Michon, pp. 162–218.

183. Eckhart, "The Nobleman" ["The Book of Benedictus: Of the Nobleman"], in *Selected Treatises and Sermons*, p. 154. See also Milbank, *Theology and Social Theory*, "Preface to the Second Edition," p. xxix.

184. Master Eckhart, *Parisian Questions*, Q. 2. 11.

185. For the entire issue of univocity in Eckhart, see Burkhard Mojsisch, *Meister Eckhart: Analogy, Univocity, and Unity*, trans. Orrin F. Summerell (Amsterdam and Philadelphia: B. R. Grüner, 2001), pp. 67–94. Mojsisch, however, describes Eckhart's teachings in anachronistic idealist language of "the self-mediation of the absolute," and unwarrantedly links infinite univocity with a transcendental subjective monism that tends to make Eckhart the precursor of Fichte. His discussion of the justice/just man paradigm is correspondingly wide of the mark, in that he declares that the justice of the just man proceeds unilaterally from the self-expression and mediation of abstract justice which is itself already fully just. So Mojsisch fails to see that this is a paradoxical account in which each term can exist only relationally through the other: without the expression of justice, the just man is not just, but without the justice performed by the just man, justice as such does not exist. This Eckhartian scheme indeed turns the univocity of infinite being into a kind of hyperbolic analogy.

186. Eckhart, "Commentary on the Gospel of John," in *Meister Eckhart: The Essential Sermons*, 120, p. 169.

187. Eckhart, *Commentary on the Book of Wisdom*, in *Meister Eckhart: Teacher and Preacher*, 148, pp. 167–168. See also Mojsisch, *Meister Eckhart*, pp. 93–99. Mojsisch has to allow that for Eckhart, the "negation of negation" is an absolute "position" (*positio*), whereas for Dietrich of Freibourg it is a kind of dynamic negative "power" (*potius*), suggesting perhaps something more like a truly void source that must later "become." Once more, then, it is Dietrich, not Eckhart, who seems proto-idealist.

188. Eckhart, Sermon 9, in *Meister Eckhart: Teacher and Preacher*, p. 257.

189. See Milbank and Pickstock, *Truth in Aquinas*, pp. 19–59.

190. See Proclus, *The Elements of Theology*, 56, 70, 71, 97; Milbank and Pickstock, *Truth in Aquinas*.

191. Eckhart, *The Book of Propositions*, Prologue, in *Master Eckhart: Parisian Questions and Prologues*, pp. 100–101.

192. Ibid., p. 102.

193. Ibid., p. 103.

194. See André de Muralt, *L'unité de la philosophie politique: De Scot, Occam et Suarez au libéralisme contemporain* (Paris: J. Vrin, 2002); Éric Alliez, *Capital Times: Tales from the Conquest of Time*, trans. Georges Van Den Abbeele (Minneapolis: University of Minnesota Press, 1996), pp. 141–239.

195. Eckhart, Sermon 30, "A Sermon for St. Dominic's Day," in *Meister Eckhart: Selected Treatises and Sermons*, p. 56.

196. One has to read paradoxically Eckhart's statements to the effect that the exterior act adds nothing to the goodness of the internal act. For he considers that an interior act itself resides truly *outside* one's ego in God, and that part of its very character is its *Logos*-imaging ecstasy which spontaneously issues forth in charitable works. Else it would not be genuinely "internal" in this sense at all. And Colledge and McGinn are wrong to say that Eckhart could not really cite Aquinas in his own defense, as he did at his trial at Avignon for heresy, on the point that external performance adds nothing to the goodness of the internal act. (See "Introduction 3: Theological Summary," in *Meister Eckhart: The Essential Sermons*, pp. 58–59.) For Thomas, in the passage cited by Eckhart, does indeed say that "If we speak of the goodness which the external action derives from the will tending to the end, then the external action adds nothing to the goodness," although he goes on to say that it does add something with respect to "the goodness which the external action derives from the matter and its circumstances" (ST I.II Q.20 a.4). Yet the latter point was also affirmed by Eckhart, both at Avignon and in his *Counsels of Discernment* (as Colledge and McGinn indeed themselves note). So he is saying only, with Thomas, that the good of the internal act is not increased in its intrinsic intentionality by external performance. Thus Aquinas adds in the cited passage that, if a good intention is involuntarily frustrated, it is equal in goodness to the unfrustrated act. Eckhart's gloss on this remains in a Thomistic spirit—namely, that if the goodness of a good intention resides in its uniting us with God in the highest manner possible, which is that of the soul, then from an absolute ontological perspective external performance really does add nothing to inward intention. Yet the latter, precisely qua intention, is utterly senseless if is not *always* proceeding outward into performance, and utterly culpable if it forgoes an opportunity to realize itself.

197. Eckhart, Sermon 39, "A Sermon on the Just Man and on Justice," in *Meister Eckhart: Selected Treatises and Sermons*, p. 50; Sermon 6, in *Meister Eckhart: The Essential Sermons*, p. 189: "In this working God and I are one; he is working and I am becoming"; Mojsisch, *Meister Eckhart*, p. 119. But this also works inversely. See Sermon 22 in *Meister Eckhart: The Essential Sermons*, p. 196: "When he [the Bridegroom, the Son] went out from the highest place of all, he wanted to go in again with his bride [the soul] to the purest place of all, and wanted to reveal to her the hidden secret of his hidden divinity, where he takes his rest with himself and with all created things."

198. See Charles Taylor, *A Secular Age* (Cambridge, MA: Harvard University Press, 2007), pp. 25–89.

199. Eckhart, Sermon 5b, in *Meister Eckhart: The Essential Sermons*, p. 183.

200. Eckhart, "On Detachment."

201. Eckhart, *Commentary on the Book of Wisdom*, in *Meister Eckhart: Teacher and Preacher*, 106, p. 160.

202. Eckhart, Sermon 15, in *Meister Eckhart: The Essential Sermons*, p. 190: "this humble man has as much power over God as he has over himself."

203. René Descartes, "Fourth Meditation," 57, in *Meditations on First Philosophy*, trans. John Cottingham (Cambridge, UK: Cambridge University Press, 1990), p. 40.

204. Milbank and Pickstock, *Truth in Aquinas*, pp. 60–87.

205. Eckhart, *The Book of Propositions*, Prologue, p. 101.

206. Eckhart, Sermon 24, in *Meister Eckhart: Teacher and Preacher*, p. 286; Eckhart, "On Detachment," p. 166.

207. Søren Kierkegaard, *Practice in Christianity*, trans. Howard V. and Edna H. Hong (Princeton: Princeton University Press, 1991), pp. 123–144; Chesterton, *The Everlasting Man*, pp. 186–213.

208. For a superbly accurate rendering of Anselm on atonement, see Hart, *The Beauty of the Infinite*, pp. 360–372.

209. See Milbank, *The Suspended Middle*, pp. 88–103.

210. Aaron Riches, of Virginia and Nottingham universities, has acutely suggested to me that perhaps Aquinas does not clearly rule out a Maximian mode of incarnation that would have taken place without the Fall in some more "universal" kind of fashion.

211. See Milbank, *Being Reconciled*, pp. 64–78. However, I would now modify my espousal of a "Thomistic" view here that the Incarnation occurred only in view of the Fall with a Maximian-Eckhartian version of the view that it would have occurred, in an altogether different fashion, without sin—for the (non-Scotist!) reasons explained in the main text.

212. See Colledge and McGinn, "Introduction: Theological Summary," in *Meister Eckhart: The Essential Sermons*, pp. 45–46; and the Encyclopedia article on Eckhart at <www. lep.utm .edu / e / eckhart.htm>.

213. Théry, "Édition critique des pièces relatives au procès d'Eckhart," pp. 230–231.

214. Sermon 5b, *In hoc apparuit charitas dei in nobis*, in *Meister Eckhart: The Essential Sermons*, pp. 182, 183.

215. Milbank, *The Suspended Middle*, passim.

216. See John Milbank, *The Religious Dimension in the Thought of Giambattista Vico 1668–1744*, Part 2: *Law, Language and History* (Lewiston, NY: Edwin Mellen Press, 1992).

217. Chesterton, *The Everlasting Man*, pp. 101–136.

218. A good example of this is C. Walter Hodges's remarkable duo of books for children (but surely also for adults) about the life of King Alfred, *The Namesake* (London: G. Bell, 1964) and *The Marsh King* (London: G. Bell, 1967).

219. Chesterton, *The Everlasting Man*, pp. 137–150.

220. Chesterton, *Orthodoxy*, pp. 38–65.

221. Chesterton, *The Everlasting Man*, pp. 250–261.

DIALECTICAL CLARITY VERSUS THE MISTY CONCEIT OF PARADOX

Slavoj Žižek

It may appear that, in a theoretical debate, one reaches a dead end when the two
opponents are reduced to their basic presuppositions—at this point, every argumentation, inclusive of "immanent critique," is superfluous; each of the two
is reduced to his/her "here I stand," about which the other cannot do anything
without relying on his/her own ultimate presuppositions, on his/her own
"here I stand." However, a truly Hegelian approach does allow for an option
here, the one of denying the obvious, of claiming: "You say this is your position, but it is not true—*you do not have a position at all*!" That is to say, one denies that
it is possible at all to truly advocate the opponent's position—something that
resembles the immortal answer of the interrogator to Winston Smith's query
"Does Big Brother really exist?" from 1984: "It is YOU who doesn't exist!"

The dialogue between Milbank and me (which, like every true philosophical dialogue, is an interaction of two monologues) seems to oscillate
between these two extremes. On the one hand, I am the first to recognize the
authentic spirituality that sustains Milbank's position, the spirituality which
is discernible in many of his formulations with which I fully agree. When, for
example, he writes that "evil is also a sin against the remedy against sin which is
always-already there," he provides a wonderful formula of the self-referential
temporal paradox of evil. And I cannot but admire his precise clarification of
how "grace is not for Eckhart merely a contingently added topmost layer to
reality": "as supremely unnecessary gift ('you shouldn't have . . .'), it is also the
most absolutely necessary thing of all."—On the other hand, there are many
points where Milbank simply attributes to me (or to Lacan) notions and statements that neither of us advocates in any sense. However, the gap that separates
us is most clearly discernible in the opposite cases: when Milbank criticizes me
simply for what I claim, as if my position is self-evidently untenable. Take the
following passage from his reply:

> God can appear only *incognito*, in a kind of playful disguise. Yet clearly, were this
> *incognito* absolute (as Žižek appears to imply, since his Christ is but a stuttering
> madman), no recognition could take place. So even if the upshot of the Incarna-
> tion is that we now see God as fully there in ordinary life, unqualified by law,
> this can first *appear to view* only through an event which combines the extraordi-
> nary with the ordinary. This is exactly what Žižek fails to see. . . . But Kierkegaard
> rightly says . . . that a miracle is only a sign that has to be interpreted, and there-
> fore that it remains a merely ambiguous indication which is still "indirect."

Of course I "fail to see" this—not because Christ is for me a mere "stuttering
madman," but because, for me, there is no transcendent God-Father who discloses himself to us, humans, only in a limited way. The reason God can only

appear incognito is that there is nothing to take cognizance of here: God is hidden not to hide some transcendent Truth, but to hide the fact that there is nothing to hide. This is, to my Hegelian view, the whole point of Christianity as the "religion of revelation": what is revealed in Christianity is not some new content, but the fact that Revelation belongs to the very nature of God, i.e., that God is *nothing but* his own Revelation to us. This is also how I read Kierkegaard's point that "a miracle is only a sign that has to be interpreted and therefore . . . a merely ambiguous indication": the Jansenists made the same point when they insisted that miracles are not "objective" miraculous facts which demonstrate the truth of a religion to everyone—they appear as such only to the eyes of believers; to nonbelievers, they are mere fortuitous natural coincidences. This theological legacy survives in radical emancipatory thought, from Marxism to psychoanalysis. In his (unpublished) Seminar XVIII on a "discourse which would not be that of a semblance," Lacan provided a succinct definition of the truth of interpretation in psychoanalysis: "Interpretation is not tested by a truth that would decide by yes or no, it unleashes truth as such. It is only true inasmuch as it is truly followed." There is nothing "theological" in this precise formulation, only the insight into the properly dialectical unity of theory and practice in (not only) psychoanalytic interpretation: the "test" of the analyst's interpretation is in the truth effect it unleashes in the patient. This is how we should also (re)read Marx's Thesis XI: the "test" of Marxist theory is the truth effect it unleashes in its addressee (the proletarians), in transforming them into emancipatory revolutionary subjects. The *locus communis* "You have to see it to believe it!" should always be read together with its inversion: "You have to believe [in] it to see it!" Although one may be tempted to oppose them as the dogmaticism of blind faith versus openness toward the unexpected, one should insist also on the truth of the second version: truth, as opposed to knowledge, is, like a Badiouian Event, something that only an engaged gaze, the gaze of a subject who "believes in it," can see. Think of love: in love, only the lover sees in the object of love that x which causes love, the parallax object, so the structure of love is the same as that of the Badiouian Event which also exists only for those who recognize themselves in it: there is no Event for a nonengaged objective observer.

This is where Milbank also misreads me when he claims that I suggest that "a revelation that there is only the finite, and that this [finite] is somehow infinite, permits the finite of itself to overcome (or somewhat quixotically to overcome) evil"—my point here is a much more precise Schellingian-Hegelian one: Evil is not finite as opposed to the infinite, so that it can be redeemed when it is disclosed that it is "somehow infinite"; Evil is, on the contrary, the Infinite itself insofar as it entertains a negative attitude toward the finite, negating or excluding the wealth of the finite content. Or, as Schelling put it, Evil is much more spiritual than Good: Evil is not the body rebelling against the spirit, but a bleak infertile spirit which hates bodily reality—there is no Goodness without accepting the "spirituality" that inheres to bodily reality. Therein lies the insufficiency of Milbank's claim that, for the Middle Ages, "evil was the 'impossible' denial of one's loyalty to the all, to being as such. It was therefore as act of privation and of self-deprivation—a matter of trying absurdly to be less than one really is." Does he not withdraw here from Chesterton's most shattering insight into how "Christianity is a sword which separates and sets free. No other philosophy makes God actually rejoice in the separation of the universe into living souls"?[1] And Chesterton was fully aware that it is not enough for God to separate man from himself so that mankind will love him—this separation *has* to be reflected back into God himself, so that God is abandoned *by himself*; because of this overlapping between man's isolation from God and God's isolation *from himself*, Christianity is "terribly revolutionary. That a good man may have his back to the wall is no more than we knew already; but that God could have His back to the wall is a boast for all insurgents for ever. Christianity is the only religion on earth that has felt that omnipotence made God incomplete. Christianity alone has felt that God, to be wholly God, must have been a rebel as well as a king."[2] Chesterton is fully aware that we are thereby approaching "a matter more dark and awful than it is easy to discuss . . . a matter which the greatest saints and thinkers have justly feared to approach. But in that terrific tale of the Passion there is a distinct emotional suggestion that the author of all things (in some unthinkable way) went not only through agony, but through doubt."[3] In the standard form of atheism, God dies for men who stop believing in him; in Christianity, God dies *for himself*. In his "Father, why have you forsaken me?", Christ himself commits what is for a Christian the ultimate sin: he wavers in his Faith. Or, to spell things out here: is the "matter more dark and awful than it is easy to discuss" not this separation of God not only from the world, but *from himself* also—in short, the explosion of an unbearable antagonism, of Evil, in the very heart of God himself? What can be more evil than a God who is a rebel against himself? How are we to combine this full assertion of a tension which tears apart God himself with Milbank's claim that, for the Catholic "paradoxical, nondialectical logic, there is never any contradiction, conflict, or tension. The origin rather *coincides* with its opposite, which is that which the origin generates, while the reverse also applies."

A brief detour through Kabbala might help us here. Kabbala locates the origin of Evil in divine self-differentiation: the source of Evil is "the superabundant growth of the power of judgment which was made possible by the substantification and separation of the quality of judgment from its customary union with the quality of lovingkindness."[4] While this thesis may appear pretty common within the mystical tradition (the source of Evil is analytic reasoning . . .), there is a further twist to it in Kabbala: prior to creating our world, God created multiple worlds which preceded it and disintegrated; these first worlds perished because of the "overly concentrated power of strict judgment that they contained."[5] However, their disappearance was not total: their "ruins"—their underground ideological features—remained, so that Evil originates "from the leftovers of worlds that were destroyed."[6] *Evil is thus in itself the proof of the multitude of worlds*—a thesis which we should apply (also) to Badiou's precise notion of "world": one cannot think Evil as a concept within a single world, one has to invoke the clash of the worlds.

This, however, should not be read in the traditional (multi)culturalist way: each "world" (as a cultural-ideological unity) is self-centered and castigates as "evil" the traces of other worlds in itself. On the contrary, the problem is that this "otherness" is inscribed into its very core. Let us take the case of monotheism: what makes it "evil" (destructive of previous religions that it dismisses as "pagan idolatry") is not its monotheist exclusivism: it is the so-called "monotheist excluding violence" itself which is secretly polytheist. Does the fanatical hatred of believers in a different god not bear witness to the fact that the monotheist secretly thinks that he is not simply fighting false believers, but that his struggle is a struggle between different gods, the struggle of his god against "false gods" who *exist* as gods? Such a monotheism is in effect exclusive: it has to exclude other gods. For that reason, true monotheists are tolerant: for them, others are not objects of hatred but simply people who, although not enlightened by the true belief, should nonetheless be respected, since they are not inherently evil.

When, dealing with the topic of Good and Evil, Milbank writes: "Žižek is entirely right to say that Sade is not the concealed and subverted truth of Kant—rather, it is a direct implication of the Kantian position," he misrepresents my precise point: Sade is not a "direct implication of the Kantian position" but, rather, a direct implication of Kant's failure to follow his position to the end: the Sadian perversion emerges as the result of the Kantian compromise, of Kant's avoiding the consequences of his breakthrough. Sade is the *symptom* of Kant: while it is true that Kant retreated from drawing all the consequences of his ethical revolution, the space for the figure of Sade is opened up by this compromise of Kant, by his unwillingness to go to the end, to sustain full fidelity to his philosophical breakthrough. Far from being simply and directly "the truth of Kant," Sade is the symptom of how Kant betrayed the truth of his own discovery—the obscene Sadian *jouisseur* is a stigma bearing witness to Kant's ethical compromise; the apparent "radicality" of this figure (the willingness of the Sadian hero to go to the end in his Will-to-Enjoy) is a mask of its exact opposite.

It is this misreading which also pushes Milbank to impute false dilemmas to me, like the following one: "But where do Lacan and Žižek themselves stand within this modern moral and sexual entanglement? It seems to me that they are caught between the egotistic imperative of impossible desire

on the one hand and an ethical regard for the rights of all, on the other."
Concretely, this means that my position ends in a deadlock: a forced choice
between fidelity to one's desire and care for others: "*Unlike* the Catholic Church,
therefore, Lacan and Žižek recommend the total abandonment of sex for the
cause of religion." Milbank's underlying idea is clear: Catholicism enables a
harmonious ethical position in which all earthly pleasures have their place
as joyful emanations or expressions of the transcendent Divine; while, from
my extreme Protestant-atheist position, I can only oscillate between the two
extremes of egotistic pleasures and radical ascetic abnegation, without any
possibility of formulating a clear criterion "*when* to persist (futilely and probably destructively) with one's desire and *when*, on the other hand, to forbear
from this out of loving concern for the other." From my (and Lacan's) position,
of course, this alternative is false: Lacan's key result of his reading of Kant is
that Kant's unconditional moral Law *is* (one of) the name(s) of pure desire, so
that desire and Law *are* one and the same thing. In his "Kant with Sade," Lacan
does not try to make the usual "reductionist" point that every ethical act, pure
and disinterested as it may appear, is always grounded in some "pathological"
motivation (the agent's own long-term interest, the admiration of his peers,
right up to the "negative" satisfaction provided by the suffering and extortion
often demanded by ethical acts); the focus of Lacan's interest, rather, resides in
the paradoxical reversal by means of which desire itself (i.e., acting upon one's
desire, not compromising it) can no longer be grounded in any "pathological"
interests or motivations, and thus meets the criteria of the Kantian ethical act,
so that "following one's desire" overlaps with "doing one's duty." The opposition is thus not between the egotist search for pleasures and ethical care for
others, but between unconditional fidelity to the "law of desire" beyond the
pleasure principle (which can assume the form of fidelity to a sexual Truth
Event of love, the form of fidelity to an ethico-political Idea, the form of fidelity to one's artistic or scientific engagement . . .) and the betrayal of this "law
of desire" on behalf of some pathological "goods."

Furthermore, when Milbank writes that "according to Jacques Lacan, as
with most of the postmodernists, there exists, 'besides' the material realm, only
the operation of signs which gives rise to subjectivity as an effect of signification," he imputes to Lacan the basic premise of what Badiou calls "democratic
materialism," against which Badiou argues and in which he sees the predominant form of today's ideology ("there are only bodies and languages"). But
Lacan does not fit this frame either—if for no other reason than because within
it, there is no place for the Real. Milbank himself admits this: "Lacan deems
that semiotics must be supplemented by mathematical set theory. And it is this
conclusion which already opens up the curious link between nihilism and
subjectivity that will later be exploited by Alain Badiou and to a degree by Žižek
himself." So yes, I fully endorse the "nihilistic mathematization of the semiotic"

as the only logical materialism. This is why, as Milbank correctly intuits, I am for Hegel against Heidegger: "Perhaps what matters to Žižek is that compared with Schelling, and even with Heidegger, Hegel points toward a more consistent nihilistic materialism, since he dispenses with all voluntarism and vitalism." It is along these lines that I agree with Milbank's claim that "materialist materialism is simply not as materialist as theological materialism"—yes, if by "materialism" one understands the assertion of material reality as fully ontologically constituted, "really existing out there," which I emphatically do not: the basic axiom of today's materialism is for me the *ontological incompleteness of reality*. But this, precisely, is why my materialism is *not* "a sad, resigned materialism which appears to suppose that matter is quite as boring as the most extreme of idealists might suppose," as Milbank asserts. Instead of "enchanting" this material reality by seeing it as interpenetrated by spiritual content, my materialism as it were undermines it from within, just as quantum physics, for example, undermines our common notion of external reality: beneath the world of simply existing material objects we discover a different reality of virtual particles, of quantum oscillations, of time–space paradoxes, etc., etc.—a wonderful world which, while remaining thoroughly materialist, is anything but boring. It is, on the contrary, breathtakingly surprising and paradoxical.

This incompleteness of reality also provides an answer to the question I am often asked by materialists: is it even worth spending time on religion, flogging a dead horse? Why this eternal replaying of the death of God? Why not simply start from the positive materialist premise and develop it? The only appropriate answer to this is the Hegelian one—but *not* in the sense of the cheap "dialectics" according to which a thesis can deploy itself only through overcoming its opposite. The necessity of religion is an inner one—again, not in the sense of a kind of Kantian "transcendental illusion," an eternal temptation of the human mind, but more radically. A truly logical materialism accepts the basic insight of religion, its premise that our commonsense reality is not the true one; what it rejects is the conclusion that, therefore, there must be another, "higher," suprasensible reality. Commonsense realism, positive religion, and materialism thus form a Hegelian triad.

How, then, is this reference to God to be taken; how do we use this term? Literally—so that there "effectively is" God, divine history, inclusive of God's death, or "merely metaphorically," so that God is ultimately a "mythical name" for a meta-psychological process? Both versions are to be rejected: it is, of course, not "literally" (we are materialists, there is no God), but it is also not "metaphorically" ("God" is not just a metaphor, a mystifying expression, of human passions, desires, ideals, etc.). What such a "metaphorical" reading misses is the dimension of the Inhuman as internal ("ex-timate") to being-human: "God" (the divine) is a name for that which in man is not human, for the inhuman core that sustains being-human.

Where does psychoanalysis stand with regard to the opposition between religious "enchantment" and scientific "disenchantment" of the world? Science is today's fundamental fact, while religion and psychoanalysis stand for the two reactions to it: the "materialist" one and the "idealist" one, i.e., a reaction at the level of scientific discourse (Lacan himself pointed out that the subject of psychoanalysis is the subject of modern science) and the hermeneutic reinscription of science into the horizon of Meaning. We should thus strictly distinguish between hermeneutics, the domain of meaningful speech, and scientific discourse which articulates what Lacan calls a "knowledge in the Real." Lacan postulates a life-and-death struggle between religion and psychoanalysis, conceding that religion plays a hegemonic role in this struggle, since a tendency to "domesticate" the Real by providing a Sense of it is part of a quasi-transcendental human disposition:

> If religion will triumph, it is because psychoanalysis will fail. . . . If psychoanalysis will not triumph over religion, it is because religion is tireless [*increvable*: can never drop dead]. Psychoanalysis will not triumph, it will survive or not. . . .
>
> Religion will not only triumph over psychoanalysis, it will also triumph over many other things. One cannot even imagine how powerful it is, religion.
>
> I have just spoken about the Real. When science deals with the Real, it will extend itself, and religion will find in it many more reasons to soothe hearts. Science means new things, and will introduce many upsetting things into the life of every one of us. But religion, above all the true [Christian] one, has resources one cannot even imagine. At this moment, one can only observe how it swarms. It is absolutely fabulous!
>
> The priests take their time, but they understood immediately where their opportunity lies with regard to religion. Their task will be to provide a sense for all the upheavals generated by science. And concerning sense, they know something about it. They are really capable of giving sense to anything whatsoever. A sense to human life, for example. They are educated to do this. From the very beginning, all that is religion consists in giving sense to things which were once natural things. If, thanks to the [scientific] Real, things will get less natural, one will not cease to extract sense from them. Religion will give sense to the most curious experiences, those which start to give to scientists themselves a little bit of anxiety. Religion will provide all this with some juicy sense.[7]

In this struggle, the relationship between religion and psychoanalysis is the one between the general field of Sense and its symptom, the point of the intrusion of the Real into this field—and Lacan comes to the sardonic conclusion that religion will succeed in "curing" humanity of this symptom:

> For a brief moment, it was possible to perceive something that was the intrusion of the Real. The analyst stays there. He is there as a symptom. He can last only as a symptom. But you will see that humanity will be cured of psychoanalysis. By drowning it in sense, in the religious sense, of course, one will succeed in

repressing this symptom. . . . Religion is made to do this, to cure people, that is to say, to make it sure that they do not note what doesn't go smoothly.[8]

Within the field of psychoanalysis itself, the hermeneutic reaction strikes in the guise of Jungian "depth psychology." One can formulate this difference between Lacan and Jung as the one between "God is unconscious" and "God is *the* unconscious": between the materialist thesis on our beliefs which, although we are unaware of it, persist in our material practices, where we act *as if* we believe, and the spiritualist-obscurantist notion of the divine dimension that dwells deep in our unconscious.

With regard to materialism itself, we are today witnessing a paradoxical reversal. In the standard precritical metaphysics, "finitude" was associated with materialist empiricism ("only material finite objects really exist"), while "infinity" was the domain of idealist spiritualism. In an unexpected paradoxical reversal, today, the main argument for spiritualism, against radical materialism, relies on the irreducibility of human finitude as the unsurpassable horizon of our existence, while it is today's forms of radical scientific materialism which keep the spirit of infinity alive. The standard line of argumentation is: we should not forget that the technological dream of total mastery over nature and our lives is a dream, that we, humans, remain forever grounded in our finite life-world with its unfathomable background—it is this finitude, this very limitation of our horizon, which opens up the space for proper spirituality. All today's predominant forms of spirituality thus paradoxically emphasize that we, humans, are not free-floating spirits but irreducibly embodied in a material life-world; they all preach respect for this limitation and warn against the "idealist" hubris of radical materialism—here the case of ecology is a good example. In contrast to this spiritualist attitude of limitation, the radical scientific attitude which reduces man to a biological mechanism sustains the promise of full technological control over human life, its artificial re-creation, its biogenetic and biochemical regulation, ultimately its immortality in the guise of the reduction of our inner Self to a software program that can be copied from one hardware to another.

It is as if, with this shift, Spinoza's old materialist insight according to which terms like "God" are false terms with no positive meanings, just terms which provide a deceptive positive form for the domain of what we do *not* know, gets its final confirmation: the religious dimension is explicitly linked to the limitation of our comprehension, i.e., this dimension is not the intimation of a "higher" knowledge, but the inverted assertion of its limitation. This is why religious thinkers are so fond of (what appears as) the limits of our knowledge: don't try to understand the biogenetic foundations of our mind, the result may be the loss of soul; don't try to reach beyond the Big Bang, this is the point where God directly intervened in material reality. . . . It was Kant who said that he limited the space of knowledge to create the space for faith.

These two sides of the same coin are clearly discernible in the work of Andrei Tarkovsky: what pervades Tarkovsky's films is the heavy gravity of Earth, which seems to exert its pressure on time itself, generating an effect of temporal anamorphosis, extending the dragging of time well beyond what we perceive as justified by the requirements of narrative movement (I should confer here on the term "Earth" all the resonance it acquired in late Heidegger)—perhaps, Tarkovsky is the clearest example of what Deleuze called the time-image replacing the movement-image. This time of the Real is neither the symbolic time of the diegetic space nor the time of the reality of our (spectator's) viewing the film, but an intermediate domain whose visual equivalents are perhaps the protracted stains which "are" the yellow sky in late Van Gogh or the water or grass in Munch: this uncanny "massiveness" pertains neither to the direct materiality of the color stains nor to the materiality of the depicted objects— it dwells in a kind of intermediate spectral domain of what Schelling called *geistige Koerperlichkeit*, spiritual corporeality. In our standard ideological tradition, the approach to Spirit is perceived as Elevation, as getting rid of the burden of weight, of the gravitating force which binds us to earth, as cutting links with material inertia and starting to "float freely"; in contrast to this, in Tarkovsky's universe, we enter the spiritual dimension only via intense direct physical contact with the humid heaviness of earth (or stale water)—the ultimate Tarkovskian spiritual experience takes place when a subject is lying stretched on the earth's surface, half submerged in stale water; Tarkovsky's heroes do not pray on their knees, head turned upward, toward heaven, but while intensely listening to the silent palpitation of the humid earth. . . . We can see, now, why Stanisław Lem's novel *Solaris* had to exert such an attraction on Tarkovsky: the planet Solaris seems to provide the ultimate embodiment of the Tarkovskian notion of a heavy humid stuff (earth) which, far from functioning as the opposite of spirituality, serves as its very medium; this gigantic "material Thing which thinks" literally gives body to the direct coincidence of Matter and Spirit. A logical materialism has to break with both these features: to get rid of Spirit, it gladly sacrifices Matter itself in its inert density.

The fundamental premise of today's advocates of the finitude of our existence is thus: we are thrown into a world which preexists us, which we did not create, and so can never fully grasp, control, or dominate; whatever we do, even in our most radically autonomous act, we have to rely on the opaque background of inherited traditions and the socio-symbolic texture which predetermine the scope of our acts. Hans-Georg Gadamer made this point in very vivid terms: the time has come to turn around Hegel's famous formula on the becoming-subject of Substance, of the subjective-reflexive appropriation of all our substantial presuppositions, and accomplish the same journey backward, from the subject to its substantial presuppositions.

This stance has to be located within the matrix of the four possible relations between the two terms. Subjectivist idealists claim that we made our world and can therefore also fully grasp it, since in comprehending it, we discern in it the traces of our own activity. Scientific materialists in the Enlightenment vein claim that although we did not make this world, although this world is an objective reality with its own independent laws, we can nonetheless understand it, and control and master it. Ecologists mostly share the premise of our finitude: we did not create our world, we are thrown into it, so we should respect it, not merely try to dominate it.

There is, however, a fourth position, rarely mentioned and the most difficult to properly understand: we created our world, but it overwhelms us, we cannot grasp and control it. This position is like that of God when he confronts Job toward the end of the book of Job: a God who is himself overwhelmed by his own creation. This is what dialectics is about: what eludes the subject's grasp is not the complexity of transcendent reality, but *the way the subject's own activity is inscribed into reality.*

I also think that Milbank misses the point of Chesterton's defense of the "extraordinariness of the ordinary": "Chesterton, like Augustine, was so astonished by the oddity of everyday reality that he found it very easy to believe in the existence of ghosts and fairies, magic and miracles, as he indicates in several places. Indeed, he considered these realities to be a matter of *popular* record, and their denial to be a product of undemocratic elitist skepticism and intellectual snobbery. . . . This is the only point where Žižek is in substantive exegetical error concerning Chesterton, but his error is nonetheless understandable." My error is not only understandable—I stand by it, since what I have in mind is Chesterton's reference to Christianity as the best defense against superstitious beliefs in ghosts, magic, and miracles: for Chesterton, the Christian God is the ultimate guarantor of ordinary reality, the Exception which sustains the rationality of the universe: "a dog is an omen, and a cat is a mystery, and a pig is a mascot, and a beetle is a scarab, calling up all the menagerie of polytheism from Egypt and old India; Dog Anubis and great green-eyed Pasht and all the holy howling Bulls of Bashan; reeling back to the bestial gods of the beginning, escaping into elephants and snakes and crocodiles; and all because you are frightened of four words: He was made Man." Indeed, as Chesterton put it, if you do not believe in God, you are ready to believe in anything. . .—There is a similar problem with Milbank's diagnosis of where psychoanalysis fails:

If, therefore, psychoanalysis can never help you to an adult fulfillment of desire (as Freud partially hoped), neither can it truly cure you of desire. For your symptomatic desire is not the sign of a psychic disease—it is rather *sinthom*, what you are, and it is this alone which analysis helps better to reveal. Therefore desire, which cannot be cured, must also be tragically persisted in—regardless of the social chaos thereby caused—because the alternative would be a suicidal abandonment of selfhood.

In an abstract sense, the first sentence is vaguely true—it points toward what Lacan formulated as *il n'y a pas de rapport sexuel*. So the question is here simply: which position is true, that of the "adult fulfillment of desire" or that of its ultimate impasse? However, what follows after "therefore," the consequence Milbank draws from it, is downright wrong: we are back at the opposition between either persisting in desire and thereby causing socio-ethical chaos, or killing (erasing, stifling) the very libidinal substance of our Self. At least two things should be added here. First, Lacan's mature theory (part of which is the notion of *sinthom*) is *not* tragic but comic; it involves a shift from the tragedy of desire to the comedy of drive: in "traversing the fantasy," one learns to enjoy one's *sinthom*. Second, the opposition Milbank construes is undermined by the very basic notion introduced by Lacan, that of *objet a* as surplus-enjoyment, which indicates the basic paradox of *jouissance*: it is both impossible *and* unavoidable; it is never fully achieved, always missed, but, simultaneously, we never can get rid of it—every renunciation of enjoyment generates an enjoyment in renunciation, every obstacle to desire generates a desire for an obstacle, etc. The ambiguity of the French expression is decisive here: it can mean "surplus of enjoyment" as well as "no enjoyment"—the surplus of enjoyment is not a remainder of enjoyment which resists no matter how hard the subject tries to get rid of it, but an enjoyment that arises out of the very renunciation itself. This is why, for Lacan (as already for Hegel), there is nothing more egotistically obscene than a radically ascetic renunciation of pleasures: the choice Milbank posits between full fidelity to desire and suicidal abandonment of selfhood is ultimately null; the two options amount to the same thing.

Although Milbank makes interesting use of psychoanalysis, his references to Lacan all too often amount to a reading which combines bits and pieces of Lacan into a construction in which I find it difficult to recognize Lacanian theory—for example, Milbank's claim that "the male subject . . . is for Lacan (again for contingent reasons both cultural and biological) initially the paradigmatic subject" is, as I have repeatedly tried to demonstrate, emphatically wrong: insofar as, for Lacan, subject as such is hysterical, it is, at its most basic level, sexed as feminine. When Milbank claims that, as a Kantian, I line up "law with freedom, but not law with 'another' desire, a transfigured natural desire for peace and harmony, as envisaged by St. Paul, which no longer requires either prohibitions or commandments," he again misrepresents my position: while I do admittedly reject as "imaginary" any notion of a "natural desire for peace and harmony," transfigured or not, I no less reject, in a Pauline way, as the ultimate ethical reality the Kantian opposition between Law and transgression ("sin"). Consequently, I fully endorse Pauline Agape (which, following Terry Eagleton, I also translate as "political love"). As a good Pauline, I claim that Law and "sin" form a vicious cycle, reinforcing each other, so that there is no way to "line up" Law and Agape: we attain Agape only when we break out of the entire cycle of Law and "sin."

It is significant how Milbank misreads my thesis on Hegel as "vanishing mediator": "Žižek admits a crucial difference between Hegel and post-Hegelian thought, and remains interestingly ambivalent about where his own loyalties here lie. His case is that Hegel was a 'vanishing mediator' who, in bringing metaphysics to a conclusion, also opened up a path beyond the metaphysical." But Hegel is for me a "vanishing mediator" in a much more radical way than just "the last of the old and the first of the new": precisely because of his unique position on the borderline between the two epochs, the traditional metaphysical and the postmetaphysical, something emerges with Hegel which his sudden eclipse and the rise of big antimetaphysicians like Schopenhauer, Marx, and Kierkegaard again covers up. In this sense there is no ambivalence, interesting or not, about my Hegelian loyalties.

So when Milbank critically remarks: "For if negativity is the driving force of reality, then a process of formally inevitable unfolding must also prevail—this being the factor that Žižek tends to play down," I cannot but agree—on condition that the quoted sentence is taken more literally than he himself takes it: "a process of formally inevitable unfolding must prevail," i.e., the conceptually determined "formally inevitable unfolding" is not there from the very beginning of the process, it gradually "prevails," and this "prevailing" is the (in itself contingent) process by means of which the conceptual necessity (I am almost tempted to say: in an autopoietic way) forms itself out of the initial contingency. In other words, there is no preexisting necessity that directs the dialectical process, since this necessity is precisely what arises through this process, i.e., what this process is about. This is why I cannot accept Milbank's description of how "Žižek's metanarrative of denominational progression fits into the Hegelian metanarrative of the necessarily presupposed development of Christianity into its own 'atheistic' truth. However, Žižek's account of denominational progression is not very historically convincing, and the facts really do not fit any dialectical mold. (In some ways I am a British empiricist. . . .)" Yes, there is a necessity, but this necessity is *retroactive*, it arises as the (*contingent*) self-sublation of contingency. And, incidentally, here also we find the key difference between Hegel and the Lukács of *History and Class Consciousness*: Lukács is not too Hegelian-idealist, but too idealist for Hegel. What is excluded as impossible in the Hegelian space is the Lukácsian historical act of the proletarian subject, a (revolutionary) act which is totally self-transparent about its own historical role, which performs it and knows exactly what it is doing. This is what Hegel's well-known metaphor of the owl of Minerva flying at dusk critically aims at: for Hegel, understanding comes after the (f)act, there is a minimal constitutive gap that separates the act and the knowledge of its scope.

As for the criticism that I simplify the actually much more complex historical development of Christianity, giving too much weight to Lossky in the Orthodox tradition, etc.: of course empirical reality is always more complex than its underlying notional structure, so that one can always play the game of pointing out what is ignored in the notional grasping of empirical reality. However, for Hegel as a notional antinominalist, the key question is elsewhere: is the notional abstraction by means of which we grasp reality a "correct" one, is it a true "concrete universality" which generates/mediates the empirical content, or a mere abstraction which reduces the living reality to its formal skeleton? In other words, while Hegel fully admits the gap between notional abstraction and empirical wealth, this gap is not merely a gap between objective reality and our abstract-reductive subjective understanding of it; it is, on the contrary, a gap inscribed into the thing (reality) itself, a tension (antagonism, "contradiction") which triggers the thing's development. As Hegel often repeats, no thing fully fits its (inherent) notion, and this discord ("self-contradiction") is the motor of dialectics. So, along these lines, I continue to claim that my abstraction is the "true" one.

However, to pursue this line of argumentation is a futile scoring of points. I should focus on the level at which things are really decided—what I am tempted to call, in the old inadequate language, the basic metaphysical vision of reality that serves as the background of our argumentation. It may seem relatively easy to formulate this difference between our basic positions: a Christianity which fully asserts the paradox of the *coincidentia oppositorum* in the transcendent God in whom all creatures analogically participate versus the atheist-Hegelian Christianity which treats paradox "as merely a logical moment to be surpassed: its stasis must advance toward the dynamism of negative dialectics." So while Milbank advocates a postsecular reenchantment of reality, I claim that we should learn to "live in a disenchanted world without wanting to reenchant it."[9] However, Milbank sometimes supplements this pure confrontation of irreducible positions with immanent critique, reading me against myself, claiming that, beneath the "official" Hegelian-atheist Žižek, there is "a different, latent Žižek: a Žižek who does not see Chesterton as sub-Hegel, but Hegel as sub-Chesterton. A Žižek therefore who has remained with paradox, or rather moved back into paradox from dialectic." This supplement is necessary, since a pure confrontation of positions is never possible: no formulation of differences is neutral, every attempt to delineate the confronted positions already formulates them from the standpoint of one position. My strategy will therefore be similar to Milbank's, combining three procedures. I will endeavor to formulate as precisely as possible our difference; I will enumerate some points where I see Milbank simply misreading my position; and—most important—I will also read him against the grain, arguing for a very strong claim: that our difference is not the one between (his) Christian orthodoxy and (my) atheist heterodoxy, since his basic position does not really allow for what Chesterton called "a matter more dark and awful than it is easy to discuss," the traumatic *skandalon* of the Christian experience. To put it even more bluntly: my claim is that it is Milbank who is in effect guilty of heterodoxy, ultimately of a regression to paganism: in my atheism, I am more Christian than Milbank. —So let me begin with Milbank's basic vision or experience of reality to which any "holistic" pagan would subscribe: the opaque (back-)Ground which is the abyssal mysterious Origin of everything, and in which the opposites that characterize our phenomenal world coincide:

> If to be hidden is to be shown (against the background of "mist," as including a misty density proper to the thing itself), and therefore to be shown is to be hidden, then this implies not an impossible contradiction that must be overcome (dialectics) but rather an outright impossible *coincidence of opposites* that can (somehow, but we know not how) be persisted with. This is the Catholic logic of *paradox*—of an "overwhelming glory" (*para-doxa*) which nonetheless saturates our everyday reality.

Milbank is very precise in outlining the cognitive paradox of this scene: it is not merely that the known things emerged against their misty back-Ground—things can be known only insofar as they are embedded in the "vague density" of their back-Ground, i.e., insofar as they are ultimately unknowable. If they were to be deprived of this impenetrable back-Ground, they would lose their very reality and become transparent specters of our solipsistic imagination:

> To accept that all truth is mediated by beauty is once more to remain with immediately given paradox. In this instance the paradox is that we can know only the unknowable—that only the vague density of things grants them at once their specificity and their external knowability, so freeing our claims to understand from the taint of solipsistic self-reflection.

Note here also the precise reference to beauty, which has to be given its full weight: a totally transparent rational structure is never beautiful; a harmonious hierarchical edifice which remains partially invisible, grounded in an opaque foundation, is beautiful. Beauty is the beauty of an order mysteriously emanating from its unknowable center. . . . Again, while I fully recognize the spiritual authenticity of this vision, I see no place in it for the central Christian experience, that of the Way of the Cross: at the moment of Christ's death, the earth shook, there was a thunderstorm, signaling that the world was falling apart, that something terrifyingly wrong was taking place which threw the very ontological edifice of reality off the rails. In Hegelese, Milbank's vision remains that of a substantial immediate harmony of Being; there is no place in it for the outburst of radical negativity, for the full impact of the shattering news that "God is dead."

But, one can reply, this is precisely Milbank's point: to acknowledge such a radical disturbance in/of the divine harmony is foreign to Catholicism; it pertains to the Protestant "disenchantment" of the world which admits a gap between the earthly and the divine, which sees only a cold material reality where Catholicism sees the wealth of a magical universe endowed with spirituality. And this brings us to the sociopolitical consequences of Milbank's intuition of reality: Milbank advocates a version of alternate modernity whose possibility is embodied in the line of Christian thought from Aquinas through Eckhart, Cusa, and Kierkegaard, up to Chesterton and Milbank himself. In refusing the Protestant narrative of the progress of Christianity from Orthodoxy and Catholicism to Protestantism (and then, if one goes to the end, Hegel's atheism), he outlines the possibility of an alternate development:

> It is easy, for example, to imagine that a more humanist reformation might have taken place (in fifteenth- and sixteenth-century Spain this had at one stage more or less already occurred) such that, while lay life and piety would have moved more center-stage, the specifics of Reformation and Counter-Reformation dogmatics would not have dominated the European future. . . . Why is it not legitimate to imagine "another" Christian modernity that would be linked to the universal encouragement of mystical openness and productivity, rather than the separation between a forensic faith and an instrumentalizing reason?

Let us first note how this reading implies that history is not a necessary logical/conceptual progress but a contingent narrative with multiple trends, so that it could also have turned out otherwise—Milbank's anti-Hegelian point is that "narrative structure refuses dialectics in the Hegelian sense": "it is not governed by determinate negation, since this would undo contingency." Against this, Milbank advocates "the narratalogical principle of alternative opposites and multiple dualities." —While opening up the space for individual freedom and creativity, this alternate modernity would constrain them to— and (re)inscribe them into—the only Ground on which they can really thrive and avoid nihilistic self-destruction, that of justice as "identical with objective social harmony," as a proportional order of cosmic hierarchic balance—a dimension missing in liberalism and Marxism:

> Liberalism (and Marxism, which is but a variant upon liberalism) knows of no justice—only mutual agreement to agree or, more likely, to differ. But justice involves an objectively right proportionate distribution, as Aristotle taught, and

beyond this a will to encourage all in their infinite fulfillment within their appropriate social roles, as St. Paul taught.

The dream here is the one of "balance between the democracy of reason on the one hand and the esoteric hierarchy of the poetic on the other": Catholicism opens up the space for an alternate modernity in which democratic universality and individual freedom remain grounded in a hierarchic proportional order in which each member is in its own place, thereby contributing to global harmony—a soft-Fascist vision, if there ever was one:

> Would it not be more plausible to suppose that one needs to modify paternalism with a greater humility and attentiveness to populist feedback rather than to remove it altogether? Especially as it is clear that, since we are always "educated" animals (even in order to become language users), the role of the parental *in principle cannot be elided*.

This is the heart of Milbank's "Red Tory" utopia: a democratic patriarchy in which opposites are reconciled, in which we have market freedom, but within hierarchic harmony, in which we have corporatist democracy, in which we have a secular order organically grounded in the sacred:

> Protestantism was not a necessary stage on the way toward enlightened liberal market freedom . . . burgeoning "modern" aspects of the Middle Ages, emerging both with and against "feudalism," can be returned to as having a different potential from the one which liberal democracy has emphasized—a more pluralist, more corporatist, more distributist, more lay-religious potential which refuses the modern duality of the economic and the political as much as the modern duality of secular and sacred.

Along these lines, Milbank celebrates Eckhart as "the 'Red Tory' who radicalizes the old establishment itself, by elevating the divine monarch out of sight, and so into kenotic proximity": "Since all derives from a topmost source that is above any conceivable ontic height (and so deeper than any ontic depths), everything is equal in relation to this ontological summit, thereby relativizing all merely ontic degrees. In a sense, as Eckhart declares, a stone proclaims as much of God as does a man; it simply cannot articulate this." It is this balance between ontological equality with regard to the unknowable transcendent God *and* ontic inequality and (ordered) hierarchy which enabled Eckhart to remain democratic-egalitarian *and* avoid

> the extreme proto-individualism of the Franciscan-inspired "spirituals" of his time, who rejected any necessity for order or hierarchy in the ecclesial or secular realms. This, one could say, was tantamount to refusing a burgeoning contractualist version of democracy, since the contract is the only thing that

can distill order out of an individualist anarchy. Yet at the same time, Eckhart in effect proposed an alternative kind of democratic leveling that is linked with his mystical sense of the equality of everything in relation to God, even though an ontic inequality remains.

Instead of the usual (implicit) notion of democratic equality as an appearance sustained by a "deeper" hierarchic order, we have here a hierarchic phenomenal order sustained by a "deeper" equality with regard to the unknowable Origin. Milbank finds in Eckhart a similar balance between contemplative withdrawal from the world and practical worldly engagement: they are not opposed, as in Protestantism; on the contrary: "Going 'inward' to attain contemplative unity is not, for Eckhart, the final goal—as it never is, for all authentic Christian mystics. . . .The 'emptied' soul is also the fertile soul, the soul open to perform- ing God's will as its own and so of acting creatively, which means precisely to act without egotism, although still with personal distinctness." Detachment thus enables authentic engagement—not only in the sense that it allows us to maintain a proper distance toward worldly phenomena, i.e., that it protects us from getting caught in the worldly whirlpool. Detachment brings us in contact with the unknowable Origin with regard to which we are all equal, and it is only with reference to this abyssal Ground that we can attain "an attitude of 'justice' which is one of equal concern for all." What gets lost here is nonethe- less the very core of democracy, which has to appear phenomenally, to posit itself as such in contrast to all hierarchic orders—the core of democracy which found its most radical expression in Christ's "scandalous" words from Luke: "if anyone comes to me and does not hate his father and his mother, his wife and children, his brothers and sisters—yes even his own life—he cannot be my disciple" (14:26).

Milbank also waters down the subversive edge of "Eckhart's extreme state- ment of identity with God—according to which we can judge God, exer- cise power over God, and so forth, as much as the other way around": "this is not a modern Kantian or Hegelian doctrine of human autonomy, accord- ing to which man is *substituted* for God. Rather, it is a *paradoxical* doctrine of divine-human identity which cuts both ways. We are identical with God only because God (following Augustine) is our own deepest identity." But Eckhart's explicit point is, precisely, that this identity does *not* cut both ways: we are not substituted for God, the gap and asymmetry remains, but an uncanny one: God cannot command us, we command God; it is God's nature to be good to us, so we do not have to be grateful to him.

Such "scandalous" messages are grounded in the way Christ relates to the Old Testament and its Law: he took nothing away from it, and only added himself to it. This gesture of subjectivization of the (source of the) Law is cru- cial, it is the secret motive of all obvious change to the content of the Jewish

Commandments that occurs in Christ. In his famous dialogue with Christianity, Jacob Neusner[10] rejected the claim that Jesus merely completes the Law, far from undermining it; his main example is the fourth Commandment, which tells a Jew to respect his father and his mother, etc.: when Jesus is told that his mother and brothers are outside the house and want to talk to him, he points to his disciples around him and says: "Look, these are my mother and my brothers!" (Matthew 12:46–50). The sense of the Commandment is thereby totally subverted: the Jewish Law prescribes the continuation of the rigid social order, with its customs and hierarchy: what is negated is not only the relation of parenthood, but the entire social edifice. From a particular social group, we pass to singular universality; the "transubstantiation" of the Jews as a particular nation into the universal family of believers is sustained by the emergence of the singular subjectivity extracted from its particular group. What happens with institutionalized Christianity is that it wants to have its cake and eat it: the tension between the particular and the universal is lost, the universal frame of the community of believers turns into a kind of protective umbrella of our particular groups, the disruptive aspect of universality is obliterated.

And—back to philosophy—it is easy to see how this ethico-political opposition to liberalism is grounded in an attitude to contradiction that differs from the Protestant-Hegelian one: for Hegel, contradiction means tension, conflict, the violence of negativity, i.e., the Hegelian Whole is a Whole kept together by the process of internal antagonisms; whereas the Catholic Whole is one of divine transcendence in which opposites miraculously coincide, in which "the incompatible are at one." We are thus dealing with two completely different ways of "ontologizing the contradictory":

> the medieval thinkers did so in a Catholic, paradoxical, and still analogical (or metaxological) rather than dialectical manner. This means that they did not on the whole take the violation of identity to mean "contradiction" . . . but, rather, "coincidence." They did not, then, take it to imply the agonistic, but rather an eschatological peace so extreme that even the incompatible are now at one, like the lion lying down with the lamb.
>
> Hegel, by contrast, remains in a stronger negative agreement with Ockham, which reflects his Lutheran inheritance: if something is also that to which it is related and so is not, then this is a source of continuous tension.

This difference between the two versions of the coincidence of opposites can also be put in more formal terms: for Milbank's Catholic view, the contradiction is that of the opposite poles which coincide in a higher third element encompassing them both, their unknowable Origin and Ground; while for me, as a Hegelian, there is no need for a third term: the difference between the two "poles"—species—coincides with the difference between the species as such and their encompassing genus; genus is one of its own species, and it is this overlapping, not any "eternal struggle of the opposite poles," which gives us a properly dialectical contradiction.

When Milbank refers to Kierkegaard as the advocate of unresolvable paradox in contrast to the Hegelian dialectical contradiction, he ignores the immense gap that separates Kierkegaard from the medieval paradox of *coincidentia opposi-torum* in Eckhart, Cusa, etc.: this paradox situates the coincidence of opposites in the absolute transcendence of God—basically, it remains a Christian version of the old pagan idea that, in the mysterious Absolute, our human opposites lose their meaning. The level at which opposites coincide is the level at which, detached from human struggles, one finds inner peace and release. For Kierkegaard, on the contrary, the "paradox" of Christian faith is far from the idea of peace in the Absolute: the Christian "paradox" resides in the breathtakingly traumatic fact that we, human mortals, are trapped in a "sickness unto death," that anxiety is our a priori condition, that our existence is radically torn—and, even more, as Chesterton pointed out, that strife is integral to the very heart of God himself, that God is the greatest rebel against himself, that he himself has to turn atheist and blasphemer. The paradox is not that finite oppositions coincide in the infinity of the Absolute, but that the Absolute itself has to take upon itself the pain of Difference, and rebel against itself—only such strife truly personalizes God, as Schelling saw clearly.

In a Catholic Whole, harmony prevails between God and his creatures, as well as between creatures themselves, which are ultimately ordered into an organic hierarchy: "Creatures are given to be in order to return to God, in order to return to God through gratitude." And—now we come to the (theological) crux of the matter—in such a close circle of harmonious and balanced exchange between God and his creation, the divine Incarnation loses its traumatic character of a radical antagonism at the very heart of divinity (of which Chesterton is, as we have just seen, fully aware) and turns into an index of the "coincidence of finite and infinite." The consequences of such a position are crucial to the way we conceive of Trinity: more precisely, the relation between the "immanent" Trinity (the trinity in / of God-in-itself, independently of God's relation to his creation, to spatiotemporal reality) and the "economic" Trinity (the trinity of God-for-ourselves, the way God relates to his "household," incarnates himself in the mortal body of Christ visible and palpable to us, and then, after dying, rises again as the Holy Spirit, as the spirit of love between believers, i.e., as the collective of believers): for Milbank, "the eternal, 'immanent' Trinity should have priority, as Christian orthodoxy declares, over the 'economic' Trinity, or the Trinity as mediated to the Creation in space and time." If God is already in himself, independently of the vicissitudes of creation (the Fall, etc.), Trinitarian, i.e., if "grace would always have been the grace of Christ, even without the Fall," if "there would always have been an incarnation process even without the incursion of sin," then the Christ who walked as a human among humans in Palestine two thousand years ago was not the "true" Christ, God himself, but a secondary figure, a kind of Platonic copy of the "original" true Christ who dwelled in the immanence of the Trinity-in-itself, independently of human history—or, as Milbank puts it, "Christ's human existence is entirely derived from the divine person of the *Logos* by which he is enhypostasized." For me, on the contrary, it is the "economic" Trinity which is the truth, the true site, of Christianity, and the "immanent" Trinity is nothing but its "reification" into an independent process; more precisely, there is absolutely no gap between the "immanent" Trinity and the "economic" Trinity: what was going on in the earthly reality of Palestine two thousand years ago was *a process in the very heart of God himself*; there was (and is) no higher reality backing it up.

This, finally, brings us to the core of the politico-theological gap that separates me from Milbank: Milbank claims that, in demanding from Chesterton the admission that Law as such is universalized crime, that Order as such is grounded in chaotic violence, I am imposing on him a foreign dialectical reasoning. However, I am in fact simply reproaching him for his illogicality, for not taking fully into account what he himself formulates in a brilliant way elsewhere—when, for example, he claims that "morality is the most dark and daring of conspiracies," or that "God, to be wholly God, must have been a rebel as well as a king." So my reply to Milbank's final question—"If law as such . . . is also crime, then wherein lies the good for Žižek?"—is an easy Pauline-Protestant one: not in the domain of law, which is by definition caught in a self-propelling vicious cycle with crime, but in love—not in sentimental love, but in love on account of which, as Kierkegaard put it with his matchless radicality, I am ready to kill my neighbor.

FROM THE DEATH-OF-GOD THEOLOGY TO POSTSECULAR THOUGHT . . . AND BACK

It is this same "further extreme" which, I think, separates me from the postsecular version of deconstructionism. A new field is emerging to which the well-known designations "poststructuralism," "postmodernism," or "deconstructionism" no longer apply; even more radically, this field renders problematic the very feature shared by Derrida and his great opponent, Habermas: that of respect for Otherness. In spite of their irreconcilable differences, its main figures are at this moment Giorgio Agamben and Alain Badiou (and if I may, I would immodestly include myself in this series). Their predecessors, the two Janus-faced figures who belong both to the previous "poststructuralist" field and to this new field, are Deleuze and Lacan—not the anti-Oedipal Deleuze recuperated by the definitely "postmodern" Negri, but the Deleuze of *Difference* and *Repetition* and *The Logic of Sense*; not the standard Lacan of signifying games, but what Jacques-Alain Miller called the "other Lacan," the Lacan of the "other *écrits*." The main feature of this field is its theologico-political turn: a decidedly materialist focus on theological topic (in a mode that totally differs from the late-Derridean negative theology of Otherness); a radical political stance, inclusive of a critical attitude toward democracy—to put it in a vicious way, democracy is not to come, but to go. . . . What if this is the first true taste of the "thought of the twenty-first century"?

So when Milbank reproaches me for ignoring altogether "the fact that a legitimate 'postmodern' critique of negative dialectics as dogmatically metaphysical itself newly legitimates a belief in transcendence along with a new primacy for the 'positive,'" my answer is that not only I am not ignoring it, I am actively fighting it—let me summarize my main points, starting from a succinct formulation of the problem that defines the postmodern "theological turn": "*How do we get from the post-Christian, post-Holocaust, and largely secular death-of-God theologies of the 1960s to the postmodern return of religion?*"[11] The answer is that the "death of God," the secularization of modern Europe, clears the slate by obliterating the moral-metaphysical God of onto-theology, and thus paradoxically opens up the space for the new authentic postmetaphysical religion, a Christianity focused on Agape. The presupposition of this "death of the death of God" is that the consequent Enlightenment leads to its self-negation: the critique which first targets religious and all other metaphysical superstitions has to end up by negating its own metaphysical presuppositions, its own trust in a rational deterministic world which inexorably leads to progress:

> In Kierkegaard and Nietzsche, the world of Enlightenment Reason and Hegelian Absolute Knowledge is left far behind. They each foresee in his own way the madness of the twentieth century whose genocidal violence made a mockery of Hegel's sanguine view of history as the autobiography of the Spirit of time.[12]

In this way, as one can expect, even Nietzsche, the fiercest critic of Christianity, can be enlisted to support the postmodern "theological turn":

> When Nietzsche says "God is dead," he's saying that there is no center, no single, overarching principle that explains things. There's just a multiplicity of fictions or interpretations. Well, if there's no single overarching principle, that means science is also one more interpretation, and it doesn't have an exclusive right to absolute truth. But, if that's true, then non-scientific ways of thinking about the world, including religious ways, resurface.[13]

It is indeed true that the now predominant "skepticism" about secular narratives of Enlightenment is the obverse of the so-called "postsecular" turn in which religion appears as a key "site of resistance" against the alienations of what is perceived as a singularly Western modernity. Religion stands here for an "auratic" belief in "God," a word which should be read as deprived of any positive onto-teleological status: God is no longer the Highest Being watching over our destiny, but a name for radical openness, for the hope of change, for the always-to-come Otherness, etc. Illustrative of this attitude is John Caputo's *On Religion*, which could be called the ultimate formulation of Derridean deconstructive messianism: Caputo is horrified at the very idea of a religious dogma, i.e., the notion of a God who decided to address a particular group of people at a particular moment, according them privileged access to absolute Truth. Religion is thus reduced to its pure desubstantialized form: a belief that our miserable reality is not all there is, the ultimate truth; that "there is another world possible," a promise/hope of redemption-to-come betrayed by any ontological positivization.

It is at this point that I should reiterate the shift from Judaism to Christianity: to assert the moment of closure, the dogma that sustains openness, the brutal and violent cut, rupture, that sustains reconciliation, or, more radically, *is* reconciliation. The "truth" of Christianity is that, in our earthly universe, things have to appear, to reveal themselves, as (in the guise of) their opposite: eternity is an ecstatic moment that cuts into the temporal flow; the work of love is a ruthless struggle; our rise to divine eternity is God's Incarnation, his acceptance of the mortal body; etc. When, in a postmodern mode, we ignore this "truth," we cannot but reject the death-of-God theologies as all too Christian, still committed to the basic Christian notions of the passage from (the Jewish) Law to love, from letter to spirit, from alienation to reconciliation, from transcendence to immanence: they remain

> theologies with a *Christian* pedigree that turn on the doctrines of the Trinity and the Incarnation. . . . The death of God is a *grand récit* all its own that is complicitous with Hegel's story about the Jews and a certain quick reading of Saint Paul on the Jews. That is the supersessionist story of the transition from the alienated Old Law of the Pharisees to the benign New Law of love and the gift, from the dead letter of literalism to the living Spirit, from the legalism of slaves to the religion of the children and friends of God, from an eye-for-an-eye economy to the gift, etc.[14]

Therein also lies Caputo's critical distance from Vattimo, who repeats the death-of-God theologies' move from transcendence to immanence (from Father to Son, who rises again in the communal Spirit), celebrating secularization as the becoming-world of the Holy Spirit: "The tolerant, nonauthoritarian and pluralistic democratic societies in the West are the translation into real political structures of the Christian doctrine of neighbour love."[15] This is the core of the Christian notion of the *kenosis*, self-emptying, of God: God "empties" himself by transposing the focal point of his message—neighborly love—into the secular world; and this is also why Vattimo rejects the Levinasian transcendence of God. For Caputo, however, Vattimo misses the point of Levinas's assertion of God's transcendence: the inaccessibility of God means that

> every time we attempt to direct our glance to God on high it is "deflected" by God to the face of the neighbour here below. The pragmatic meaning of the transcendence of the *tout autre* in Levinas is service to the neighbour. Levinas's Jewish deflection does the work of Vattimo's kenosis.[16]

Does it really? As Caputo is quick to admit, the problem is, of course, that there is no neutral ground between Judaism and Christianity—his rejection of the Christian "narrative" automatically gives priority to the Jewish position:

> Deconstruction is something more of a Jewish science, that is, a deconstruction of idols that, while affirming flesh and the body—the Jewish Scriptures are all about land and children—is constantly worried about divine incarnations, because incarnations are always local occurrences.[17]

What, then, happens with the basic Christian theme of the death of God within this perspective? What is allowed to "die" in a "deconstruction" of Christianity? As expected, just the temporary-contingent historic-symbolic specification/determination of God:

> So my theology of the event is prepared to concede, if not exactly the death of God, at least the mortality or historical contingency of the name of God, the separability in principle of the event from the name, like a spirit leaving a lifeless body behind.[18]

It is difficult to miss the irony of these lines: after rejecting the Christian opposition between the dead Letter and the living Spirit, Caputo has to mobilize this very opposition to sustain the "separability" of the event from its name. But does this not entirely miss the truly new traumatic dimension of the Christian death of God: what dies on the Cross is indeed God himself, not just his "finite container," a historically contingent name or form of God? If we claim the second, we reduce Christianity back to the pagan-Gnostic topic of a nameless divine Real which takes different shapes in different times. Caputo relies here on the opposition between God as *ens supremum et deus omnipotens*, the highest Entity, the creator and ruler of the world, the highest Power, etc., and God as a totally desubstantialized promise, the source of an unconditional claim on us, a spectral life that "stirs within the name of God," but is already betrayed by each positive determination. To designate the encounter with the authentically transcendent divine dimension, Caputo has recourse to Badiou's notion of Event—the event is an irreducible possibility, a potentiality that can assume various forms of expression and instantiation. The event is not reducible to the actual, but stirs as a simmering potentiality within the name or the state of affairs, incessantly seeking an outlet, constantly pressing for expression in words and things. The event is irreducible; indeed, . . . it is the very form of irreducibility itself. For what is irreducible is what resists contraction into some finite form or other, what seeks to twist free from the finite containers in which it finds itself deposited.[19]

The move from metaphysics to postmetaphysical postmodernism is the move from substantial entities to events. An event is not something that happens, but "something going on in what happens, something that is being expressed or realized or given shape in what happens."[20] We should thus distinguish

> between a *name* and the event that is astir or that transpires in a name. The name is a kind of provisional formulation of an event, a relatively stable if evolving structure, while the event is ever restless, on the move, seeking new forms to assume, seeking to get expressed in still unexpressed ways. Names are historical, contingent, provisional expressions in natural languages, while events are what names are trying to form or formulate, nominate or denominate.[21]

This opens up the space for deconstruction: its task is to maintain the gap between the spectral unconditional Event and its contingent instantiations. In this "deconstructive" way, every particular taking sides, every instantiation of the Divine, is relativized, has to be taken and practiced with ironic distance: whenever we focus on a particular formulation of the divine, *ce n'est pas ça*. Within this space, there is simply no place for the paradox of Christian Incarnation: in Christ, this miserable individual, we see God himself, so that his death is the death of God himself. The properly Christian choice is the "leap of faith" by means of which we take the risk to fully engage in a singular instantiation as the Truth embodied, with no ironic distance, no fingers crossed. "Christ" stands for the very singular point excluded by Caputo: a direct short circuit, identity even, between a positive singularity and the divine Event. Caputo professes his love for Kierkegaard—but where here is the central insight of Kierkegaard's *Philosophical Fragments*, his insistence on the central paradox of Christianity: eternity is accessible only through time, through the belief in Christ's Incarnation as a temporal event?

What Caputo misses here is the "reflexive" move by means of which the very excess of the Event over its embodiment in name(s) has to be re-marked in a name, a name that functions as a "signifier without signified," as an empty name, not the fullness of Meaning but a promise, an obligation. The excess of the signified (spirit) over the signifier (letter) has to be registered / contracted in an empty letter. And this is the function of Christ's Incarnation: the contraction of the void.

The basic problem with Caputo's theology of the Event is that it shrinks from performing the (Hegelian) move from reflection to reflexive determination. First, the Event appears as the unintegrable excess that stirs things up but can never be caught in its effects, its positive determinations: it shines through its effects, it is reflected in them, but always in a displaced/distorted way. The next crucial step is to conceive this excessive X itself as an effect of its effects, as the presupposition which is itself posited—determined—by its distorted reflections: the Event is a retroactive effect of the act of naming: there is no Event prior to its name. The logic is here the same as with Einstein's passage from special to general theory of relativity: from space curved by matter to matter itself as an effect of the curvature of space. In other words, the Event is nothing but the distortion of the space of its effects—this is the (Hegelian) passage from idealism to materialism. The point is not to pass from inadequate/distorted reflections to a fully adequate and transparent (self-)reflection: the gap that separates reflection from the (distortedly) reflected X remains, it is just itself displaced into the heart of this X. (Note that Badiou himself is ambiguous here, shrinking from this step of conceiving the Event itself as a retroactive effect of its inscriptions.) If, however, we follow Caputo and "deconstruct" the paradox of the unique divine Incarnation, the dimension of absolute Truth also has to go, since Incarnation is in Christianity its only ontological guarantee—Caputo is completely logical in taking this step:

> In Christianity there is a fundamental commitment to freedom. And, to add a bit of scandal, by standing for freedom, this includes freedom from (the idea of) truth. After all, if there really is an objective truth, there will always be someone who is more in possession of it than I and thereby authorized to impose its law obligation on me.[22]

This inevitably brings us to the self-referential paradox Caputo heroically assumes: "The truth that shall set us free is true precisely because it frees us."[23] The "truth" that sets us free (from truth itself) is thus the well-known postmodern meta-truth: the insight into the fact that there is no final Truth, that every "Truth" is the effect of contingent discursive mechanisms and practices. . . . How, then, after admitting that every figure of God is culturally conditioned, can Vattimo go on praying? His answer cannot but surprise us by its unintended objective cynicism:

> when I pray, I know precisely that the words I am using are not intended to convey some literal truth. I pray these words more for the love of a tradition than I do for the love of some mythic reality. It is like the relationship you have with an aged relative.[24]

The only way to redeem the subversive core of Christianity is therefore to return to death-of-God theology, especially Thomas Altizer: to *repeat* its gesture today. What gets lost in "soft" postmodern theology is the dimension indicated by the very concept "death of God"—the traumatic core of the divine kenosis, of God's self-emptying. In postmodern theology, kenosis affects only us, humans: it turns out to be the deconstructive drawing of the line of separation between the unconditional Promise and its contingent instantiations; in and through it, the divine dimension is "emptied" of its onto-theological fetishization.

This, perhaps, accounts for the strange fact that, although Caputo understands his position as a postsecular reassertion of religion (against the death-of-God endorsement of secularization as the actualization of the Holy Spirit), his "religion without religion" appears much too aseptic, lifeless, bloodless, lacking the properly religious passion (I am even tempted to say: the stirring power of the Event), in comparison with someone like Altizer, whose vision of the death of God retains a properly apocalyptic shattering power. Caputo's reading of the death of God reduces it to a happy "deconstructive" event: the God who dies is the onto-theological Master of creation, the supreme Entity, and the field is thereby open for the (re)assertion of the true abyss of Divinity as a spectral Promise—to a death like this, one can only say "Good riddance!" For Altizer, on the contrary, what "dies" on the Cross is not just the false (positive, ontic) envelope of Divinity, which was obfuscating its eventual core; what dies is God himself, the structuring principle of our entire universe, its life-giving force, the guarantee of its meaning. The death of God thus equals the end of the world, the experience of "darkness at noon."

It is thus not that death-of-God theology is a middle-of-the-road phenomenon, partially negating the classical onto-theology while remaining within its horizon, which is truly left behind only with postmodern deconstructive religion; it is rather that something traumatic erupts in death-of-God theology, something that is covered up by postmodern theology. We should go even further here: what if the entire history of Christianity, inclusive of (and especially) its Orthodox versions, is structured as a series of defenses against the traumatic apocalyptic core of incarnation/death/resurrection? What if Christianity comes near to this core only at its rare apocalyptic moments? This is Altizer's thesis.[25]

Today, apocalypse is near at many levels: ecology, informational saturation ... things are approaching a zero point, "the end of time is near," so that the only serious question for an authentic Christian is today the following one:

Ours is surely a truly apocalyptic situation, the most apocalyptic situation in our history, one transcending even an original Christian apocalypticism in the totality of its historical enactment. All past historical worlds are now being dissolved, and even all truly natural and sacred realms as well. Yet could such a dissolution be in genuine continuity with an original apocalyptism? Could our contemporary dissolution ultimately be a kenotic and self-emptying dissolution? (204)

Nothing seems stranger to us today than apocalyptism which is dismissed by the (liberal) majority as a pathological reaction to the deadlocks of (capitalist) modernization, as a sign of the total failure of our "cognitive mapping" of social reality: "Nothing is a deeper mystery today than apocalypse, and this despite the fact that ours is so clearly an apocalyptic time, the deepest and most comprehensively apocalyptic time in our history" (xiii). What we find so difficult to grasp is that apocalypse is not merely a catastrophe of creatures: "Ultimately apocalypse is the apocalypse of God" (xxv). The crucified Jesus is the apocalyptic Jesus: it stands for the end of the world as we knew it, the end of time, when God himself dies, empties himself; at this point of apocalypse, opposites coincide, the lone Jesus is Satan himself, his death is the death of Evil, so that crucifixion and resurrection are one event.—Such an apocalyptism has been from its very beginning till today

> a profoundly revolutionary force in Western history, perhaps our most purely revolutionary power. Just as apocalyptism played a decisive role in all of the great political revolutions of the modern world, from the English Revolution to the Russian Revolution and beyond, nothing has been more revolutionary in world history than apocalyptism, which not only made possible the original triumph of Islam, but also has been a fundamental ground of Marxism, and even of Asian Maoism. (2)

Here we should recall the utopian fervor that sustained the Bolsheviks around 1920: despair and true utopia go together; the only way to survive the catastrophic times of civil war, social disintegration, hunger and cold, is to mobilize "crazy" utopian energies. Is this not one of the basic lessons of the much-maligned "millenarian" movements, exemplarily of the German peasants' revolt in the sixteenth century and their leader Thomas Muntzer? Catastrophe itself has to be read in the apocalyptic mode, as a sign that "the end of time is near," that a new Beginning is around the corner. Such an authentically Pauline apocalyptic atmosphere is clearly discernible in passages like the following one from Trotsky:

> What the Third International demands of its supporters is a recognition, not in words but in deeds, that civilized humanity has entered a revolutionary epoch; that all the capitalist countries are speeding toward colossal disturbances and an open class war; and that the task of the revolutionary representatives of the proletariat is to prepare for that inevitable and approaching war the necessary spiritual armory and buttress of organization.[26]

We should read such outbursts of apocalyptic revolutionary fervor also against the background of its expressions in poetry—recall the most famous poem of the October Revolution, Alexander Blok's "The Twelve" (1918), about twelve Red Guardists patrolling a desolated nighttime city. The apocalyptic atmosphere clearly echoes Blok's earlier symbolist link of catastrophe and utopia:

> To get the bourgeoisie
> We'll start a fire
> a worldwide fire, and drench it
> in blood—
> The good Lord bless us!
> You bourgeoisie, fly as a sparrow!
> I'll drink your blood,
> your warm blood, for love,
> for dark-eyed love.

The famous finale directly identifies the twelve Red Guardists with the apostles led by Christ:

> So they march with sovereign tread . . .
> Behind them the hungry dog drags,
> and wrapped in wild snow at their head
> carrying a blood-red flag—
> soft-footed where the blizzard swirls,
> invulnerable where bullets slice—
> crowned with a crown of snowflake pearls,
> a flowery diadem of ice,
> ahead of them goes Jesus Christ.

In early Christianity, before Orthodoxy established itself, the first counter-movement to an apocalyptic Jesus occurred in Gnosticism, whose traces can be discerned already in the Gospel of John. Gnosticism promoted the figure of "Cynical Jesus, understanding the historical Jesus by way of a radical wisdom tradition, as present in the Gnostic Gospel of Thomas":

> flights from the apocalyptic Jesus are also thereby flights from the revolutionary Jesus, or flights from any kind of historical revolution. . . . Gnosticism not only dissolves every possible humanity of Jesus, but also, and even thereby, dissolves every possibility of historical or even human transformation. (4)[27]

There are thus, *grosso modo*, three main currents in Christianity: Centrist "Legal" Christianity (the ideology of the Church as a State Ideological Apparatus), "Rightist" aristocratic Gnosticism, and "leftist" apocalyptism. This triad loosely fits the historical triad of Orthodoxy–Catholicism–Protestantism: in its understanding of Christ, Orthodoxy focuses on the Gnostic topic of the divinization of man ("God became man so that man could become God"); Catholicism is clearly legalistic, and keeps God-Father at a distance as the Creator; Protestantism violently reasserts the centrality of the Crucifixion as the death of God.—Further distinctions are to be drawn here, of course: Hans Jonas clearly outlined the difference between the two basic orientations of Gnosticism: they both conceive history as the history of Godhead itself, as an immanent divine "devolution"; in both cases, the Fall is not only the Fall from Godhead, but simultaneously the drama of the Fall (and recuperation) of Godhead itself; in both cases, the loss of unity between God and his creation, the gap that separates them, makes God himself evil (the elevated Master of the world):

> Both dramas start with a disturbance in the heights; in both, the existence of the world marks a discomfiture of the divine and a necessary, in itself undesirable, means of an eventual restoration; in both, the salvation of man is that of the deity itself. The difference lies in whether the tragedy of the deity is forced upon it from outside, with Darkness having the first initiative, or is motivated from within itself, with Darkness the product of its passion, not its cause. To divine defeat and sacrifice in the one case, corresponds divine guilt and error in the other; to compassion for the victimized Light—spiritual contempt of demiurgical blindness; to eventual divine liberation—reformation through enlightenment.[28]

So while, in the first case, we have what Kant would have called a "real opposition" between the two active/positive divine forces (of Light and Darkness), in the second case, "the fall is quite simply forgetfulness, a cosmic forgetfulness that is the very creation of the world, and the material universe passes into nothingness when the Father is truly known" (56). What both versions of Gnosticism cannot accept is precisely the fact that "he was made man," i.e., the full humanity of Christ—this refusal went even to such intimate details as, to put it bluntly, the claim that Jesus did not piss and shit:

> He was continent, enduring all things. Jesus digested divinity; he ate and drunk in a special way, without excreting his solids. He had such a great capacity for continence that the nourishment within him was not corrupted, for he did not experience corruption.[29]

A further consequence of the Gnostic stance is the Platonic subordination of ethics to cognition: Evil is ultimately not a question of our (free) will, but is rooted in our ignorance (of the Good), i.e., you cannot know the Good *and* remain evil. (This is why, in the Gnostic reading of Genesis, the serpent which seduces Eve into eating the fruit from the Tree of Knowledge is not evil, but a good agent of self-cognition.) In contrast to the Platonic notion of Evil as deficient knowledge, as ignorance of the good, Christianity tells us that a truly evil person is not ignorant of goodness, he knows it from within and is thus able to exploit it. This anti-Platonic point was nicely made in the classic Hollywood version of *The Three Musketeers*: when Athos is about to send Countess de Winter, his utterly corrupt but still beloved wife, to her death, he remarks: "What is the essence of your evil? That you know the secret of the good."

All the same, a thin but nonetheless crucial line separates this authentically Christian subordination of knowledge to ethics from the properly *perverse* denigration of knowledge as dangerous and an obstacle to ethics. In an old Christian melodrama, a temporarily blinded ex-soldier falls in love with the nurse who takes care of him, fascinated by her goodness, forming in his mind an idealized image of her; when his blindness is cured, he sees that, in her physical reality, she is ugly. Aware that his love would not survive permanent contact with this reality, and that the inner beauty of her good soul has a higher value than her external appearance, he intentionally blinds himself by looking for too long into the sun so that his love for the woman will survive . . . if ever there was a false celebration of love, this is it.—What, then, is the problem with Gnosticism? Let me begin with Harold Bloom's definition of the gap that separates Gnosticism from Christianity: "If you can accept a God who coexists with death camps, schizophrenia, and AIDS, yet remains all-powerful and somehow benign, then you have faith. . . . If you *know* yourself as having an affinity with the alien, or stranger God, cut off from this world, then you are a Gnostic."[30] We can see how the solution of Gnosticism is the easy one, an easy way out of the paradox of true faith quite adequately described by Bloom ("If you can accept a God who coexists with death camps, schizophrenia, and AIDS, yet remains all-powerful and somehow benign, then you have faith.")—faith always implies a *credo qua absurdum*.

Here I have to raise a naive question: but why God at all? Why not heroically accept the world with death camps, schizophrenia, and AIDS as the only reality? Why should there be a higher Reality above it? The counterargument is that our immediate self-experience tells us that we are not "at home" in this miserable reality. Heidegger's notion of *Geworfenheit*, of "being-thrown" into a concrete historical situation, could be of some help here. *Geworfenheit* is to be opposed both to standard humanism and to the Gnostic tradition. In the humanist vision, a human being belongs to this earth, he should be fully at home on its surface, able to realize his potential through an active, productive exchange with it—as the young Marx put it, earth is man's "anorganic body." Any notion that we do not belong to this earth, that earth is a fallen universe, a prison for our soul striving to liberate itself from material inertia, is dismissed as life-denying alienation. For the Gnostic tradition, on the other hand, the human Self is not created, it is a preexisting Soul thrown into a foreign and inhospitable environment. The pain of our daily lives is the result not of our sin (of Adam's Fall), but of the fundamental glitch in the structure of the material universe itself which was created by defective demons; consequently, the path of salvation lies not in overcoming our sins, but in overcoming our ignorance: in transcending the world of material appearances by achieving true Knowledge.—What both these positions share is the notion that there is a home, a "natural" place, for man: either the realm of the "noosphere" from which we fell into this world and for which our souls long, or earth itself. Heidegger shows us the way out of this predicament: what if we are in effect "thrown" into this world, never fully at home in it, always dislocated, "out of joint," in it, and what if this dislocation is our constitutive, primordial condition, the very horizon of our being? What if there is no previous "home" out of which we were thrown into this world, what if this very dislocation grounds man's ex-static opening to the world?

I am therefore tempted to turn around the standard theological metaphor of God who sees the entire picture in which what we perceive as a stain contributes to global harmony: the devil is not in the detail but in the global picture, the world in its entirety is a meaningless cruel multiplicity, and the Good is always partial, an island of fragile order. . . . What is nonetheless a deep truth of Gnosticism is the idea of a "self-saving" God, a God who himself falls and then enacts his own redemption: the redemption through Christ's sacrifice is not only the redemption of humanity (which fell into sin because it misused its freedom), but God's redemption of himself. The death of Christ is thus the death or self-annihilation of God himself who, at this climactic coincidence of opposites, is identical with Satan: only if Christ is Satan can his death be the defeat of Evil, and thus Redemption. It was only William Blake who dared to draw this ultimate consequence of the process of crucifixion as redemption, conceiving the death of God as "the self-sacrifice of God, a kenotic emptying that is the embodiment of a total compassion, the love that is finally the deepest depths of actuality itself" (137).

In the history of thought, this speculative identity of opposites was intuited by Eckhart and fully enacted/conceptualized by Hegel: they both "refuse every final distinction between the eternal generation in the Godhead and the kenotic incarnation of Godhead or Spirit" (170), i.e., for both of them, the Father/Creator is ultimately the Son/Christ, and Christ is ultimately Satan. There is no substantial difference between entities here, just a processual differentiation of the divine Substance emptying itself and thus becoming Subject. Orthodox Christianity cannot accept "even the possibility of the redemption of the Godhead":

Then only humanity is redeemed; the redemption has no effect whatsoever upon God as God, who is and only is an absolutely immutable and ineffable God. Thereby the passion and death of God is only the suffering and death of the humanity of Christ, for while the Son of God underwent a real death, Christ died as man and not as God. . . . Thus Christian orthodoxy knows a Redeemer who suffers and dies only in his humanity or human nature. The divine nature of Christ is wholly unaffected by his death, and redemption can only be the redemption of a fallen humanity. (66–67)

The death of Christ is thus only the death of his carnal body—it has no effect upon God as God, who is absolutely transcendent, "absolutely immutable and impassive, absolutely unaffected by the suffering and death of Christ"(68). The whole point of Gnosticism is to oppose this transcendence: for Gnosticism, the transcendent God-Master is the evil (or, at best, clumsy) Creator, i.e., Satan himself. I should mention here the central exegetic insight of Milton, the greatest of all Protestants: his insistence on the "absence of any real scriptural foundation for the dogma of the eternal generation of the Son of God, demonstrating on the contrary that such a generation could only be a temporal generation"(117). Here we are at the furthest possible point from Orthodoxy: the Son is not part of some eternal Trinity which is God's eternal mystery; on the contrary, the Father and the Son differ in essence, since the infinite essence of God cannot become incarnate. Protestantism thus fully asserts the death of Christ: when Christ died on the Cross, he died there totally, "his divine nature succumbed to death as well as his human nature"(118); it is only such a full death that is the true Event, the sole source of Redemption. However, the price paid for this assertion is that the God-Father himself withdraws into absolute transcendence, turning into a superego figure of a capricious Master predestining our destinies, much more severe than the Catholic God of law and just punishment.[31]

So how does the Christian apocalypse, its absolute ending (the death of God), stand in terms of the Buddhist attainment of nirvana? Their difference concerns not so much content as form itself. With regard to content, the difference is smaller than it may appear: in both cases, the ending (the end of the world we know, of the Law or of samsara) immediately reverts into its opposite, the eternal blessing of Love. What is much more crucial is the form itself:

> If the crucifixion fully parallels the absolute "selflessness" of the Buddha, it nevertheless is an absolute act or enactment, and therefore the true opposite of an absolute and primordial nothingness. Therefore an apocalyptic Kingdom of God can be known as the true opposite of a Buddhist nirvana or sunyata, just as the kenotic Christ can be known as the true opposite of the kenotic Buddha. (167)

In other words, the Christian Crucifixion confronts us with the absolute contradiction between content and form: its content (the self-annihilation of God, of any substantial Truth) is asserted in the form of a crucial act, a cut between "before" and "after." This absolute contradiction reveals itself in another key feature. When crucifixion is conceived as the crucifixion of God himself, a crucial difference nonetheless persists between Gnosticism and authentic apocalypticism: in Gnosticism, the identity of the opposites, the reversal of crucifixion into the eternal bliss of redemption, is an immediate one, the pain of crucifixion immediately reverts into bliss, since, in the Gnostic enlightenment, man is directly divinized, and the material world thus literally disappears. The same goes for Buddhism, which represents the absolute calm of Buddha, the calm of nothingness, in numerous paintings and other works of art. However:

> neither the New Testament nor any subsequent Christian visionary can enact an actual story of the resurrection. The only real action or plot the Christian can narrate is the passion story, for the passion and the death of God are the deepest center of Christianity. . . . Buddhism can know a full reversal of the resurrection in which passion and death fully and wholly disappear. But even the most exalted Christian art has never been able to envision the actuality of the resurrection, an actuality that is overwhelming in Christian images of the crucifixion. (173)

This is why Hegel is authentically Christian—for him, the only actuality of Spirit is the actuality of finite life: "it is in the finite consciousness that the process of knowing spirit's essence takes place and that the divine self-consciousness thus arises. Out of the foaming ferment of finitude, spirit rises up fragrantly."[32] This is why, for Hegel, the reversal of crucifixion into redemption is a purely formal one: the art is to see redemption in (what appears as) crucifixion itself—or, as Hegel put it apropos of Luther, to see the Rose in the Cross of our present. The reality of the Cross is the only reality there is. And, as is usual with Hegel, this formal reversal has the simple form of universalization: resurrection is nothing but "the universalization of the crucifixion" (173). In his poetic terms, Blake intuits this speculative high point when he formulates the passage from Law to Love as the passage from external to self-relating negativity:

> Satan! My Spectre! I know my power thee to annihilate
> And be a greater in thy place, & be thy Tabernacle
> A covering for thee to do thy will, till one greater comes
> And smites me as I smote thee & becomes my covering.
> Such are the Laws of thy false Heavns! But Laws of Eternity
> Are not such: know thou: I come to Self Annihilation
> Such are the Laws of Eternity that each shall mutually
> Annihilate himself for others good, as I for thee.[33]

This self-reflexive turn is, of course, the passage from "spurious infinity" to true infinity, from relating to others (interacting with them) to self-relating: Christ is "actual infinity" because he turns the act of violence back upon himself, sacrificing himself (thus breaking the endless vicious cycle of reaction and revenge, of the "eye for an eye"). In this way, he already enacts universality: he becomes universal in his very singularity, acquiring a distance from his particularity as a person among others, interacting with them. In other words, when "each annihilates himself for others good," sacrifice self-cancels itself and we enter universal Love.

All difficult questions should be raised here, including the standard reaction: can the horror of the Holocaust, etc., be conceived as a divine kenosis? Does such a notion not blur its scandalous edge, making it into a moment of divine self-sacrifice and self-redemption? Our answer should be: it all depends on how we understand the divine kenosis. What if this kenosis should be taken literally, as a true self-sacrifice, not as a game God is playing with himself, remaining its master throughout? In other words, what if the horror of being an impotent witness to an event like the Holocaust, in which the world falls apart, is divine kenosis at its purest?

LAW, LOVE, AND DRIVE

How, then, are we to reply to the argument (repeated by Caputo, among others) that the death-of-God theology comes much too close to the (potentially anti-Semitic) "overcoming" of Law in love? Let us begin with the figure usually evoked as the counterpoint to Christian supersessionism: Emmanuel Levinas. What one should reproach Levinas with is, paradoxically, the very opposite of his apparent "excessive" Judaism: on the contrary, his Judaism is all-too-Christianized, colored by the Christianized notion of "neighbor" who primordially stands in front of me alone, not as part of a collective. No wonder Levinas is so popular among Christians: he enables them to recognize *themselves* in the Jewish otherness. (His popularity is thus analogous to the popularity of Kurosawa's *Rashomon* in the West in the early 1950s: the very film that, for us in the West, functioned as the discovery of Japanese spirituality, failed in Japan, where the main criticism of the film was that it was perceived as far too Westernized. . . .) And, in a further paradoxical twist, this very Christianization prevents Levinas from grasping the most radical core of the Christian experience itself, since this experience can take place only against the background of the "impersonal" Jewish notion of the Law. This Jewish legacy—in Lacanese, the passage from the big Other qua the abyss of subjectivity to the big Other qua the impersonal structure of the symbolic Law—found what could be said to be its most radical expression in the Talmud, in the story about the two rabbis who basically tell God to shut up:

There was once a dispute between Rabbi Eliezer and the Mishnic sages as to whether a baking oven, constructed from certain materials and of a particular shape, was clean or unclean. The former decided that it was clean, but the latter were of a contrary opinion. Having replied to all the objections the sages had brought against his decision, and finding that they still refused to acquiesce, the Rabbi turned to them and said, "If the Halacha (the law) is according to my decision, let this carob tree attest." Whereupon the carob tree rooted itself up and transplanted itself to a distance of one hundred, some say four hundred, yards from the spot. But the sages demurred and said, "We cannot admit the evidence of a carob tree." "Well, then," said Rabbi Eliezer, "let this running brook be a proof" and the brook at once reversed its natural course and flowed back. The sages refused to admit this proof also. "Then let the walls of the college bear witness that the law is according to my decision," upon which the walls began to bend, and were about to fall, when Rabbi Joshua interposed and rebuked them, saying, "If the disciples of the sages wrangle with each other in the Halacha, what is that to you? Be ye quiet!" Therefore, out of respect to Rabbi Joshua, they did not fall, and out of respect to Rabbi Eliezer they did not resume their former upright position, but remained toppling, which they continue to do to this day. Then said Rabbi Eliezer to the sages, "Let Heaven itself testify that the Halacha is according to my judgment." And a Bath Kol or voice from heaven was heard, saying, "What have ye to do with Rabbi Eliezer? for the Halacha is on every point according to his decision!" Rabbi Joshua then stood up and proved from Scripture that even a voice from heaven was not to be regarded, "For Thou, O God, didst long ago write down in the law which Thou gavest on Sinai (Exod. xxiii. 2), 'Thou shalt follow the multitude.'" We have it on the testimony of Elijah the prophet, given to Rabbi Nathan, on an oath, that it was with reference to this dispute about the oven God himself confessed and said, "My children have vanquished me! My children have vanquished me!"[34]

No wonder this passage from the Talmud was endlessly exploited by anti-Semites as proof of the Jewish obscene-manipulative relationship to God! To cut a long story short, what happens here is already the death of God: once the act of creation is accomplished, God dies, he survives only in the dead letter of the Law, without retaining even the right to intervene into how people interpret his law—no wonder this anecdote recalls the well-known scene from the beginning of Woody Allen's (another Jew!) *Annie Hall*, where a couple waiting in line for cinema tickets debate a point about Marshall McLuhan's theory, and then McLuhan himself appears in the queue, intervening in the debate by brutally siding with the Woody Allen character. . . .

David Grossman once reported[35] a weird personal memory: when, just prior to the 1967 Israeli–Arab war, he heard on the radio about the Arab threats that they would throw the Jews into the sea, his reaction was to take swimming lessons—a paradigmatic Jewish reaction if ever there was one, in the spirit of the long talk between Josef K. and the priest (the prison chaplain) that follows the parable on the Door of the Law in Kafka's *The Trial*. Such a Jewish art of endless interpretation of the letter of the Law is thus profoundly materialist, its implication (and maybe even true goal) being (to make sure) that God is (and remains) dead. This is why Christianity could emerge only after and from within Judaism: its central theme of the death of Christ only posits as such, "for itself," the death of God which, "in itself," takes place already in Judaism.

The reference to this aspect of Judaism enables us to reject the "fundamentalist" religious suspension of the ethical whose formula was proposed long ago by St. Augustine: "Love God and do as you please." (Or, another version: "Love, and do whatever you like."—from the Christian perspective, the two ultimately amount to the same, since God is Love.) The catch, of course, is that if you really love God, you will want what he wants—what pleases him will please you, and what displeases him will make you miserable. So it is not that you can just "do whatever you like": your love for God, if genuine, guarantees that, in what you want to do, you will follow the highest ethical standards. It is a little bit like the proverbial joke "My fiancée is never late for an appointment, because if she is late, she is no longer my fiancée": if you love God, you can do whatever you like, because when you do something evil, this is in itself a proof that you do not really love God. . . . However, the ambiguity persists, since there is no guarantee, external to your belief, of what God really wants you to do—in the absence of any ethical standards external to your belief in and love for God, the danger is always lurking that you will use your love of God as the legitimization of the most horrible deeds.

How, then, are we to grasp the overcoming of the Law in love in a nonfundamentalist way? In his reading of St. Paul, Badiou provides a perspicuous interpretation of the subjective passage from Law to love. In both cases, we are dealing with division, with a "divided subject"; however, the modality of the division is completely different. The subject of the Law is "decentered" in the sense that it is caught in the self-destructive vicious cycle of sin and Law in which one pole engenders its opposite; St. Paul provided the definitive description of this entanglement in Romans 7:

> We know that the law is spiritual; but I am carnal, sold into slavery to sin. What I do, I do not understand. For I do not do what I want, but I do what I hate. Now if I do what I do not want, I concur that the law is good. So now it is no longer I who do it, but sin that dwells in me. For I know that good does not dwell in me, that is, in my flesh. The willing is ready at hand, but doing the good is not. For I do not do the good I want, but I do the evil I do not want. Now if I do what I do not want, it is no longer I who do it, but sin that dwells in me. So, then, I discover the principle that when I want to do right, evil is at hand. For I take delight in the law of God, in my inner self, but I see in my members another principle at war with the law of my mind, taking me captive to the law of sin that dwells in my members. Miserable one that I am!

It is thus not that I am merely torn between the two opposites, Law and sin; the problem is that I cannot even clearly distinguish them: I want to follow the Law, and I end up in sin. This vicious cycle is (not so much overcome as) broken, one breaks out of it, with the experience of love—more precisely: with the experience of the radical gap that separates love from the Law. Lacan's extensive discussion of love in *Encore* is to be read in the Pauline sense, as opposed to the dialectic of the Law and its transgression: this second dialectic is clearly "masculine"/phallic, it involves the tension between the All (the universal Law) and its constitutive exception, i.e., "sin" is the very exception which sustains the Law. Love, on the contrary, is not simply beyond Law, but articulates itself as the stance of total immersion in the Law: "not all of the subject is within the figure of legal subjection" equals "there is nothing in the subject which escapes its legal subjection." "Sin" is the very intimate resistant core on account of which the subject experiences its relationship to the Law as one of subjection, it is that on account of which the Law has to appear to the subject as a foreign power crushing the subject.

This, then, is how we are to grasp the idea that Christianity "accomplished/fulfilled" the Jewish Law: not by supplementing it with the dimension of love, but by fully realizing the Law itself—from this perspective, the problem with Judaism is not that it is "too legal," but that it is not "legal" enough. A brief reference to Hegel might be of some help here: when Hegel endeavors to resolve the conflict between Law and love, he does not mobilize his standard triad (the immediacy of the love link turns into its opposite, hate and struggle, which calls for an external-alienated Law to regulate social life; finally, in an act of magical "synthesis," Law and love are reconciled in the organic totality of social life). The problem with the Law is not that it does not contain enough love, but, rather, the opposite: there is too much love in it, i.e., social life appears to me as dominated by an externally imposed Law in which I am unable to recognize myself, precisely insofar as I continue to cling to the immediacy of love which feels threatened by the rule of Law. Consequently, Law loses its "alienated" character of a foreign force brutally imposing itself on the subject the moment the subject renounces its attachment to the pathological *agalma* deep within itself, the notion that there is deep inside it some precious treasure which can only be loved and cannot be submitted to the rule of Law. In other words, the problem (today, even) is not how we are to supplement Law with true love (authentic social link), but, on the contrary, how we are to *accomplish* the Law by getting rid of the pathological stain of love.

St. Paul's negative appreciation of Law is clear and unambiguous: "For no human being will be justified in his sight by deeds prescribed by the law, for through the law comes the knowledge of sin" (Romans 3:20). "The sting of death is sin, and the power of sin is the law" (1 Corinthians 15:56), and, consequently, "Christ redeemed us from the curse of the law" (Galatians 3:13). So when Paul says that "the letter kills, but the spirit gives life" (2 Corinthians 3:6), this letter is precisely the letter of the Law. The strongest proponents of this radical opposition between the Law and the divine love moving one to grace are Lutheran theologians like Bultmann, for whom

> the way of works of the Law and the way of grace and faith are mutually exclusive opposites. . . . Man's effort to achieve his salvation by keeping the Law only leads him into sin, *indeed this effort itself in the end is already sin.* . . . The Law brings to light that man is sinful, whether it be that his sinful desire leads him to transgression of the Law or that *that desire disguises itself in zeal for keeping the Law.*[36]

How are we to understand this? It is not only the logic of the forbidden fruit (the Law, by prohibiting something, creates the desire for it); more radically, man's effort to keep the Law *in the end is already sin*—it is sinful desire itself disguised as Law, converted into zeal for the Law. This is why Western Christian fundamentalists are sinners in disguise: what they lack is a feature that is easy to discern in all authentic fundamentalists, from Tibetan Buddhists to the Amish in the USA—an absence of resentment and envy, a deep indifference toward the nonbelievers' way of life. If today's so-called fundamentalists really believe they have found their way to Truth, why should they feel threatened by nonbelievers, why should they envy them? When a Buddhist encounters a Western hedonist, he hardly condemns him. He just benevolently notes that the hedonist's search for happiness is self-defeating. In contrast to true fundamentalists, terrorist pseudo-fundamentalists are deeply bothered, intrigued, fascinated, by the sinful life of nonbelievers. One can feel that, in fighting the sinful other, they are fighting their own temptation. Christian fundamentalists are a disgrace to true fundamentalism.

That is the radical difference between the couple Law/sin and the couple Law/love. The gap that separates Law and sin is not a real difference: their truth is their mutual implication or confusion—Law generates sin and feeds on it, etc., one can never draw a clear line of separation between the two. It is only with the couple Law/love that we attain real difference: these two moments are radically separate, they are not "mediated," one is not the form of appearance of its opposite. In other words, the difference between the two couples (Law/sin and Law/love) is not substantial, but purely formal: we are dealing with the same content in its two modalities. In its indistinctness/mediation, the couple is the one of Law/sin; in the radical distinction of the two, it is Law/love. Is love, then, sin which is no longer mediated by Law? This formula remains much too close to sexual liberation: love becomes sin when it is subordinated to the Law. . . . It should thus be supplemented by its opposite: *love is Law itself extracted from its mediation by sin.*

Why, then, did God proclaim the Law in the first place? According to the standard reading of St. Paul, God gave Law to men in order to make them conscious of their sin, even to make them sin all the more, and thus make them aware of their need for salvation, which can occur only through divine grace—however, does this reading not involve a strangely perverse notion of God? The only way to avoid such a perverse reading is to insist on the absolute identity of the two gestures: God does not first push us into sin in order to create the need for Salvation, and then offer himself as the Redeemer from the trouble into which he got us in the first place; it is not that the Fall is followed by Redemption: the Fall is identical to Redemption, it is "in itself" already Redemption. That is to say, what is "redemption"? The explosion of freedom, the breaking out of the natural enchainment—and this, precisely, is what happens in the Fall. We should bear in mind here the central tension of the Christian notion of the Fall: the Fall ("regression" to the natural state, enslavement to passions) is stricto sensu identical with the dimension from which we fall, i.e., it is the very movement of the Fall that creates, opens up, what is lost in it. I can even go a step further, drawing on the parallel between the believer and the adulteress evoked by St. Paul in Romans 7—here is this strangely sexualized comparison of the believer delivered from the Law with an adulteress who, after her husband dies, is free to consort with her lover:

> Are you unaware, brothers (for I am speaking to people who know the law), that the law has jurisdiction over one as long as one lives? Thus a married woman is bound by law to her living husband; but if her husband dies, she is released from the law in respect to her husband. Consequently, while her husband is alive she will be called an adulteress if she consorts with another man. But if her husband dies she is free from that law, and she is not an adulteress if she consorts with another man. In the same way, my brothers, you also were put to death to the law through the body of Christ, so that you might belong to another, to the one who was raised from the dead in order that we might bear fruit for God.

Does this not mean that love is sin itself, once it is extracted from the vicious cycle of its inherent opposition to Law? Life is sin when submitted to Law, and love is pure life extracted from the domain of Law. —The key Hegelian lesson here is that it is wrong to ask the question: "Are we then forever condemned to the split between Law and love? What about the synthesis between Law and love?" The split between Law and sin is of a radically different nature than the split between Law and love: instead of the vicious cycle of mutual reinforcement, we get a clear distinction of two different domains. Once we become fully aware of the dimension of love in its radical difference from the Law, love has in a way already won, since this difference is visible only when one already dwells in love, from the standpoint of love. In this precise sense, there is no need for a further "synthesis" between Law and love: paradoxically, their "synthesis" already is the very experience of their radical split. And exactly the same goes for the Hegelian love which is the dialectical "synthesis": it resolves the mess of "contradiction" by asserting a clear difference. This is why I cannot endorse Milbank's characterization of Hegelian dialectics as

> a kind of [counterfeit] *parody* . . . of the orthodox Catholic idea that Creation really exists even though it is impossible. Paradox affirms the full reality of the impossible and the contradictory, whereas dialectics declares that an existing contradiction, because it is a contradiction, must be destroyed even though it exists. Dialectics is like a civic bureaucrat who says that a bizarre building put up in the town without permission can really be there at all because it stands upright without legal warrant, and therefore must be discreetly pulled down at dead of night, to ensure that a bright dawn will reveal that it had only ever appeared to be there, on an earlier day of mists and mirages.

As a description of the elementary logic of the dialectical process, this passage misses two key points. First, since, for Hegel, the failure of empirical reality to fit its notion is always also an indication of the failure of this notion itself, the dialectical civic bureaucrat would have not only to pull down the unwarranted building, but also to discreetly change the very rules of what is legally warranted. Second, for Hegel, the "resolution" of a contradiction is not simply the abolition of difference, but its full admission: in dialectical "reconciliation," difference is not erased, but admitted as such. It took even Lacan a long time to reach this insight. Throughout his development, Lacan was looking for a "quilting point," a link that would hold together, or at least mediate between, S (the symbolic semblance) and J (the Real of *jouissance*); the main solution is to elevate the phallus into the signifier of the lack of signifier which, as the signifier of castration, holds the place of *jouissance* within the symbolic order; then, there is *objet a* itself as the surplus-enjoyment generated by the loss of *jouissance* which is the obverse of the entry into the symbolic order, as *jouissance* located not on the side of the real *jouissance* but, paradoxically, on the side of the symbolic. In "Lituraterre," he finally drops this search for the symbolic pineal gland (the gland which, for Descartes, marks the physical point at which body and soul interact) and endorses the Hegelian solution: *it is the very gap which forever separates S and J that holds them together*, since this gap is constitutive of both of them: the Symbolic arises through the gap that separates it from full *jouissance*, and this *jouissance* itself is a specter produced by the gaps and holes in the Symbolic. To designate this interdependence, Lacan introduces the term *littorale*, standing for the letter in its "coast-like" dimension, and thereby "figuring that one domain [which] in its entirety makes for the other a frontier, because of their being foreign to each other, to the extent of not falling into a reciprocal relation. Is the edge of the hole in knowledge not what it traces?"[37] So when Lacan says that "between knowledge and jouissance, there is a *littoral*,"[38] we should hear in this the evocation of *jouis-sense* (enjoymeant), of a letter reduced to a *sinthom*, a signifying formula of enjoyment.

—This is Lacan's final late "Hegelian" insight: the convergence of the two incompatible dimensions (the Real and the Symbolic) is sustained by their very divergence, i.e., difference is constitutive of what it differentiates. Or, to put it in more formal terms: it is the very intersection between the two fields which constitutes them. That is why, in psychoanalysis, there is no repression without the "return of the repressed": the symptom (in which the repressed returns) sustains the repressed content (what it is a symptom of). The domain of this intersection is that of "ex-timacy" (intimate exteriority)—we should recall here Winnicott's concept of the "transitional object" as a bridge between inner and outer worlds, a place where the two interact uninterruptedly with the help of the first "not-me" possession: the infant assumes rights over an object which is affectionately cuddled as well as excitedly loved and mutilated. This object never changes, unless changed by the infant; it must seem to the infant to give warmth, or to move, or to have texture, or to do something that seems to show it has a vitality or reality of its own. It comes from without from our point of view, but not so from the point of view of the baby, neither does it come from within. Its fate is to be gradually allowed to be dis-invested, so that in the course of years it becomes not so much forgotten as relegated to limbo: it does not "go inside," nor does the feeling about it necessarily undergo repression; it is not forgotten and it is not mourned. It loses meaning, and this is because the transitional phenomena have become diffused, have become spread out over the whole intermediate territory between "inner psychic reality" and "the external world as perceived by two persons in common." These objects, again, sustain the division, they separate, by functioning as "bridges."

Popular imagination is fascinated by the minimal element which, in a disabled body, sustains the link between external reality and the psyche, and thus serves as the tiny fragile "door into the soul": Stephen Hawking's little finger, the only part of his paralyzed body that Hawking can move; or the even more extreme condition of Jean-Dominique Bauby, who, after a three-week coma, woke up in hospital with "locked-in syndrome," an extremely rare condition where one is completely physically paralyzed, but mentally normal; in this state, he wrote a book describing his life, *The Diving Bell and the Butterfly*. His only link with the external world was blinking his left eyelid: for every letter an attendant recited him the French frequency-ordered alphabet (E, L, A, O, I, N, S, D . . .), until Bauby blinked to choose the letter; the book took about 200,000 blinks to write, and each word took approximately two minutes. He died ten days after the book was published.

The direct link between the brain and a computer will dispense with the need for such a minimal intermediary: with my mind, I will be able to directly cause objects to move, i.e., it is the brain itself which will directly serve as the remote-control mechanism. According to a CNN report from May 29, 2008, monkeys with sensors implanted in their brains have learned to control a robot arm with their thoughts, using it to feed themselves fruit and marshmallows: in the experiment at the University of Pittsburgh School of Medicine, a pair of macaque monkeys were fitted with electrodes the width of a human hair that transmitted signals from areas of the brain linked to movement. Scientists behind the experiment say it will lead to the creation of brain-controlled prosthetic limbs for amputees or patients with degenerative disorders. Even the proverbial Stephen Hawking's little finger—the minimal link between his mind and outside reality—will thus no longer be necessary. What looms at the horizon of the "digital revolution" is nothing other than the prospect that human beings will acquire the capacity of what Kant and other German Idealists called "intellectual intuition [intellektuelle Anschauung]": the closing of the gap between mind and reality, a mental process which, in a causal way, directly influences reality. This capacity that Kant attributed only to the infinite mind of God is now potentially available to all of us, and we are thus potentially deprived of one of the basic features of our finitude. And since, as we learned from Kant as well as from Freud, this gap of finitude is at the same time the resource of our creativity (the distance between "mere thought" and causal intervention into external reality enables us to test hypotheses in our mind and, as Karl Popper put it, let them die instead of ourselves), the direct short circuit between mind and reality implies the prospect of a radical closure.

In other words, the disappearance of the intermediary between the two domains will entail the disappearance of these domains themselves: when the distance between soul and body disappears, when our psyche can directly act upon external physical reality, we not only no longer have a soul, we also lose a body as "our own," as separated from external objects. Here enters the properly philosophical intervention of psychoanalysis: it designates a dimension which resists and undermines the very terrain of the duality of soul and body: of the subject (which is not a soul) and the "partial object" (which is not part of a body). The subject persists in the guise of an autonomous object with a spectral life of its own, like the palm that runs around all on its own in early surrealist films.

In the middle of David Fincher's *Fight Club* (1999), there is an almost unbearably painful scene, worthy of the weirdest David Lynch moments, which serves as a kind of clue to the film's final surprising twist. In order to blackmail his boss into continuing to pay him even after he quits working, the hero throws himself around the man's office, beating himself bloody before the building's security officers arrive. In front of his embarrassed boss, the narrator thus enacts upon himself the boss's aggression toward him. The self-beating begins with the hero's hand acquiring a life of its own, escaping the hero's control—in short, turning into a partial object, *an organ without a body*. The hand acting on its own is the drive ignoring the dialectic of the subject's desire:

drive is fundamentally the insistence of an undead "organ without a body," standing, like Lacan's lamella, for that which the subject had to lose in order to subjectivize itself in the symbolic space of sexual difference. And perhaps we should reread from this perspective of the Freudian partial object Derrida's insistence on the monstrosity of the hand from his reflections about "Heidegger's hand": "The hand will be the monstrous sign [le monstre], the proper of man in the sense of Zeichen."[39] So when Heidegger writes that "only a being who can speak, that is, think, can have hands and can be handy in achieving works of handicraft,"[40] he is in effect saying that thought is a corporeal event: one does not "express" thoughts through hands, one thinks with one's hand. The formative gesture of thought, the autonomous rejection of reality, "is" the middle finger defiantly pointed up ("Up yours!"). It is in this sense that we should read Hölderlin's famous line "We are a monster/sign void of sense [Ein Zeichen sind wir, deutungslos]": we are subjects only through a monstrous bodily distortion, only when part of our body, one of its organs (hand, phallus, eye . . .) subtracts itself from the body and starts to act as an autonomous monster. (I cannot but recall here Heidegger's remark from the mid-1930s to a colleague who complained about Hitler's vulgarity: that one should look at Hitler's hands, what he does with them, to see his greatness.)

It is thus quite appropriate that the final gesture of the dying hero in John Carpenter's They Live is that of giving the finger to the aliens who control us—a case of thinking with a hand, a gesture of "Up yours!", the digitus impudicus ("impudent finger") mentioned already in Ancient Roman writings. The hand is here, yet again, an autonomous "organ without a body." It is difficult to miss the Christological resonances of this scene of the dying hero who saves the world. No wonder, then, that, in a unique moment in the history of art, the dying Christ himself was portrayed in a similar way. Wolfram Hogrebe proposed such a reading of Michelangelo's unfinished drawing of Christ on the Cross which he first gave to Vittoria Colonna, his passionate intimate friend, and then inexplicably asked her to return it to him, which she refused to do, since she was enthusiastic about the drawing, and is reported as studying it in detail with mirror and magnifying glass—as if the drawing contained some forbidden half-hidden detail Michelangelo was afraid would be discovered.[41]

The drawing illustrates the "critical" moment of Christ's doubt and despair, of "Father, why have you forsaken me?" For the first time in the history of painting, an artist tried to capture Christ's abandonment by God-Father. While Christ's eyes are turned upward, his face does not express devoted acceptance of suffering, but desperate suffering combined with . . . here, some unsettling details indicate an underlying attitude of angry rebellion, of defiance. His legs are not parallel, one is slightly raised above the other, as if Christ is caught in the middle of an attempt to liberate and raise himself; but the truly shocking detail is the right hand: there are no nails to be seen, and the index finger is stretched out—a vulgar gesture which, according to Quintilian's rhetorics of gestures probably known to Michelangelo, functions as a sign of the devil's rebellious challenge. Christ's "Why?" is not resigned, but aggressive, accusatory. More precisely, there is, in the drawing, an implicit tension between the expression of Christ's face (despair and suffering) and of his hand (rebellion, defiance)— as if the hand articulates the attitude the face doesn't dare to express. Did St. Paul not make the same point in Romans? "I take delight in the law of God, in my inner self, but I see in my members another principle at war with the law of my mind, taking me captive to the law of sin that dwells in my members." Should we therefore not apply here to Christ himself his own "antithesis" from Matthew 18:9—"And if thy right hand scandalize thee, cut it off, and cast it from thee: for it is expedient for thee that one of thy members should perish, rather than that thy whole body go into hell"? A passage which should none-theless be read together with an earlier one (6:3) in which a hand acting alone stands for authentic goodness: "But when thou doest alms, let not thy left hand know what thy right hand doeth." Is Christ at this moment, then, the devil; does he, for a moment, succumb to the temptation of an egotistic rebellion? Who is who in this scene of Goethe's formula *Nemo contra deum nisi deus ipse*—no one but God himself can stand against God? But what if we follow, rather, the Gnostic line and conceive the God-Father himself, the creator, as the Evil God, as identical with the devil?

The ambiguous status of such "immortal" persisting is clearly discernible in Heinrich von Kleist's *Michael Kohlhaas*, whose hero is a sixteenth-century decent horse dealer whose two horses are mistreated while in the possession of the arrogant Junker von Tronka. Kohlhaas first patiently seeks justice in the courts; however, when this fails, he gathers an armed band, hires militia, destroys the Junker's castle, burns down whole cities, and involves the whole of Eastern Germany in a civil war—all because he does not want to compromise his demand for recompense for his two famished horses. At the end, Kohlhaas is captured and beheaded, but accepts his punishment, since his claims against the Junker are also to be met in full, and the Junker will have to spend two years in prison. At the place of his execution, his two horses are presented to him, fully restored to health, and he dies completely satisfied, as justice is done. Ger-man interpreters are deeply divided about Kohlhaas: is he a progressive figure fighting feudal corruption, or a proto-Fascist madman, a case of the German petit-bourgeois legal pedantry elevated into the absurd? Terry Eagleton is right to point out that we are dealing here with the "ethics of the Real" beyond (social) reality:

> As Kohlhaas's actions become increasingly extravagant and bizarre, and the frantic political intrigues of the state over a couple of knackered horses deepen by the page, the grotesque discrepancy between the horse dealer's obdurate

demand for justice and its trifling causes reveals plainly enough that this is a narrative not of realism, but of the Real. . . . It is not the horses as such which are the object of his desire. Nobody would burn down Wittenberg just because someone neglected his nags. The horses are perhaps better seen as an instance of Lacan's *objet petit a*—that modest, contingent scrap of matter which becomes invested with all the formidable power of the Real. If Kohlhaas perishes in tragic joy, plucking victory from his death in the act of bowing an obedient knee to it, it is not because of a welcome addition to his livestock, but because he has managed not to give up on his desire.[42]

Perhaps a more appropriate way to put it would have been that the two horses are "sublimated," insofar as, for Lacan, what happens in sublimation is that an ordinary object is "elevated into the dignity of the Thing," the unconditional object of *jouissance*. The Real resides in this very incommensurability between the vast catastrophe and the trifling matter that triggered it—more than the ridiculous object itself, the Real is the gap itself, the line that separates the object-cause from the texture of ordinary reality. This is why love is also of the Real: if I look at the reality around me with a neutral gaze, I see objects that form one and the same texture; if, however, I look at it with the lover's eye, something that appears as just another object sticks out, derailing the balanced whole: "this miserable woman (or man) is to me more than my career, honor, happiness, even my life." Does Badiou not make the same point when he insists that, "so as not to succumb to an obscurantist theory of creation *ex nihilo*, we must accept that an Event is nothing but a part of a given situation, nothing but a *fragment of being*"?[43] There is thus nothing miraculous in the reality of an Event—in its reality, an Event is "nothing but a *fragment of being*," a moment of the endless multiplicity of Being; what makes it an Event is the mode of its subjectivization, the way the subject for which a fragment of reality is an Event "elevates" this fragment into a stand-in for the Void. —This same tension is reflected in Kohlhaas himself—or, to quote Eagleton's sarcastic formulation: "Apart from the fact that he is a brutal mass murderer who sells his own family into poverty to raise funds for his cause, Kohlhaas is really quite a reasonable character."[44]

Is, then, the Real the incalculable excess, the shattering trauma, which disturbs the domain of (symbolic) justice as equivalent exchange, appropriate punishment, etc.? The lesson of Kleist's *Kohlhaas* is, rather, the opposite one: Kohlhaas's monstrous "lunatic stubbornness" does not stand in contrast to his being a "paragon of civil virtues"—what makes him monstrous is precisely the way he sticks to his sense of civil virtue and justice to the end, whatever the cost. The "ordinary" object elevated into the "dignity of the Thing" is here *the demand for justice itself*, a modest demand for proper restitution for the abused horses. Ideological "common sense" would enjoin us to display a little bit of "wisdom" here: does it really serve the cause of justice to burn half the country and bring suffering and death to thousands because of the maltreatment of two horses? But are things really as simple as that? E. L. Doctorow retold the same story in *Ragtime*: in New York of the early 1920s, a white racist trash of a man shits on the front seat of the nice new car of a proud, law-abiding, upper-middle-class black; when the black returns, he insists to the attending policeman on a proper punishment; the policeman displays the required "wisdom" and advises the black to simply clean the seat of his car and forget all about it; the proud black insists, and his insistence leads to rioting, destruction, and death. Does ultimately the same not also hold for Rosa Parks, a modest black lady who, on December 1, 1955, was ordered by a bus driver in Montgomery, Alabama, to give up her seat to a white passenger? When she refused, she was arrested and taken to jail. Rosa Parks occupies the honorable mythical place of the "zero" fighter for black equality (in the sense of the infamous Canadian promiscuous gay flight attendant who was proclaimed the zero-AIDS-patient): a trifling cause, elevated into an object of unconditional demand, triggered a disproportionately vast movement.

It is here, then, that Eagleton is perhaps much too quick in his rejection of the Kohlhaas figure as an example of the suicidal madness of the "ethics of the Real," as an insistence on justice which turns its partisan into its opposite, into a mass murderer terrorizing an entire population. In order to break the stalemate of an oppressive status quo, every radical emancipatory movement requires such an "excessive" starting point in which a vast cause of injustice gets embodied in a trifling demand (to repeal a tax on salt, to liberate a journalist, etc.). It is those in power who, in such cases, utter words of wisdom: "Let's talk reasonably: we admit that many things are wrong, but let's not get caught up in a game which may bring havoc to us all because of such a trifling matter. . . ." And it is the protesters who insist with "lunatic stubbornness," stick to their demand, rejecting all calls for a reasonable compromise. The reason is not only that people are primitive, that every universal cause has to be compressed into a pseudo-concrete particular demand; it is simply that the very discrepancy between the true Cause and the trifling demand that embodies it bears witness to the fact that we are fighting not over the true Cause, but over our freedom itself.

No wonder Eagleton praises the Aristotelian ethics of moderation which abhors extremes: the gap that separates him from the radical Freudian and Marxist tradition is insurmountable here. To put it briefly: for Aristotelians, the normal provides the key to (understanding) the pathological, while for Marx, as well as for Freud, the pathological provides the key to the normal: economic crises enable us to understand the normal run of capitalism; psychopathological symptoms enable us to understand the normal functioning of the psychic apparatus. *Mutatis mutandis*, one should say that extreme ethical situations of the type of Abraham and Isaac, Antigone and Oedipus at Colonus, etc., provide the key to the understanding of our everyday ethics. In other words, it is much too simple to reduce the gesture of focusing on such limit-situations to "French" academic eccentricity and contempt for the ordinary.

It is for this reason that Eagleton, an Irish Catholic like Chesterton, falls short of Chesterton's radicality when he deals with the Christian passage from Law to love: first, there is the "destructive antagonism-cum-collusion between law and desire, and what breaks this vicious circle, in which the law obtusely provokes a desire which it then goes on to punish, is the recognition that the law or Name-of-the-Father is itself desirous—but desirous in the sense that it wants our well-being, and is thus a kind of love" (28–29).[45] This may look like a very Hegelian move: to recognize Love in the very "cross" of the Law that oppresses us: "The moment of conversion comes when love dispels the false consciousness which blinded us to the realization that love was what the law was about all along" (38). How? Through self-change: law is for immature people who need an external master; when we can act spontaneously, we no longer need the Law: "It is not, then, that the moral law is pernicious, but that if we could really live according to its injunctions we would no longer have need of them. The technical term for this is grace" (35). The existence of Christ is a demonstration that God loves us, that God is not a supreme cruel sovereign but a lover, with us in our suffering; not aligned with the Power of Tyrants, but on our side against it. Only anti-Semitic Christians see the opposition between callously legalistic Law and love (30). Agape emerges thus as universal, indiscriminate love, "or political love as we might translate the term" (31).

God as the supreme Tyrant who plays cruel superego games with us, demanding payment for our sins, etc., is Satan himself. This is why the legalistic reading of the Crucifixion that sees it as Christ paying the price exacted by the justice of the cruel Father is the "Satanic reading" (40) to be opposed to the proper non-Satanic reading: Jesus is put to death not by his father, but by the State. So, insofar as Jesus stands for Justice, it means that Justice itself is transgressive with regard to the social order of Power: God is on our side against the powers of this world. Radical as this reading appears, Eagleton does not go far enough here: the tension, the *madness* of Christ's gesture, is thereby lost, everything ends well in the reconciliation of Law and love—as if a God who takes care of our well-being is not the ultimate monster. We can thus fully agree with Eagleton's claim that "it is the law which is transgressive, not the subversion of it" (xxvi)—with the proviso that we conceive "transgression" not as a true liberation from the existing order, but as its immanent obscene supplement which is the condition of possibility of its functioning. Law is in itself subversive of the existing order, because this order already implies and relies on its own transgression, so that the way to truly subvert it is to stick to its letter and ignore its obscene transgression. If we accept this paradox, then Eagleton's notion of the "law of love" becomes problematic:

The idea that [Jesus] stood for love against law, inner feeling against external ritual, is a piece of Christian anti-Semitism. For one thing, Jesus is interested in what people do, not in what they feel. For another thing, the Judaic law is itself the law of love. It belongs to the law, for example, to treat your enemies humanely. (xxv)

However, when we read in the Gospels: "You have heard that it was said to the people long ago, 'Do not murder, and anyone who murders will be subject to judgment.' But I tell you that anyone who is angry with his brother will be subject to judgment. . . . You have heard that it was said, 'Do not commit adultery.' But I tell you that anyone who looks at a woman lustfully has already committed adultery with her in his heart," does this nonetheless not imply a shift from what you do (kill, commit adultery) to what you think and feel (anger, lust)? Furthermore, it is clear from St. Paul's explanations that—for him at least—the problem is not the content of the Law, but its *very form*: it is the form of prohibition as such which gives rise to sin (I desire what is prohibited because it is prohibited). Is there anything more terrifying, then, than the "law of love"? A law which enjoins me to love my neighbors? Will such a law, on account of its very form, not give rise to a desire to hate and hurt one's neighbors?

This is why Christianity, at its most radical, does not posit the unification of Law (judgment) and love (grace, salvation), but the suspension of (legal) judgment: "For God didn't send his Son into the world to judge the world, but that the world should be saved through him. He who believes in him is not judged. He who doesn't believe has been judged already, because he has not believed in the name of the one and only Son of God" (John 3:17–18). So there is no judgment: you are either *not* judged, or you have *already been* judged. —Furthermore, Eagleton links early Christian apocalypticism to the self-perception of human beings as passive objects of change, and (in a nice dialectical paradox, true) proposes that it was the later institutionalization of the Church which opened the space for human agency:

> There was no room in the first-century outlook for the idea of men and women as historical agents capable of forging their own destiny, or at least assisting in it. This would have been no more part of the evangelists' vision of things than the belief that the earth is round. Once Christ failed to return, however, the church began to develop a theology for which human efforts to transform the world are part of the coming of the New Jerusalem, and prefigurative of it. Working to bring about peace and justice on earth is a necessary pre-condition of the coming of the reign of God. (xxi–xxii)

There is, however, a third position between these two extremes, that of the Holy Spirit, of the apocalyptic community of believers, of the self-organization of believers who drew from Christ's nonreturn after his death the correct conclusion: they were awaiting the wrong thing, Christ already had returned as the Holy Spirit of their community. The very meaning of Christ's death is that the work to be done is theirs, that Christ put his trust in them. Once we accept this, Eagleton's reading of Jesus' "ethical extravagance" also becomes problematic:

> What one might call Jesus's ethical extravagance—giving over and above the measure, turning the other cheek, rejoicing in being persecuted, loving one's enemies, refusing to judge, non-resistance to evil, laying oneself open to the violence of others—is . . . motivated by a sense that history is now at an end. Recklessness, improvidence and an over-the-top lifestyle are signs that God's sovereignty is at hand. There is no time for political organization or instrumental rationality, and they are unnecessary in any case. (xxiii)

But is this "extravagance" really constrained to the end-of-time atmosphere in which all we can do is wait and get ready for the Second Coming? Is it not that, in an apocalyptic time—the time of the end of time, as Agamben put it—we have both aspects, "ethical extravagance" as well as political organization? The specificity of the Holy Spirit, the apocalyptic emancipatory collective, is that it is precisely an organization which practices these "ethical extravagances," i.e., which lives its life in an apocalyptic "state of emergency" in which all ordinary legal (and moral) commitments are suspended, practiced in the mode of "as if not." The problem with the Church is that it betrayed original Christianity not by its organization, but by the type of this organization: the apocalyptic community of believers which lives in the emergency state of a "permanent revolution" is changed into an ideological apparatus legitimizing the normal run of things. In other words, with the Church, we are not active enough: the pressure of the Second Coming is eased, all we have to do is to lead our daily lives following the prescribed ethico-religious rules, and Salvation will come by itself. —So let us take a closer look at the exemplary case of Christ's "ethical extravagance," the parable on the Good Samaritan in Luke 10:25–37, when Jesus is asked by an "expert in the law": "And who is my neighbor?" His reply is:

> A man was going down from Jerusalem to Jericho, when he fell into the hands of robbers. They stripped him of his clothes, beat him and went away, leaving him half dead. A priest happened to be going down the same road, and when he saw the man, he passed by on the other side. So too, a Levite, when he came to the place and saw him, passed by on the other side. But a Samaritan, as he traveled, came where the man was; and when he saw him, he took pity on him. He went to him and bandaged his wounds, pouring on oil and wine. Then he put the man on his own donkey, took him to an inn and took care of him. The next day he took out two silver coins and gave them to the innkeeper. "Look

after him," he said, "and when I return, I will reimburse you for any extra expense you may have."

As is well known to all historians, there was great animosity between Jews and Samaritans: the Samaritans were despised by the Jews, and they themselves were taught to hate the Jews. So, in today's terms, one could put a Palestinian in that role (or a member of Hezbollah aided by an orthodox Jew, or a racist helped by a member of another race, or a Nazi helping an old Jew, or a devoutly religious person helped by an atheist, or any reverse or combination thereof).

There are two ways to avoid this "excessive" conclusion—or to water it down, at least. The first is simply to claim that the Samaritan was added later to give the parable an anti-Semitic twist: the original series consisted of the priest, the Levite, and an ordinary Jew, representing the three great classes into which the Jews were divided; later, "Jew" was changed to "Samaritan," which introduces an element of historical inconsistency, since no Samaritan would have been found on the road between Jericho and Jerusalem. One can also shift the focus to the expert in the law who is questioning Jesus: his goal is to learn what to do to obtain eternal life, i.e., he wants the confirmation that he is good enough to qualify for eternal life. So when Jesus tells him to love his neighbor, he wants a definition of neighbor that is not too challenging for him to say that he loves that person. Jesus, however, sets the standard extremely high: the one you should consider your neighbor is the person you believe is the most undesirable—you have to love that person as yourself if you want to qualify for eternal life. The point of Jesus' statements was to drive the lawyer to despair of his own efforts to qualify for eternal life, and this conclusion is applied to all people: none can be good enough to meet God's standard.

The key question here is: how can we not read this in the sense of the superego injunction? We are in effect dealing with the limit of an impossible-real; however, this does not mean that Jesus simply imposes a norm which we cannot fulfill and which thus makes us guilty—it is not that we should spend our days looking for those who are most undesirable to us, dismissing those who are too close to our lifestyle with: "Sorry, but I can't spend too much time helping you—I like you, and this disqualifies you as a candidate for my ethical work!" (Are Politically Correct fighters for the rights of minorities not often caught in this trap? They like nothing more than worrying about the restricted human rights of terrorists, serial killers, etc.) There is a way out of this predicament: what if, if the impossible norm drives us to despair, there is something wrong in its very form, the form of a norm? I remember fondly how, months before her sad death, after reading my *Fragile Absolute* where I celebrate the figure of Medea, Elizabeth Wright asked me, with genuine concern: "Something disturbed me in your book. Do you really mean that, in order to be truly ethical, one should murder one's children?" *Antigone* confronts us with the same problem: Antigone's fascinating beauty explodes when she is elevated into the position of the living dead on account of not compromising her unconditional desire. If, however, this implies that in "real" life we should follow the "safe" path of remaining within the symbolic coordinates and allowing the radical stance of "going to the end" only in the guise of an aesthetic image, does this not reduce art to the aesthetic contemplation of a radical ethical stance, as a supplement to our "real-life" compromising attitude of "following the crowd"? If there is one thing foreign to Lacan, it is such a stance.

There is a way to avoid the debilitating dilemma of either the impossible superego injunction or neutralization into an excess not to be followed in "real life." What if we refer to Jesus' "excessive" commandments (and to Medea, to Antigone . . .) as to "paradigms" (in the Kuhnian sense): exemplary models, indications of an attitude, which are not to be followed, but to be reinvented/repeated in each specific situation? In this precise sense, Sethe from Toni Morrison's *Beloved* reinvents/repeats Medea.

Another (as a rule overlooked) aspect of the "excess" of turning the other cheek, etc., is that it is a double-edged weapon: we should read it together with Jesus' unsettling statements that he brings the sword, not peace; that those who do not hate their parents and siblings are not his true followers, etc. Following an inner necessity, the "excess" of goodness (excess over equitable justice) has to appear as evil. There is an underlying extreme violence in Jesus' "excessive" injunctions. —There is a refined sense in which Jesus only brings to completion the Law: his "excesses" should makes us aware that the "golden rule" position of a balanced exchange of justice (a tooth for a tooth, an eye for an eye) is inherently impossible: in order to establish the space of this equivalence, the subject has to commit to it by means of an "excessive" gesture. It is in this sense that Jacques-Alain Miller pointed out how the Pascalian wager "only makes sense if what is put into the game is understood as already lost"[46]—in Pascal's case, what is lost are life's earthly pleasures.

When Eagleton emphasizes that Christian salvation is "performative rather than propositional"—"What distinguishes [Christ] from other Jewish prophets is not his heralding of the kingdom (the Baptist, for example, is all about that), but his insistence that it was faith in his own person that would determine how you stood with that regime"(xxix)—we should give this statement all due weight: the key thing that Christ added to the Old Testament teaching was himself. This is his true "extravagance"; all his other "ethical extravagances" are grounded in and follow from this one: that he is not merely God's prophet, but is himself God—this is why his death is so shattering, an ontological (not only ethical) scandal. How, then, do we pass from this death to the Holy Spirit?

THE NECESSITY OF A DEAD CHICKEN

Early in Christopher Nolan's The Prestige (2006), when a magician performs a trick with a small bird which disappears in a cage on the table, a little boy in the audience starts to cry, claiming that the bird was killed. The magician approaches him and finishes the trick, gently producing a living bird out of his hand—but the boy is not satisfied, insisting that this must be another bird, the dead one's brother. After the show, we see the magician in the room behind the stage, bringing in a flattened cage and throwing a squashed bird into a trash bin—the boy was right. The film describes the three stages of a magic performance: the setup, or the "pledge," where the magician shows the audience something that appears ordinary, but is probably not, making use of misdirection; the "turn," where the magician makes the ordinary act extraordinary; the "prestige," where the effect of the illusion is produced. Is this triple movement not the Hegelian triad at its purest? The thesis (pledge), its catastrophic negation (turn), the magical resolution of the catastrophe (prestige)? And, as Hegel was well aware, the catch is that, in order for the miracle of the "prestige" to occur, there must be a squashed dead bird somewhere.

We should thus fearlessly admit that there is something of the "cheap magician" in Hegel, in the trick of synthesis, of Aufhebung. Ultimately, there are only two options, two ways to account for this trick, like the two versions of the vulgar doctor's joke of "first-the-bad-news-then-the-good-news." The first one (which I already mentioned in my first contribution to this volume) is that the good news is the bad news, just viewed from a different perspective ("The bad news is that we've discovered you have severe Alzheimer's disease. The good news is the same: you have Alzheimer's, so you will have forgotten the bad news by the time you get back home."). There is, however, another version: the good news is good, but it concerns another subject ("The bad news is that you have terminal cancer and will die in a month. The good news is: you see that young, beautiful nurse over there? I've been trying to get her into bed for months; finally, yesterday, she said yes and we made love the whole night like crazy . . ."); The true Hegelian "synthesis" is the synthesis of these two options: the good news is the bad news itself—but in order for us to see that, we have to shift to a different agent (from the bird which dies to another one which replaces it; from the cancer-ridden patient to the happy doctor; from Christ as individual to the community of believers). In other words, the dead bird remains dead; it really dies, as in the case of Christ who is reborn as another subject, as the Holy Spirit.

There is, however, a key distinction between Christ's dead body in Christianity and the squashed bird in the magician's trick: in order for his trick to be effective, to work as a trick, the magician has to hide the squashed body from the audience, while the whole point of the Crucifixion is that Christ's body is displayed there for everyone to see. This is why Christianity (and Hegelianism as Christian philosophy) is not cheap magic: the material remainder of the squashed body remains visible . . . although, of course, Christ's body disappears from the sepulcher—the element of cheap magic religion cannot resist. . . . Again, the lesson of The Prestige is relevant here: in the middle of the film, Angier, one of the two competing magicians, travels to Colorado Springs to meet Nikola Tesla and learn the secret of Tesla's teleportation machine; he discovers that the machine creates and teleports a duplicate of any item placed in it. Angier returns to London to produce a new act, "The Real Transported Man": he disappears under huge arcs of electricity and instantaneously "teleports" fifty yards from the stage to the balcony. When Borden, his competitor, inspects the scene after the show, he spots a trap door and beneath it a locked water tank with a drowning Angier inside. Angier was so committed to the illusion that every time he disappeared, he fell into a locked tank and drowned, and the machine created a duplicate who was teleported to the balcony and basked in the applause. This is how we should reread Christ's resurrection in a materialist way: it is not that there is first his dead body and then its resurrection—the two events, death and resurrection, are strictly contemporaneous. Christ is resurrected in us, the collective of believers, and his tortured dead body remains forever as its material remainder. A materialist does not deny miracles, he just reminds us that they live behind disturbing material leftovers.

Apropos of Christianity and its overcoming, Jean-Luc Nancy proposed two guidelines: (1) "Only a Christianity which envisages the present possibility of its negation can be relevant today." (2) "Only an atheism which envisages the reality of its Christian provenance can be relevant today."[47] With some reservations, I cannot but agree with these two guidelines. The first proposition implies that today, Christianity is alive only in materialist (atheist) practices which negate it (the Pauline community of believers, for example, is to be found today in radical political groups, not in churches); the second proposition implies that a true materialism not only asserts that only material reality "really exists," but has to assume all the consequences of what Lacan called the nonexistence of the big Other, and it is only Christianity that opens up the space for thinking this nonexistence, insofar as it is the religion of a God who dies. Buenaventura Durutti, the famous Spanish anarchist, said: "The only church that illuminates is a burning church." He was right, although not in the immediate anti-clerical sense in which his remark was intended: a true religion arrives at its truth only through its self-cancellation.

Nancy also points out that Christianity is unique among all religions in that it conceives its very core as the passage from the overcoming of another religious corpus, a fact palpable in the duality of its sacred texts, Old and New Testament. The only way to account for this fact is to bring it to its self-relating extreme: Christianity includes within itself its own overcoming, i.e., its overcoming (negation) in modern atheism is inscribed into its very core as its innermost necessity. This is why radical political movements, with their elementary process of "sublating" their dead hero in the living spirit of the community, are so much like the Christological Resurrection—the point here is not that they function like "secularized Christianity," but, on the contrary, that the Resurrection of Christ is itself their precursor, a mythic form of something which reaches its true form in the logic of an emancipatory political collective. At the Woodstock festival in 1969, Joan Baez sang "Joe Hill," the famous Wobblies song from 1925 (words by Alfred Hayes, music by Earl Robinson) about the judicial murder of the Swedish-born trade-union organizer and singer, which, in the following decades, became a real folk song, popularized all around the world by Paul Robeson; here are the (slightly shortened) lyrics, which present in a simple but effective way the Christological aspect of the emancipatory collective, a struggling collective bound by love:

> I dreamed I saw Joe Hill last night
> Alive as you or me.
> Says I, "But Joe, you're ten years dead."
> "I never died," says he.
>
> "The copper bosses killed you, Joe,
> They shot you, Joe," says I.
> "Takes more than guns to kill a man."
> Says Joe, "I didn't die."
>
> And standing there as big as life,
> And smiling with his eyes,
> Joe says, "What they forgot to kill
> Went on to organize."
>
> "Joe Hill ain't dead," he says to me,
> "Joe Hill ain't never died.
> Where working men are out on strike,
> Joe Hill is at their side."

The crucial thing here is the subjective reversal: the mistake of the anonymous narrator of the song who does not believe that Joe Hill is still alive is that he forgets to include himself, his own subjective position, in the series: Joe Hill is not alive "out there," as a separate ghost, he is alive here, in the very minds of workers remembering him and continuing his fight—he is alive in the very gaze which (mistakenly) looks for him out there. The same mistake of "reifying" the object of search is committed by Christ's disciples; Christ corrects this mistake with his famous words: "When there will be love between two of you, I will be there." —When, on May 18, 1952, Robeson sang "Joe Hill" at the legendary Peach Arch concert, in front of 40,000 people gathered at the US—

Canadian border in the State of Washington (since his passport had been revoked by the US authorities, he was not allowed to enter Canada), he changed the key line from "What they forgot to kill" into: "What they can never kill went on to organize." The immortal dimension in man, that in man for what "takes more than guns to kill," the Spirit, is what went on to organize itself. We should not dismiss this as an obscurantist-spiritualist metaphor—there is a subjective truth in it: when emancipatory subjects organize themselves, it is the "spirit" itself which organizes itself through them—to the series of what the impersonal "it (*das Es, ça*)" does (in the unconscious, "it talks," "it enjoys"), one should add: it *organizes itself (ça s'organise*—therein lies the core of the "eternal Idea" of an emancipatory Party). Here we should shamelessly evoke the standard scene from science-fiction horror movies in which the alien who has assumed human appearance (or invaded and colonized a human being) is exposed, its human form destroyed, so that all that remains is a formless slime, like a small pool of molten metal; the hero leaves the scene, satisfied that the threat is over—however, soon afterward, the formless slime that the hero forgot to kill (or couldn't kill) starts to move, slowly organizing itself, and the old menacing figure emerges again . . . perhaps it is along these lines that one should read

> the Christian practice of eucharist in which the participants in this love feast or sacrificial meal establish solidarity with one another through the medium of a mutilated body. In this way, they share at the level of sign or sacrament in Christ's own bloody passage from weakness to power, death to transfigured life.[48]

Is what we believers eat in the Eucharist, Christ's flesh (bread) and blood (wine), not precisely the same formless remainder, "what they [the Roman soldiers who crucified him] can never kill," which then goes on to organize itself as a community of believers? We should reread from this standpoint Oedipus himself as a precursor of Christ: against those—including Lacan himself—who perceive Oedipus at Colonus and Antigone as figures driven by the uncompromisingly suicidal death drive, "unyielding right to the end, demanding everything, giving up nothing, absolutely unreconciled,"[49] Terry Eagleton is right to point out the fact that Oedipus at Colonus

> becomes the cornerstone of a new political order. Oedipus's polluted body signifies among other things the monstrous terror at the gates in which, if it is to have a chance of rebirth, the *polis* must recognize its own hideous deformity. This profoundly political dimension of the tragedy is given short shrift in Lacan's own meditations. . . . In becoming nothing but the scum and refuse of the *polis*—the "shit of the earth," as St. Paul racily describes the followers of Jesus, or the "total loss of humanity" which Marx portrays as the proletariat—Oedipus is divested of his identity and authority and so can offer his lacerated body as the

cornerstone of a new social order. "Am I made a man in this hour when I cease to be?" (or perhaps "Am I to be counted as something only when I am nothing / am no longer human?"), the beggar king wonders aloud.[50]

Does this not recall a later beggar-king, Christ himself, who, by his death as a nothing, an outcast abandoned even by his disciples, founds a new community of believers? They both reemerge by passing through the zero level of being reduced to an excremental remainder. —This "transubstantiation," by means of which our acts are experienced as drawing their strength from their own result, should not be dismissed as an ideological illusion ("there really are just individuals who are organizing themselves"). Here is the shortest Jacob and Wilhelm Grimm fairy tale, "The Willful Child":

> Once upon a time there was a child who was willful and did not do what his mother wanted. For this reason God was displeased with him and caused him to become ill, and no doctor could help him, and in a short time he lay on his deathbed. He was lowered into a grave and covered with earth, but his little arm suddenly came forth and reached up, and it didn't help when they put it back in and put fresh earth over it, for the little arm always came out again. So the mother herself had to go to the grave and beat the little arm with a switch, and as soon as she had done that, it withdrew, and the child finally came to rest beneath the earth.

Is this obstinacy that persists even beyond death not freedom—death drive—at its most elementary? Instead of condemning it, should we not rather celebrate it as the ultimate resort of our resistance? The refrain of an old German Communist song from the 1930s is *"Die Freiheit hat Soldaten!* [Freedom has its soldiers!]" It may appear that such an identification of a particular unit as the military instrument of Freedom itself is the very formula of the "totalitarian" temptation: we do not just fight for (our understanding of) freedom, we do not just serve freedom, it is freedom itself which immediately avails itself of us. . . . The way seems open to terror: who would be allowed to oppose freedom itself? However, the identification of a revolutionary military unit as a direct organ of freedom cannot simply be dismissed as a fetishistic short circuit: in a pathetic way, this is true of the authentic revolutionary explosion. What happens in such an "ecstatic" experience is that the subject who acts is no longer a person but, precisely, an object. And it is precisely this dimension of identifying with an object which justifies the use of the term "theology" to describe the situation: "theology" here is a name for what is, in a revolutionary subject, beyond a mere collection of individual humans acting together.

Is this not Christ's message of resurrection—what "God is love" means is: "No one has ever seen God; but if we love one another, God lives in us and his love is made complete in us" (John 4:12, New International Version). Or:

"No one has ever seen Joe Hill since his death; but if workers organize themselves in their struggle, he lives in them. . . ." —There is a triple movement of *Aufhebung* here: (1) the singular person of Christ (Joe Hill) is sublated in his resurrected identity as the Spirit (Love) of the community of believers; (2) the empirical miracle is sublated in the higher "true" miracle. (This follows the well-known rhetorical figure: when Hegel talks about religious miracles, his point is that one cannot be sure if there are real physical miracles—a polite way of saying that there aren't—but the true miracle is the universal thought itself, the wonder of thinking. Today, it is popular to say that the true miracle is a moral victory: when, after a difficult inner struggle, someone makes the right difficult decision—to give up drugs or crime, to sacrifice himself for a good cause; in a similar way, for Christianity, the true miracle is not the dead Christ walking around, but the love in the collective of believers.) (3) Christianity itself is sublated in political organization. And, again, this miracle comes at a price: there is the bird's body squashed somewhere—like Christ on the Cross, this supreme squashed bird.

It is this key dimension of the Holy Spirit as the spirit of the community of believers, as something which is here only insofar as we, believers, include ourselves in it, that gets lost in the "immanent" idea of a Trinity which persists independently of the divine "economy," as an In-Itself independent of the Fall. What gets lost is the idea that the fate of God himself is at stake in the vicissitudes of human history. This is why Hegel is *the* Christian philosopher: the supreme example of the dialectical reversal is that of Crucifixion and Resurrection, which should be perceived not as two consecutive events, but as *a purely formal parallax shift on one and the same event*: Crucifixion *is* Resurrection—to see this, one has only to include oneself in the picture. When the believers gather, mourning Christ's death, their shared spirit is the resurrected Christ.

And we should go to the (political) end here: the same goes for revolution itself. At its most radical, revolutionary "reconciliation" is not a change of reality, but a parallactic shift in how we relate to it—or, as Hegel put it in his Preface to the *Philosophy of Right*, the highest speculative task is not to transform the Cross of miserable contemporary reality into a new rose garden, but "to recognize the Rose in the Cross of the present [*die Rose im Kreuz der gegenwart zu erkennen*]."[51] So what if we should return to the very beginning of it all, to the split of the Hegelian school into the revolutionary "young Hegelians" and the conservative "old Hegelians"? What if we should locate the "original sin" of modern emancipatory movements in the "young Hegelian" rejection of State authority and alienation? What if—a move suggested by Domenico Losurdo—today's left should reappropriate the "old Hegelian" topos of a strong State grounded in a shared ethical substance? Milbank (quite correctly) points out how Chesterton's Catholic perspective "permitted him to think of the importance of mediating institutions (cooperatives, guilds, and corporations) in a way not unlike that of Hegel"—from my perspective, the only problem here is that this "corporatist" solution is today, with the unheard-of advancement of capitalist "deterritorialization," no longer actual. Milbank continues that, if we reject this "corporatist" solution, " the only alternative would indeed appear to be an austere socialist dictatorship in which the forbidding of futile desire by law benignly releases us for the privacy of chastened love according to the dictates of the autonomous law of morality." I am tempted to add here: why not embrace this alternative? Why should our task not be to recognize the Rose in the Cross of the "austere socialist dictatorship"?

The relationship between Death and Life in the figure of Christ (the exemplary death on the Cross; the resurrection into eternal life given to all who believe in him and decide to "live in Christ") is thus also purely parallactic: it is not the pseudo-dialectical one between utter loss/negation (death) and its reversal into absolute life, i.e., death is not *aufgehoben* in life, since, first of all, this relationship is not a succession at all, but *one and the same event* viewed from different perspectives. Life and Death here are not polar opposites, contrasts, within the same global Whole (field of reality), but the same thing viewed from a different global perspective. The difference is not in "life" and "death" as the designated particular content of the statement, but in the very universal horizon from which this content is viewed; we are dealing not with the split of particulars within a universal frame, but with the split between two universals with regard to the same particular. To put it in Kierkegaard's terms, the difference is the one between becoming and being: the (temporal) death of Christ is his very (eternal) life "in becoming." (In a precisely analogous way, Christ's "I bring sword and division, not love and peace" is his Love in becoming.)

Today's official Catholicism shrinks from this insight no less than a vampire from garlic. Pope Benedict XVI recently gave a sign that he will endorse an interesting change in Catholic dogma: the notion of "limbo," the incomplete afterlife for infants who die before being baptized. Limbo was conceived in medieval times as a place where children would enjoy eternal happiness, but be deprived of the actual presence of God. This change, of course, does not mean that the Church will return to its original position, formulated by St. Augustine, that children who were not reunited with Christ in baptism will go to hell; the idea is, rather, that they will go directly to heaven. No wonder that, a decade ago, the same Pope—as Cardinal Ratzinger—claimed that those who are truly seeking God and inwardly striving toward unity with him will receive salvation even if they are not baptized.[52] Although this idea may seem warm and sympathetic, it is in effect a fateful concession to the New Age notion of a direct inner contact with divinity: what gets lost is the central place of baptism as the individual's inclusion into the Holy Spirit, the community of believers.

It is thus deeply problematic that Agamben reads limbo as the model of happiness. What we should question is Agamben's implicit distinction between "good" and "bad" *homo sacer*: Hitler and his kind wanted to discriminate, to draw a clear line excluding *homo sacer*, while we should persist at the point of nondecision, in a limbo. For Hitler, the scope of *homines sacres* who can be killed with impunity gradually expands: first, *homines sacres* are the Jews, then other inferior races, and in the end Germans themselves who betrayed Hitler . . . is the situation not the same with regard to anti-Semitism which culminates in Zionist anti-Semitism? Stalin dealt with the same problem of the ever-expanding group of traitors through political trials whose function was to invent fictions of treason which enabled the regime to draw the line of separation and decide who was the excremental traitor. It is a kind of mystery that Agamben never analyzes the Stalinist Gulag whose logic is not the same as that of the Nazi camps: although there were "Muslims" in the Gulag also, the Gulag prisoners were not reduced to bare life, they remained subjects of ideological indoctrination and ritual. (The exception seems to be some camps in today's North Korea.) The comatose limbo state prior to decision is the very opposite of the Pauline community of believers; if we elevate children in the undecided limbo state into emancipatory figures, does this not lead to extending the series to the unborn fetus? Is a fetus not the bare undecided life at its purest? No wonder that, for US anti-abortionists, tens of millions of aborted children are a crime worse than the Holocaust, marking our entire civilization with an indelible stigma of sin. No wonder Agamben's implicit notion of "positive" community sounds uncannily close to the dream of a "good" concentration camp.

This is why, with regard to the opposition between Catholicism and Protestantism, I am effectively on the Protestant side. Recall the difference between the standard liberal notion of "private" and Kant's paradoxical notion of the "private" use of reason as religion: for liberals, religion and state should be separate, religion should be a matter of private beliefs with no power to intervene directly with authority in public matters; while for Kant, religion is "private" precisely when it is organized as a hierarchic state institution with jurisdiction in public matters (controlling education, etc.). For Kant, religion is thus much closer to the public use of reason when it is practiced as a "private" belief outside state institutions: in this case, the space remains open for the believer to act as a "singular universality," to reach the universal domain directly as a singular subject, bypassing the frame of particular institutions. This is why Kant was a Protestant: Catholicism, with its links between religious and secular power, is Christianity in the mode of private use of reason, while Protestantism, with its subtraction of the collective of believers from the institutional "public" space, is Christianity in the mode of public use of reason—every singular subject has the right to a direct contact with the divine, bypassing the Church as an institution.

This difference is the one between abstract and concrete universality. The standard reading of Hegel would tell us that Catholicism stands for concrete universality (the Church is embedded in its particular social context), while Protestantism stands for abstract universality (the believing individual reaches universality directly, in abstraction from the "concrete" texture of a particular social order). The truth is the very opposite. What makes Catholic universality (inscribed into the very term "catholic"—all-encompassing) abstract is the very character of the Church as a great Body of believers which unites them all in a hierarchic organism. What makes Protestantism concretely universal is not the mere fact of the direct short circuit between the singular and the universal as such, but the precise nature of this short circuit: in it, universality appears as such, in its opposition, its negative relation, to the particular organic order; it cuts into every particular community, dividing it from within into those who follow the universal Truth and those who do not. Abstract universality is the mute medium of all particular content, concrete universality *unsettles from within the identity of the particular*; it is a line of division which is itself universal, running across the entire sphere of the particular, dividing it from itself. Abstract universality is uniting, concrete universality is dividing. Abstract universality is the peaceful foundation of the particulars, concrete universality is the site of struggle—it brings the sword, not love. . . .

When St. Paul says that, from a Christian standpoint, "there are no men and women, no Jews and Greeks," he thereby claims that ethnic roots, national identity, etc., are *not a category of truth*, or, to put it in precise Kantian terms, when we reflect upon our ethnic roots, we engage in a *private use of reason*, constrained by contingent dogmatic presuppositions, i.e., we act as "immature" individuals, not as free human beings who dwell in the dimension of the universality of reason. The opposition between Kant and Rorty with regard to this distinction of public and private is rarely noted, but nonetheless crucial: they both sharply distinguish between the two domains, but in opposed ways. For Rorty, the great contemporary liberal if ever there was one, the private is the space of our idiosyncrasies where creativity and wild imagination rule, and moral considerations are (almost) suspended, while the public is the space of social interaction where we should obey the rules so that we do not hurt others; in other words, the private is the space of irony, while the public is the space of solidarity. For Kant, however, the public space of the "world-civil-society" designates the paradox of the universal singularity, of a singular subject who, in a kind of short circuit, bypassing the mediation of the particular, directly participates in the Universal. This is what Kant, in the famous passage of his "What is Enlightenment?", means by "public" as opposed to "private": "private" is not one's individuality as opposed to communal ties, but the very communal-institutional order of one's particular identification; while "public" is the transnational universality of the exercise of one's reason:

The public use of one's reason must always be free, and it alone can bring about enlightenment among men. The private use of one's reason, on the other hand, may often be very narrowly restricted without particularly hindering the progress of enlightenment. By public use of one's reason I understand the use which a person makes of it as a scholar before the reading public. Private use I call that which one may make of it in a particular civil post or office which is entrusted to him.[53]

The paradox of Kant's formula "Think freely, but obey!" (which, of course, poses a series of problems of its own, since it also relies on the distinction between the "performative" level of social authority, and the level of free thinking where performativity is suspended) is thus that one participates in the universal dimension of the "public" sphere precisely as a singular individual extracted from or even opposed to one's substantial communal identification—one is truly universal only when radically singular, in the interstices of communal identities. It is Kant who should be read here as the critic of Rorty. In his vision of the public space of the unconstrained free exercise of reason, he asserts the dimension of emancipatory universality *outside* the confines of one's social identity, of one's position within the order of (social) being—the dimension missing in Rorty.

This space of singular universality is what, within Christianity, appears as the "Holy Spirit," the space of a collective of believers *subtracted* from the field of organic communities, of particular life-worlds ("neither Greeks nor Jews"). Consequently, is Kant's "Think freely, but obey!" not a new version of Christ's "Give to God what belongs to God, and to Caesar what belongs to Caesar"? "Give to Caesar what belongs to Caesar," i.e., respect and obey the "private" particular life-world of your community, and "give to God what belongs to God," i.e., participate in the universal space of the community of believers—the Pauline collective of believers is a proto-model of the Kantian "world-civil-society."

So, back to the book of Job: the three theological friends who come to harass Job are three representatives of the "private" use of reason in the Kantian sense of the term: they try to reinscribe the catastrophe that has befallen Job into the "private" ideology of their community; and Job's resistance is a minimal gesture of subtracting oneself from this communal space. By declaring his solidarity with Job, God declares himself to be the "public" God—a fact which is accomplished in Christian revelation. That is to say: what dies on the Cross is precisely the "private" God, the God of our "way of life," the God who grounds a particular community. The underlying message of Christ's death is that *a "public" God can no longer be a living God*: he has to die as a God (or, as in Judaism, he can be a God of the dead Letter)—public space is by definition "atheist." The "Holy Spirit" is thus a "public" God, what remains of God in the public universal space: the radically desubstantialized virtual space of the collective of believers.

But is there not an obvious counterargument to such a death-of-God theology which focuses on the passage from the death of God qua substance to the Holy Spirit as the community of believers, a counterargument known to anyone who is really acquainted with Nietzsche? When Nietzsche talks about the death of God, he does not have in mind the pagan living God, but precisely this God qua Holy Spirit, the community of believers. Although this community no longer relies on a transcendent Guarantee of a substantial big Other, the big Other (and thereby the theological dimension) is still there as the virtual frame of reference (say, in Stalinism in the guise of the big Other of History which guarantees the meaningfulness of our acts). Did Lacan himself not point in this direction when, in 1956, he proposed a short and clear definition of the Holy Ghost: "The Holy Ghost is the entry of the signifier into the world. This is certainly what Freud brought us under the title of death drive"?[54] What Lacan means, at this moment of his thought, is that the Holy Spirit stands for the symbolic order as that which cancels (or, rather, suspends) the entire domain of "life"—lived experience, the libidinal flux, the wealth of emotions, or, to put it in Kant's terms, the "pathological": when we locate ourselves within the Holy Spirit, we are transubstantiated, we enter another life beyond the biological one.

But is this shift from the living gods of the Real to the dead God of the Law really what happens in Christianity? Is it not that this shift already takes place in Judaism, so that the death of Christ cannot stand for this shift, but for something much more radical—precisely for the death of the virtual-dead big Other itself? So the key question is: is the Holy Spirit still a figure of the big Other, or is it possible to conceive it outside this frame? It is here that the reference to the undead remainder of the dead Father becomes crucial: for Lacan, the transmutation of the dead Father into the virtual big Other (of the symbolic Law) is never complete, the Law has to remain sustained by the undead remainder (in the guise of the obscene superego supplement to the Law). It is only Christianity which properly completes the Law by, in effect, getting rid of the undead remainder—and, of course, this completion is the Law's self-sublation, its transmutation into Love.

The problem of shofar—the voice of the dying father rendered in the Jewish ritual by the low, ominously reverberating sound of a horn—is that of the rise of the Law out of the Father's death: Lacan's point is that, in order for the Law to arise, the Father should not wholly die, a part of him should survive and sustain the Law. This is why shofar occurs in Judaism, the religion of the dead God—monotheism is as such the religion of a dead God. Shofar is not a pagan remainder, a sign of the death of the pagan God, but something generated by the monotheist turn. The shift from Judaism to Christianity is discernible precisely in the shift from shofar—the cry of the dying God-Father—to "Father, why have you forsaken me!", the cry of the dying son on the Cross.

With regard to atheism, there is a radical change between Lacan's Seminar VII (1959–1960, on the ethics of psychoanalysis) and Seminar XI (1963–1964, on the four fundamental concepts of psychoanalysis): in Seminar VII, Lacan draws the consequences from the proposition "God is dead," which constitute, for him, the atheist content of the Freudian myth of Oedipus, as well as of the Judeo-Christian legacy. From Seminar XI, however, he insists that the true formula of atheism is not "God is dead," but "God is unconscious," and this renders the question of atheism much more difficult and complex: to be an atheist, it is no longer sufficient to declare that one "doesn't believe (in God)," since the true site of my beliefs is not my conscious acts, but the unconscious. This, of course, does not mean the psychological claptrap that "even if I try to deny God, deep in myself I continue to believe"—the unconscious is not "deep in me," it is out there, embodied in my practices, rituals, interactions. Even if I subjectively don't believe, I believe "objectively," in and through my acts and symbolic rituals. This also means that religion, religious belief, is much more deeply rooted in "human nature" than it may appear: its ultimate support is the illusion of the "big Other" which is in a way consubstantial with the symbolic order itself. The true formula of atheism is not "I don't believe," but "I no longer have to rely on a big Other who believes for me"—the true formula of atheism is "there is no big Other."

To conclude, I would like to tackle directly the question which resonates beneath all Milbank's critical remarks: with all the paradoxes of universalized evil reverting to good, etc., what would the ethical stance that I imply actually look like? The first thing to emphasize is that it is a resolutely and ambiguously *materialist* ethics, where it is not enough to say that it does not rely on any (religious) belief—we should be much more precise and radical here: what do we really believe when we believe? Is it not that, even when our belief is sincere and intimate, we do not simply believe in the direct reality of the object of our belief; in a much more refined way, we cling to a vision whose status is very fragile, virtual, so that its direct actualization would somehow betray the sublime character of the belief. You believe only in things whose status is ontologically suspended, which is why a friend of mine, a devout Catholic, was shocked when Cardinal Joseph Ratzinger[55] was elected Pope Benedict XVI: "This is a man who really believes in what he is saying . . ."—as if it is normal not to believe, or, to paraphrase the Marx Brothers: "This man looks and acts as if he believes, but this shouldn't deceive you. He really does believe." (We should not forget that the same goes also for atheists: "This man acts and looks as if he is an atheist, but this shouldn't deceive you. He really is an atheist.") This is why Graham Greene didn't go far enough when, in some of his plays and novels (*The End of the Affair*), he writes of the traumatic impact on a nonbeliever when he witnesses a sudden miracle, a direct divine intervention (as a rule, the miracle of saving a dying man from certain death). I should add a further twist: the true paradox is that such a direct miracle shatters a believer even more—as in *Leap of Faith* (1992), in which Steve Martin plays the Reverend Jonas Nightingale, a revivalist preacher with a road show of Gospel music, miracles, and wonders. He's a cynical hustler who knows how to read people and make money out of their vulnerabilities, using every trick in the book to prey upon the hopes and dreams of the townsfolk. He even rigs up a life-sized statue of Christ so that tears stream down its face. However, at the climactic moment of the film, when Jonas is challenged to cure the crippled younger brother of a woman he wants to seduce, he produces a real miracle—the boy regains the ability to walk. His entire universe shattered, Jonas runs away from the town. . . .

So Chesterton was right: if we do not believe in God, we are ready to believe in anything. Belief in God is a constitutive exception which enables us to assert the factual rationality of the universe. We are dealing here yet again with the Lacanian logic of the non-All: God allows me to not to believe in vulgar miracles and to accept the basic rationality of the universe; without this exception, there is nothing I am not ready to believe.

In a kind of almost symmetrical reversal, atheism is the secret inner conviction of believers who externalize their belief, while belief is the secret inner conviction of public atheists. This is why Lacan said that theologians are the only true materialists—and, I might add, this is why materialists are the only true believers. Umberto Eco is right here: "I frequently meet scientists who, outside their own narrow discipline, are superstitious—to such an extent that it sometimes seems to me that to be a rigorous unbeliever today, you have to be a philosopher. Or perhaps a priest."[56] These lines cannot fail to bring to mind what a leading Slovene conservative-Catholic intellectual wrote in a polemic against my defense of atheism:

> There are no proofs—and there can be none—that God doesn't exist. Instead of the proofs, the atheist is driven only by the desire that there would be no God. This, however, is the best proof that God exists, since it is only about things which exist that one can desire that they would not be. Atheism is the best proof of God's existence.[57]

It is not enough to laugh at the all too obviously circular nature of this weird "proof of God": atheists do not pretend to provide a positive proof that God doesn't exist; what they do is (among other things) to render problematic the proofs that he does exist; moreover, they do not "desire" that God shouldn't exist—what they desire, at the limit, is that religion (the illusory belief in God) shouldn't exist. Much more important is to reject the central premise, namely that "it is only with relation to things which exist that one can desire that they should not exist": at its most fundamental, desire relates to something which does not exist. The basic lesson of psychoanalysis is that one can not only desire but even prohibit something which doesn't exist, and that such a prohibition is a cunning strategy to make it (appear to) exist. Prohibition at its most radical—prohibition of incest—is the prohibition of something which is in itself impossible.[58]

Furthermore, we can easily turn the argument around: "There are no proofs—and there can be none—that God exists. Instead of proofs, the believer is driven only by the desire that there should be a God. This, however, is the best proof that God doesn't exist, since it is only with relation to things which do not exist that one can desire that they should exist. Theism is the best proof of God's nonexistence." This, again, is what Lacan effectively claims: theologians are the only true atheists.

The premise that underlies this conundrum is that it is impossible to do it directly—either to believe fully and directly, or to be a full and direct atheist. As if ashamed to openly declare their belief, believers take refuge in externalized phrases and rituals—if they are asked directly about their beliefs, their faces go red and their gazes turn down. And the same holds for the majority of atheists: even if they publicly declare themselves atheists, when they are directly asked about it, they start to mumble: "Of course I don't believe in a personal God, or in the Church as an institution, but maybe there is some kind of higher power, a spiritual entity. . . ." This symmetry, however, is not perfect; it is even deeply misleading, since both sides *believe*, only at a different level: each of them covers a different aspect of the big Other. The atheist who officially doesn't believe is, today, the one who assiduously checks his horoscope in the newspaper, with an embarrassed laugh which indicates that he "doesn't take it seriously"; the believer observes external ritual, says his prayers, gets his children baptized, etc., convinced that he is simply displaying a respect for tradition . . . in short, they both rely on the big Other. To be truly an atheist, one has to accept that the big Other doesn't exist, and act upon it.

How, then, does such a materialist ethics look? Let me begin with *Baden Learning Play on Consent [Badener Lehrstueck vom Einverstaendnis]*,[59] in which Brecht provides his most poignant formulation of how an emancipated human being should relate to death. First, in a refined dialectical way, he formulates the loss in dying as giving up not only what you know or have, but also what you do not know or have; not only your wealth, but also your poverty:

> The one of us who dies also knows this: I give up what is present there, I give away more than I have. The one of us who dies gives up the street he knows, but also the street he doesn't know. The riches he has and also those he does not have. His very poverty. His own hand. (601)

This means that what one has to give up if one is to consent to dying cannot be brought under the designation of "sacrifice." In sacrifice, one gives up what one has, while here, one has to give up what one *is*, an "is" of extreme poverty, deprived of all one "has"—in short, in the authentic gesture of "giving up," one sacrifices nothing, because one has already renounced all content one could have sacrificed:

> To encourage a man for his death, the interveningly thinking one [*der eingreifend Denkende*] asks him to give away his goods. When the man gives away everything, what is left over is only life. Give away more, says the thinking one.
>
> When the thinking one overcomes a storm, he overcomes it because he knew the storm and consented to [*einverstanden war*] the storm. So when you want to overcome dying, you overcome it when you know dying and you consent to dying. And the one who wishes to consent sticks to poverty. He does not stick to things! Things can be taken away, and there is thereby no consent. He also does not stick to life. Life will be taken away, and then there will be no consent. He also does not stick to thoughts, thoughts can also be taken away and then there is also no consent. (602)

This "give more" is a true ethical answer to the false spirit of sacrifice: it hits the narcissistic satisfaction provided by sacrifice in the eye. Brecht's real target here is the pathetic gesture of sacrifice, where one stages a spectacle which enables the subject to gain surplus-enjoyment from his very renunciation. The truly difficult thing is not to reach the impossible *jouissance*, but to get rid of it, i.e., to renounce it in a way which will not generate a surplus-enjoyment of its own. What one should sacrifice is sacrifice itself, or, as Brecht put it, prior to giving oneself up, one should reduce oneself to the point of "smallest greatness," so that one has nothing to give away—in this way, *no one dies when you die*:

THE LEARNED CHORUS:
Who then dies, when you die?

THE THREE FALLEN MECHANICS:
No one.

THE LEARNED CHORUS:
Now you know:
No one
Dies, when you die.
Now you have
Reached your smallest greatness. (606)

So, again: what kind of ethics does such an acceptance of "being no one" imply? It is an *ethics without morality*—but not in Nietzsche's sense of immoral ethics, enjoining us to remain faithful to ourselves, to persist on our chosen way beyond good and evil. Morality is concerned with the symmetry of my relations to other humans; its zero-level rule is "do not do to me what you do not want me to do to you"; ethics, on the contrary, deals with my consistency with myself, my fidelity to my own desire. There is, however, a totally different way to distinguish ethics and morality: along the lines of Friedrich Schiller's opposition of naive and sentimental. Morality is "sentimental," it involves others (only) in the sense that, loooking at myself through others' eyes, I like myself to be good; ethics, on the contrary, is naive—I do what I have to do because it needs to be done, not because of my goodness. This naivety does not exclude reflexivity—it even enables it: a cold, cruel distance toward what one is doing. The best literary expression of such an ethical stance is The Notebook, the first volume of Agota Kristof's trilogy The Notebook—The Proof—The Third Lie.[60] When I first heard someone talk about Agota Kristof, I thought it was an East European mispronunciation of Agatha Christie; but I soon discovered not only that Agota is not Agatha, but that Agota's horror is much more terrifying than Agatha's. Although her universe is "postmodern" (the three books are written in totally different styles, and they often contradict each other in talking about the same events, presenting different versions of a traumatic "thing" that must have happened), her writing is totally anti-postmodern in its clear simplicity, with sentences which recall elementary-school reports.

The Notebook tells the story of young twins living with their grandmother in a small Hungarian town during the last years of World War II and the early years of Communism. (Later we learn that it is not even clear if there really are two brothers or merely one who hallucinates the other—the Lacanian answer is: they are more than one and less than two. The twins are $1 + a$: a subject and what is in him more than himself.) The twins are utterly immoral—they lie, blackmail, kill—yet they stand for authentic ethical naivety at its purest. A couple of examples should suffice. One day, they meet a starving deserter in the forest , and bring him some things he asks them for:

> When we come back with the food and blanket, he says:
> "You're very kind."
> We say:
> "We weren't trying to be kind. We've brought you these things because you absolutely need them. That's all." (43)

If ever there was a Christian ethical stance, this is it: no matter how weird their neighbor's demands, the twins naively try to meet them. One night, they find themselves sleeping in the same bed with a German officer, a tormented gay masochist. Early in the morning, they wake up and want to leave the bed, but the officer holds them back:

> "Don't move. Keep sleeping."
> "We want to urinate. We have to go."
> "Don't go. Do it here."
> We ask:

"Where?"
He says:
"On me. Yes. Don't be afraid. Piss! On my face."
We do it, then we go out into the garden, because the bed is all wet. (91)

A true work of love, if ever there was one! The twins' closest friend is the priest's housekeeper, a voluptuous young woman who washes them and their clothes, playing erotic games with them. Then something happens when a procession of starved Jews is led through the town on their way to the camp:

Right in front of us, a thin arm emerges from the crowd, a dirty hand stretches out, a voice asks:
"Bread."
The housekeeper smiles and pretends to offer the rest of her bread; she holds it close to the outstretched hand, then, with a great laugh, brings the piece of bread back to her mouth, takes a bite, and says:
"I'm hungry too." (107)

The boys decide to punish her: they put some ammunition into her kitchen stove, so that when she lights the fire in the morning, the stove explodes and disfigures her. Along these lines, it is easy for me to imagine a situation in which I would be ready, without any moral qualms, to murder someone in cold blood, even if I knew that this person had not killed anyone directly. In reading reports about torture in Latin American military regimes, I found particularly repulsive the (regular) figure of a doctor who helped the actual torturers conduct their business in the most efficient way: he examined the victim and monitored the process, letting the torturers know how much the victim would be able to endure, what kind of torture would inflict the most unbearable pain, etc. I must admit that if I were to encounter such a person, knowing that there was little chance of bringing him to legal justice, and be given the opportunity to murder him discreetly, I would simply do it, without a vestige of remorse about "taking the law into my own hands." . . . What is crucial in such cases is to avoid the fascination of Evil which prompts us to elevate torturers into "demoniac" transgressors who have the strength to overcome our petty moral considerations and act freely. Torturers are not "beyond" Good and Evil, they are *beneath* it; they do not "heroically transgress" our shared ethical rules, they simply *lack* them. —Back to *The Notebook*: the two brothers also blackmail the priest: they threaten to let everybody know how the priest sexually molested Harelip, a girl who needs help to survive, demanding a regular weekly sum of money from him. The shocked priest asks them:

"It's monstrous. Have you any idea what you're doing?"
"Yes, sir. Blackmail."

"At your age . . . It's deplorable."

"Yes, it's deplorable that we've been forced to this. But Harelip and her mother absolutely need money." (70)

There is nothing personal in this blackmail: later, they even become close friends with the priest. When Harelip and her mother can survive on their own, they refuse further money from the priest: "Keep it. You have given enough. We took your money when it was absolutely necessary. Now we earn enough money to give some to Harelip. We have also taught her to work" (137). Their cold serving of others extends to killing them when asked: when their grandmother asks them to put poison into her cup of milk, they say: "'Don't cry, Grandmother. We'll do it; if you really want us to, we'll do it'" (171).

Naive as it is, such a subjective attitude in no way precludes a monstrously cold reflexive distance. One day, the twins put on torn clothes and go begging; passing women give them apples, biscuits, etc., and one of them even strokes their hair. Then another woman suggests that they come to her home and do some work, for which she will feed them.

> We answer:
> "We don't want to work for you, madam. We don't want to eat your soup or your bread. We are not hungry."
> She asks:
> "Then why are you begging?"
> "To find out what effect it has and to observe people's reactions."
> She walks off, shouting:
> "Dirty little hooligans! And impertinent too!"
> On our way home, we throw the apples, the biscuits, the chocolate, and the coins in the tall grass by the roadside.
> It is impossible to throw away the stroking on our hair. (34)

This is where I stand—how I would love to be: an ethical monster without empathy, doing what is to be done in a weird coincidence of blind spontaneity and reflexive distance, helping others while avoiding their disgusting proximity. With more people like this, the world would be a pleasant place in which sentimentality would be replaced by a cold and cruel passion.

NOTES

1.   G. K. Chesterton, *Orthodoxy* (San Francisco: Ignatius, 1995), p. 139.

2.   Ibid.

3.   Ibid.

4.   Gershom Sholem, *Kabbalah* (New York: Meridian, 1978), p. 123.

5. Ibid., pp. 123–124.

6. Ibid., p. 124.

7. Jacques Lacan, *Le triomphe de la religion* (Paris: Editions du Seuil, 2005), pp. 78–80.

8. Ibid., pp. 82, 87.

9. Jean-Luc Nancy in *Le Monde*, March 29, 1994.

10. See Jacob Neusner, *A Rabbi Talks with Jesus* (New York: Doubleday, 1993).

11. John D. Caputo and Gianni Vattimo, *After the Death of God* (New York: Columbia University Press, 2007), pp. 12–13.

12. John D. Caputo, *On Religion* (London: Routledge, 2001), p. 55.

13. Caputo and Vattimo, *After the Death of God*, p. 133.

14. Ibid., pp. 79–80.

15. Ibid., p. 76.

16. Ibid., pp. 78–79.

17. Ibid., p. 80.

18. Ibid., p. 70.

19. Ibid., pp. 51–52.

20. Ibid., p. 46.

21. Ibid., pp. 47–48.

22. Ibid., p. 37.

23. Ibid., p. 45.

24. Ibid., p. 42.

25. Thomas J. J. Altizer, *The Contemporary Jesus* (London: SCM Press, 1998). Numbers in brackets after extracts refer to pages in this volume.

26. Leon Trotsky, *Terrorism and Communism* (London: Verso, 2007), p. 74.

27. From here on, numbers in brackets refer again to pages in Altizer, *The Contemporary Jesus*.

28. Hans Jonas, *The Gnostic Religion* (Boston: Beacon Press, 1958), p. 237.

29. *The Gnostic Scriptures* (New York: Doubleday, 1987), p. 254.

30. Harold Bloom, *Omens of Millennium* (London: Fourth Estate, 1996), p. 252.

31. In the sixteenth century, to help Cardinal Albert of Mainz pay off his loan, and also to help with the expenses for St. Peter's Church in Rome, the Pope gave Albert a ten-year license to sell indulgences of unprecedented potency. What triggered Luther's fury was the promise that these indulgences would actually work even on future sins. It was thus possible to be preemptively absolved of future sins: having paid the required price, you could commit a sinful act, even a murder, with a clear conscience—a patent encouragement to sin. No wonder Luther was so enraged by this preemptive absolution: the basic Protestant attitude is "anything is permitted *on condition that you feel guilty about doing it*"—here, you dispense with the guilt before the act.

32. G. W. F. Hegel, *Lectures on the Philosophy of Religion*, vol. 3 (Berkeley: University of California Press, 1987), p. 233.

33. William Blake, *Jerusalem* 38:29–36.

34. *Bava Metzia*, fol. 59, col. 1.

35. Personal conversation, Madrid, 2007.

36. Rudolf Bultmann, *Theology of the New Testament*, vol. 1 (London: SCM Press, 1952), pp. 264–265.

37. Jacques Lacan, "Lituraterre," in *Autres écrits* (Paris: Editions du Seuil, 2001), p. 14.

38. Ibid., p. 16.

39. Jacques Derrida, *"Geschlecht II: Heidegger's Hand,"* in *Deconstruction and Philosophy* (Chicago: University of Chicago Press, 1987), p. 169.

40. Martin Heidegger, *What Is Called Thinking?* (New York: Harper and Row, 1968), p. 16.

41. Wolfram Hogrebe, *Die Wirklichkeit des Denkens* (Heidelberg: Winter Verlag, 2007), pp. 64–72.

42. Terry Eagleton, *Trouble with Strangers: A Study of Ethics* (Blackwell, forthcoming 2008).

43. Alain Badiou, *Theoretical Writings* (London: Continuum, forthcoming).

44. Eagleton, *Trouble with Strangers*.

45. Terry Eagleton, *Holy Terror* (Oxford: Oxford University Press, 2005). Numbers in brackets refer to the pages in this volume.

46. Jacques-Alain Miller, "From an Other to the other," *lacanian ink* 30, p. 37. Numbers in brackets refer to the pages in this volume.

47. Jean-Luc Nancy, "La déconstruction du Christianisme," *Etudes Philosophiques* 4 (1998).

48. Eagleton, *Trouble with Strangers*.

49. Jacques Lacan, *The Ethics of Psychoanalysis* (London: Routledge, 1992), p. 176.

50. Eagleton, *Trouble with Strangers*.

51. G. W. F. Hegel, *Grundlinien der Philosophie des Rechts* (Frankfurt: Fischer Verlag, 1968), p. 41.

52. See David Van Biema, "Life after Limbo," *Time*, January 9, 2006, p. 48.

53. Immanuel Kant, "What Is Enlightenment?," in Isaac Kramnick, *The Portable Enlightenment Reader* (New York: Penguin, 1995), p. 5.

54. Jacques Lacan, *Le séminaire, livre IV: La relation d'objet* (Paris: Editions du Seuil, 1994), p. 48.

55. Pope Benedict's face is in itself provoking—as if, beneath the smiling surface, one can discern, through darkened eyebrows and other details, the weird contours of a vampire. . . . A truly Hegelian coincidence of opposites: the broad benevolent smile concealing obscene Evil.

56. Umberto Eco, "God Isn't Big Enough for Some People," *Sunday Telegraph*, November 27, 2005, p. 20.

57. Janko Kos, "Islam in ateizem," in *Demokracija*, April 13, 2005 (in Slovene).

58. According to some anthropologists, in the prehistory of humanity this was quite literally true: in that early age, parents as a rule died before their children became sexually active, so the prohibition of incest between parents and children was practically void. One can reconstruct the underlying reasoning in these terms: "In order to discipline people and make them work harder, we have to prohibit something; however, we are so poor that all that we have is necessary for survival, there is no surplus that can be renounced; so let us play it safe and prohibit something that is already in itself impossible—in this way, we will instill a spirit of sacrifice and prohibition without really losing anything. . . ."

59. Bertolt Brecht, *GesammelteWerke*, vol. 2 (Frankfurt am Main: Suhrkamp, 1967). Numbers in brackets refer to pages in this volume.

60. Agota Kristof, *The Notebook—The Proof—The Third Lie* (New York: Grove Press, 1997). Numbers in brackets refer to pages in this volume.